DRUG WARS: THE FINAL BATTLE

RESCUING AMERICA FROM DRUG VIOLENCE

DON E. MILLER, Ph.D.

SPERANZA PRODUCTIONS
CHULA VISTA, CALIFORNIA

Publisher's cataloging in Publication Data

Miller, Don E.

Drug Wars: The Final Battle
Rescuing America From Drug Violence
by Don E. Miller, Ph.D. First Edition

    Bibliography.
    Includes Index.

ISBN: 0-9640695-0-4

1. Prevention of Substance Abuse. 2. Crime and Drug Abuse.   3. Drug Abuse Counseling.
4.Prison Reform.   5. Narcotics, Control of.
HV5825   362.2917

Library of Congress Catalog Card No.: 94-66003

Cover design, logo, moral support, most of Chapter Four and computer entries of several drafts by Annette Miller.

Speranza is the Italian word for Hope.

10 9 8 7 6 5 4 3 2

Dedication

This book was written for our children, for their children, and for their children's children. This book was written for all of America's children. The hope is that it will be possible for all of them to live out their full lives in a world that has become a little less violent because of this book. We must pass civilization on to our children.

Much of the credit for bringing this project to final completion must go to my wife Annette Miller. In every project of this nature it is almost always imperative to have a least one other person who believes in the project as strongly as the author. She was that person in this project.

TABLE OF CONTENTS

CHAPTER ONE *THE FINAL BATTLEGROUND* 1

THE BATTLE FOR THE HEART* MILLIONS FOR DEFENSE*
HOW TO BALANCE THE BUDGET IN FOUR YEARS*
RETURNING FROM A LIVING HELL* A NATION IN DECAY*
SOBERING UP AMERICA* FINDING THE LOST SHEEP*
HOW LOW WILL A DOPE FIEND GO?* SUPPLY AND
DEMAND* JUST SAYING "NO" ISN'T ENOUGH*
THE PRISON FRONT* A WHOREHOUSE IN TIJUANA*
DOING MY TIME GOT EASY* TEN PERCENT OF THE
INMATES ARE ALWAYS LOADED* CUTTING A DEAL*
GETTING A LIFE* SINCE MY WIFE ONCE LOVED A
HEROIN ADDICT I BECAME ONE TO IMPRESS HER* TIRED
OF BEING A FUGITIVE* I LOST MY TEETH AND I'M DYING
OF A LIVER DISEASE* NO ONE REACHING OUT FOR
ROBBY* 200 DOWN WITH 99,800 TO GO*
JUMPING FROM TWO MILES UP WITH NO PARACHUTE*
STAY'N OUT OF JAIL* HIGH PRICED NURSING HOMES*
DISAPPEARING INTO ADDICTION* THE GANG FRONT*
TAGGER BATTLES* NO GANG BANGERS ALLOWED*

CHAPTER **TWO** *GETTING SOBER:
STAYING SOBER* 27

SUCCESS AND DRUGS DON'T MIX* DEATH FOR
DEALERS* VOLUNTARY PATIENTS CHOOSE DRUGS
OVER TREATMENT* THE PILLAR OF SALT* FEW
STAY SOBER AFTER TREATMENT WITHOUT FOLLOW-UP
DRUG TESTING* YOU DON'T HAVE TO "HIT BOTTOM'
TO QUIT DOPE* WITHOUT TREATMENT, FEAR OF JAIL
WON'T STOP DRUG USE* STOP DRUGS - STOP CRIME*
WHERE THERE'S DOPE, THERE'S CRIME*
DECRIMINALIZATION VS. LEGALIZATION* DO NOT
REDUCE SUPPLY WITHOUT REDUCING DEMAND*
CALIFORNIA FARMERS GROW POT* STOP BLAMING THE
GENES* CHANGING PLAYMATES AND PLAYGROUNDS*

CHAPTER **THREE** *THE HIGH COST OF
BEING HIGH* **4 8**

DOESN'T SOBERING UP ADDICTS COST TOO MUCH?*
EX- ADDICTS PAYING TAXES*   A SOBER AMERICA MEANS
EMPTY JAILS*   DRIVE-BY SHOOTERS: LOADED GUNS
AND LOADED ON DRUGS*   DRUG ADDICTS AND
ALCOHOLICS COLLECT SOCIAL SECURITY*   GETTING ON
SOCIAL SECURITY*   MORE GOOD NEWS FOR DRUG
ADDICTS*   BUYING A BEER FOR YOUR FAVORITE
ALCOHOLIC*   DRUGS AND MENTAL ILLNESS*
EFFECTIVE PAIN CONTROL*   A SUBSTANCE ABUSE
"DISABILITY" IS NOT A LICENSE*   JAILS: THE NEW
ASYLUMS*   A PLEASANT SURPRISE!*   DRUGS AND
HOMELESSNESS*   WHAT IF WE JUST SAY NO TO DRUGS
A LITTLE LOUDER?*   WHAT'S FIRST, JOBS OR SOBER?*
DROPPING CRIME TO CONTROLLABLE LEVELS*

CHAPTER **FOUR** *SUBSTANCE ABUSE
AND MURDER* **7 3**

KEEP AWAY FROM DANGEROUS NEIGHBORHOODS*
DEATH AND THE FLOWER CHILDREN*   THE KILLER
CLOWN*   BETRAYED BY MOM*   THEY DON'T RUN OUT
ON ME NOW*   SOBERING UP SERIAL KILLERS*

CHAPTER **FIVE** *NATIONAL DRUG POLICIES: POOR
PARENTING WORST CASE SCENARIO* **8 3**

TEACHING HATE IN OUR JAILS*   LEARNING SOBRIETY
IN JAIL*   SEVENTY-EIGHT PERCENT STAYED SOBER*
SOBERING UP ONE ADDICT SAVES MILLIONS*   DRUGS
EASIER TO GET IN JAIL THAN DRUG TREATMENT*   EVEN
WARDENS LIKE DRUG REHAB*   A QUICK FIX FOR OUR
SOCIAL ILLS?*   THE LOST GENERATION?*   ONE MORE
BOLOGNA SANDWICH*   GETTING LOST IN THE SYSTEM*
THE REVOLVING DOOR TO THE JAIL*   MORE MISSPENT
MONEY*   SOME VERY ACTIVE CRIMINALS*   THE

TIME FOR BOOT CAMPS HAS COME (AND GONE)*   WHEN
SHOULD INTERVENTION START?*   SOBER UP OR DO
YOUR TIME*   "GETTING TOUGH ON CRIME"*
DON'T CODDLE CRIMINALS!*   RED RAG AND
BANDANNA*   SOBERING UP THE HOMIES*

CHAPTER **SIX**   *WHERE DO WE START*   **112**

STEALING A TANK OF GAS*   LESS VEGETABLES TO
TEND IN THE NURSING HOMES*   DRUNKS COVERED
WITH THEIR OWN VOMIT*   "I WAS SO STRESSED OUT
BY COURT I GOT LOADED"*   THE LEGALIZATION
DEBATE*   PRESCRIPTION FOR DISASTER: LEGALIZED
DRUGS*   "GIVE ME THE HOLY WEED"*   AMERICA
LOVES ITS JAILS*   EUROPE AHEAD OF U.S. IN DRUG
POLICIES*   DRUGS: THE EQUAL OPPORTUNITY PATH
TO RUIN*

CHAPTER **SEVEN** *INTERVIEW WITH*
            VICKI MARKEY, DEPUTY CHIEF
            PROBATION OFFICER OF
                SAN DIEGO COUNTY   **133**

THE PAPER CHASE*   THE WARRANT BANK: LIMBO OF
THE ABSCONDED*   THEY CAN BE FOUND IF SOMEBODY
LOOKS FOR THEM*   SENATE BILL 38 FOR DRIVING
UNDER THE INFLUENCE*   DWINDLING SUPPORT
SERVICES*   PENAL CODE 1000 DIVERSION PROGRAM*
THE PIR PROGRAM: PROBATIONERS IN RECOVERY*
DRAGGING THE LOST SHEEP BACK TO THE FOLD*
PREDATORY OFFENDERS WALK A THIN LINE*   BRAIN
BLOCKERS FOR CRACK COCAINE*   CUBANS AND AIDS*
SOBER LIVING HOUSES*   HOMELESS SCHIZOPHRENIC
SUBSTANCE ABUSERS*   NO DRUNKS OR DOPE FIENDS
ALLOWED*   THE NEW RAGE: BOOT CAMPS FOR DOPE
FIENDS*   TEACHING CONVICTS TO READ AND WRITE*
HIDING PROBLEMS AND PAIN WITH DRUGS*   SOBER
LIVING HOUSES MAKE GOOD NEIGHBORS*

CHAPTER **EIGHT** *INTERVIEWING ART FAYER*
AT MITE **164**

TOOLS FOR SOBRIETY*   NO MONEY FOR A HAMBURGER
AT MCDONALDS*   BREAKING THE JAIL CYCLE WITH A
SAFETY NET*   ELIGIBILITY FOR DIVERSION*
SPEEDY DIVERSION*   "NOPE, THAT'S NOT MY DOPE"*
TO TEST OR NOT TO TEST*   SOBERING UP THE
HOMELESS*   THE FCP OR FIRST CONVICTION PROGRAM*
CHEATING ON URINE TESTS*   KEEPING UP WITH
PROGRESS*   WORKING WITH TRUST*
MAKING SOBRIETY LOOK GOOD*   MARIJUANA KILLS
THE DESIRE TO ACHIEVE*   YUPPIE AMERICA AND THE
DOPE DEALER ON THE CORNER*   RUNNING FROM THE
PROBLEM*   LEARNING TO HAVE FUN WHILE SOBER*
DIGGING INTO THE PAIN*   PROTECTING PRIVACY VS.
SAVING LIVES*

CHAPTER **NINE** *THE LOST BATTLES:*
AMERICA'S DISGRACE **193**

BINGO PLAYERS HELP SOBER UP SAN DIEGO*   THE
MOST ADDICTED SLIP THROUGH THE CRACKS*
SPEEDIER PROCESSING PLEASE*   KEEPING HELP
WITHIN ARM'S LENGTH*   FEELING GOOD FAST*
PREVENTING THE DESCENT INTO HELL*   FIRING
PAROLE OFFICERS WHILE BUILDING MORE JAILS *   THE
RIGHT HAND DOESN'T KNOW WHAT THE LEFT HAND IS
DOING*   THE SHOTGUN WEDDING*   NOWHERE
TO GO AFTER JAIL*   PARENTS' RIGHTS TO SOBER
KIDS*   NO SHORTAGE OF PEOPLE NEEDING HELP*
CRIPS AND BLOODS: AMERICA'S NEW OWNERS*
REHABILITATION WORKS: FOR THE FEW WHO GET IT*
THE LEGAL SYSTEM AT A BREAKING POINT*   UNCLE
SAM'S SHARE OF THE DOPE MONEY: ZERO*   BUYING
OLYMPIC SIZE SWIMMING POOLS FOR COLOMBIANS*
WE CAN'T TREAT YOUR COLD YET: LET'S WAIT UNTIL IT
TURNS INTO PNEUMONIA*   PREGNANT AND ON
DRUGS? LOCK THEM UP AND TAKE THEIR BABIES*

SOBER LIVING FOR ONE TENTH THE COST OF JAIL*   A STITCH IN TIME SAVES NINE*   TEETERING ON THE EDGE OF A SOCIOLOGICAL ABYSS*   WATER BUFFALO HEROIN ADDICTS*   WE MUST PASS CIVILIZATION ON TO OUR CHILDREN*   HUMAN TOXIC WASTE*   GIVE ME YOUR HUNGRY, YOUR POOR - AND I'LL LOCK THEM UP*   NOT EVERYONE NEEDS LONG TERM REHABILITATION*   SANCTUARY TRAUMA* "WE HAVE MET THE ENEMY AND THEY IS US"*   DOPE DEALER NEEDED: APPLY IMMEDIATELY*   7-ELEVEN SELLING COCAINE AND VITAMINS*   60 MINUTES ON METHADONE*

CHAPTER **TEN** *MEMORY HEALING*   2 3 1

CONGRESSIONAL MEDAL OF HONOR WINNER*   SAYING GOODBYE*   ALONE IN THE FIELD OF BATTLE* TURNING INTO THE HULK*   CHOOSING CHRIST TO MUFFLE THE BLOWS*   TANKS BUT NO TANKS* GETTING RID OF NIGHTMARES*   TALKING TO THE DEAD* THE REUNION*   THE DOUBLE TECHNIQUE*   ALL ALONE WITH NO ONE TO LOVE YOU*   THERE IS NO FATE BUT THAT WHICH WE MAKE*

CHAPTER **ELEVEN** *THE RETURN FROM HELL: THE SOBER FOREVER PROGRAM*   2 4 7

DRUGS ARE ROTTING THE AMERICAN DREAM* "SOBER FOREVER" OPENS FOR BUSINESS*   THE FIRST ANGUISHED HOWL AFTER GETTING SOBER* LEARNING NEW SOLUTIONS TO OLD PROBLEMS*   I DON'T HAVE A PROBLEM*   LIFE MEMBERSHIP IN THE "SOBER FOREVER" PROGRAM*   NO MORE WAITING LISTS FOR TREATMENT*   "A FEW GOOD MEN"*   DRUGS IN THE SOBRIETY CENTER*   THE RIGHT TO PRIVACY*   DRUGS IN JAIL* "VOLUNTARY" CLIENTS*   THE HAND IN THE COOKIE JAR*   RETURNING THE LOST SHEEP TO THE FOLD*

KEEPING OUR PROMISE*   YOU CAN'T GO HOME
AGAIN*   LEARNING TO WORK TOGETHER*
TRACKING THE STRAYS*   THE POSSE*   FOR
WANT OF A NAIL*   THE JOB LADDER*   THE
ELECTRONIC "BIG BROTHER"*   THE ROAD BACK GETS
LONGER*   NOT ONE CENT FOR TRIBUTE*   DOUBLING
THE PUNISHMENT*   CRUEL AND UNUSUAL
PUNISHMENT*   FINANCING THE "SOBER FOREVER"
PROGRAM*   ABANDONING OUR YOUTH*   SOBER
FIRST, THEN BASKETBALL*   MULTIPLE
INTERVENTIONS AT MITE*   THE CLUB YOU CAN'T QUIT*
BRING YOUR BABY WITH YOU*   CENTRALIZED STATE
LEVEL TRACKING*   THE "DOPE OPERA" MENTALITY*
EMPTY COURTROOMS, EMPTY JAILS*

CHAPTER **TWELVE** *THE LAST FIELDS OF BATTLE:*
                      HOME AND WORK   **300**

CLEAN AND SOBER AT HOME*   TOOLS FOR PARENTS:
URINE TESTING BY MAIL*   DRUGS AND WORK*
KEEPING GOOD WORKERS SOBER*   THE NEW NUCLEAR
FAMILY*   REBUILDING NEIGHBORHOODS FROM
SCRATCH*   CRACK HOUSES: THE NEW SODOM AND
GOMORRAH?*   PRESCRIPTION DRUGS*   THE
FIRST FLIGHT OVER THE CUCKOO'S NEST*   THE
REBIRTH OF TALK THERAPY*   YOU CAN MAKE A
DIFFERENCE*   GETTING YOUR BABY BACK*
THREE STRIKES AND EATEN BY THE WOLVES*   TELL
YOUR LEADERS*   LET'S WAIT UNTIL YOU NEED A
HEART TRANSPLANT*   "DRUG WARS: THE FINAL
BATTLE"- THE MOVIE*   THE FINAL EXAMINATION*
HOMEWORK ASSIGNMENT*

REFERENCES, REVIEWS AND NOTES   **331**

ABOUT THE AUTHOR   **399**

INDEX   **400**

POSTSCRIPT   **403**

CHAPTER ONE

THE FINAL BATTLEGROUND

Where will the final battle of the drug wars be fought? Will it be on the high seas, with our superior Naval forces capturing and confiscating one boatload after another of illegal drugs? Will it be at our borders where people smuggle in Marijuana and Cocaine in a million clever containers? Will it be in the high Andes of Peru? There, the Indians are finding that growing the poppy is a way to stave off starvation in a country that is in economic ruin. Will we fly in legions of bombers and dump paraquat on those poppy fields, or on the coca crops in Colombia? Or will we go in with flame-throwers, utilizing a scorched earth policy?

Will the final battle in the drug wars be someplace in Mexico, where cannabis abounds? Or will it be in Northern California, where cannabis has become a major cash crop? Or, will the final battle in the drug wars be fought in those Pacific Rim nations growing poppies and exporting Heroin? Will we invade those countries to teach them that they better stop growing the dope that is ruining America?

We could spend billions of dollars storming through one third-world country after the other. Then, we could drag one third-world country dictator after another back to America for a trial. Will that be our final battle in the drug wars? No, these are all merely very costly skirmishes. There is more and cheaper dope coming out of Panama than before we locked up Noriega.

The final battle will not be fought in Colombia, nor in the Peruvian poppy fields, nor won by the dope-sniffing dogs on the Tijuana-San Diego border.

THE BATTLE FOR THE HEART

America's final battle in the drug wars is going to be fought in America. The final battle in the drug wars will be fought for the hearts and souls of our lost brothers and sisters and our addicted sick children. And sometimes our mothers and fathers. In the final battle of the drug wars, we will turn our loved ones, our substance abusing families, friends and neighbors into human beings again. In the final battle of the drug wars we will bring all the substance abusers back from their living hell. When we do this, and nobody is buying drugs anymore, the drug wars will be over. And, we will have won.

We will say to America's substance abusers, "We don't want to lock you up or punish you. We want to help you find the heart and soul you have lost. The search for these precious items begins the moment you are sober." We will take back our lost brothers, sisters and children on drugs who have been stolen from us. We have suffered far too long the pain of losing so many of those we love to substance abuse.

Drugs steal the mind, the body, the soul and the heart. Drugs dehumanize. Drugs give their users a few moments of bliss, a brief feeling of total and absolute power, followed by a living hell. The conscience of the substance abuser is destroyed by the very same substances designed to make them feel good. While under the influence they stop worrying about what's right and wrong. The major concern of the substance abuser is to make sure they never run out of this wonderful chemical.

The longer and heavier the substance abuse, the further from human the user has become. Without a conscience, drug addicts do despicable things with no remorse to make sure they keep supplied with drugs. They would never commit such unspeakable acts when sober. Once sober, they slowly become human beings again and their consciences return.

MILLIONS FOR DEFENSE

In 1798 the French offered to stop robbing American ships if we paid them enough money. Robert Harper said, "Millions for defense, not one cent for tribute." The battle cry hasn't changed. We are willing to spend billions of dollars going all over the world burning up poppy fields. We spend billions more building new jails to lock up our citizens. But we are not willing to spend one cent for tribute.

Translate the word "tribute" to prevention and treatment. Out of every dollar dedicated to the drug wars, more than ninety cents goes to cover the non-treatment costs connected to drug abuse. These costs include police, courts, judges, lawyers, stolen property, medical and social services. Less then ten cents of every dollar in the drug wars is spent on prevention, treatment, or stopping people from taking drugs. If nobody was using drugs think of the billions that could be spent somewhere else.

HOW TO BALANCE THE BUDGET IN FOUR YEARS

Nobody is paying taxes on the billions being spent on illegal drugs. If all that money was spent on goods and services, taxes would be paid on every transaction. Once sober, the $15 a former drug addict spent on dope will take him and a friend to the movie. The theater pays taxes on that money and pays the ticket taker, who pays income taxes. Then he buys a hamburger which is taxed. Get it? Every dollar put in the economy can earn a dollar in taxes. We could go a long way toward paying off the $4.5 trillion national debt if the billions of dollars changing hands in the underground drug economy were taxed.

Most of the $600 billion in goods stolen in America each year goes to buy dope.[117] Imagine what a $600 billion transfusion would do to our economy when we don't have to keep replacing stolen goods. That's twice our yearly $300 billion budget deficit.

Billions of underground and untaxed dollars are going to other nations to supply Americans with illegal drugs. When America is sober we will move those billions out of the underground and into our economy. Why should America's precious dollars end up in Colombia? When the Drug Wars are over and nobody is buying drugs those billions now spent on dope will jump-start our sluggish economy. Hundreds of thousands of new jobs will be created by those billions that will be staying in America.

This new money flowing into our economy would provide cheaper capital for new businesses, money to finance new homes at low interest rates.   When the money now spent on drugs is spent for goods, the millions of dollars collected in taxes could start retiring the national debt. It is time to stop mortgaging our children's future.

RETURNING FROM A LIVING HELL

Our battle cry used to be "The British are coming." That has been changed to the "The Dope Fiends are coming." We are out to get them. Half the movies are about catching dope dealers and dope smugglers. How many hundreds of dope busts have we seen on "Cops?" We all feel really good when kilo after kilo of that white powder is loaded into the police vans. We cheer when the long haired degenerates are lined up in handcuffs and dragged away. But let's stand close enough to the front lines in our drug wars to see who is really on the other side. We will not see the British, not even the Colombians.

We will see our sons and daughters, our brothers and sisters, and sometimes our mothers and fathers. What Pogo said has never been truer - "We have met the enemy and they is us." Isn't it time that we brought our loved ones back from a living hell?

A NATION IN DECAY

Substance abuse is the direct or indirect cause of most of the major horrors that are rotting away the soft under-belly of the American Dream.   These horrors include escalating violence and crime, homicide, child abuse, gang warfare, drive-by shootings, and most of the homeless problem. Our medical resources are being exhausted with crack babies and drug-related emergencies. The emotional and financial resources of our great nation are being drained and exhausted by substance abuse.

There is no speculation involved in the statement that substance abuse plays a major role in virtually every social problem that we face. This book offers a solution: The "Sober Forever" Program, which is an involuntary sobriety program. The promise of this book is that, once implemented, the "Sober Forever" Program will greatly reduce most of this nation's crippling social problems. The "Sober Forever" Program can and will reverse most of the horrors that have caused a pervasive sadness over our land. Documentation will be given in this book to back up these promises.

SOBERING UP AMERICA

There is no alternative to a program of involuntary sobriety. Everything else has been tried. We have played endless variations of the cops and robbers game. We have caught dope boats coming in from Colombia. We have shouted at the dope dealers on the corners with megaphones. We have crammed as many substance abusers as we can into packed prisons. Yet, the drug/alcohol abuse problem continues to escalate on a daily basis.

Wherever an involuntary sobriety program has been tried it worked. But such programs have been tried only sporadically and inconsistently. There has never been enough understanding of the problem to implement such a program on a broad, nation-wide basis.

Nobody seems to get it. The simple fact is that if substance abusers sober up, they stop buying drugs. When nobody is buying drugs, there will be no drug wars. There will be no turf battles with dope dealers shooting it out. When America is sober, there will be no Colombians getting rich by pouring poison into the veins of our children.

The proof is there. Sobering up criminals stops five out of six of them from committing crimes. The step by step procedures to implement the "Sober Forever" Program are given in Chapter 11. That program will reverse most of the horrors now haunting America. After you have read the first two or three chapters, jump to the chase, or Chapter 11. You'll be curious to know how we will sober up America. There, you will read about the program that will give us back our hope and the American dream. Then come back and slowly read the other chapters. There, you will find all the sad details about America's out of control substance abuse problem. You will see the costs, in dollars, emotions and lives that we pay for this problem. But also in this book you will find hope as the results are given of the programs that work.

FINDING THE LOST SHEEP

America's parents are sick to death of their sons and daughters trading the family's heirlooms and possessions for drugs. Our fellow Americans are selling their bodies for drugs. They are murdering for drugs. Drug-crazed devil worshipers are sacrificing babies. We cannot keep building more jails and hiring more police officers forever. It is time to bring our lost sheep back into the fold.

If only one person wants to take illegal drugs to temporarily feel a little better than they have been feeling, there will be someone to sell them what they want. Many say that we can solve the problem by locking up drug dealers for life. They say that the risk of a life sentence will convince dope dealers to get out of the business. But 95% of all dope dealers are dope users.[119] Dopers often use poor judgment. They can't be counted on to quit selling dope even if it gets more risky. They can be counted on to do whatever is necessary to guarantee their drug supply. It won't matter if we increase the risk of selling drugs by locking up drug dealers for life. There are very large amounts of money involved. There will always be a supplier to take that increased risk as long as there is a consumer.

A husband and wife on drugs had their children removed from their home. The children's grandmother applied to be their guardian and began raising them. She brought the children to me for family counseling to help them recover from the chaos drugs had made of their lives. Their mother had died of an overdose.

HOW LOW WILL A DOPE FIEND GO?

The children's father promised he would sober up. His mother allowed him to come home to be with his children. But he slipped badly, and at Christmas time. His mother had saved money to buy bicycles for her son's children. On Christmas morning when the children got up and ran to see what was under the Christmas tree, their bicycles were gone. Their father explained, "I needed a fix real bad." Let's make a promise to America's children: "Your drug addict parents will never steal another Christmas from you."

SUPPLY AND DEMAND

There was a time when even the smallest of towns had at least one smithy who shod horses. What if it was against the law to make horseshoes, but people still had horses instead of cars? There would be a thriving black market business in horseshoes. Any time there is a highly desired product, substance or service which is illegal, a black market and underground supply system will emerge to fill that demand. This is the law of supply and demand.

If people stopped buying illegal drugs, drug suppliers would be out of business. We need to eliminate the demand for illegal drugs. The focus on eliminating the supply of illegal drugs has never worked in the past. It will not work in the future.

Natives in Colombia spend all night stomping on coca leaves treated with lye. They work with bare feet because they cannot afford protective foot wear. They earn ten dollars a night and have severe foot ulcerations. When they are too sick to work or they die of their infections, ten other natives are there to take their place.

The astronomical amounts of money involved guarantee that each drug peddler/supplier/grower locked up for the rest of their lives will be replaced by others. What would happen if just half of the money now spent trying to cut off the supply of drugs was spent on sobering up America? The demand for illegal drugs would almost vanish within a few months. Law enforcement would then need much less money to make a serious dent in a much lower volume of illegal drugs.

JUST SAYING "NO" ISN'T ENOUGH

Aren't we focusing on demand now? What about the anti-drug messages such as, "Just say no." The educational campaign is working on some populations. The groups influenced by media and school educational campaigns tend to be professionals, middle class, caucasian junior high school, high school, and college students. Many of them are getting the message.

But the illegal drug problem is intensifying in ghettos and gangs, in the poor and in the minorities. They are not getting the message. Who is using illegal drugs might be changing, but the number of people using illegal drugs is increasing. Extensive media efforts do educate people, but not the ones using or most likely to use drugs.

I heard a black woman in a ghetto apartment building say, "It is not the drug dealer who beats, robs, rapes and kills you. It is not the drug dealer who urinates and defecates in the building where he lives and I live. It is the one who buys drugs from the drug dealer."

THE PRISON FRONT

As in any large scale battle, we will be fighting The Final Battle in the Drug Wars on several fronts at the same time. In World War II, we had many fronts. There was the Italian front and the Russian front. On the African front we chased Rommel across the desert. In the new Drug Wars, we will be battling to win back the hearts and souls of our addicted brothers and sisters. In the new Drug

Wars, there will also be many fronts. One will be in the prisons.

Raoul's story: "At the age of fourteen I was strung out on I.V. (Intravenous) morphine. Over the years, I've abused every drug there is. When I couldn't get the drugs it was alcohol. I was married at the age of 18. The marriage lasted less than two years. If I had to blame the failure of the marriage on any one thing, it would probably be the drinking. But even after we were divorced we had gotten back together and split up again off and on for seven years. I think my wife loved me. I'd stop by to visit her during those years and our sexual relationship continued even though we were divorced.

"During one of my drinking episodes, during a time we were separated, I called her. I asked her to stop by. She must have been able to tell over the phone I was drunk. But she came anyway. But instead of coming in, she just stopped outside and honked the horn. She wanted me to come out there to talk. Usually when she came by we ended up having sex.

"When she honked I hollered out the window 'Just a minute!' I went and got a knife and went down to her car with it. I said, 'You're coming up.' But she screamed. Some policemen having lunch at the Taco Bell across the street came running over and arrested me. I went to jail for assault with a deadly weapon and for threatening my wife."

A WHOREHOUSE IN TIJUANA

"After a few years I got out of jail and I did real good for awhile. I had never really been able to talk to a woman all those years. I was not sure what I was afraid of. When I had been out for seven months I still hadn't met a girl. I didn't know how to speak to them. Just a month before I got arrested again I went to one of the whorehouses in Tijuana. But it was like nothing, there was no satisfaction. Masturbation would have been more satisfying.

"I had a son. I had even arranged visitation. He came and spent all summer with me one time. It was great. But after he went back home I got depressed. I went and had a drink. When I did, that led to several days of binge drinking. I got very drunk. I left the people I was staying with. I was sleeping in my car. I'd wake up, drink, and pass out. Then I'd do it all over again. One of the times I was awake I kidnapped a woman and raped her. I ended up getting sentenced to 21 years. I did 11 years.

DOING MY TIME GOT EASY

"Here's what happened in prison. I was at C.M.C., The California Men's Colony, by San Louis Obispo. That's the biggest prison in California. It has 5,000 inmates. It is built like four separate prisons. There are four yards, four chow halls. At first, in spite of my other time in jail, it was very hard on me. But after two and one-half years I got institutionalized. I didn't think about the outside anymore. You can almost be as happy in there as you can out here, once you get used to it for so many years. If I was arrested again, I could take that many years again.

"You're locked in with these people. But there's more drugs in prison and easier to get than drugs on the outside. The first two and one-half years I was there, I drank home-made wine and used some drugs, but mostly I smoked marijuana. Then I got in with the people using I.V. drugs, speed, heroin. I was using all that stuff for about five years. But then about three years before I got out, it dawned on me that if I was ever going to make it on the outside I had to quit. So I did.

TEN PERCENT OF THE INMATES ARE ALWAYS LOADED

"I'd estimate that at any one time, about ten percent of all the prisoners in there were loaded when I was there. That's about 500. A lot more than that use off and on. But ten percent is probably the number who basically stay loaded all the time.

"How do you get drugs in there? It was brought in by the guy's girlfriends, or their wives. Women usually put it in their vagina, in several small balloons. Sometime during the visit, they would excuse themselves to go to the bathroom. They'd take the dope out and put it in their bra and come back out. They would slip the little balloons to their husband or boyfriend. After awhile during the visit, the husband or boyfriend would tell the guards they had to go use the bathroom. Once they got there they would use Vaseline to insert the little balloons in their rectum.

"You're only put behind the glass to visit if they suspect you of smuggling drugs. Or if they caught you smuggling drugs. If you're caught, you can't have any contact with your visitors for a year. It has to be visits behind glass.

"If they suspect that somebody brought you in some drugs they assign you to the potty watch. An officer watches you 24 hours a day until you go to the potty twice. Of course they check to see if there was anything in your stool. The 24 hour period is because some of the guys swallow the little balloons. I guess they figure it will all come out after 24 hours. Come to think of it, they would keep them on potty watch and in restraints up to 48 hours. They'd give them a pan to use to go to the bathroom.

CUTTING A DEAL

"My cell mate was on potty watch several times. He was bringing in large quantities of methamphetamine, or speed. He must have been caught but he always had some way of getting out of it. I think he was telling on the higher ups. The bigger dealers who were in the prison. It's the same in there as on the outside. Sometimes you can cut a deal by fingering someone else.

"A lot of the guys who were the heaviest users paid for their dope by selling drugs to the other prisoners. They would send the money back out with their wives or girlfriends so they could buy more. They got a lot more selling it in there than you could sell it for on the outside. But then it was more available inside the prison. They were very active selling it on the inside. Long after I quit using entirely, they would still come up to me and say, 'Some good stuff is coming in.'

"I was good with my hands and I made these cute little things. Then I would put them in the gift shop. Visitors could go to the gift shop and buy stuff the prisoners made to take home with them. I used to get enough money from that to buy all the dope I wanted in there.

"It was very rare that the guards were involved in the drug deals. I'm not sure, but I think a teacher was involved once. They took the hobby store manager out in handcuffs once.

GETTING A LIFE

"I've been out of prison for five years. I'll be off parole pretty soon. I haven't drank or used drugs for eight years now. I've had to test twice a month in the five years I've been out. I got remarried four years ago. To a good woman. She has never drank or used drugs. I've got a good job. All my life, I never had anything. Now I have cars, stereos, anything I want. Both my parents are alcoholics who finally sobered up. They go to five meetings a week. It's a way of life for them.

"For me, once I decided to give it up, it was easy. I've been out for five years and in all that time I have had no desire to drink or drug. At the tender young age of 43 I finally got a life. My son is 22 and lives with a girlfriend. My ex-wife still drinks and drugs off and on. She's been in and out of the nut house several times. That stuff can really get to you."

Raoul either got lucky or smart or both. He had a drug/alcohol-free environment to come home to from prison. Also, he had been sober for three years when he left prison. His first prison sentence was for threatening his wife with a knife. Too bad he wasn't watched very closely and enrolled in a fail-safe sobriety program after he got out of jail the first time. If he had been, prison term number two would never have happened. A few sober buddies, a support group he met with regularly, would have kept him from drinking that summer when his son went back home. Not drinking would have prevented the kidnap/rape and the second prison sentence.

SINCE MY WIFE ONCE LOVED A HEROIN ADDICT I BECAME ONE TO IMPRESS HER

Robby wasn't as lucky. His story is more typical. I saw him just after he was released from jail for the second time at the age of 46. He had a lot more than jail on his rap sheet but he ended up doing time just twice. He said, "I met this girl in the fourth grade. I started going with her in high school. We started living together when I was 17. I married her when I was 20. We stayed together another six years after we got married. We got along better before we got married.

"My dad was a drunk. There was always a lot of shouting and fighting in the house. At the age of 12, when I was in the fifth grade, I occasionally took diet pills. I started using more speed when I was in high school. I started smoking marijuana when I was 15. I only took acid six to twelve times in my whole life. I didn't like it. I jumped off a roof on acid once. Reality escapes me easy when I'm on acid. I preferred speed in high school though I experimented with downers.

"My wife used to have a crush on this guy who used heroin. So when I was 18 I thought if that's the kind of person she wants, I'll use heroin. I quit meth (speed) from the age of 18 to 25 and just used heroin on weekends for a few years. But from the age of 23 to 25 I got really strung out. I was hooked bad. I guess that ruined our marriage. We weren't getting along. I got divorced and went to Alaska.

"I was off drugs for three years. I came back to California and started using meth again. I committed my first crime. I robbed a drug dealer with a gun. I handcuffed a guy to some pipes in an abandoned building. They were selling drugs there, marijuana and meth. I went in to rob them with three other people. A shotgun went off, that scared us off. We ran out but one of the people who was driving by at that time saw me. We got away, but the other three guys got caught later. Somebody informed on me and I got picked up. But I bailed out before they took me to trial. I went back to Alaska.

TIRED OF BEING A FUGITIVE

"I came back three years later and turned myself in. I was tired of being a fugitive. I did two years at San Quentin. Right after I got out I started using a lot of speed again. I was dealing drugs, that's how I lived, selling meth. I had basically sold dope for a living since the age of 18. I did have a regular job off and on for a few months when I was in my twenties.

After San Quentin I had a girlfriend living with me. I was in a small town. I didn't have a lot of traffic coming to my place. I'd drive to a big city and get the dope and just drop it off to some other locals.

"But my girlfriend went someplace for a couple days. She either got caught with some dope or was picked up for doing something illegal. She had made a deal. She had promised to help them catch me for a lighter sentence. She had dumped all my bleach out. I had bottles of bleach to stash the dope in, in case of a raid to make it disappear. She walked into town and took my keys. I was supposed to be trapped there. But I had an extra set of keys. So I drove into town.

"This cop came toward me and said 'Come here.' I said, 'Just let me cut off my engine.' I jumped in my truck and drove off. There was a chase. I threw the drugs out. The cop blocked me off. I accidentally hit his police car. He hurt his arm. They found the drugs. I was charged with assault and bodily injury. I got four years but served two. I got high about 15 to 20 times when I was in prison."

I LOST MY TEETH AND I'M DYING OF A LIVER DISEASE

"I'm on general relief now. I lost all my teeth because of drugs. I'm supposed to get false teeth later sometime. I got hepatitis a few times from drugs and needles so now I have this liver disease. I'm weak, tired and this disease gives me sharp pains. The doctor says I am disabled from this disease. It is a virus that attacks your liver.

"I've used heroin maybe four times in the six months I've been out of prison. I'm being tested every two weeks for drugs. Tomorrow is the day. I clean up for 72 hours before the tests. I drink a lot of water for three days. It's worked so far. I haven't gotten caught. But then I'm not using like I used to. I'm playing it cool. I'm mostly using Tylenol 3, or Tylenol with codeine now, 8 to 12 tablets a day. I have a friend who gets them with a prescription for pain. I basically get them for free. What are friends for?

"I've used a little speed, but not like I used to. I can't afford it. I'm not dealing now. I've gotten very paranoid and depressed. I stay in the house. I try to stay out of trouble.

"Even if I could work and got a job, I think the parole people would go over there and ask questions and make me lose my job. The DEA (Drug Enforcement Administration) would make sure I wouldn't work so I would have to go back to dealing drugs because they want to see me back in prison.

"The agency that is supposed to work with you to get you a job is a joke. The guy gives you a big speech about places you can go look for work, like CalTrans. But CalTrans isn't hiring. Even if I wasn't sick, I couldn't work. I just don't get along with people very well. I get mad easy. I don't like taking any bullshit off anybody. If anybody thinks that they're Mr. Uppity I get upset. I don't like authority figures.

"My disease makes me weak, tired, sleepy, and I'm in a lot of pain. I sleep 14 to 16 hours a day. I sleep a straight 12 hours at night, then I take a two to three hour nap during the day. If I get some speed I have a little more energy. But when I take speed, it runs me down even worse when it wears off. But then I get so tired and I'm not feeling good, so I take some speed. I can't seem to concentrate on anything anymore."

Were DEA agents determined to get Robby back in jail? Very unlikely. We know how drugs, especially speed, create paranoia.[15]

NO ONE REACHING OUT FOR ROBBY

Upon release from expensive incarceration which taught Robby no new skills, parole supervision was haphazard and ineffective. The system was still failing Robby. He had been thrown out with no parachute, no meetings he had to attend, no support group, no buddy system to help him stay sober. No one had tried to change his values, teach him morality or a work ethic. He sat alone, figuring how to clean up long enough to beat his very predictable urine test every other week.

He grew more paranoid, more depressed. His drug-caused physical and psychiatric problems were growing worse daily. His sole goal and ambition for the future? To try to prove he was totally disabled, unable to work, so he could collect social security benefits. Our failure to sober up Robby when we first had the chance about 24 years ago has cost us millions. The continued failure to sober Robby up will cost us millions more.

Art had just gotten out of Westfork, an "honor camp" in rural San Diego County when he came to see me in 1993. While in Westfork, he had helped to build bridges and repair drainage ditches. He made fire trails and repaired roads. His sordid story is so much like many others it is not worth telling in detail. Briefly, drugs cost him two jail terms, loss of one eye and getting shot in the hand by his father. He said, "I lost interest in my family." The street/drug life proved to have much more allure than home. He had two boys in their late teens he had not seen or heard from for years. In the past 20 years he had been sober one year, the year he had just spent at the Westfork prison honor camp.

The time Art went to jail in 1980 for four years did not interfere with his getting high on drugs as often as he wanted. He didn't do drugs in 1993 at Westfork because they did periodic urine testing inside the prison. He didn't want to come up dirty on a test and have four months tacked onto his sentence, which is what happened to several people Art knew at Westfork who had come up dirty on their urine tests.

As soon as Art was released he got back on cocaine. Nobody bothered him about going to treatment or taking urine tests. He had to mail in a report to a probation officer once a month. He did not come to my office to seek treatment. He came to ask if I could help him get on Social Security by certifying that he was a hopelessly addicted and totally disabled drug addict. If you pass that test you basically have an income and hassle free highs for life.

"Dr. Miller, please help me get back on Social Security," Ron Begged. Ron slouched on the couch and could hardly keep his eyes open. "I have been a hopeless diabetic since childhood. I was on Social Security for 10 years. But after I got out of jail after a two year term they had lost all my records and I had to reapply all over again. It's been hell for the last two years with no money and no way to take care of myself or treat my illness. I get my insulin from this same pharmacy I've been going to for a long time. They know I am a diabetic and I can die if I don't get insulin. My girl friend pays for it. I have to inject myself twice a day."

To explain why he wasn't being followed by a doctor he shouted, "I don't have any money. No one will help me!" He woke up a little. His eyes even opened up for a short time. Surely, I thought, he must know about C.M.S., or County Medical Services, the program designed to provide medical care for those with no funds. I have seen many people receive excellent care through the C.M.S. program.

When I started to inform Ron about C.M.S. he exploded again. "I can't wait in those stupid lines for three days! I'll just go out and sell dope rather than stand in those lines!" I wasn't aware of any lines to get into the

C.M. S. program. It turned out that Ron couldn't get G.R. or General Relief for the same reason: too many lines.

Ron said that he had to sell dope to supplement his Social Security money before he went to jail in 1988. He had to take dope because of his pain about life and his condition. He had to sell dope after he got out because his Social Security money had been cut off. That got him his second jail term.

Ron said that he was trying very hard to not sell or take dope. He said that with the new "Three strikes and you're out" law he would go to jail for the rest of his life if he was caught again. So instead, he drank every day "Because of my joint pain." He admitted that the times he was in jail were the only times his diabetes was under control. In jail he had eaten regularly and had been given medicine regularly. Out of jail, drugging or drinking tore up his body. Substance abuse kept his blood sugar level in chaos. His many near death diabetic comas had resulted in very expensive ambulance trips to emergency rooms.

The system failed them all: Raoul, Art, Robby and Ron. Raoul was lucky enough to finally make it on his own. The system consistently failed to help Robby for 34 years. Someone should have noted Robby's diet pill use at age 12 and got him help. Probation did nothing at all to impact on Art's Ron's and Robby's use and sales of drugs, their primary life-long career. Every arrest and jail time since then, since nothing was done to keep them sober, was one more system failure.

200 DOWN WITH ONLY 99,800 TO GO

Of the over 100,000 people locked up in California prisons in 1992, two hundred were involved in a therapeutic community treatment program at Donovan Prison in San Diego. Only 200 in the whole state were in a program that would make a difference in their drug/crime rate when they get out. Two hundred down and 99,800 to go.[43]

The need for a combination of programs involving inside prison job training and a Stay'n Out type in-prison drug rehab program is critical and very cheap. Such programs keep people out of jail after they are released. Combine those programs with the "Sober Forever" Program described in Chapter 11, and we will see our nation-wide rearrest rate drop to around five percent.

The "Sober Forever" Program focuses not only on what happens to prisoners after their release, but on everyone else after their first arrest which involved substance abuse in any way. This includes all the people who were drunk or loaded at the time of their arrest. This includes anyone who was caught with drugs in their possession or caught selling drugs. This includes people who didn't commit any crime except to be noticeably under the influence of an illegal substance.

JUMPING FROM TWO MILES UP WITH NO PARACHUTE

Imagine that there is a plane full of prisoners with a few guards flying at 10,000 feet and this conversation takes place:

Guard: "Okay you guys, it's time to jump."

Prisoners: "When do we put on the parachutes?"

Guard: "Sorry, guys, we had a real budget problem. We had to cut costs somewhere. There are no parachutes. But here's $35."

Prisoners: "What are we supposed to do with that?"

Guard: "Don't spend it all in one place."

This happens thousands of times every day all over America. Only it isn't an airplane they are ejected from. Thousands are released from jail or prison daily with $35 and no parachute. What can you do with $35? Can you pay first and last month's rent on an apartment and fill it with food? Can you go to school and learn a trade? Can you start a small business? No.

These prisoners are leaving 'three hots and a cot' for the unknown and the scary. There is something you can do to take care of that fear with the $35. That's just enough money to get drunk or high. After that? If you're lucky enough to have done something stupid while you were loaded, you may be able to get back to the security of 'three hots and a cot' right away.

There are very few programs designed to catch the prisoner on his way out the jailhouse door. It is rare that the prisoner is provided a parachute so he doesn't splatter on the concrete 10,000 feet below. Where such programs do exist they do work.

Without a parachute, the prisoner heads for the only place he knows, which is where he was before he went to jail. He goes back to his gang, his 'hood,' his old dope-using girlfriend, to his drugs and alcohol. How do they survive? They do what they did before, which usually involves drugs and crime. That's the only way they know to earn a living. In jail 85% of them were given no new social, educational, or job skills. Most of them sharpened their criminal skills in jail.

STAY'N OUT OF JAIL

A few prisoners, but less than 15%, are exposed to some kind of drug rehabilitation program in jail. A frequently quoted model is Stay'n Out, based in the New York prisons. The few lucky enough to be in that program were housed separately from other inmates. They were supervised by a staff of recovered addicts and ex-cons. Counseling, encounter sessions and group seminars were designed to build respect for authority, discipline, confidence, and self-awareness. They were assigned work in the program. Half continued treatment in residential programs in the community after leaving jail. Prison costs were $35,000 per inmate. Stay'n Out costs another $4,000 a year.

On follow-up, after being out three years, Stay'n Out program graduates were being arrested one-third to one-half less often than non-participants. Offenders with the most serious drug problems are each responsible for as many as 90 robberies and burglaries a year. Without treatment, nine out of ten return to crime and drugs after prison and the majority will be rearrested within three years. The threat of rearrest does not deter addicts from using drugs or committing crimes after they are released from prison.[27, 44]

The general public's idea seems to be that if we lock up people longer, they will stop committing crimes. This is a fallacy. It is true that while they are in prison they are not doing as much robbing, stealing, killing and usually not as much drugging. But while in jail they earn their advanced C.A. (Criminal Arts) degree.[133] The longer they are in the joint the less likely they are to commit crime when they get out. Right? Wrong. Whether the time served is long or short, without treatment in jail, the chances of committing more crime and going back to jail are the same.[14]

Anyone who thinks that the best way to keep people from committing more crimes is to keep them in jail must be willing to give up our park system, road maintenance, garbage collection, etc. It costs a lot of money to lock people up. The longer you lock them up the more it costs.

HIGH PRICED NURSING HOMES

Many of our prisons have been turned into nursing homes. Prisoners given absurdly long sentences years ago are growing old, senile and decrepit. Many of them are in wheelchairs and have Alzheimer's disease. They must be wheeled to the chow hall and are spoon fed and they don't remember their names. But we must continue to spend $30 to $70 thousand a year protecting the public from these dangerous felons. We all know what they would do if released to the outside world. Within 24 hours they will have tooled down to the nearest 7-Eleven, jumped out of their wheelchairs and pulled the heist of the century. Give me a break. Nursing homes outside of prison do not cost $30 to $70 thousand a year.

The Federal Bureau of Prisons reported on studies of its Federal Prison Industry's $343 million business that employs over one-fourth of America's 58,000 federal prisoners. Of 7,000 federal prisoners released between

1984 and 1986, the ones who were trained for jobs behind bars were more likely to work when they got out of prison. They were less likely to slide back into a life of crime.

This program is available to perhaps 15,000 of America's 1.2 million prisoners, and is operated only in federal prisons. Goods produced (including office furniture, gloves, optics, etc.) could be sold only to the federal government.[115]

DISAPPEARING INTO ADDICTION

Over and over I have seen people stop cooperating with probation or parole when they were slipping back into drugs. Many prisoners show up for their tests for a couple of months after release from prison, then they "disappear" when they know they will fail their tests. Whether we are talking about ex-prisoners with a substance abuse history or people with just one substance abuse related arrest, none should be allowed to "disappear."

They must be provided with a support system consisting of a place to live, food to eat, sober buddies to guarantee their sobriety, job training and **random**, not predictable testing. We will know about their first slip within minutes or hours after it happens (not months or years). A series of steps will be taken to guarantee that that person is returned to and kept in the fold of sobriety. We do not need so many lost sheep. Probably 20 to 40 million Americans fit this category, though only 1.2 million are locked up at this time. For each one in jail, it is safe to say that another 20 are on their way to or from jail or the hell of substance abuse.

Robby could work through his authority conflicts in therapy. Robby could get over his paranoia. Robby could learn that though the world **is** against him and other substance abusing criminals who prey on society, it doesn't have to be that way. Robby could learn to work through the lingering pains of a childhood with a drunken, abusive father. Those were the childhood experiences that have left him resenting and fighting orders of any kind. If the "Sober Forever" Program described in Chapter 11 is implemented, these good things can and will still happen to Robby.

Robby could still become sober and stay sober. He can still use what is left of his body and mind to make whatever contributions he can to a good life for himself and to society. Without the "Sober Forever" Program, Robby, and the millions like him who were ejected from 10,000 feet with no parachute, are going to splatter on the pavement. They will go deeper into drugs. They will try to disappear. They will die early deaths. They will return to jail over and over.

It is easy to say that all Robby and the millions like him have to do is start making phone calls and going to meetings and reaching out for help. The help is there, for the persistent. But Robby and millions like him are not going to reach out for help. That is what this book is all about. We must reach out to them with the help. And when we get hold of them, we must never let go, lest they slip back into the substance abuser's hell.

THE GANG FRONT

Another major battleground for the hearts and souls of our substance abusers will be fought in the gangs. Here is Terry's story: "I got jumped into that gang three years ago, when I was twelve. I had to fight three guys to jump in. They beat me up. But I didn't feel it till the next day, because I was drunk. I had a headache and a fat lip.

"There were 150 members in that gang. They were mean and rough. They would go shoot people, jump people, drink, smoke weed, and go look for trouble. Of the 150 members, about 30 were dealing in drugs. About 75 of the 150 used cocaine. They were tweakers (heavy drug users). One guy didn't use drugs, but he drank heavy. I had to dress different to be in that gang. But it got dangerous because they got into big fights with other gangs.

"I guess I got scared when another gang drove by and shot at my house. Nobody was hurt but it could have killed my brothers or sisters or my parents. Another time a car was parked in front of my house. As I walked by they pulled out a gun and aimed it at me. I jumped into the bushes and ran up a hill.

"Most of my friends are taggers. They go around with spray paint. All this time they've been telling me 'Don't gang bang, it's too dangerous. You'll get killed.' Finally my friends told me 'You better decide, you have to pick: The gang or us.' By then I was scared of the gang. There's a bunch of crazy guys in that gang. Always looking for trouble. So about five months ago I got jumped out of that gang. This time I had to fight four guys. Getting jumped out, they beat you up even more than when you get jumped in. But I was drunk this time too. But I sure hurt the next day.

TAGGER BATTLES

"Now I'm 15 and after three years in that rough gang I'm in this tagger gang. It's a lot better. And safer. There's about 100 members in our gang. We will have tagger battles. Like maybe in a one block area. We work in crews of six to ten. A crew is a smaller bunch of taggers. All 100 members of the gang out there at once would be too much. Then the tagger gang that has left the most marks gets the highest number of points and wins. The marks are like the symbols for your gang. We have judges who decide who wins.

"Sometimes there are tagger battles at different places where there is a big wall. Like if you go to the Euclid trolley station, at Euclid and Market. You walk along the trolley tracks then jump a fence. You go down about 100 feet from the trolley station and there is a half mile long wall. It is completely filled from taggers spraying it. They let you tag (spray paint) in there. The media has been there taking pictures. But don't try to go in there by yourself.

"About an hour before a big tagger battle at the trolley station wall, someone will go down and roll a big section. They paint it over with fresh white paint. Then the battle starts. And after an hour the judges decide who won. We'll paint people, dogs or clowns jumping out of a box. Some people draw in what they're going to paint with a marker pen before they start. Some just start spraying. The judges decide whose is best. Like whose looks the best, whose has less paint dripping, whose is cleaner. The group that loses has to change the name of their gang.

NO GANG BANGERS ALLOWED

"Being a tagger is a lot better and safer than being a gang banger. We have parties. But we have to be careful. Nobody knows where the party is until the last minute. First you hear that you should make a phone call to somebody. Then if that guy thinks you are okay, he'll tell you that you should go to a certain store in the big shopping mall. When you get there you'll see a couple guys standing out in front of that store. If they know you and think that you are okay, they give you the address of the party. If you look at them bad, they don't tell you. They don't like gang bangers. If gang bangers get into the party they always mess up the parties. They cause the fights. They take guns. That's why they don't let them go to the parties.

"I haven't drank anything for six weeks. Before, I was drinking three or four 40 ounce bottles of malt liquor a night. I beat up my girlfriend a few times when I was drinking. She had two black eyes. I was arrested. I was in juvenile hall for three days. Me and my girlfriend are getting along really good since I haven't been drinking. It turns out that she is pregnant. She'll be 14 when she has the baby. She wants me to quit the tagger gang. She said that we do vandalism. Some of the guys in a gang that my old gang used to fight are still looking for me. They said they want to kill me. I hope they forget about me pretty soon. My dad is still drinking."

It costs easily over a million dollars a year to clean up after the estimated 1,000 taggers in San Diego County. That would amount to costs of about $1,000 to clean up after each tagger. The trolley spends $400,000 a year and CalTrans spends $240,000 a year to scrub or paint over freeways and roads. Business owners in San Diego County spend thousands on security, paint, and floodlights.[150]

The amount and degree of violence in Terry's two different gangs is directly related to the amount and degree of drug usage. High cocaine usage in Terry's first gang resulted in murder, drive-by shootings and random assaults on whoever was available. Lower amounts of substance abuse in Terry's tagger gang resulted in 'hide-and-seek' tagger games with authority. Terry's tagger gang did graffiti and vandalism but not the gross mayhem of the high cocaine-using gang.

The prisons can be sobered up. The gangs can be sobered up. Chapter 11 tells how.

Charles Murray, "a darling of the Reagan right," in a book titled "Losing Ground" said we must give up hope of trying to solve the underclass problem of drugs, AIDS and crime. We must settle for "containment" or "custodial democracy" where the poor will be provided medical care, food, housing" much as we do for American Indians who live on reservations."[58]

But on the other hand, if the Indian gambling casinos continue to flourish, they may close down Las Vegas, finance a repurchase of their stolen lands with money earned from gambling-addicted Americans and evict us all.

CHAPTER TWO

GETTING SOBER: STAYING SOBER

Once hooked on drugs, the junkie knows that it's "until death do us part" from his dope. Right? Once an addict, always an addict. The best we can hope for is to keep the drug addict happy with Methadone. Right? Wrong! Hundreds of studies prove that "hopeless" addicts can sober up and stay sober. Many addicts have sobered up on their own with no outside intervention. Many addicts have sobered up and remained sober after involvement in a voluntary substance abuse program. But the highest rate of continued sobriety is reported by involuntary treatment programs. Intense follow-up and monitoring of the addict on a long-term basis is crucial. This intense follow-up/monitoring is referred to as having a "long tail."

Not only do involuntary sobriety programs work, they are the only intervention that works most of the time. Thousands of addicts are sobered up every day in expensive 30 day live in sobriety programs. When they graduate, they have to decide: Stay sober, or go back to drugs. Unfortunately, most addicts choose to go get high. They don't necessarily get high on the first day or even in the first month after they graduate from a treatment program. But, without close follow-up/monitoring (the "long tail") most of them will return to using illegal drugs within a few months. Studies show that keeping very close tabs on the newly sober substance abusers is essential in order to keep them sober.

SUCCESS AND DRUGS DON'T MIX

An international study of drug abuse in 29 countries revealed that the typical abuser of most illegal drugs is a young male. He is unemployed, relatively unskilled, and living in lower-class circumstances. Females often outnumber the males in abusing legal drugs, such as tranquilizers. Almost all countries report increased drug use and abuse in the past twenty years.[134]

In countries keeping records, negative effects are almost universal by-products of illegal drug abuse. These include higher school dropout rates among drug users. Unemployment and absenteeism is higher among illegal drug users. In other words, by all standards of success (education, career, jobs) drug abusers are handicapped and do not live up to their potential.[134]

The economic costs associated with thefts connected to illegal drug use and abuse in the United States is estimated to be at over $600 billion a year.[145]

The National Academy of Sciences claimed that 5.5 million Americans have serious drug problems.[49] At least half of the 1.2 million criminals locked up in America's jails and prisons are substance abusers.[19] We will see that their drug abuse is what got them there.

DEATH FOR DEALERS

Singapore has an extensive program for the early identification of illegal drug abusers. Their laws allow urine testing of suspected users and treatment of drug users. Few countries have programs to identify high risk illegal drug users. Most countries do have treatment programs for drug abusers and addicts. Singapore's maximum penalty for possession of illegal drugs is ten years. In the Philippines it is twelve years. Both Singapore and the Philippines may impose the death penalty for illegal drug trafficking and for importing illegal drugs. These two countries have the most severe penalties.[134]

Treatment was effective in reducing intravenous illegal drug abuse. The longer you manage to keep the illegal drug abuser in treatment the higher the chances are he will stay sober. When people can choose whether they will stay in treatment or not, the success/sobriety rate is much lower than in programs where they don't have that choice. In voluntary programs drug addicts trying to sober up are confused, angry, and hurting (missing their dope). They leave if one counselor or fellow addict says anything that rubs them the wrong way. They say "I'm out of here! I don't have to take this shit!" They say "I hate to spill my guts in front of a group" or "What a bunch of nerds." The various complaints about the program are a cover-up for the real reason they leave which is to go get high.

We must recognize that illegal drug dependence is chronic. That means that drug users keep going back to their dope, in spite of multiple treatment programs and in spite of doing sober time in jail. There need not be multiple, very expensive treatment programs. Only one is necessary. See Chapter 11.

I have seen many addicts who had been in many treatment programs on an off and on basis for years. They had quickly relapsed upon release from each of these drug treatment programs. There was always inadequate follow-up/testing. An easy half million treatment dollars can be spent on one addict who has been in and out of treatment programs for years.

Involuntary or compulsory treatment means close supervision and penalties for dropping out of treatment. Federal, state, and civil commitment programs were in full operation from 1965 to 1975. Drug abusers were forced into treatment. In the 1965-1975 time period federal monies were made available to provide drug treatment throughout the nation. But in the next ten years federal support was drastically reduced. Individual states were expected to pick up the costs of the various programs which had been in operation. Many states did take over support of some programs. But many programs were dropped as the over-all level of financial support fell.[78]

These civil commitment programs were replaced by a system of community drug treatment programs which were cheaper to run. They didn't call for all the burdensome administrative costs of federal levels of civil commitment drug treatment programs. When public attention began focusing on the drug abuse/crime problem in the 1980's the federal government did appropriate money to deal with the problem. But this time, instead of backing treatment, most of the new monies went toward trying to stop supply by catching and jailing drug traffickers. Some monies went toward prevention among non-user groups. Over the years the federal government got further from treatment and closer to law enforcement as a solution - with disastrous results. For one thing, the prison population doubled in the last ten years.[78, 134]

Federal drug law enforcement budgets went from $800 million in 1981 to $1.9 billion in 1985. In the same time period, education and treatment funds were cut from 404 million to 338 million.[42] In 1991, only 14% of the $10.5 billion federal drug budget went to treatment. Ten years ago 25% of the $800 million Federal drug budget went to treatment and that was before the cocaine epidemic. In most cities, addicts must wait months for treatment.[43]

The community treatment programs available are not drawing enough high risk/high drug use people into treatment. Addicts who are deepest into drugs don't get treatment. They don't want treatment. They want their dope. The jails are filled with prisoners with extensive drug abuse histories. Most of these prisoners with drug abuse histories had managed to avoid treatment/sobriety programs before going to jail.[78]

VOLUNTARY PATIENTS CHOOSE DRUGS OVER TREATMENT

The primary role of two public health service hospitals was to treat federal prisoners who had abused drugs. The one in Lexington, Kentucky opened in 1935, another opened in 1938 at Fort Worth, Texas. These treatment centers also accepted voluntary drug abuse patients. However, most voluntary patients did not stay long enough to complete the treatment program. In fact, most left a few days after their arrival.[78]

Before passage of the Narcotic Addiction Act (NAA), drug abuse treatment did not provide for community after-care. Without follow-up there was an extremely high relapse rate. Abstinence was best guaranteed in the confirmed illegal drug user through the availability of compulsory parole supervision.[149]

The NACC (Narcotic Addiction Control Commission) which emerged from the New York State Narcotics Control Act of 1966 resulted in a very extensive civil commitment drug treatment program. Addicts could be committed to treatment for three to five years. People eligible for the program included those addicted to illegal drugs and those arrested for drug-related crimes. Voluntarily committed drug addicts were accepted into the program. Also, family members were able to petition the courts to get their kin into treatment. Parents didn't have to stand by and watch helplessly as their children drifted deeper into the hell of drug addiction.

A period of incarceration was followed by a period of community after-care. But the success rate was not astounding. That experience should teach us that how treatment programs are implemented is important. Also, monitoring of the drug abuser must be carefully carried out. Without compulsory parole supervision, the confirmed illegal drug user is very likely to keep using.[64,149]

Compulsory drug treatment should utilize existing, appropriately designed treatment programs rather than creating a whole new separate system. The new system created by NACC apparently was rather rigid and too authoritarian in nature, in addition to not having a really effective follow-up component.[64]

THE PILLAR OF SALT

The relationship between heroin addiction and crime is well established, as is the relationship between IV (intravenous) drug use and AIDS. About 30% of all AIDS cases in the United States are related to IV drug use. IV drug abusers constitute a major conduit for the heterosexual spread of AIDS into the general population. There is a high probability that infected individuals will transmit the HIV virus to their regular sexual partners. The number of AIDS cases has more than doubled every thirteen months. Many IV illegal drug users are sexually active. Many HIV positive females resort to prostitution to support their drug habits. This is one of the ways AIDS is spreading from IV drug users to the general population.[51] High on cocaine, male and female druggies in crack houses engage in marathon sex with multiple partners. Remember Lot's wife? When you drive by a crack house, don't look back or you might turn into a pillar of salt. Or, if the homie guarding the door thinks you looked at him wrong, you'll get shot.

Treatment for illegal drug abuse is effective in reducing intravenous illegal drug use.[130] A variety of treatment methods in many different settings generally resulted in reductions in illegal drug use and associated criminality. Many studies also show improvement in employment status and other positive behavioral outcomes following treatment. Because many clients had multiple treatment experiences in varying programs, the question of which treatment is superior becomes clouded. But, when there is a "long tail" or tight follow-up, less than twenty percent of the treated abusers continued their daily or near-daily opioid use at follow-up six years later.[6]

FEW STAY SOBER AFTER TREATMENT WITHOUT FOLLOW-UP DRUG TESTING

Relapse prevention is a critical part of any drug abuse treatment program. Without it, success rates, or the number of people who stay sober, go way down. The greatest risk of relapse after leaving treatment occurs during the first ninety days. This is the time when a structured relapse prevention program is most critical. Many after-care programs teach stress reduction and help clients work on the development of coping skills. Unfortunately, most drug treatment programs offer little once you've graduated from the more intense part of their program. That part usually lasts thirty days. Virtually none can do anything about it if their graduated clients decide to go back to using.

Thirty-five states have existing civil commitment statutes. This does not necessarily mean jail. Civil commitment means that someone can be ordered into treatment. Jail is a possibility if they still refuse to go.[78]

A thousand drug addicts who entered the California Civil Drug Addict Program were studied. They had been treated at various clinics between 1970 and 1973. They were all on probation or parole. Probation is community supervision instead of jail. Parole is supervision in the community after release from jail. One of the conditions of their probation and parole was that they had to get into treatment.[6]

It was discovered that there usually had been "an out of control" period of very heavy drug abuse for about two years before admission to treatment. But by eleven to thirteen years following admission, significant changes were noted. These changes showed that civil commitment had the effect of suppressing daily illegal drug use and criminal involvement.

Forty Seven Percent of the previously unemployed drug users got jobs when they sobered up. Only ten percent were rearrested. The rearrest rate for untreated and unsupervised druggies after release from jail hovers around 70%. Even more dramatic was the reduction in antisocial behavior. After treatment and sobriety, crime was greatly reduced even in those who hadn't found a job.[6]

A "long tail" or some variation of parole must be used to monitor illegal drug addicts to prevent relapse. Supervision without drug testing is virtually useless and produced nearly the same results as no supervision at all. Without concrete laboratory evidence showing whether the individual is clean or not, drug rehab counselors as well as probation and parole officers can be conned.

Outpatient supervision with testing resulted in major reductions in narcotic use. It follows that supervised after-care with objective monitoring is the most important component of any civil commitment drug treatment programs.

It costs between $20,000 to $60,000 a year to keep a drug addicted criminal in jail. Out of jail, he can be watched closely, tested frequently, and his sobriety guaranteed, for a couple thousand dollars a year. And sober, it is very unlikely he will do any more crime. The California Civil Commitment Drug Addict Program proved to be very effective in changing criminal behaviors. The New York and NARA (Narcotic Addiction Rehabilitation Act) programs were not as effective. This may have been because they were administered through agencies other than the criminal justice system. They lacked the legal clout to demand that the illegal drug abuser get into and stay in treatment. Without any real power to insist on sobriety, the number of drug abusers who stay sober goes way down.[78]

YOU DON'T HAVE TO "HIT BOTTOM" TO QUIT DOPE

Many people in the drug abuse treatment system say that the illegal drug abuser has to "hit bottom" before he or she is ready for drug treatment. That is simply not true. This is another way of saying "Don't try to get addicts sober until they are ready." For many long term addicts, "bottom" is death.

In actuality, the earlier in his drug abuse career the drug abuser is forced to sober up the easier it is to keep him sober. The sooner the newly addicted are pried away from their dope, their brains and coping skills are less deteriorated. Dope does cause permanent brain damage and tears up the body in multiple ways. Drug induced heart attacks killed a young Elvis and an even younger Jim Morrison. Add River Phoenix to the list of dead celebrity junkies.

We need to get people off drugs as quickly as we possibly can after their first experience with drugs. That way we don't have to wait until five or ten years later or until he or she "hits bottom" to treat him or her.

Many people insist that involuntary drug treatment never works. This also is a fallacy. Involuntary drug treatment works as well or better than voluntary drug treatment. This is in spite of the fact that voluntary drug abusing patients are supposedly highly motivated and want to change. This is because of the high rate of drop out in voluntary programs. Of each six people entering voluntary therapeutic community drug treatment programs, only one finished. The other five dropped out. Only one in four stayed over three months. The first 90 days sober is the hardest.[5]

When is the best time to force addicts into treatment by using the power of the criminal justice system? Studies show that addicts are helped the most when this referral occurred at an early stage of their substance abusing career.[78]

As we will see, the substance abusers most in need of treatment avoid it the longest. Involuntary treatment, in spite of many people's belief to the contrary, works better than voluntary treatment. If you voluntarily enroll in a treatment program you can leave as soon as you get bummed out, bored, or want to go get high. You can't do that in involuntary programs. Forcing substance abusing people into treatment isn't enough. They also have to be forced into after-care or follow-up treatment.

Most opioid (e.g., heroin) users enter drug treatment only with some type of coercion. Civil commitment is useful in bringing narcotic addicts into treatment, but civil commitment alone is not drug treatment and cannot take the place of drug treatment. Drug addicts have to fix what's wrong inside to stay sober. The role of the law must be to keep them in treatment until that 'fixing' has progressed enough to guarantee sobriety.[78]

WITHOUT TREATMENT, FEAR OF JAIL WON'T STOP DRUG USE

Drug treatment was effective in producing positive behavioral outcomes. Twenty five percent of a sample of 405 male drug addicts never once returned to daily opioid use during a twelve-year follow-up period. By year twelve, sixty three percent of that total sample had not used opiates daily for at least three years. Data indicate that while they were in a drug treatment program, fifty percent of the sample stopped using opiates.

The drug addicts who entered drug treatment programs were usually being pressured by the legal system and their families. They admitted that without pressure, they probably would never had sobered up. The drug users said that probation, parole, and their legal problems had been important incentives for entering drug treatment.

STOP DRUGS - STOP CRIME

The TASC (Treatment Alternatives to Street Crime) program was established in 1972. This program identified drug-and/or alcohol-dependent, nonviolent offenders. Next, they referred them to treatment and monitored their progress. The treatment program was backed by court authority to keep illegal drug abusers in treatment. They showed that drug treatment served as an alternate or supplement to the criminal justice system. The TASC linkage provided a much less costly alternative to incarceration. The TASC clients remained in drug treatment longer. Most important to the success of TASC was the case management aspect which "tracked" (i.e., followed) illegal drug abusers through their drug abuse careers.[78]

The Drug Abuse Reporting Program (DARP) did a twelve year follow-up study of a large sample of drug abuse clients admitted into treatment programs between 1969 and 1971.[130] The Treatment Outcome Prospective Study evaluated 10,000 clients who had been admitted to 41 different treatment programs between 1979 and 1981.[61]

What did these massive studies show? Remember, that basically we are talking about voluntary treatment programs, though some clients were under pressure from the legal system to participate. People who remained in treatment for less than three months didn't do very well later as far as sobering up was concerned. Of those who stayed in treatment three months or longer, drug consumption and criminal behavior was greatly reduced. The most progress was made while people were actually in treatment. After treatment, they didn't do as well, but they still did better (in terms of drugs consumed and crimes committed) than they did before treatment.

Some treatment programs were better than others but all programs studied had at least some effectiveness. Length of time in treatment was the major predictor of success. Those who stayed in treatment the longest did the best later, in terms of quitting crime and drugs, having jobs, etc. We will see that in-prison programs like "Stay'n Out" can have an incredible success rate. Seventy eight percent of those who went through this in-prison program quit drugs and crime and did not get rearrested. The "Stay'n Out" program was lengthy, a year or two. This shows that it can take quite awhile (up to two years) of intensive work on sobriety to really make sobriety stick.[27, 45]

Even when participants in the mostly voluntary programs did not achieve total abstinence, drug consumption and criminality were reduced by treatment. Any way the numbers are run, treatment pays back society many fold for the dollars spent, on at least a ten to one ratio. With even the partially recovered addict, there are reductions in crime and victim losses, less foster home placements, less jail time and less police time required. Every treatment dollar easily saves ten that we would have had to spend elsewhere.

Treatment works. Even a little bit of treatment pays off. Longer time in treatment often brings total sobriety and an amazing turn-around in the lives of the addicted. Chapter 11 tells how we will guarantee that all of those with addiction problems will remain in treatment and follow-up as long as it is necessary in order to sober them up.

Reducing illegal drug abuse reduces crime. It's that simple. This is because heavy users of illegal drugs engaged in six times as much criminal activity as drug abusing criminals who had quit using.

WHERE THERE'S DOPE, THERE'S CRIME

More crime is committed by druggies because they need money to feed their drug habits. Drugs have eroded the addict's concept of what is right or wrong. Drug testing for all illegal drug abusing offenders is important to identify who has quit and who hasn't.[153]
Why many leaders in the criminal justice system cringe at the idea of drug rehab can be appreciated to some extent when we review the results of some disappointing studies. In one, the success rate (how many stayed sober after treatment) was only thirty eight percent.[36] But involvement was voluntary. Druggies were able to decide whether they wanted to continue in treatment or not. Unfortunately, we know the route taken by most drug addicts when given that choice. The treatment program studied involved what is referred to as a therapeutic community. This is one type of program utilized in drug treatment. The concept involves peer support, peer confrontation, and a 'healing' process which can emerge when a group is working on the same goals.
Most dropouts from one voluntary "therapeutic community" treatment programs occurred within the first 120 days. The highest dropout rate occurred within the first fifteen days. We see again that legal pressure plays a very important role in keeping people in drug treatment programs.[5]

DECRIMINALIZATION VS. LEGALIZATION

This book does not at any point recommend legalizing drugs which are now illegal. Hopefully there will never be a time when you can pick up your daily supply of heroin and cocaine along with your morning coffee at a 7-Eleven. This book **does** recommend decriminalization of drug charges. This means we by-pass the courts and jails and focus **hard** on sobriety. It is very important for addicts in compulsory drug treatment to receive legal protection. Once a drug user is in a drug treatment program, he should be obligated to go to his meetings and testings to guarantee that he is sober. The court system should not be involved, except to provide the legal backup to guarantee the drug abuser's continuation in the treatment program.

Someone in drug treatment should not have to make court appearances. If they do, they will be worried constantly about their legal status instead of focusing on getting sober. Then, the treatment program will not be effective. Some people may say we're coddling criminals if people don't do time for their crimes. There will be some crimes which will not be excused or forgiven even by drug treatment involvement.   But, the sober criminal is six times less likely to commit further crimes than the illegal drug user.

Stopping the illegal drug user from drugging goes a lot further toward crime prevention than continued involvement with courts and jails. People often say "Don't coddle criminals, lock them up!" But we have seen that doing time in prison does not stop people from doing drugs and crime. Some things do reduce crime but jails are not one of them.

Most prisoners, in spite of the hard-liners attitude, do get out of jail sooner or later. And as it is, most criminals (if all they got was jail, and no treatment and no follow-up) go back to drugs and crime. Many people maintain that since someone currently in jail isn't robbing anyone, keep him locked up longer. As it is now, people are not even doing time for their crimes. The reason for this is that judges keep emptying the jails of desperate felons because of the inhumanitarian overcrowding in the jails. In response to this people say "Build more jails." This book will prove that the "more and bigger jails" solution is exorbitantly costly, foolish, and plain doesn't work.

The rearrest rate for new crimes is between sixty to eighty percent when no attempts to guarantee sobriety are made after release from jail. Clients in drug treatment programs who are offered legal protection appreciate the end to the legal hassles. This legal protection from further prosecution needs to continue as long as they're sober, and of course don't commit any more crimes. This legal protection enhances treatment. The alternative of doing the time will still be there if the individual refuses to become involved in a diversion/involuntary sobriety program.

Many writers suggest that repeated interventions will probably be needed for most clients. The details of the "Sober Forever" Program can be found in Chapter 11. This program does **not** propose repeated interventions but **one long intervention** from the first time a pattern of drug abuse is identified. Involvement in the "Sober Forever" Program will end only when proof of sobriety has been provided for several years. Random testing as infrequently as once a year may be all that is needed after a few years of sobriety. Random means that the ex-druggie will never know when someone will show up and ask them to donate a urine sample.

Long-term client after-care and monitoring are essential parts of drug treatment programs. Compulsory treatment in the form of civil commitment increases treatment retention for drug abusers. The cost for treatment may appear high but treatment/prevention costs are only a small fraction of the cost of courts and incarceration.

There is overwhelming proof that compulsory treatment works. Not only that, compulsory treatment is the only intervention that works on a consistent and predictable basis. After compulsory treatment there is less drug and alcohol use, less criminal behavior and more clean and sober addicts working. Urine testing is an important tool in keeping addicts sober.[78]

Some writers say that if you reduce availability of drugs without reducing the demand for drugs, you increase crime. This is because when drugs are scarce, drug users will still obtain the higher-priced illegal drugs. They do this either through criminal activity within the illicit drug market or through other money-producing crimes.[95]

DO NOT REDUCE SUPPLY WITHOUT REDUCING DEMAND

Here are some standard assumptions of law enforcement: By making drugs harder to get through vigorous law enforcement we drive up the price of drugs and then less people will use drugs. At times this has been true. But often when the supply of drugs was reduced while demand was still high the result was higher-priced illegal drugs and more crime. Druggies often steal more to get their higher priced dope when it is harder to get.

Mostly, all the money spent on stopping supply has been wasted. The high priced helicopters, surveillance balloons, Coast Guard runs, paraquat spraying, have come to naught. In 1981 a kilogram of cocaine sold for $60,000 in Miami. In spite of the seizure of many tons of cocaine, in 1987 a Miami kilo of cocaine sold for $12,000.[42]

Sometimes disrupting street markets makes it harder for drug users to find dealers. A druggie who can't find a dealer can't buy drugs. Areas where street dealers have been driven out report lower property crime and drug use.[155]

Citizen patrols have been effective in disrupting street markets. Street markets (300 have been identified in New York City) are areas where drugs are sold openly on the streets.[25]

The drug abuse situation continues to deteriorate in most parts of the world, not just in the U.S. There are major escalations in the use of opiates and cocaine. There is a general sense that current approaches are not going to be effective, and that drug trafficking and drug use will continue to increase. A higher success rate in reducing supplies from sources outside the country is likely to result in the increased growth of a domestic industry.

This could include the cultivation and manufacturing of a variety of substances.[94]

CALIFORNIA FARMERS GROWING POT

Pot, or marijuana, is a big cash crop for many Northern California farmers. The economic vitality of unrelated businesses often become heavily dependent on the illicit drug industry. Most South American countries have national economies and foreign exchanges based primarily on the production of coca. Most of the coca goes to America.[94]

The supply reduction effort alone won't solve many problems. The risk of being identified or apprehended is seen among illegal drug users and sellers as being very low.

There are those who insist that, based on the above facts, we legalize drugs. This author opposes that solution because chaos reigns whenever it has been tried. We can stop the drug crime cycle by reducing demand. Educating people will help. Programs designed to reduce the acceptance of illegal substances have been popular. Until informed otherwise, many people still consider pot relatively harmless. So far, educational programs have been effective in some small ways, more so in certain populations. None have been effective in really reducing illegal drug demand.

There have been successful attempts at controlling epidemic illegal drug use in the past. Opium use in China was greatly reduced after World War II as a result of a massive government effort. Many people in the United States think the drug rehabilitation in China simply involved lining up and shooting all the illegal drug users and pushers. This is not true. Changes in the Chinese youth's view of drugs after World War II was accomplished by providing massive treatment and drug rehabilitation programs for all drug users. This stopped the creation of a new drug addict population. The drug addicts were encouraged to seek medical care in a nonpunitive atmosphere with a great deal of support from the community.[94]

The major thrust of current approaches to solve the drug problem include: (1)   Efforts to keep illegal drugs away from the user. (2) Publishing information about the horrors of the illegal drug menace. These approaches have had some minor impact. But the massive amounts of money spent on non-treatment approaches has mostly been wasted. On a dollar-for dollar-basis, comparing treatment with all other approaches, a dollar spent on treatment sobers up ten times more people than spending that dollar on any other approach. We need to keep people away from illegal drugs, not vice versa.

The facts are clear: Only reducing the demand for drugs is going to work. This can be done, and done much cheaper than the major efforts to control this epidemic which are now underway. Information about the involuntary sobriety program that will do this, called the "Sober Forever" Program, will be given in skeletal form through this book. Complete details of the plan are presented in Chapter 11.

STOP BLAMING THE GENES

Some researchers contradict some of the standard assumptions regarding substance abuse. For example, illegal drug addicted behavior is not necessarily progressive from mild to severe, though this frequently is the case. Also, genetics play a minor role in that development of illegal drug addicted behavior. It is still popular to blame substance abuse on the genes.[59]

Fraternal twins who lived together were more likely to share a drinking problem than identical twins who lived apart. A genetically transmitted characteristic is more likely to show up in identical twins, who have very similar gene pools. But fraternal twins, with fewer shared genes, are more likely to be alcoholics if they shared the same environment. It would follow that children growing up in a sober environment are less likely to be substance abusers than children whose parents drank alcohol or used drugs.[70]

The fact that substance abusing parents have a higher percentage of substance abusing children then the general population was used to prove the 'genetic connection.' The implication was that if substance abuse was in the genes, growing up in a sober world wouldn't change anything. The bad news is that we can't blame the genes anymore for drug and alcohol addiction. The good news from these studies is that sobering up parents, and of course keeping them sober, greatly increases the probability that their children will be grow up sober and stay sober.

Unfortunately, actual research evidence for the treatment success of the twelve step programs does not exist. A.A. does not keep records on the percentage of people who, after showing up for at least one meeting, stay sober. Less than twenty percent of those who are referred to A.A. (Alcoholics Anonymous) attend on a consistent basis.[59] Though records don't show it, we all know that many millions who have gone to and stuck with the 12 step programs (A.A., N.A.) have turned their lives around.

What is needed is a way to guarantee that people needing help get help. The way to do that is described in Chapter 11. There may come a time when A.A., as an organization, may find it has become a key link in an involuntary sobriety program. **Then** A.A. **will** help a much larger percentage of the people who show up to get sober. Even now, many people are ordered by the courts to show proof of attendance at A.A. or N.A. meetings.

Collaboration, rather than confrontation, is more likely to be effective as an illegal drug treatment intervention. For alcohol, hospital treatment programs are typically no more effective than shorter or less intense treatment programs. For drugs, the effectiveness of hospital treatment programs is hard to demonstrate.[93]

William Bennett, America's former drug czar, promised to work on a plan to cut demand. In spite of his promises, most of the new money ($1.2 billion dollars) he managed to pump into the "drug wars" went for law enforcement and new jails. Treatment funds in 1989 went from $621 million to $925 million out of a total federal drug wars budget of around $10 billion.[11]

How the addict performs in treatment is not nearly as important as what happens afterwards. Getting addicts off drugs is not nearly as hard as keeping them off drugs. Drug abusers seek treatment voluntarily, if they do so at all, only after the problem has been chronic for many years and has caused them legal, job and family problems.[18]

Treatment works well in the short-term, but permanent abstinence and complete social rehabilitation is achieved in only a minority of the patients who enter treatment voluntarily.   Most of those now being "forced" into treatment by the courts find that nobody seems to really notice or do anything if they quit going. They find that getting high is a lot more fun than being sober. It is no fun sitting in a group with other addicts all squirming in their chairs with their nerves jumping and raw. On top of that they are supposed to listen to all these people who are trying to find out why they are hurting inside. Boring! The newly sober druggie knows why he is hurting and what to do about it, and quickly. "Just ask Alice, when she's ten feet tall."

There are some universal drawbacks to the current almost completely voluntary treatment systems. These include late entry (after years of addiction) into attempted sobriety.   This late entry into treatment is usually followed by aftercare programs which are completely voluntary. With the exception of those few programs in which follow-up was done, they rarely worked. This means that when these people who were not forced to get into and **stay in** treatment were tracked down later to see how they were doing, most had gone back to drugs. For the little extra money spent on a hard "tail," or long-term tracking, the many thousands of dollars spent on treatment would not have been wasted.   It is useless to return sobered-up substance abusers, even after long absences, to an environment which supports drug abuse.[18]

CHANGING PLAYMATES AND PLAYGROUNDS

Should the newly sober drug user just coming out of a live-in treatment program be allowed to return home? If there is a good chance he/she will start using again when they get there, the answer is no. Alternate housing must be arranged for the newly sober druggie until their home environment has also become sober and supportive of sobriety.

Some researchers have tried to devise strategies to prevent relapse in drug abusing teens who can't go to a drug free environment. It has been suggested that they give their old friends plausible reasons for quitting drugs. For example, they could say they must be clean on urine tests or they will lose the privilege of using the car.[75]

In the "Sober Forever" Program proposed in Chapter 11 of this book, a new sober peer group will be provided for the teens trying to sober up. Everyone in this group will be working on sobriety. Once enrolled in the "Sober Forever" Program the ex-substance abuser **can** hang around with his old friends again - anytime his old friends decide (or it is decided for them) that they will be sober. To stay successfully sober, most substance abusers find they must "change playmates and playgrounds" (where you hang out, whom you hang out with).

A major problem for the newly sober and drug free teen is rebuilding trust and family relationships. Both of these are often destroyed during the addicted state. Selling sex for drugs or performing in pornographic movies is something many addicted teenagers will do, but something they would never do sober. Some writers still maintain that adolescents should be allowed to participate in treatment willingly since risk of failure is greater with an uncooperative teen.[75]

The problems with this kind of conclusion are that: (1) Involuntary treatment has a better success rate then voluntary treatment and (2) We cannot wait until people (teens, adults) decide to get sober. By the time this decision is made voluntarily, most addicts have done irreparable damage to their bodies, their lives, and to everyone whoever loved them. When sobriety is an option and not a firm demand, most substance abusers don't stay sober very long.

The decaying value system of a large sub-culture of mostly drug involved inner city youth is described. There, the goal of males is to get as many girls as possible to have their babies. The more times they can brag that they have just become a new father results in higher levels of esteem from peers.[73]

The results are illegitimacy rates of 70% to 80% in some populations, intergenerational poverty, social and family breakdown.

We are descending to the level of animals because the description of mating behavior in these subgroups resembles descriptions of mating behaviors of many animal species. The elk who has fought all the other elks and won gets to have exclusive sexual use of all of the female elks in the herd. He spends the whole season fighting and mating and is usually dead a few months later. But he has left his mark.

CHAPTER THREE

THE HIGH COST OF BEING HIGH

Can we afford to sober up America? We can't afford to not sober up America. What does it cost to have one individual on dope and stealing to support his habit? If he has a five hundred dollar-a-day drug habit, he has to steal $2,000 to $5,000 a day in property. This is assuming that the stolen goods can be fenced for ten to twenty percent of their actual value. This adds up to between $875,000 and $1,750,000 worth of goods that the druggie must steal from innocent victims a year in order to support his $500 dollar-a-day drug habit. Most of the $600 billion of goods stolen each year is used to buy drugs.[117]

Five out of six criminals who take dope stop stealing when they are forced to sober up.[152] Sixty-five to seventy percent of all placements of children in foster homes are a result of parental substance abuse.[31,135] Foster home placement for one child costs taxpayers $1,000 or more per month. It costs taxpayers up to $2,500 or more a month per child for a group home placement. Some children too disturbed to be placed in foster homes must go to highly structured but very expensive group homes.

If a family of six is broken up because of substance-abusing parents and the four children are placed in foster homes, this costs taxpayers a minimum of $4,000 a month. This adds up to a total of $48,000 a year. When sobered up, most of these parents can function successfully in the role of parent. While under the influence they neglect, abuse, molest or abandon their children. Drunk and loaded parents have mood swings. They are irresponsible. They give birth to drug addicted children.

The whole foster care system is plagued with multiple problems. One of the biggest problems is the permanent trauma that children suffer due to the

separation from their parents. A new, very costly program is being tried. Social workers with a case load of only two families each are providing multiple supportive services designed to help keep families together.[68]
 In spite of huge costs, this new program is still cheaper than the $48,000 a year cost of foster care for four children. That job of keeping shaky families together will be much easier when sobriety is guaranteed. Most of the parents in these costly programs are substance abusers. The social workers seldom have the power they need to enforce sobriety. With intensive involvement and family support services, they manage to talk a lot of parents into getting sober. What if we coupled that support system with an involuntary sobriety program in which sobriety would be guaranteed? Meaning, sobriety would not be contingent upon how good a sales person the social worker was. When that is the case, the social workers' success rate in patching up broken families will soar to nearly 100 percent.

DOESN'T SOBERING UP ADDICTS COST TOO MUCH?

 Let's drop in on Joe. He is the father in a marginally functioning drug abusing family. Foster placement has not yet occurred. Joe has been using drugs for two years. He has had six arrests, a couple for the possession of illegal drugs, the rest for miscellaneous infractions. Druggies get in more trouble than non-users. All Joe's arrests have gone to warrants because he never showed up for his court hearings. Since the jails are full and everyone is busy, no one has bothered yet to make him settle up on his "debt" to society.
 Joe lost his full-time job due to excessive absences. Substance abusers often have trouble getting up in the morning. Joe now works part-time off and on at odd jobs. Sometimes he helps a buddy haul away trash or do yard clean-up. He pays for much of his drugs by being a middleman between his dealer and a few friends. Without quite realizing it, Joe has become a small time dope dealer.

He is a participant in America's fastest growing multi-level marketing system and it isn't Amway.

His family is receiving welfare assistance at a cost to taxpayers of $10,000 or more a year. Some of that, often a lot of that, goes to buy dope. Double that $10,000 figure if you want to include other services, such as medical care. The police have come several times to Joe's home because of domestic violence. This has cost taxpayers several thousand dollars in police time. Drug addicts often have rages over little or nothing. Joe's four children are failing in school. They are confused, angry, and can't concentrate well because of stress. This is the result of the neglect and violence children often experience in the substance abusing home. Special tutors and expensive educational programs have been implemented for the children at their schools. This can add another $10,000 a year to the cost of educating Joe's children. Add the cost of free breakfasts and lunches at school because dope buying cuts into the home food budget.

Child Protective Services is closely monitoring the family situation. They haven't yet put the children in foster homes. The foster home system is jam-packed already. So, Child Protective Services has provided additional support services to the family costing taxpayers another $10,000 a year. The social workers are trying to prevent foster placement. The schools have reported strange bruises on the children. One more incident will trigger removal of Joe's children to foster home placement at a cost to taxpayers of $48,000 a year.

After he finally does something bad enough, Joe will go to jail for at least a year, costing taxpayers somewhere between $30,000 to $50,000. It will cost taxpayers at least $20,000 or more just to process Joe through the courts and the legal system. Joe's substance abuse addiction is costing taxpayers anywhere from $100,000 to a half million dollars a year.

What would happen if we sober up Joe? The chances are that if he has been stealing, he will stop stealing. Five out of six criminals stop stealing when they sober up. There is a fifty percent chance that sobered up, Joe will be back to work in a couple of years.

EX-ADDICTS PAYING TAXES

When he's back to work, Joe will be paying taxes of $4,000 to $6,000 a year. Sober, Joe can most likely function well in the parent role. His sobriety could save taxpayers $100,000 to a half million dollars a year. This is because the wide array of the above-listed services/costs (e.g., foster homes) are no longer incurred by the county/city/state.

What will it cost to sober up Joe? If his wife has ejected him from the family home, room and board must be provided for him. This can be done for as little as $250 a month in "sober living" homes, or even less in other settings. Detailed cost estimates are presented in Chapter 11, but it would cost about $4,000 a year or less to keep Joe sober for a year. Joe's second year of guaranteed sobriety would cost maybe half that.

By the third year of Joe's sobriety, there is a fifty percent chance that he would be working and starting to pay back, in taxes, the money or loans spent sobering him up. Once sober, any stealing Joe was doing to support his drug habits stops. The annual savings to society by sobering up Joe could be over a million dollars. Can we afford to sober up Joe? We can't afford not to. The least expensive way of sobering him up would be in his own home. To make that work, there would have to be at least a once a day contact with Joe. These contacts could include surprise visits to his home to collect urine samples. Possible other supports for his sobriety would be group meetings, electronic monitoring, buddy calls, etc. See Chapter 11 for more details of the "Sober Forever" Program.

A SOBER AMERICA MEANS EMPTY JAILS

If Joe fights sobriety, he may periodically have to spend a few days in jail. These short stints in the slammer are designed to help convince Joe that total and permanent sobriety is the way to go. These brief periods of jail time, after all else has failed, will help Joe realize he **will** be sober: Joe can choose whether his sobriety will happen in confinement or in freedom. Joe's first slip might result in five days in jail. His next slip could result in ten days in jail, then thirty days. This will be a special jail, where at least eight hours a day are spent in study on how to become sober and how to stay sober.

The first thing all our criminal justice system leaders will claim is that we have no room in the jails. They will say we can't give Joe his few days a year of incarceration even if it becomes necessary. The solution? Empty jail beds can be produced by phasing substance abusers currently in jail into the "Sober Forever" Program. The petty criminals whose alcohol or drug abuse was the major reason they went to jail would be excellent candidates for such an out-of-prison program. The data is clear: Most of the people in jail who did crimes while under the influence stop doing crime when they sober up and stay sober.

Fifty to eighty-five percent of all people arrested for any reason are under the influence of drugs/alcohol at the time of their crime and at the time of their arrest. Multiple studies cited in the section in this book on "References, Reviews and Notes" confirm this fact. Cities on the West Coast report the highest rates. Five out of six substance abusers who sober up do not get rearrested. Most people who commit crimes are under the influence. If they are not kept sober, when they get out of prison they keep committing crimes. Sobering up America will reduce the number of crimes and criminals moving through the criminal justice system by at least 50%.

Let's jump to five years down the road when the "Sober Forever" Program being proposed in this book is fully operational at all levels. The billion plus dollars now spent by San Diego County on its criminal justice system every year will be cut at least by half. Only a small portion of the savings needs to be used to continue to guarantee San Diego County's sobriety. The rest could be used for parks, housing, libraries, etc. We will be able to rip the bars off the empty jails and finally have someplace to house the homeless and a place where the addicted among them can sober up.

In 1992 seventy percent of the San Diego County's total yearly budget was spent on public protection, including the Sheriff's Department, courts, probation, District Attorney's Office, and the Public Defender's Office.

DRIVE-BY SHOOTERS: LOADED GUNS AND LOADED ON DRUGS

Worried about gangs, drive-by shootings? Illegal drugs are involved in almost all gang slayings in one way or another. Turf wars are fought over who is going to sell drugs to whom. Most of the drive-by shooters were under the influence of drugs/alcohol at the time of the shootings. Sobering up America's teenagers will cut the juvenile violence/homicide rate by fifty to eighty percent.

Costs to run the criminal justice system have risen astronomically in the past ten years because of substance abuse. Cops, jails, justice systems and security businesses are truly the growth industries of the decade. And these costs are just the beginning of what substance abuse costs America.

Substance abuse drains our finances in many other ways. Locking up druggies/alcoholics who have committed crimes while under the influence is very expensive. Three youths could be sent to Harvard for a year for what it costs to keep one youth locked up in prison for a year. Millions of dollars are lost in tax revenue because most substance abusers cannot work and therefore don't pay taxes. Many more millions of dollars are spent to support the increasingly larger number of totally disabled individuals whose disabilities have been completely produced by substance abuse.

DRUG ADDICTS AND ALCOHOLICS COLLECT SOCIAL SECURITY

Most Americans are probably not aware that drug addiction and alcoholism are considered as legal disabilities. Not many people are aware that if you can prove you are a hopeless alcoholic or drug addict you can collect a monthly Social Security check from the government. SSI stands for supplemental security income. If you have never paid a dime into the social security system you can still collect SSI if you can prove you are disabled. There were 5.4 million people in America on the SSI roles as of December, 1992. Fifty four thousand thirty nine of them were receiving these monthly checks because of a "disability" caused by substance abuse. Thirty thousand four hundred sixty seven were alcoholics, 8,595 were drug addicts. Fourteen thousand nine hundred seventy seven were dual diagnosed, meaning they were "disabled" because of abusing both alcohol and drugs.

The SSA or regular Social Security program applies to disabled people who have paid into the program. In December 1992 there were 26,000 alcoholics and 5,500 drug addicts in that program. The total number of "disabled" substance abusers in both programs is 85,539. With an average monthly payment of $316, SSI substance abusers are paid over $17 million a month or almost $205 million a year. SSA payments are usually higher. If we assume that the SSA payments average $500 a month, another almost $16 million a month or $188 million a year is paid out. A rough total of benefits paid to substance abusers in both programs is $393 million a year. There are some 270,000 individuals who are labeled as mentally disabled also receiving Social Security benefits who have substance abuse problems. Costs of paying out money to people who use a good portion of their government provided Social Security disability benefits for drugs or alcohol runs over a billion dollars a year.

Someone called a "payee" may handle the "disabled" drug addict's and alcoholic's money. Substance abusers can be very obnoxious and insistent people. Most of the payees I have met give the substance abuser his money on the first of the month when the checks come in. Sometimes this payee will pay the druggie's rent some place, and perhaps even try to provide food for the druggie. That leaves the "disabled" druggie free to focus on getting drugs. They don't have to worry about eating or sleeping anymore.

If they get sick, they have access to medical care which they qualify for since they are "disabled." They may spend their time collecting and selling things out of dumpsters.

They are free to make a few drug deals in order to keep themselves supplied with illegal drugs. Many thanks to our generous Americans who have supplied the rest of their needs.

Not all "disabled" drug addicts and alcoholics have payees. Some have managed to never have a payee, or have managed to get off payee status by having a doctor write a letter saying they can now manage their own funds. Many of the "homeless" receive Social Security disability payments for alcoholism and drug addiction. They may have their checks go to a bank or to a friend's house. For a few days at the beginning of each month many of them "party" (abuse drugs and/or alcohol) until the money is gone. They prefer this to paying rent. Many substance abusers with payees have gone to the Social Security office to gripe about how their payee was handling their money. They have talked their worker into switching them to a new payee whose name they provided. **SURPRISE!** That new payee often turned out to be a fellow drunk or dope fiend whose only payback for being a "payee" is "a little help from his friend" to get high when the checks come in.

The citizens of the United States are contributing to the incomes of the liquor industry and our friendly neighborhood dope dealers. The liquor industry plows some of their revenues back to the government through taxes. The dope dealers do not. The general public may not be aware that each tax paying citizen, through their contributions to the Social Security fund, are buying a drunk a jug of wine or a six pack of beer each month. Or, they're buying a line of coke for a drug addict. The Social Security Administration has become one of the biggest "enablers" in the history of mankind. An enabler is one whose actions make it possible for substance abusers to keep abusing substances. The Social Security Administration has claimed that they are going to correct that problem. At the time of the first printing of this book they had not yet done that. Our Social Security contributions do also, of course, provide needed housing and care for the truly disabled.

GETTING ON SOCIAL SECURITY

The following is a typical legal brief, much like those presented by lawyers in the Social Security Administration courtrooms of America and heard by administrative law judges on a daily basis. The brief argues that the individual in question is disabled due to substance abuse. Appropriate legal precedents are cited. The result of this legal brief: One more substance abuser started receiving monthly Social Security disability checks.

"The developing case law on alcoholism under the Social Security Act reflects the increasingly accepted view of alcoholism as a disease.

"Even before the change in regulations, 20 C.F.R. 404.151 (c)2(iii) 1975 repealed, the law in California is that alcoholism by itself, could be disabling.

"In 1975, the Ninth Circuit ruled in Griffis v. Weinberger 509 F. 2d 837 (9th Cir. 1975) that alcoholism itself could be disabling without any underlying impairments.

"The opinion refers to the Mays court's statement in 206 F. Supp. 170 (S.D.W. Va. 1962), that the claimant would have the capacity to work if he would simply stop drinking. The Griffis court said:

"'Insofar as Mays can be read as holding that an alcoholic can never be found disabled because all that he need do is 'stop alcohol,' we think it's wrong. Some alcoholics can stop; more cannot.'

"The Griffis case was remanded for a new administrative hearing at which the proper standard should be applied.

"The court in Stevens v. Califano, CCH U.I.R. Para. 16.099 (N.D.N.Y. 1978) noted that the older Osborne and Mays (409 F 2d 37, 6th line 1969). Supra, cases relied, at least in part, on administrative regulations which have now been repealed. The court stated:

"'The more modern view is that acute alcoholism is a disease, and, in certain circumstances, can, itself, be a physical or mental impairment within the meaning of the Act.'

"The court also noted that the Administration must look at alcoholism in combination with all other impairments of a claimant.

"Summary judgment for the claimant was ordered in <u>Lewis v. Weinberger</u>, 402, F. Supp. 632 (D. Md 1975) where the A.L.J. (Administrative Law Judge) had found the claimant's alcoholism prevented him from performing gainful activity but no associated physical manifestations from the disease had developed until after the claimant's insured status had expired. Since he was disabled from the alcoholism itself before the insured status expired, the court awarded him benefits.

"It should be noted that the Listing of Impairments refers to alcoholism and drug addiction in section 12.04 20 CF 2 Subpart P. App 1 P B 11: 12.00 Mental Disorders (c) Other functional non-psychotic disorders, including 'alcohol addiction and drug addiction.'

"Claimant made a prima facie showing that he was disabled by <u>alcoholism</u> which Secretary of Health and Human Services failed to rebut by showing that his alcoholism was not disabling, or by presenting any evidence of specific jobs in the economy which claimant could perform; thus, claimant was entitled to Social Security Disability Benefits. See Johnson v. Harris, 625 F. 2d 311 (9th Cir. 1980). Severe alcoholism alone may be disabling within the meaning of the Social Security Act. Johnson v. Harris, supra."

MORE GOOD NEWS FOR DRUG ADDICTS

In February, 1994, there was even more good news for drug addicts. One of the criteria for getting on Social Security disability as a drug addict is that you have not earned enough money in the past year to support yourself. One drug addict had been denied Social Security benefits because he had taken in substantial income in the past year through his sales of illegal drugs. However, since he used most of that money to buy more drugs to feed his habit, it was ruled that that money could not be considered as income, and instead, was part of his addiction pattern.

The Social Security Administration maintains that all of the 54,039 substance abusers receiving SSI (Supplemental Security Income) payments have "payees." The 31,500 "disabled" substance abusers on SSA or regular social security have been assigned payees on a case by case basis. These "payees" supposedly handle the substance abusers money. The Social Security Administration also maintains that there are requirements that the substance abusers involve themselves in treatment. In my experience, I have yet to see any substance abusers on the SSI or SSA roles being made to follow through on getting treatment or getting sober.

I tried to counsel Ruth who was receiving Social Security disability income due to her alcoholism. She was ordered to attend A.A. meetings. She did for a time. She said that she hated those "damn meetings." So, she began forging signatures on her monthly attendance reports which she mailed to a Social Security Office in Burbank, California, 120 miles from her home. At no time, whether or not she was attending A.A. meetings, was there any change in her drinking pattern. She was drunk every day by noon. That fact didn't stop her Social Security "disability" checks from coming each month like clockwork.

She went to jail three times in 1993 for 30 to 90 day stints for various out of control behaviors. One trip to jail was for stabbing her boyfriend. "But I hardly made a mark, just a little tiny one on his arm and another one on his leg," she insisted. She was ordered to pick one of perhaps 20 programs in San Diego for spouse/significant others abusers. She said she couldn't afford to pay the $50 a month they wanted for these programs. This was because all she got was her Social Security disability check for about $600 a month for her alcoholism. She was afraid she would be sent back to jail for not participating but she couldn't stand to hear other people tell their problems.

The court had completely missed the fact that alcohol was driving all of Ruth's out of control behavior. The court's assumption had obviously been that the spousal abuse classes would stop Ruth's violence. Quitting drinking is the only thing that would stop Ruth's violence. I offered to write the judge a letter and ask to substitute counseling with me for the spousal abuse program. Ruth liked this idea until I said, "I called the pharmacy near your home and as soon as we get a prescription they are willing to administer liquid antibuse to you every morning." I had suggested liquid antibuse because I have seen alcoholics go to pharmacies and pretend to swallow the pills so they could continue drinking.

"Isn't that the stuff that makes you sick if you drink?" Ruth asked.

"Yes," I answered.

"That's the stupidest thing I ever heard!" Ruth said. "You know I have to have a couple beers to get going in the morning."

Ruth and the other addicted will give us ten million excuses as to why they can't get to a sobriety center to start attending their meetings. "I didn't have the money for the trolley/subway/bus to get to the meetings," or "My friend's car broke down," or "My parakeet died."

After the "Sober Forever" Program begins, we will go to the homes of people like Ruth and tell them "You don't live here anymore." Then they will be taken either to a detox center, jail, or a sober living home, depending on their level of toxicity, violence, and degree of cooperation.

In Ruth's case, diverting her money to a sober living home for perhaps a year would give her a chance to sober up and see how much of her brain was left. She said, "It took me a year to learn my new phone number since I got hit on the head" (in one of her many drunken skirmishes).

Implementation of rehabilitation programs to enforce sobriety among those who are "disabled" because of substance abuse requires no new legislation. There already are legal mandates in the Social Security Codes.

These require that those individuals who are identified as disabled due to substance abuse obtain treatment. These requirements, to my knowledge, are either not enforced at all, or are enforced only inefficiently and sporadically. It appears to me that qualifying as a "disabled" substance abuser at this time guarantees an indefinite period of hassle-free highs.

BUYING A BEER FOR YOUR FAVORITE ALCOHOLIC

I maintain that the individuals receiving public monies should not be allowed to use these monies to stay under the influence of drugs and/or alcohol. The taxpayers should be able to decide who they would like to treat to a beer or a line of cocaine. I maintain that we can enroll these "disabled" substance abusers into a sobriety program that will guarantee that they get the help they need to sober up. If, even sober, the hundreds of thousands "disabled" substance abusers now receiving Social Security benefits are still disabled, so be it.

Sometimes, even after sobering up, the damage to the brain and body is too extensive to allow the substance abuser to ever work again. But, after they sober up, we may end up with some nice surprises from many of our "disabled" druggies and alcoholics. I would gamble that, sober, a good percentage of them would return to work within a year or two. We need to sober up even those addicts who will remain disabled after they are sober. Even if they can't work, after they sober up, we will have added dignity, self-worth, and years to their lives. Also, they won't be going around doing "Just little" stabbings of their friends.

Many mentally disabled individuals, some with diagnoses of depression or schizophrenia, have a secondary diagnosis of substance abuse, drugs or alcohol. Many people suffering from emotional problems feel that they can experience some relief from their disturbing symptoms of emotional distress, (paranoia or depression) through chemicals. They may claim that marijuana or alcohol relaxes them and helps them sleep. Or the depressed person may claim that "speed" or methamphetamines make them feel better.

DRUGS AND MENTAL ILLNESS

For two years, from 1986 to 1988, I ran a halfway house/independent living center for schizophrenics. The project failed and I lost a $40,000 investment. I found that I wasn't dealing with just schizophrenia, I was dealing with a population of illegal drug/alcohol abusing schizophrenics who tore everything apart. That's what got us evicted. If those drug abusing schizophrenics had been sober, I think I could have helped some of them.

I have met many emotionally disabled individuals who entered the mental health system after extensive substance abuse. These are individuals whom I believe never would have become schizophrenic or psychotic or depressed had they never abused substances. Many drug abusers experience paranoid episodes after long and heavy "speed" runs. Once they become paranoid, they will often remain permanently paranoid and schizophrenic, with or without further illegal drug usage. Research confirms these impressions.[9,15] I have seen mentally ill substance abusers whose symptoms disappeared when they were cut off from their substances for example, if they ended up in jail for a time. I have seen these same individuals become completely psychotic again a short time after they got reconnected with their favorite substances.

The fact is that alcohol, marijuana, and a wide variety of other "feel good" chemicals can cause a resurgence of psychiatric symptoms.[9] These symptoms can include hallucinations and dangerous depressions. Alcoholics have a much higher suicide rate than the general population. If we enlarge our ambitions to sober up even the people with secondary diagnoses of substance abuse, many of them will stop being disabled because their psychoses and depressions will disappear when they sober up. Of course, many individuals displaying symptoms of mental illness who are abusing substances will still have their mental illness even after getting sober. But substance abusing schizophrenics often lead chaotic and dangerous lives. Sober, their lives and their psychiatric symptoms such as hallucinations and delusions are much more controllable. Their danger to others will reduce.

EFFECTIVE PAIN CONTROL

I have seen many individuals who were light users of illegal drugs/alcohol until they received a work injury. After such injuries, they found that using larger amounts of the same alcohol or drugs which they used before would kill the pain. In fact, alcohol and/or heroin worked better than anything they could get from their typically conservative physicians. These are special cases, and may have to be treated differently than those cases not involving physical injury. Fortunately, this is a small minority of drug/alcohol addicted individuals. Even so, they will have to become sober with the rest, with perhaps stronger medications prescribed for pain relief.

American doctors typically under-prescribe for pain. They seem to think that giving strong narcotics for pain control will turn people into drug addicts. The truth is that less than one in 1,000 pain sufferers try to get pain relieving drugs once their pain is gone. For individuals with a prior drug abuse history the addiction rate after being prescribed pain relievers is a bit higher. Thoughts about pain control are gradually changing. The morphine pump is coming into its own. **Untreated** pain causes much more physical and emotional damage than the slight risk of addiction when appropriate pain killing medications are prescribed.[100, 123]

The morphine pump is a self administered pain control instrument. Such a device has allowed many individuals to keep working who otherwise would have been unable to even think because of their pain.

On a talk show, I heard two gay men talk about a black boy who had been born with AIDS whom they had adopted. Two weeks before he died the AIDS infected youth was skiing. His pain, which would have kept him in cold sweats and flat on his back till his death, was controlled on the ski slopes with a morphine pump. The boy was going to die, whether he was in pain or not in pain. With the pain killers, it is very clear that his quality of life in his last days was immensely improved.

The sobriety plan outlined in Chapter 11 can now begin to be applied to our "disabled" substance abusers receiving Social Security. Here's how this would be done: All the "disabled" substance abusers would receive notice with their monthly check that they were going to be enrolled in a new program. They would be told that they had three months to sober up. They will be given a list of programs that help people become sober and stay sober. They can enroll in any of these programs which will attest to and help them attain sobriety any time within the next three months. The staff at the program they choose (not the substance abuser) will submit proof that they are attending meetings and testing sober twice a week.

If that proof is submitted, everything continues as before. Their checks keep coming. If such proof of sobriety is not received, with their next check they are told that they have two months left. If they haven't gotten started on their sobriety by the third month, they will receive a notice that this will be their last check. In order to qualify for any further benefits they must go sign up at one of the "Sober Forever" Program Centers.

Maybe they will have managed to sober up on their own in the three months since their first notice. If so, all they have to do is come in to test periodically to prove continued sobriety. The "Sober Forever" Program Center in which they have enrolled will decide what is needed in each case to guarantee sobriety. In cases of alcohol abuse, daily testing might be required, possibly breathalyzer tests to check B.A.C. (Blood Alcohol Content). They might be required to take liquid antibuse in front of a witness on a daily basis. Their mouth should be open with no liquid dripping out after taking the antibuse. When antibuse is in the system, drinking alcohol causes severe nausea. Twice a week urine testing will pick up most drug abuse. Even so, this should be done on a random basis. That is, the substance abuser should never know on what day he is to be tested.

A SUBSTANCE ABUSE 'DISABILITY' IS NOT A LICENSE

Law does not give the right to stay drunk or loaded on drugs from then on just because someone begins to receive Social Security benefits as a "disabled" substance abuser.

Since his checks are to be cut off if he doesn't go to a "Sober Forever" Program Center, the "disabled" substance abuser probably will show up there. But when he does, if he is under the influence of alcohol or drugs, he will be charged with public intoxication. Then, he will be tried and sentenced to probation via a closed circuit TV connection to the court room. This will all be done in a few minutes. Conditions of his probation will be successful involvement in the "Sober Forever" Program. Now, he is enrolled in a sobriety program he can't quit. How his case is handled from that point on will be up to the "Sober Forever" Program Center in which he enrolled. See Chapter 11 for the variety of options to be utilized at that point.

In brief, he may be sent to detox, he may have his funds diverted to a sober living center. There, he and other sober buddies will help each other to work on sobriety. He may be assigned to a remote desert "Sober Forever" Program Center. If all else fails and he keeps not showing up to work on his sobriety, we will go look for him. When we find him, if he is under the influence, brief periods in jail might be required. It is a fail safe system that guarantees sobriety.

What if these "disabled" substance abusers ignore all the notices about the new program? What if they never show up to work on getting sober and their money is cut off? What if they choose continued substance abuse over sobriety, even if they somehow have to finance it themselves? Then, taxpaying citizens will no longer be in the role of enablers by supplying the "disabled" substance abuser with money to purchase their favorite 'feel good' chemicals.

What do we say to the people who will exclaim "Oh, they will turn to crime and they will prey on society if we don't pay for their dope and booze." That is bribery. That would be like paying the French to not rob our boats in 1798.   We refused to succumb to bribery then.   Why should we give in to threats now?

Others may say that we will create a whole new population of homeless alcoholics and drug addicts. They may maintain that if the "disabled" substance abusers' funds are cut off, that could well force them onto the streets and into trouble (e.g., public drunkenness or arrests for being under the influence).   If those kind of brushes with the law do occur, that will change their legal status and make them eligible for participation in our "Sober Forever" Program. The laws to do this are already on the books.

JAILS: THE NEW ASYLUMS

Sheriff Jim Roache said his seven jails in San Diego County are really warehouses for the mentally ill. In addition to the mentally ill, the jails were filled with homeless people who were repeatedly drinking in public.[56]

Sobering up drug/alcohol abusing schizophrenics would result in large numbers of them permanently graduating from the mental health system.   The spontaneous remission rate for schizophrenia is as high as 60%.[16]   But there is little hope that the drug/alcohol abusing schizophrenic will escape the mental health system as long as they are using/abusing substances which are so toxic and damaging to the brain and the body.

Even if substance abusing "schizophrenics" are prescribed large doses of antipsychotic drugs such as prolixin or haldol, these drugs are often relatively ineffective.   Their usefulness is reduced because of the other chemicals (illegal drugs/alcohol) being used by these individuals.

Sobering up the mentally ill is not going to completely solve the problems created by our abandonment of that population. We closed down most of the treatment centers for the mentally ill and discharged them onto the streets. But sobering up the substance abusing mentally ill will make a very large dent in that population.

Some schizophrenics who are drug/alcohol abusers will still be psychotic even when sober. But they will still fare better in society. Why are so many substance abusing schizophrenics in the homeless population? For one thing, landlords get into this nasty habit of expecting the rent. When these substance abusing schizophrenics no longer have first-of-the-month drug/alcohol rampaging binges, landlords won't be kicking them out into the streets. (The Social Security disability checks come on the first of the month.)

A significant percentage of schizophrenics are dual diagnosed (alcohol/substance abuse and schizophrenia). The dual diagnosed population of schizophrenics ends up on the streets much more often than the sober mentally ill. The behavior of sober schizophrenics rarely produces the societal anger caused by the out of control behaviors of the substance abusing schizophrenic.

A PLEASANT SURPRISE!

I believe that America has no other choice but to implement the "Sober Forever" Program described in Chapter 11, or one much like it. I believe that the substance abusers receiving Social Security should be and will be required to sober up. When that happens, some of them are going to surprise us. After a time, some will have recovered enough to be able to return to work. Others, even without continued substance abuse, will never be able to work again. They will be too damaged in body and mind after their long-term abuse of substances. But sober, they will live longer, cost less to care for, and have a greatly improved quality of life.

Substance abuse doesn't just cost money.   The emotional costs and losses in human resources are so high they can never be fully measured or appreciated.   The child who ends up alone and afraid in a foster home because his parents are substance abusers experiences terrible emotional pains.   For most of the over a million men or women locked up in jail in the United States, there are heartbroken parents, brothers and sisters.   Prisoners leave parents, wives, husbands and children behind who grieve over the loss of their loved ones in jail.

How can you measure the pain caused by the shattering of the lives and families left behind?   What do parents always want for their children?   A good life!   The pain and wounds caused by having a son or daughter in jail leave emotional scars that never heal.   How could you ever say you succeeded as a parent if your child is in jail?   What a horrible waste to have over a million Americans locked up in jail.   Especially since we know that jail could have been prevented in far more than fifty percent of those cases.   How?   If that   person in jail had been helped to sober up much earlier in their substance abuse career they never would have become involved in crimes, courts and jails.

Substance abuse is a factor in easily over fifty percent of the arrests of all people currently serving time in jails across the United States.   In some places, 85% of all people arrested for any crime are loaded at the time of their arrest.[17]   It is likely that even a large percentage of those who tested sober at the time of their arrest had been drunk or high a few hours or days before.   The anger and anti-social attitude caused by substance abuse do not instantly end with sobriety, especially sobriety of a few hours or a few days.   Of course, people are the most dangerous when they are actively under the influence.

It is likely that substance abuse was a factor in much more than the 50% to 85% figures reported.   People under the influence of drugs or alcohol are much more likely to commit crimes.   Five out of six drug abusing criminals quit doing crime when they sober up.   Many of the people who were sober when they were caught in the middle of a crime were not sober because they wanted to be sober. Many crimes are committed to get money for drugs. If the accidentally sober junkie hadn't been caught in the middle of a crime, they wouldn't have stayed sober for very long.

Substance abuse can continue to produce problem behavior for weeks after people sober up. In fact, it probably takes a year or two for the substance abuser's dead conscience to make a fair recovery. However, after even hours or just a week of sobriety we will see some major improvements in the behavior of substance abusers and a great reduction in their levels of violence.

If all the drug addicts and alcoholics who are causing so much damage are sobered up, crime will not cease. There will still be a small, residual population of dangerous offenders. Even sober, even with attempts at rehabilitation, a small percentage of our criminals will probably need to spend the rest of their lives in jail in order to protect the public.

As it is now, less than 15% of all criminals get any rehabilitation while they are in jail.[87,120] When that disgraceful situation is corrected our jail population will decline to a tenth of what it is now.

DRUGS AND HOMELESSNESS

Does substance abuse cause homelessness? The answer is a resounding **"YES."** Some researchers estimate that 38% of the homeless are severe alcoholics and 15% are drug addicts. Some homeless are both alcoholics and drug addicts. Other researchers estimate that substance abuse problems in the homeless range between 12% and 60%. Homeless women with children are thought by some to have low rates of substance abuse, but other investigators have reported that 45% of these mothers were abusing drugs or alcohol.[10, 89, 124]

Deteriorated behavior occurs when people are under the influence of drugs and/or alcohol. They rampage in, and even burn down their own living quarters. The substance abuser uses available finances, even his general relief welfare payments, to buy alcohol/drugs instead of paying the rent.   All of the above irresponsible and out-of-control behaviors result in his being evicted from his residence, rendering him homeless.   If we sober up the homeless, will that act alone reduce the number of homeless people by fifty percent?   There is evidence attesting to this.   What about homeless women and their children?   Are drugs again to blame for a large part of the problem?   **YES!**[124]

Many sober women are homeless because they are escaping dangerous substance abusing spouses or companions.[10]   What if these substance abusing men were enrolled in the involuntary sobriety program from the time of the first 911 domestic violence call?   In most cases, the abuse would stop.   Most child beatings would stop.   Much homelessness would be prevented.   If mom is the one on drugs, once sober, she can usually function in the role of mother.   Mom and her husband or live-in boyfriend can be a family, get a life, and a chance at the American dream.

WHAT IF WE JUST SAY NO TO DRUGS A LITTLE LOUDER?

How about a speaker's bureau to put out the anti-drug message?   Ex-addicts and drug counselors could go to industries, schools,   Rotary Clubs and many other places to share the anti-drug message.   What if each time they gave a speech, we rounded up one hundred homeless drug addicts and bussed them in to listen?   Will these one hundred homeless drug addicts we drive to each anti-drug speech immediately start saying "No" to drugs?   The homeless druggie might go to the meetings if he is promised a free meal.   But he would be nodding out during the anti-drug speech and if he can get it, he will shoot up immediately afterward.

The point is, we are not reaching the people we need to reach through media campaigns.   For the homeless druggie, getting drugs and getting high is a higher priority than jobs, housing or even food. Free food is available to the homeless druggie at the soup kitchens. As a society, we have inadvertently become enablers. We help the homeless druggie remain a homeless druggie by giving him free food and free shelter. That way he can focus on getting more dope instead of worrying about hustling enough food to avoid starvation. Should we stop feeding our drug addicts? No, but we should also sober them up if we want to have the hope that they will one day learn to feed themselves.

There are those among the poor who use drugs and live in the ghetto who say "If I sober up, what's in it for me? There are no jobs. Besides, when I'm sober I'm reminded of my poverty and misery. I can forget those things when I have numbed my pain with drugs."

WHAT'S FIRST, JOBS OR SOBER?

It sounds simple, give them jobs and money and they will sober up. A neat bargain. But we've gone that route before and it doesn't work. The druggie can't do an eight to five job even if it pays $15 an hour. The druggie can't get up in the morning. The druggie can't remember what the boss told him to do. If the boss tells him again what to do, this time with a little irritation in his voice, the druggie is likely to shout "Get off my back!" and walk off the job. If the druggie does manage to get to work, his mood swings and irritability on the job get him fired or cause him to quit in a tantrum.

Some say it's society's fault that there are substance abusers. Let's face it, there is not true equal opportunity in America or anywhere in the world. Someone with a higher I.Q.. (Intelligence Quotient) who has a rich family and an education has a higher probability of success than someone who was born and raised in poverty. But the chances of success are reduced to near zero for **both** the smart rich boy and the ghetto dweller if they are substance abusers. Only when sober will **either** the ghetto dweller or the more advantaged individual be able to maximize their ability.

Only sober can they make the most of what their respective environments have to offer. There are many success stories of ghetto graduates who have left poverty and crime behind. They became part of the American Dream. They studied and found excellent jobs. Many if not most of those who have found the American dream beyond their reach have been left behind in the ghetto because of substance abuse.

DROPPING CRIME TO CONTROLLABLE LEVELS

Sobering up our criminals will return America to a level of crime that could be easily handled by the current judicial system. We need to sober up criminals early in their criminal and substance abuse careers. Drunk and high petty offenders commit more and more serious crimes as time goes by and as they sink deeper into substance abuse. When America has sobered up its substance abusing criminals, we won't be wasting money catching and locking up the bad guys. We will be able to focus on rehabilitation and retraining. When rehabilitation has been tried, it worked.[45,152] The one-two punch of involuntary sobriety, combined with job training and counseling, is an unbeatable combination. Providing job training and rehabilitation to the individual who is still thinking about sobering up (but hasn't yet) is very likely to fail. This is a quick quiz to see if you are following the gist of the argument in this book so far. If we were forced to choose between sobriety and job training, which is best?

(A) We put the offenders into an involuntary sobriety program and hope for the best.

(B) We offer multiple support services such as job training, housing, food and hope. They decide if they want to sober up or not. They decide if they want to make use of what we have offered.

If you picked "A" you chose the right answer. Sober, the individual may look around him and make use of those resources available, minimal as they may be. But we don't have to choose between sobriety or support services/job training. We can do both. First, sober up our substance abusers. Then, offer them rehabilitation, training and jobs. Only sober will they be able to take advantage of our offers. Only sober can they get in line for their share of the American dream.

I talked to Charles Swafford, an African American, and a former operator of a work furlough center. He said blacks are not released to the work furlough program because they don't have money and they don't have jobs. So they do their time in the slammer. I asked him why didn't they just use their G.R. or general relief funds to stay in a work furlough center, and spend that time out of jail testing sober, and training for or looking for work. He said that he would have accepted black clients for the $400 a month G.R. money. But he told me that judges would never approve of that. This was because the pledge of allegiance had been changed, and it now read "with liberty and justice for all THE RICH." I told him I was unaware of the addition of the two new little words at the end. He said most people weren't because they were slipped in so "gradual-like." "And besides," he asked "Where except in America can two rich boys get away with killing their parents with the help of scriptwriters, acting coaches and a director orchestrating a wonderful drama of molest?"

CHAPTER FOUR

SUBSTANCE ABUSE AND MURDER

At least half the grisly murders of the past few years could have been prevented. How? By sobering up the killers early in their substance abuse careers. There is evidence that most murders are committed while the killer is under the influence of one or more substances. Drunk and loaded people do things they would never do sober - even murder. There is proof that when five out of six criminals who were substance abusers sobered up, they stopped committing crimes.[152]

Richard Speck killed eight nurses. He was under the influence of multiple substances at the time. He later maintained that if he had been sober, he never would have committed such atrocities. I believe he was right. He died of a heart attack in prison at the age of forty-nine.

Jeffrey Dahmer's grisly, cannibalistic murders back the main thesis of this book. That is, substance abusing people are much more prone than sober individuals to break the law. Many murderers, in spite of long-term involvement in the legal system, had still not sobered up. Very often long periods of criminal activity co-exist with substance abuse while the criminal is on probation or parole.

Jeffrey Dahmer was a periodic binge drinker. He found many of his victims dead in the same room with him when he woke up from a drinking binge. Often he couldn't remember the events of the murder because he (and often the victims) had been drunk. On May 23, 1989, Dahmer was in court to be sentenced on a conviction of second degree sexual assault and enticing a child for immoral purposes.[37]

He had already committed several murders which had not yet been linked to him. He had been convicted of disorderly conduct in 1986. He had exposed himself to twenty-five people while drunk. The prosecuting attorney in the 1989 sentencing argued for a strong prison sentence. He said that Dahmer had simply gone through the motions of receiving therapy when he was put on probation for disorderly conduct in 1986.

Dahmer's probation did not involve the close follow-up necessary to guarantee sobriety. He had not been sober for years except for his brief period of time in jail. At his May 23, 1989 hearing Dahmer said, "I am an alcoholic, not the sort that has to have a drink every day, but when I do drink, I go overboard."[37]

The judge, unaware of Dahmer's already impressive body count, decided that Dahmer needed treatment for his emotional problems and his alcoholism. Since prison would not provide treatment, the judge ordered that Dahmer obtain help outside of prison. Dahmer was sentenced to five years for second-degree sexual assault. The sentence was stayed and Dahmer was given five years of probation. He was also ordered to spend one year in the House of Corrections with work release so that he could keep his job.

During that year, he was not only able to go out to work during the day, he had other passes. He got drunk on a twelve-hour leave on Thanksgiving in 1989. He petitioned for early release from the program. Jeffrey's own father, Lionel Dahmer, argued against early release from the House of Corrections work release program. He said that Jeffrey still needed to receive treatment for his alcoholism. He said, "Every incident, including the most recent conviction for a sex offense, has been associated with and initiated by alcohol in Jeff's Case."[37]

Jeff's father sought strict alcohol treatment and follow-up for his son. His request was ignored. On March 2, 1990, Jeffrey was free to go after serving ten months of his year sentence. Within weeks he was a regular in the bar scene. A very tight follow-up would have made that kind of immediate plunge back into substance abuse impossible. He murdered again on May 29, 1990, not quite three months after his release from the house of corrections.

When Jeffrey Dahmer showed up for his meetings with his probation officer Donna Chester, he was usually a mess. He was dirty and unshaven. He talked to Donna about his homosexuality, his drinking, his anger and his thoughts of suicide. He admitted to being drunk and in violation of his probation. But he was never sent back to jail even for brief periods to reinforce sobriety. This was in spite of the fact that substance abuse was obviously behind most of Dahmer's problems and irrational behavior. Alcoholics kill themselves and others at a much higher rate than sober people.

KEEP AWAY FROM DANGEROUS NEIGHBORHOODS

Dahmer's probation officer was supposed to visit him every thirty days. Donna Chester had too full a caseload and could not visit him very often. Dahmer's neighborhood was so bad she was afraid to visit him alone. There were no spare Probation Officers to go with her. During the time he was on probation, Dahmer received counseling. The binge drinking more than wiped out any possible benefits to be gained in counseling.[37]

What if Dahmer had been forced to sober up in 1986 when he was first on probation? Would he have stopped killing? When violent substance abusers sober up, most stop committing violent crimes. What might have happened if Dahmer had been forced to participate in an involuntary sobriety program similar to the one proposed in this book? At Dahmer's first sign of continued alcohol abuse, he would have been sent for a ten day detox experience.

At detox he would have been exposed to eight to ten hours a day of educational tapes, group sharing and reprogramming. Such a program can and does change attitudes and behavior. He would not have been sent back to serve the five year prison sentence which had been stayed by the judge. If he returned to jail, it would have been for brief periods and as part of a program to guarantee sobriety.

Dahmer had already killed at least five people before he was placed on probation in 1986. He killed twelve more before he was caught in 1991. If he had been sober from 1986 on, there is an excellent chance he would not have killed again.

The bad news is that if he had been sober from 1986 on, he might never have been caught for the five or more murders he had already committed. The good news is that if he had been forced to sober up in 1986, he probably wouldn't have killed twelve more people. In 1991 he was falling apart. He had lost his job. He had sunk into a deep depression. He tried to feel better by using even more alcohol. You choose: Would it have been better if he was a sober free man after five murders, or in jail for life after seventeen?

Depression is frequent among chronic alcoholics. Their suicide rate is very high. They have lost everything. Alcohol saps emotional resources. Treatment for the depression is rarely going to work unless they stop drinking.

DEATH AND THE FLOWER CHILDREN

Remember the Haight-Ashbury Section in San Francisco and the flower children? They were against the Vietnam War. They were going to lead America to new depths of understanding. We saw them on the news flashing us the peace sign. They were going to teach Americans how to tame our violent, aggressive nature. So what if their search for truth, light and nirvana was aided by a little chemistry?

The flower child movement folded in on itself. Death began to stalk them. For a couple of years, the few block area of Haight-Ashbury reported one of the highest per capita death rates in history. They died in droves of murder, suicide and drug overdoses. Like others in the past who sought enlightenment through chemicals, the flower children found disaster, not nirvana. One might say the flower child movement was one more failed experiment in better living through chemistry.

THE KILLER CLOWN

John Wayne Gacy is another example of a human being sinking to the depths of a bizarre, twisted, grotesque hell through the use and abuse of alcohol and drugs. He was not only a substance abuser but he was himself a victim of an abusive, alcoholic father. He suffered severe emotional ridicule and humiliation as well as physical beatings at the hands of his cruel, stern father. John's father had been a heavy binge drinker since John was a toddler. When John was six, in a drunken rage his father shot and killed his pet dog, Pal, to punish him. John's father died early of the alcoholic's plague, cirrhosis of the liver.

John Wayne Gacy was literally "a clown who got away with murder." He enjoyed dressing up as "Pogo" the clown and entertaining the hospitalized children. Never can the saying "Looks can be deceiving" be as appropriate as in this individual's life. Outwardly, he was an outstanding member of high society and a successful businessman. He belonged to many reputable charitable organizations. He was involved with local politics. He was even photographed with First Lady Rosalynn Carter. He was a member of the local Jaycees and had many upstanding business connections. He was admired by many of his peers. He threw lavish parties at his home which were attended by some of the community's most elite. Inwardly, he was a twisted, tortured psychopath.

No matter what John did as a child to try to please his father it was to no avail. At the age of five, John began suffering from seizures and was prescribed dilantin and phenobarbititol. Early in life John was introduced to drugs to help relieve and/or numb his pain and make him feel good. At the age of ten, he was diagnosed as having psychomotor epilepsy.

Even at this time, John's abusive, perfectionist father did not believe that John was ill. He would say that John was faking his illness to get out of going to school. His mother Marion was a pharmacist. She tried to protect John and acted as a buffer between John and his father. John's father's response to this was to taunt his son by calling him a "mama's boy" and telling him he was "going to be queer." John's father hated homosexuals. Even though she was a pharmacist, John's mother apparently never realized that her son was growing more dependent on the mood-altering drugs being prescribed for him.

BETRAYED BY MOM

When John was a toddler, he was sexually abused by a mildly retarded fifteen year old girl. When he was nine, he was continually sexually abused by a male friend of his father. He could not tell his father of this abuse for fear of being labeled "queer." The ultimate blow, or the straw that broke the camel's back, may have been the betrayal and humiliation by his only protector and confidant: his mother.

To escape the physical, verbal and sexual abuse, John would go to his secret hiding place. This was the "crawlspace" under his father's house. Many years later the grisly remains of his 29 victims would be found in a dark massive grave in the "crawlspace" of his house. While still a boy, John had taken his mother's underwear (he stated he liked the feel of it) to his hiding place in the crawlspace. He kept it there in a paper bag. His mother found it and related this discovery to his father. As a punishment, his mother made him wear the women's panties to school under his clothes. This devastated John.

John had given in to homosexual feelings in his early 20's. He had sex with an acquaintance after both of them became intoxicated after heavy drinking. This sickened John and he tried to put this incident out of his mind. Later that same year he married his first wife. He had two children, Michael and Christine, in an endeavor to maintain normalcy.

In spite of his marriage, John's homosexual feelings and thoughts reemerged. His homosexual desires became overwhelming and uncontrollable the more substances he abused. At the peak of his addictions, he was gulping handfuls of pills daily. He took valium to calm down and amphetamines to pep himself up. He also swilled down beer and whiskey every evening in increasing amounts in addition to smoking marijuana regularly. During some of his binge drinking episodes he would give in to his homosexual feelings. At first he would occasionally procure young, caucasian males for sex and would pay them for their services. He began luring males to his house, partying with them. He would supply them with drugs and alcohol and show them pornographic homosexual films. He would then torture and murder them hideously.

He was already getting away with murder but was convicted in 1968 of sodomy. He served 18 months at Iowa State Reformatory for Men at Anamosa. He was a model prisoner. His wife divorced him while he was in jail. He never saw his family again. By then, his father loathed him. His release from jail marked the beginning of the end for John Wayne Gacy, and many others.

On 6/22/72 he was charged with aggravated battery against one of his sex partners. The charges were dropped for lack of evidence. In March 1978 John again left a bruised victim of his torture games. Jeff Rignall, a 26 year old homosexual, survived a brutal beating by Gacy and sued Gacy in civil court. Rignall obtained a $3,000 settlement. At this time the police were gathering evidence and were close on Gacy's tail. On December 22, 1978, he was formally charged with murder.

The drugs and alcohol had destroyed John's mind. He made irrational statements such as "I want to clear the air, I know the game is over." He also said that all his victims had deserved what they got since they were hustlers and homosexuals who sold their bodies for cash. In spite of his thousands of homosexual acts, Gacy kept denying his own homosexuality and held himself totally blameless. He had used lime to cover the smell in the house.

Despite the severe beatings, sexual and emotional abuse, John Wayne Gacy did manage to become a very successful businessman. If it wasn't for the use and abuse of mind-altering drugs and alcohol, John could have overcome the horrible trauma of his abusive childhood with long term professional counseling.

Is it possible that at the time of one of his earlier arrests, there was some mention somewhere of substance abuse? Of course there was. And what was done with that information? Nothing. Yet, if that information had triggered involvement in an involuntary sobriety program, many lives would have been saved. Like Dahmer, Gacy killed only while under the influence of massive amounts of drugs and alcohol.[76,77,142]

THEY DON'T RUN OUT ON ME NOW'

Dennis Nilsen was born in Fraserburgh, Scotland on November 23, 1945.   In many ways his personality was similar to that of Jeffrey Dahmer's.   They could almost have been clones.   Both were timid loners and both despised their homosexuality.   Both had been abandoned as children and both had abused alcohol to escape from their pain.   The alcohol also allowed them, in a sick psychopathic frenzy, to release their rage and seek comfort with their dead victims.

Dennis was abandoned by his father when his younger sister was born.   Young Dennis loved and idolized his grandfather with whom he had spent a great deal of time.   When he was almost six years old, his grandfather died.   His mother told him that his grandfather was only sleeping in the coffin.

Dennis waited for his grandfather to come back for several months.   When he did not return, Dennis was devastated.   Years later in his prison cell, he stated that all of his destructive tendencies had sprung from this childhood trauma.   "I have spent all my emotional life searching for my grandfather."   Dennis also loved animals.   But if an animal was suffering, he would kill it to save it from further suffering.   Dennis related to the suffering animals.   He felt that he was suffering in the same way.

A common thread runs through the history of many serial killers.   Many of them had tortured and killed animals as teenagers.   They later switched to humans. Watch out if your neighborhood cats start to disappear.   Be especially careful if the local pets start showing up hanging on clotheslines around the neighborhood.

In his teen years Dennis began to have homosexual fantasies.   He was sexually attracted to other boys.   At the age of fifteen he enlisted in the army.   That was where he had his first sexual experience, with an Arab boy.   In 1972 he fell in love with an eighteen year-old private but this love was not reciprocated.   Thus, he was rejected again.

Dennis' failure in his quest for companionship and acceptance was a strong contributing factor to his sick deterioration into depravity.   He looked for love in all the wrong places. In June 1974 he took a seventeen year old boy to his tiny room. There they drank large amounts of alcohol and got drunk. The boy crawled into bed. Nilsen took pictures of the boy, who objected and then became hysterical and smashed his arm through a glass partition. Nilsen panicked and summoned an ambulance to take the boy to the hospital. The boy's parents did not press charges. Nilsen felt rejected again. His self-esteem plunged to new depths. He wallowed in self-pity and started thinking that maybe he deserved nothing better than to stay forever friendless and socially detached.

He became more wary of people. His evenings became more sordid and aggressive. He met a blatant homosexual named Twinkle with whom he lived for two years. Nilsen was looking for stability in this relationship but this was not to be. Nilsen adopted an increasingly harsh attitude toward his roommate. Twinkle retaliated by bringing his lovers home to the apartment for sex. Nilsen brought a woman to the apartment and had a one-night stand. He bragged about this conquest. He had a conflict within himself between being bisexual and homosexual. When the relationship with Twinkle fell apart, Dennis felt rejected again.

Drinking even heavier, he began cruising the gay bars. Most of the time he would go home alone, drink himself into a stupor and fall sleep. He drifted into a deep depression. He began to have love/death fantasies which stemmed back to the death of his grandfather. Then the killing began. Killing induced by his rages and fueled by his consumption of large amounts of alcohol. He committed fifteen horrific murders while in drunken stupors.

Dennis Nilsen admitted that he was a psychopath who became violent when he drank too much. The alcohol removed all human emotions. The alcohol turned him into a monstrous, mindless creature. The alcohol allowed him to act out his rage over his loneliness and feelings of rejection. He fixed it so that people would not walk out on him anymore. After killing them, he kept his dead victims for weeks. He would clean them and love them with tenderness. They didn't try to leave now. They didn't talk back or cheat on him like Twinkle had done. Nilsen was not alone, but his mind was gone. When his mind left, it took fifteen victims with it.[76,77,78]

SOBERING UP SERIAL KILLERS

Could America be freed of serial killers if everyone committing a crime while under the influence was sobered up? Probably not. Some people who have never gotten high on drugs or alcohol are perfectly capable of committing atrocities. For example, Ted Bundy, who brutally raped and murdered over 30 women was not an alcoholic or drug addict. But most serial killers **are** substance abusers. The homicide rate **would** drop to half or less than it is now if the "Sober Forever" Program was implemented. Substance abusing criminals will be sobered up after their first brush with the law. This will stop the deterioration that has led so many to murder.

You might be surprised at what a small percentage of homicides are committed by sober people. You probably know that perhaps only one in thirty motorists driving along the road is drunk at any one time. Yet half of all vehicular deaths involve substance abuse. Did you also know that over half of the people who drown every year are drunk or loaded when they slip under the waters? Yet half of all swimmers are not drunk or loaded. The perhaps one in thirty who get drunk while on these recreational outings are at the highest risk for accidents. Substance abuse takes its toll in every arena.

We have seen that the chance of committing atrocities increases many fold when a person is abusing substances. We know that after we sober up violent criminals, 85% of them stop committing crime and violent acts.[152]

We have seen that the United States treats its poor, mentally ill, and children, the groups least able to engage in self advocacy, worse than any industrialized nation in the world.[109]

CHAPTER FIVE

NATIONAL DRUG POLICIES: POOR PARENTING WORST CASE SCENARIO

If you are one degree off and you are traveling in a jet airplane you are going the wrong way in a very big hurry. America is 180 degrees off in its handling of drugs, crime, disturbed people and substance abuse in general. We have thus gone a long way in the wrong direction very rapidly and for a long, long time. As a result, we teeter on the edge of a sociological abyss and slip daily deeper into a dangerous morass. We helplessly watch all of our time honored American values decay and crumble in front of our eyes.

Are there any similarities between our current national drug and crime intervention programs and really bad parenting? The answer is yes! Here's what some really misguided parenting looks like: Joan tells her five year old son, Mark, over and over, to turn off the TV and clean up his room. She gets louder with each repetition of her demand. Though she is screaming, Joan's lack of any real action encourages Mark to do nothing. This raises Joan's anger to the boiling point. She finally acts, but it is an over-reaction. Her tantrum not only doesn't get the room clean, but leaves an angry, rebellious and possibly abused son.

If Mark goes to school with bruises a Child Protective Services involvement could be triggered. Mark has not learned how to follow the rules. He has learned to be wary of an inconsistent and dangerous parent. He has learned to manipulate his mother and others to survive in an unpredictable world. He does not incorporate his mother's values nor does he develop respect for authority.

Joan could have tried a lot of different things which would have worked. Here is an example of one: Simultaneous with giving Mark the order to clean his room, she walks to the TV, turns it off, then walks over to Mark. Gently but firmly, she tells him again to clean his room, adding "and right now." She then takes him by his elbow and escorts him to his room. Then, gently but firmly, she guides and talks him through the room cleaning process.

She praises him for each bit of progress he makes in the cleaning. After several repeats of the same series of actions by Joan, Mark will realize that he is going to follow her orders when they are given. Finally, following Joan's orders becomes automatic. Mark is now dealing with a predictable system which he can trust. It is a system that makes reasonable demands. It is a system that will guarantee compliance by Mark but will not scare him or hurt him. Because he has been praised for cleaning his room, he will grow to like and feel good about a clean room.

TEACHING HATE IN OUR JAILS

Like Joan, society spends years yelling at its substance abusing addicts but doing nothing. Currently, drug/alcohol addicts must have at least fifteen outstanding warrants to be brought into the criminal justice system in San Diego County. Some city's jails are not as crowded as San Diego's. But in general, San Diego's problems and approaches to the drug/crime problem are duplicated across the nation.

When society's anger is strong enough, we over-react. Like Joan, we do not try to teach the right behavior, we punish. We have no plan to really address and change the problem behavior. We lock up the substance abusing criminal for increasingly longer prison terms, when we have the jail space. When locked up, substance abusers generally sit and do nothing, and learn nothing, except how to be better criminals. They do not grow in any way. They become increasingly discontented and rebellious.[65, 133]

Like Joan's son Mark, our substance abuser becomes wary of the system. By system is meant the recognized laws and authority. In Mark's case it was his mother. The substance abuser rejects society's recognized authority and its authority figures. He, like Mark, learns to survive outside the system. He does not adopt the values of the system.

We, like Joan, need to create a different outcome. Joan wants Mark to obey her rules. As the example shows, parents can teach their children to obey them and follow the rules without ever raising their voices - without ever getting angry. Criminals and substance abusers respond to the same firm but caring approach. We need to start by gently taking our substance abusing addicts and firmly divesting them of their drugs and alcohol. Then we will train them for work. Finally, we will let them pay their fair share of taxes. Training prisoners for jobs works better than spending jail time in idleness.

Rehabilitation works. We need job training and drug/alcohol rehabilitation inside the jails. Such programs, rare as they are, drastically reduce recidivism or the rate of rearrest and return to jail. These in-prison programs still worked even when there was little or no after jail enforcement of sobriety. Most of the people locked up in our jails have a substance abuse history. An unbeatable combination would be to first do the inside-the-jail job training and drug rehabilitation. If we add the involuntary sobriety program proposed in this book we might drop our recidivism rate (rate of return to jail for new crimes) from 65% to 5% or 6%. Incidently, 6% is the recidivism rate claimed by China. The in-jail drug rehabilitation and job training won't be wasted because drug/alcohol abuse relapse upon release from prison will be virtually impossible in the "Sober Forever" Program described in Chapter 11.

LEARNING SOBRIETY IN JAIL

Longer sentences do not affect the rearrest rate. Longer sentences means crime only stops while the prisoner is locked up. If they are let out in two years or ten years, 70% go back to crime. In fact, "shock" sentences of one month result in lower rearrest rates than those sentenced for longer sentences for the same crime. Longer jail terms means habituation to jail and getting an advanced degree in the criminal arts.[133]

There is a proven way to keep ex-prisoners from being rearrested. This is through an in-prison rehabilitation program referred to as the therapeutic community approach. One of the first applications of the therapeutic community treatment method to drug rehabilitation was done in the fifties by Charles Dederich. He was an ex-alcoholic. He ran encounter groups which he found helped heroin addicts to quit drugs. Synanon was created as a result of Dederich's discovery.

Synanon and most therapeutic community programs since then have been live-in programs where everyone there was working on getting and staying sober. Synanon was one of the first applications of the therapeutic community concept to help heroin addicts get sober. Even skeptics could soon see that Synanon was having success in an area where failure was the norm.

Many variations of the therapeutic community have been utilized since the founding of Synanon. The therapeutic community approach stresses firm behavioral norms. There is a system of rewards and punishments clearly defined within a communal economy of housework and other roles. Participants engage in reality-oriented group and individual therapy. Included were lengthy encounter group sessions which focused on current living issues and deep-seated emotional problems. They worked up a 'ladder' of tasks from admission to graduation. This simulated the way the real world works. You might have to be the floor sweeper at Jack-In-The-Box for awhile before they make you the district manager.

The Amity therapeutic community program added workshops on recovery topics and video playback so members could see what they looked like and sounded like in the encounter sessions.[97]

Graduates from several in-jail treatment programs had a much lower than average rearrest rate. That was achieved in spite of the haphazard follow-up most released prisoners experience. Four hundred inmates had participated in the Amity Therapeutic Community program in Pima County, Arizona in a three year time period.

Graduates had a 36% rearrest rate, compared to the average rearrest rate of 65%. This was in spite of the fact that many of the program participants were involved in the program for only a few months. The Oregon therapeutic community program called Cornerstone had similar success rates.[45]

SEVENTY-EIGHT PERCENT STAYED SOBER

The New York based in-prison therapeutic community program called Stay'n Out claimed that 78% of their graduates stayed off drugs and were not rearrested. Stay'n Out program participants on the average spent up to two years in that program. That was much longer than the average stay in the Amity program.[27]

To successfully quit drugs, addicts almost always need to "change playmates and playgrounds." One reason so many people fail in their fight with drugs is that stopping drugs often means they are alone. When that loneliness gets bad, they go see an old friend or two, who almost always are still using. When you are an addictive personality, not drinking and not doping is always hard. It becomes near impossible to stop using if everyone else around you is loaded and praising the values of their latest high.

The therapeutic community provides an answer to the loneliness. A bunch of people living and working together to give up drugs learn new work and job skills. That way there is someone there to help them fight the urges to use again when these urges come up. Good drug rehabilitation can take a couple years of intensive program involvement in a live-in therapeutic community-type treatment program. This is especially true when there is a long history of criminality and addiction.

We will see that length of time in outpatient (non live-in programs) treatment is also very important. Longer time in treatment translated to a higher success/sobriety rate on follow-up years later.[61, 130]

Old habits and attitudes die hard. But they can be changed. It may just take a little longer in some cases. When we are talking about saving the addicted criminals from their own personal hell and the hell they put society through, we must never give up. We must take as long as it takes.

It costs $25,000 and up to lock up someone in jail for a year. Many criminals cost up to $430,000 a year when they are outside of prison robbing people.[55] That figure comes from adding up victim losses, police costs, private security costs, court and attorney costs. Advocates of the "lock-em-up" mentality say "Look, we save society $405,000 a year by keeping them locked up!" (That is $430,000 a year minus the $25,000 a year cost of jail). Some have estimated that the total value of goods stolen each year is $600 billion.[117]

Let's move to math problem number two: We will add $4,000 year to the cost of keeping someone in prison for the last two years they are there. This is what it will cost per year to run a Stay'n Out type drug treatment program. When that has been done in the past, 78% of the participants quit drugs and crime. Now let's say we spend another $4,000 a year for the first two years after they get out. This it what it costs to follow them, provide them with food and housing if they don't have it, and to thus guarantee their sobriety. By doing that we can up the odds. Around 98% will stay sober and quit crime. Since length of time in prison has no bearing on whether they commit more crime after release, take 90% of the prisoners, all except the really dangerous psychopaths, and put them in the in-prison rehabilitation program. That means that they spend only two more years behind bars learning how to get sober. That means we drop anything over two years off their sentence.

Let's run the new numbers: We've saved $25,000 a year for an average of five years or so for each prisoner. These are the years we don't have to spend money on keeping them in jail. Here we are assuming that the average sentence was seven years. That's $125,000 saved per prisoner in jail costs.

We save $430,000 a year for an average criminal career lasting fifteen years. Even if he's in jail a lot, he's going to be out a lot also. That $430,000 is the Justice Department's estimate of what an active career criminal costs on the outside per year. Since we know he quits crime when he is sober we have cut his criminal career short. Fifteen years times $430,000 equals close to $6.5 million. He pays $50,000 in taxes over the fifteen years because he's working, not stealing.

SOBERING UP ONE ADDICT SAVES MILLIONS

Our savings ($6,450,00 plus $125,000, plus $50,000) total $6,625,000. Our costs? Twenty five thousand dollars a year for the last two years in prison, plus the treatment costs of $16,000. That's for the $4,000 a year for four years to keep him sober. Those treatment costs cover the last two years he's still in jail and the first two years after he gets out. In most cases, only periodic monitoring will be necessary after that. We have turned his life around in four years at a bargain rate. It is rare that it would ever actually take a full four years as described here to sober up a drug abusing career criminal. For many, sobriety will be able to be guaranteed after a few months in a sober living house after release from prison. Each case is different but in each case we will work with the substance abuser for as long and as intensely as it takes to guarantee sobriety.

Fortunately, many addicts, especially those earlier in their addiction career, sober up a lot easier. So far America has not been willing to finance the four years of drug treatment when it was necessary to do the job right. Thinking that "drug treatment" can be an occasional A.A. or N.A. (Narcotic's Anonymous) session is why America is in such a horrible mess. That's why people are scared to death of all the substance abusing predators. Getting money out of an ATM (automatic teller machine) should not be the scariest thing you do. But that's what it has come to. In one recent movie spoofing modern times, ATM customers lined up on one side and the robbers on the

other.   As the customers left the machine the robber
introduced himself saying "I'm your designated robber for
the evening."

Now we know what can be done and what needs to be
done. Let's see what is being done. Good solid drug
rehabilitation programs like Stay'n Out are rare in the
federal prison system. They are almost nonexistent in
county and state jails. A survey was conducted to find out
how many of the 1,687 jails offered drug treatment.
Seven percent of the inmates were supposedly involved in
drug treatment. This "drug treatment," it turned out,
often consisted of as little as an occasional class with a
drug counselor. Sometimes "drug treatment'" involved
only the periodic viewing of a videotape on how to sober
up.

Only two percent of the 1,687 jails surveyed had
more that ten hours a week of treatment activities.[87,120]
If those are the figures used to prove rehabilitation doesn't
work, no wonder. The Stay'n Out program, which does
work, is a 24 hour a day program that lasts for about the
last two years of a prison sentence. Working on sobriety
is the main thing they do. In the process, they work on
building the skills needed to maintain that sobriety. These
are work skills, social skills, and psychological skills. In
the latter category we would include increased self esteem,
understanding our feelings, etc. The best and most
successful in-prison program in existence costs only
$4,000 a year. This is a pittance compared to the savings
in money and lives which are the results of graduating
those sobered-up former criminals back into society.[27]

DRUGS EASIER TO GET IN JAIL THAN DRUG TREATMENT

We have already seen that out of jail drug
treatment/rehabilitation also works. We have seen that
the longer people stay in a therapeutic community type of
treatment program the better these programs work to
turn people's lives around. People who stay in these
voluntary outside-of-prison programs for two years have

about the same success rate as the Stay'n Out program. The problem is that hardly anyone stays that long. By twelve months after admission 71% had left treatment and only 5% ever completed their treatment plan.[130] When given the choice of getting better or getting high, the druggie almost always chooses getting high. At this writing, it is much easier to get drugs in prison than it is to get drug treatment in prison. In some jails you can get anything you want anytime you want, provided you have the cash. Some prisoners still operate large dope rings on the outside from inside the prison and have plenty of cash. This book tell how we are going to steal all their customers away from them.

There are many advantages to starting drug treatment in prison. The first is that we know almost everybody is there because of substance abuse and because of the behaviors or actions their substance abuse caused. They are in prison with others who have the same problem. We know that they rarely get involved in treatment outside of prison on their own. From the time of their release from prison up till the time they get rearrested, they rarely obtain the truly effective kind of supervision that guarantees sobriety. For those who do sober up in jail, their brains can begin to work again. They think more clearly. For many it is the first time in years they have not been loaded all the time. Sober people get more out of treatment.

Another advantage to in-prison rehabilitation programs is that the prisoners can't use denial. Substance abuse led to their breaking the law. They **are** in jail. They can't say "I don't have a problem." Prisoners entering the two year in-prison treatment program will be told: "Here are the facts. You are in jail. Substance abuse got you here. Nothing else. Not your mother, not your girlfriend, not poverty and not some cops who had it in for you. If you want to stay out after you get released next time, you're going to have to sober up. In the next two years we're going to show you how."

The in-prison rehabilitation/treatment programs help break down staff stereotypes and reduce conflict between guards and inmates and between the inmates themselves. Remember, one of the things the prisoners are learning in their rehab/treatment program is conflict resolution through discussion, negotiation and bartering. Many of them had learned that violence and power were how to resolve conflicts.[23]

EVEN WARDENS LIKE DRUG REHAB

Prison administrators are not against drug treatment programs. In fact, most would like such programs in their jails and prisons. They said they would like these programs even if it did not affect inmates' behavior after they are released. Why? Because drug treatment programs provide good security, good working conditions for correctional staff and good publicity. They also provide a resource through which crisis intervention can be done in the jail. Such programs can win brownie points in attempts to get American Correctional Association accreditation.

As of January, 1994, Donovan Prison in San Diego had had a therapeutic community treatment program for three years. In describing Donovan Prison, Rod Mullen, one of the directors of the Donovan Amity Therapeutic Community Program, said, "The name correctional institution is a joke! It's a graduate school for crime. When we first went there it was very hostile. Now, when you walk into and through the yard, it is still scary. But when you get over to where there are 200 inmates in the drug rehabilitation program it is a different world. People are polite to each other. It is a safe and healthy place. There has not been a single violent incident among the program participants since we started the program. The staff loves to work in that part of the prison. The administrators love the program. Each stabbing out in the yard costs them $85,000."[99]

"Seventy percent of the men who leave the program go out and do not get rearrested. When a man is on drugs we see a ripple effect. His kids go on welfare or in foster homes when he goes to jail. When the graduates of this program get out of jail there is a reverse ripple effect.

They go get their women and pull them out of addiction. They get jobs. They take their children out of foster homes and off welfare. They get health insurance. Programs can be mounted in prisons that make a difference! If wardens were rewarded for the numbers of people who don't come back to their prison because they have succeeded on the outside, wardens would be taking a very close look at what works."99

A QUICK FIX FOR OUR SOCIAL ILLS?

Cities all across America have felons on the loose. Los Angeles has 20,000. Denver has 10,000. These are criminals known to have committed usually multiple felonies. They have been positively identified by victims of rape or assault or by witnesses as murderers. But the police are too busy responding to each day's new crises. They don't have the few hours it would usually take to track down each of these felons.

San Diego Judge Robert Coates said we cannot use the criminal justice system to cure social ills. He claimed that the criminal justice system is being asked to do what other institutions in our society have been unable to do. This includes teaching accountability for their behavior to children at a young age. He said the courts are somehow supposed to fix the erosion of social values and stop the break up of the family unit. He recognized that the neglected adult misdemeanor offender is part of a salvageable group. He said that they should be both punished and treated before they graduate to doing more serious crimes. Judge Coates maintained that many misdemeanor offenders became felons simply by not being caught and punished in the misdemeanor stage.52

THE LOST GENERATION?

The misdemeanor offenders are almost completely left out of the criminal justice system. Some public officials such as San Diego County Supervisor (and later

Mayor) Susan Golding seemed to feel that there may be no hope for a whole generation of criminals who have been reared in a drug-crazed culture. She was quoted as saying, "We may not have a choice other than to incarcerate and punish. I don't want to lose another generation."[52]

Juvenile crime is up all across the nation. People under eighteen committed a third of the San Diego County's crimes in 1985. In 1990, juveniles accounted for 14% of all arrests for violent acts. Robert Amador, a San Diego Deputy District Attorney, said the kids keep committing crimes and the criminal justice system doesn't know how to deal with them.[21]

Drugs are behind the juvenile crime wave. The percentage of juveniles under the influence when arrested is close to the adult rate of 85%. We have seen that people under the influence are many times more likely to break the law than sober people. Drugs and alcohol destroy their conscience and their sense of what is right and wrong. People under the influence do what feels good right now.

Juvenile arrests in San Diego County increased 13% from 1986 to 1990 or from 16,546 to 18,664. The largest increase was in felony categories. During the same time period arrests for violent offenses almost doubled, from 682 to 1,303. These statistics reflect nation-wide trends, though some cities have been hit harder by the juvenile crime wave than others.[21]

Who is toughest on crime often translates to who gets the most votes. Congress has expanded the number of crimes which are subject to federal prosecution. Penalties for drug offenses have been tightened. A first time offender convicted of a drug charge in federal court could be sent to 30 years in prison without parole. In state courts, a similar offense may mean only a few years in prison with parole. In San Diego County a similar offense will typically mean nothing at all in terms of punishment, though ten to fifteen of the same offenses may result in court action and incarceration.[22]

Even so, all the wrong people are going to jail. Small time dealers are the ones being sent away. They almost always are users who deal to keep themselves supplied with drugs. When they are sober they will have no need to deal drugs. Judge Harold Greene refused to impose the mandatory thirty year sentence on a 25 year old repeat offender drug dealer. He felt stiff sentences handed down in federal court violated the Eighth Amendment, which bans cruel and unusual punishment.[30]

Fifty other federal judges refused to hear drug cases because they felt that the penalties were too excessive. The harsh federal guidelines took effect in 1987. By 1993, 17,000 drugs offenders had been sent to jail for ten years or more. Fewer than one in ten were management level dealers. People higher up the ladder have more information and can cut a deal with federal prosecutors. The little guys, small time dealers, have no information with which to dicker. They do the hard time and their bosses get off easy.[30]

Here we have more examples of an inconsistent and dangerously unpredictable system. Did we think that Joan's parenting was harsh and inconsistent? Depending on who catches you and what judicial system you are processed through (federal, state, county) the same crime can result in getting anything from a ticket which you can ignore to as much as life in prison.

ONE MORE BOLOGNA SANDWICH

Misdemeanor offenders in San Diego County get lost in the limbo of nearly 700,000 unserved warrants for arrest.[52] A drunken driver caught driving on a suspended license served twelve hours and fifty-eight minutes before his release from jail. He was unlikely to comply with the orders to participate in various rehabilitation programs. Even so, he probably wouldn't be back to court until rearrested. A homeless man arrested for 115 outstanding warrants for such things as drinking in the wrong place was sentenced to 45 days in jail. He stayed in jail for two weeks. Deputy Public Defender Richard Gates said, "The sheriff probably tries to figure out how to release them, while they (the inmate) are doing everything they can to stay in for one last bologna sandwich."[54]

In 1990, San Diego County spent over two million dollars to send sixty teenage substance abusers to VisionQuest, known for its covered-wagon excursions and confrontational methods. More than 900 substance abusers are in the VisionQuest Rehabilitation Program, 250 are from California. A probation department study reported that 90% of a group of 80 hard-core offenders released from VisionQuest were rearrested within a year of their release. Ninety-five percent of CYA (County Youth Authority) releasee's get in trouble again within a year of their release.[21]

San Diego County, using mostly State of California funds, supports several drug rehabilitation programs. Nobody knows how effective these programs are because there is no follow-up data on these programs. Many of those in treatment are on probation. If they decide to stop treatment and get back into drugs, they can disappear for months and years. If they never check in with their probation officer, usually nothing happens.

GETTING LOST IN THE SYSTEM

The San Diego County Probation Department is hopelessly overwhelmed. Chief Probation Officer Cecil Steppe said that aggressive violent offenders should be supervised in small numbers. He admitted he didn't have the resources to do it. Eighty-seven probation officers were assigned to handle all 20,000 cases in 1992. Of these, 6,200 were felons, robbers, drug dealers, and some child molesters. These criminal offenders rarely had contact with a Probation Officer. They simply went about their usual business.[20]

Two thousand felons on probation in San Diego County had no contact with officials whatsoever because they had "absconded." They were supposedly being sought by police agencies. How were they hunted down? They weren't. Three or four phone calls were made to try to track down these individuals before they were labeled "absconded."

Bill Swank, a probation officer for 26 years, claimed that the criminal justice system was on the verge of collapse. A Rand Corporation study concluded that "without stringent monitoring, probationers pose a serious threat to the public." The Probation Department is uncertain about who gets rearrested. They don't conduct studies on rearrest rates. They feel that the more serious felons should have their probation revoked, but this doesn't occur because they don't know where they are.[22]

More than 50% of all the substance abusers on probation who were required to undergo random drug testing never showed up even once for testing. Of those who did show up to be tested, most had to fail drug tests repeatedly before their probation was revoked.[22]

It gets worse. When the probationers did bother to show up, the accuracy of the drug tests were questionable. San Diego County paid $230,000 in 1991 for the urinalysis tests which have been criticized as inadequate by the National Institute of Drug Abuse. The Department of Justice said that the Western Clinical Laboratories, who had the contract, "performed poorly in identifying the presence of illegal drugs."[22]

Judge Frederic Link complained that many people he put on probation were never seen by a probation officer. He had tried other programs because probation generally resulted in no action whatsoever. He had used work furlough programs. In one case of a pregnant woman tested positive for cocaine, Judge Link personally made periodic checks to determine whether she was following through on the drug counseling program he had ordered.[22]

THE REVOLVING DOOR TO THE JAIL

There are various levels of supervision in the San Diego County Probation Department. Level two is close supervision, level one is more infrequent supervision. Another level consisted of the 6,000 who were in the "felony bank" in 1992.   They received no face-to-face supervision.

Supposedly, the people in the "bank" were not serious offenders.   This wasn't always the case.   Many people in the "bank" were rearrested for a new crime. They did some time, then went back out on probation. Again, they were not seen until rearrested for a new crime and put back in jail.   The cycle repeats itself.   Four thousand dollars a year could keep most of these people sober and away from crime.   The system claims we can't afford the $4,000 a year.   So instead we end up spending up to a half million dollars apiece on them to process them through the criminal justice system and keep them in jail for a few years.

Level one probationers are the most closely watched cases in the County Probation Department.   Even at this level, only two face-to-face meetings are required each month.   Each probation officer must handle 600 probationers a month.[22]

There are doubts in everybody's mind as to whom should be on probation.   A man repeatedly raped a 30-year-old mother of three children.   He admitted to being dependent on alcohol and drugs. He said they made him feel like a "superman."   He was placed on probation in spite of the objections of probation officers.[22]

Drugs and alcohol do make people feel better, for awhile.   That's why people use them.   These same people can learn that life can be much better without abusing substances.   But, they are rarely going to voluntarily give up the chemicals that make them feel so wonderful.   The criminal justice system seems to be continually surprised that America's addicted keep abusing drugs and alcohol. Questions typically asked by those not familiar with the addiction process are "Can't these druggies see that their lives are being destroyed?   Can't they see that they are ruining their lives and the lives of everyone around them?"   It is true that the ones who love and are loved by the drug addicts are hurt the most.

James Galhey, a former law professor said that the war on crime may call for spending a lot of money.   After all, Desert Storm wasn't cheap.   But Paul Sutton, a

Criminal Justice Professor at San Diego State University disagreed.   He said that the belief that money and willpower were all that was needed to win the war on crime had nearly bankrupted America.[56]

MORE MISSPENT MONEY

A jury spent five days listening to the trial of a man who was trying to get a job washing windows. Because the man looked strange, the police were called.   He was arrested.   He was mentally ill and under the influence of drugs.   After just ten minutes of deliberation the jury decided that the man needed help, not punishment.   They wondered why the case had ever been brought to trial.   It cost taxpayers $2,000 a day to try the man whose crime was trying to get a job washing windows.   It would have cost taxpayers $4,000 to keep him sober for a year.[56]

What are "true root causes" of crime?   The declining economy, joblessness and homelessness?   They are often said to cause the problems which have overloaded and thus paralyzed the criminal justice system.   But wherever we see major social problems, we find a high percentage of people who are involved in daily substance abuse.   This includes the jobless, the homeless, parents of children in the foster care system, spousal abusers and the criminals.   Did these "root causes" result in substance abuse?   Or did substance abuse actually cause most of the homelessness, criminality and the splintering of the American family?   A strong case can be made for the latter explanation.   I challenge America to sober up its citizens and discover the same facts.   Eighty-five percent of drug abusing criminals who are forced to sober up quit committing crimes.

Substance abuse is a preventable and curable problem.   The criminal justice experts are noted to say "there are no quick fixes" for a system that has for years been growing bigger and more overwhelmed.   The influence of substance abuse on crime, homelessness and most of the other major ills of society is recognized but has not been truly addressed.   The experts are wrong when they say there is no quick fix. Sobering up America's troubled and troubling substance abusers would be a quick fix. Doing so would cost somewhere between a tenth to a fiftieth of what we are spending now on courts and jails.

The sagging economy would receive a tremendous financial boost because the billions of dollars spent on drugs would end up in the economy of the United States. This would create more jobs. As it is now, America's addiction is providing a financial boost to the criminal population of many third world countries.

Paul Pfingst, a San Diego defense lawyer and former prosecutor said, "The emphasis needs to be on fortifying the family structure and rehabilitating those mired in drug addiction. People without values will commit crimes. People whose brains are totally fried are deadly."[56]

People are frightened of the decay in our cities, our dangerous streets and the high murder rate. Yet everyone keeps proposing the same tired solutions. They scream "Take the dangerous people off the street, lock them up!" But if we take the drugs out of the dangerous people, most of them won't be dangerous anymore. After we sober our criminals up, then we will find out who is going to still be a bad guy, with or without drugs. We would have only about 15% of our criminal population left to deal with. That will be the time to focus on some serious rehabilitation programs. We'll have billions of dollars to squander that we now spend on cops, courts, lawyers and jails. This would be money saved by keeping the substance abusing criminal out of the criminal justice system. By sobering up the substance abusing criminal we have stopped his criminal acts.

SOME VERY ACTIVE CRIMINALS

The Rand Corporation reported that only a small percentage of criminals are responsible for a large amount of crime. Eight percent of the prisoners studied had committed more than sixty crimes a year.[56] There are a few criminals who are going to be criminals sober or not.

They will have to be locked up. But when all of the substance abusers committing crime are sobered up and quit crime, the figures will change drastically. As it is, many repeat offenders leaving the jail are routinely sent back to their old neighborhoods with no job skills, no drug abuse counseling and no education. They go back to their streets of origin where gangs using and dealing in drugs is a way of life.

We have seen that the jails have become the new mental hospitals. The schizophrenics wandering the streets for the past few years, since most treatment facilities were closed, keep having brushes with the law. But instead of beefing up treatment for the mentally ill, nine million dollars was cut from an $83 million budget for mental health programs in San Diego County in 1992.[56] This means that even more mentally ill schizophrenics ended up in the jails and on the streets. There and in the homeless shelters, they are prey for the psychopathic drug addicted predators of society. This was the theme of the movie "The Saint of Fort Washington."

The jails and justice system suck up a larger and larger percentage of our tax dollars. All other services end up getting cut. The libraries are open fewer hours. The parks close sooner. Trash piles up in the parks because of budget cuts. Needed repairs on the parks and recreational facilities are postponed because of staff cuts. We are financing our growth boom in the justice system by slashing more each year from education, from kindergarten through graduate school.

The State of California claims to be broke and is drastically raising the fees at the University of California schools each year. The goal has been established to have the schools in the State educational system totally self-supporting within a few years. After another recent doubling of tuition at the University of California system, the students were gathering to protest on the various campuses. If he had not been so busy, Pete Wilson, California's governor in 1994, should have gone to some of those meetings and explained to the students "We wanted to help you with your education, but we had to use that money to build more jails to lock up more people." I'm sure the students would have understood.

How are you going to explain to **your** children that the government took the tax dollars that used to be set aside for their education? Will **your** children be satisfied that that money will now be spent to lock up more of their friends and neighbors in a place where they get raped and turned into drug addicts and animals?

Earlier in this book I promised that the "Sober Forever" Program would make it so that dope fiends could never steal another Christmas from their children. I add to that the promise that the "Sober Forever" Program will stop the criminal justice system from stealing Americans' right to an education. There was a time when America could be proud of its educational policies. Compared to almost anywhere else in the world, America was way ahead in providing a free or low cost education to anyone who wanted one. As education budgets are slashed and college tuition fees double almost every year the chance for anyone to get an education is yet another American dream that is slipping slowly away.

There are many gross inconsistencies in how the criminal justice system responds to crime and criminals. The system often clamps down hard on the wrong people for the wrong reasons. Dale Akiki spent thirty months in jail in San Diego being tried for child molest at a cost of many millions of dollars in a trial lasting many months. Some in the media said this was because district attorney Ed Miller was a friend of the father of an alleged victim. There was no evidence though there was a lot of hysteria. The jury acquitted Akiki in just a few hours when they were finally given the chance to deliberate after months of testimony. On the other hand, others are ignored for years while they commit one major crime after another with no steps taken to stop them. "False Memories," a process by which information is planted in the memory then believed to be true, were major factors in the Akiki fiasco. False memories are discussed in greater detail elsewhere in this book.

San Diego Police Sergeant, Terry Degelder, said it costs money to take officers out of service to deal with the problems caused by people who are mentally ill, alcoholic or drug addicted, but who are not criminals.[56] When you stop providing services for, and stop taking care of the mentally ill, they don't just go away.   Others, the police, the shopkeepers and the general public end up dealing with the homeless schizophrenics.   In tattered clothes they stand on corners shouting at the voices that tell them the end of the world is coming.   Maybe they are right this time.   In the meanwhile, the police have to try to herd them out of the public's eye.

Everyone knows how the mental health system has changed over the years.   Maybe there were times when people got locked up for years in "Snake Pit" types of facilities. It made sense to shut down those cruel inpatient treatment facilities to stop this "disgrace."   But discharging the mentally ill into the streets and not putting a new system in its place is just another kind of disgrace.   There is a middle road somewhere which we are not even considering.   Now, the homeless, hallucinating underweight schizophrenic who has become enough of a nuisance is taken briefly into a county run locked mental ward.   There, he is pumped full of drugs, fed a couple meals, and discharged back to the streets.

I can remember the sixties when I worked in psychiatric hospitals and the hallucinating schizophrenics were kept more than three days in order to allow them to stabilize.   Then they were placed in board and care homes where they could have a place to eat and sleep while they worked on recovery.   Now the social workers don't have the time to do a good job.   They are too busy doing the necessary paperwork on the massive numbers of psychotics rotating through the psychiatric wards.   There isn't time to even begin looking after or processing them into the dwindling "aftercare" resources.

That term "aftercare" is a joke unless you somehow think that you can call it "care" or "treatment" when you have heavily drugged someone for three days before kicking them back out into the streets.   Sometimes in America, but more often in other parts of the world, humane and comprehensive care is provided for the severely mentally ill.   This care results in much higher rehabilitation rates than we have in the U.S. America needs to implement these treatments. They are described in detail in Dr. Peter Breggin's book "Toxic Psychiatry."[16]

THE TIME FOR BOOT CAMPS HAS COME (AND GONE)

Sergeant Degelder suggested work camps, not jail, for alcoholics who committed petty crimes so they could work and get sober. If the "work camps" actually taught work skills and provided job training, fine. But usually people like Degelder are not talking about true drug or alcohol treatment or even job training. They want a sort of "Boot Camp" that isn't quite like jail but somehow is supposed to sober people up (but doesn't).[56]

The idea of "work camps" or "boot camps" for treatment of substance abusers has become very popular. Americans have watched many tough celluloid drill sergeants shape up errant humans in "boot camps." It is an idea with appeal, an idea whose time has come. There's only one problem: It doesn't work. "Work camps" or "boot camps" could be dubbed as the "march in a circle theory of substance abuse rehabilitation." It is a popular idea. People think that this practice is going to solve the problem.

There are no studies anywhere showing that marching substance abusing people in a circle stops them from being substance abusers. There are studies showing "boot camps" don't work. A military type boot camp, without treatment, without soul searching, without confronting your internal demons, doesn't work.[106] Just what do the boot camps do for drug addicts and drug dealers who graduate from them? They go back out to their businesses of dealing drugs with a good idea of discipline and order. They are able to militarize their own drug operations. They have their "Sergeants," "Lieutenants" and "Captains." Because of their "boot camp" experience they proceed with the business of making and selling dope in a very orderly, militaristic fashion.[99]

There is a substantial body of research which shows that substance abuse rehabilitation does work. Not only that, many varieties of substance abuse rehabilitation programs work. None of these programs which have proven that they can sober up substance abusers rely on the "boot camp" or "marching in a circle" principle. The research articles reviewed also pointed out over and over that without the "long tail" or very close follow-up, very few rehabilitation programs are effective in the long run. This includes those programs deemed to be the best. Those who advocate some variation of "boot camps' or "work camps" have not reviewed the drug rehabilitation literature. If they take a close look at the information presented in the body of this book and in the "References, Reviews and Notes" section, they will be forced to give up some of their pet theories.

There was a study by the public defenders office in 1991 of 50 North County jury trials. One of them involved possession of an aerosol paint can. Twenty-four of the fifty trials resulted in 24 acquittals. Each of these 50 cases cost taxpayers between $35,000 and $50,000. It is safe to assume that at least 25 to 40 of those 50 cases involved substance abuse.[56] We know that 50% to 85% of all people arrested for any crime are under the influence of drugs or alcohol at the time of their arrest.

Two million dollars was spent to try those 50 cases. Almost all of the 26 out of 50 who were convicted served a few hours in jail. Then they were released to probation. But they probably didn't see a probation officer until they were rearrested somewhere down the line. The large majority of those cases should not have been put into the criminal justice system at all. The county spent two million dollars on a series of go-nowhere trials. For $200,000 all 50 of these people could have been followed very closely for a year. Their sobriety could have been guaranteed for a year. This would have been a savings of $1.8 million. Even greater savings would occur as these petty offenders stopped committing costly crimes. Five thousand dollars a day must be stolen to feed a $500 a day habit. They would have also stopped the other problems created by their substance abuse: spousal abuse, assault, etc.

Want to know where another few hundred million of your tax dollars go? By now, probably not. Every day across America people already serving 25 years to life sentences for murder, rape, or other crimes are tried for new crimes. These are new murders or assaults committed in prison, new charges for drug dealing in prison. Or in these new trials they may be tried for crimes discovered after the criminals had already been tried and sentenced for something else. By the time they had gotten through serving their first sentence they would have been in wheelchairs. The new sentences guarantee they will die in prison and guarantee paychecks for the bevy of lawyers prosecuting and defending these cases.

WHEN SHOULD INTERVENTION START?

A focus on sobriety should begin the very first time the substance abuser enters the criminal justice system. The same day he is arrested, tested and found to be loaded or high, he should be enrolled in a diversion program. It would not be a diversion program that would start in six months, a year or five years, but one in which his first meeting would be within 24 hours. This procedure would save multiple court appearances and the many hours of expensive lawyer time. It is very costly to even get to the pre-trial plea bargain phase.

Ninety-five percent of the cases are plea bargained without a trial. The plea-bargain can include expensive jail time. The time and money now spent processing one petty criminal through the initial phases of the criminal justice system could be spent to sober up ten who were diverted into a sobriety program. The courts would be by-passed altogether. People might object because someone who beat up his wife when loaded or drunk didn't get punished with a few months in jail. But jail has little or no impact on whether he'll do it again.

Guaranteeing his sobriety will almost certainly guarantee he won't do it again. Also, he'll still be home taking care of his kids instead of being locked up in jail with the county welfare department feeding his kids. Immediate and successful involvement of the substance abuser in a diversion program must stop any further legal action against him.

If the two million dollars spent on the 50 trials had been spent instead on sobering people up, 500 people could have been substance-free at an estimated cost of $4,000 a year per person. It would be even cheaper to keep them sober the second year. By the third year of sobriety, half of them would be working and paying taxes. They would have started paying back what society had spent to sober them up. To increase the chances of success we will need to have a tight follow-up period for as long as ten years. After a time, random testing as infrequently as once a year may be enough to guarantee sobriety.

SOBER UP OR DO YOUR TIME

Substance abusing criminals should be given a choice: (I) Go through the regular criminal justice system and do your time; (2) Avoid the criminal justice system entirely by participating in the involuntary sobriety program for ten years. Those choosing sobriety, for the most part, would never be seen again in the overloaded criminal justice system. The only time they would become involved with law enforcement is when they mess up: Fail a urine test (test dirty) or miss a meeting. The involuntary sobriety program called the "Sober Forever" Program is described in detail in Chapter 11. Once that program is implemented, probation officers would be left to do quality probation work with smaller, manageable caseloads consisting of the more problematic criminals.

"GETTING TOUGH ON CRIME"

Our leaders across the nation are trying to impress their voters by taking a tough stand on crime and drug offenders. Unfortunately, getting tough on crime doesn't work. Sobering criminals up does work. Filling our prisons to overflowing is the worst way to combat the rise in violent crime. California has spent $4.5 billion dollars building new prisons in the last ten years.[60] It is the most extensive prison building program in the nation. Why is California broke? One of the reasons is because locking up people is very expensive. In 1991 over 100,000 people were housed in 23 different California prisons. Yet there still was not enough room. The prisons were operating at 175% of capacity. Almost 8,000 of the 100,000 inmates in California prisons were from San Diego County.

The average cost to house an inmate in a California prison is $20,562 per inmate per year. It costs taxpayers $158 million a year to keep San Diego's 7,712 prisoners locked up. The prison department's total budget in 1991 was 2.5 billion dollars. A San Diego Public Defender, attorney Francis Bardsley, questioned whether this was the most effective way of dealing with the problem. He pointed out that halfway houses for convicted felons or treatment programs for drug offenders cost about $4,000 a year.[55]

DON'T CODDLE CRIMINALS!

We know what works. Jails don't. Rehabilitation and sobriety do. But rehabilitation instead of jail is seen as coddling criminals. That attitude of many public officials keeps us from doing what really works. Politicians cannot get elected if they are perceived as coddling criminals. San Diego's District Attorney, Edwin Miller, Jr., wanted more prison space, and said, "The need for more prison bed space is unavoidable."[55]

Edwin Miller said that many critics of the judicial system complained about the cost keeping an offender in jail. He felt that these critics were unaware that it could cost up to $430,000 a year to let one active criminal stay out of jail.[55]

Apparently Edwin Miller never considered the alternative of sobering up these criminals, whose crimes are almost all drug/alcohol abuse related. He also must not be aware that research proves that the large majority of the criminal population, once sobered up and kept sober, will stop doing crimes. The advocates of more jails and locking up more criminals are highly focused on prisons as a solution. An inmate spends either a short time or a long time in jail. How long he is in jail does not affect his rearrest rate.[14] Whether or not he gets drug treatment in jail **does** affect his rearrest rate. As it is now, as soon as he is released from jail, he can do almost anything illegal that he wants. And he can do this for a long time before the criminal justice system catches up with him again.

The basic alternatives to deal with crime currently being utilized by the criminal justice system are: (1) Criminals are either in jail, or (2) Criminals are allowed to remain on the streets, unsupervised by an overloaded probation department. They are free to do whatever they want, take all the drugs they want, commit all the crimes they want for long periods of time. Alternative number two is not acceptable to either the public or the criminal justice system. Alternative number one is breaking the nation's back financially and emotionally. The advocates of a "tough stand on crime" say criminals should not to be allowed to remain on the streets committing more crime. They say that the only solution is to lock them up.

There is a third alternative, and that is simply insisting on the substance abusing criminal's sobriety in exchange for his continued freedom. A program to guarantee sobriety can be carried out at a very reasonable cost to taxpayers. This third alternative involves the spending of $4,000 a year for a couple of years to sober up the substance abusing criminal. During this two year sobering up time period the substance abusing criminal will not be costing taxpayers $20 to $60 thousand a year to keep them in jail. And they won't be costing society up to a half million dollars a year in stolen goods, police and judge time, etc.

RED RAG AND BANDANNA

Garland Peed, who headed the San Diego District Attorney's gang unit, claimed there was a correlation between the San Diego Police Department drug operations in 1991 and a decrease in violent crime in black gang territories.[55] There were 300 arrests in three major crime sweeps by the police, with a reduction in violent incidents involving gang members by 75%. Drug charges were used to get the gang members off the streets. The "sweeps" were given colorful code names such as "red rag" and "bandanna." The unit was disbanded in 1992 and drive-by shootings jumped from 81 in 1991 to 107 in 1992. The sweeps reduced drive-by shootings and took a lot of the dope business from local gangs and gave it to illegal aliens.[69]

I was told by San Diego police officers that the gang member dealers who were locked up were replaced by a new breed of dope dealers. Ninety-five percent of them were illegal aliens who operated out of a whole new string of crack/dope houses. These new dope dens had two steel doors. Potential customers were ushered past the first steel door into a narrow hallway. There they stood and conducted their business with the seller who stood behind yet another steel door with small openings. What if the police decided to raid these new crack/dope houses? By the time they smashed through the double set of steel doors, the drugs had been flushed down the toilet. Mexican criminals had prepared themselves to do a lucrative drug dealing business on dangerous American turf. Their "soldiers" were trained in street guerrilla tactics before coming across the border.

As long as there is one person who wants to buy drugs, there will be someone willing to sell drugs to that person. These 300 drug involved gang members should have been taken off the streets, but not put in jail. They should have been put in detox. Then they should have been told that they could either get sober or go to jail. They should have been told that they could not go back to their old gang members until those gang members had also been sobered up. They would have to prove every single day of their lives that they were sober in order to stay out of jail.

SOBERING UP THE HOMIES

An involuntary sobriety program would have saved the $20,000 to $40,000 spent to process each of these 300 gang members through the prison system. It would have saved the high costs of locking them up. The cost to guarantee sobriety would have been $4,000 a year each. That $4,000 cost would cover a new place to live to keep the gang member away from his drug-riddled homie crowd. After implementation of the "Sober Forever" Program, one by one, the homies will be pulled out of their drug-infested worlds, sobered up, and trained for work. They will be allowed to go back home when both they and their home turfs are sober.

CHAPTER SIX

WHERE DO WE START?

Who do we sober up first?   Do we break down the doors of suspected alcoholics or drug addicts and give them breathalyzer or urine tests?   That's not necessary. We do not beat down doors to find drunk drivers to put in the drunk driver programs.   The drunk drivers literally crash into the criminal justice system by banging into other cars or trees or by weaving down the road. The four million people in America either in jail or on probation or parole weren't dragged from their quiet homes where they were unobtrusively getting loaded.   Their intoxication caused them to engage in violent or otherwise illegal behaviors over and over.

We have extensive lists of those who need help. We know who will experience major improvements in behavior, morality, health, finances and in their overall quality of life as soon as they sober up.   Hundreds of thousands of our fellow citizens' lives have been devastated by substance abuse.   The problem will not be to decide where to start looking for people needing to sober up.   The problem we will have when the "Sober Forever" Program is implemented on a broad scale: To choose from the legions of the addicted who desperately need help, whom to help first.

We could start with those three million people on probation or parole, many of whom, if they are ever tested for drugs, show up positive for drugs on their urine tests.[120]   What happens to those people now if they keep getting loaded?   Usually nothing. But depending on the whims of the judicial system, a dirty urine test could mean five to 20 years in jail.   Instead, the positive or dirty urine test should trigger full involvement in an involuntary sobriety program which will guarantee sobriety.   Sober, the probability of repeat offenses, even by the "predatory" offender, reduces drastically.   How can we find these thousands of "absconded" drug addicted felons who "can't" be found? With a tiny bit of effort, as we shall see later in this book, they can be found.

The most important group of all to sober up we can find very easily. These are the over a million people locked up in America's jails. Most of them are there because of substance abuse. Almost all of them, if sobered up, would never go back to jail. As it is now, 65% or more of them will return to jail. If we ever want to change that, the last two years they are in jail must be spent in a "Stay'n Out" type therapeutic community drug rehabilitation program. Less than 15% have any kind of drug rehabilitation while in jail. At the most, a few thousand of the 1.2 million Americans behind bars are receiving the kind of intense in-jail treatment that would keep them sober and out of jail after they have done their time. As it is, going to jail does not mean getting sober. You can often get whatever drugs you want in jail. In jail, many inmates engage in an intensive body building program with a regimented weight lifting routine. If they get tough enough they might not get raped. In jail, they get advanced training in their criminal careers.[133]

Another very important group to sober up are new entrants into the world of substance abuse. That is, those who are just beginning to engage in erratic and illegal behavior because of substance abuse. This population will sober up easier than the addict of a few years or more. Also, when sober, these recent entrants into the world of substance abuse will have more of their intellectual faculties still intact. Their brains will recover sooner.

STEALING A TANK OF GAS

Example: Harry beats up his girlfriend and drives off with squealing tires. He stops at a gas station and fills up his tank, steals a cigarette lighter, then leaves without paying. When caught, the pupils in Harry's eyes look funny. Sure enough, he is experiencing a high. He has taken drugs. After he got loaded, he did a bunch of dumb things which he never would have done if he had been sober. The **longer** he is sober, the **less** likely it is he'll ever do those dumb things again. It takes awhile for the mentality and morality of an individual who is sinking deeper into illegal drug usage to deteriorate. It takes awhile for the mentality and morality to come back after the individual is off illegal drugs.

Harry can now be charged and tried for assault, petty theft, driving under the influence, public endangerment, etc. This is the usual procedure. It will cost an easy $20,000 to get Harry convicted. Then, since there is no room in jail, Harry will be put on probation but never be seen by a probation officer. Or at least not until he has committed another whole series of crimes, has lost his job, his car and his girlfriend. Instead of filing charges after he beat up his girlfriend why don't we tell Harry "You're mine. You did something illegal while you were high. So you can't use illegal drugs or alcohol anymore."

We know Harry is very unlikely to commit any more crimes if he is sober. We can sober Harry up for a tiny fraction of the cost of prosecuting him for his first offense. Since Harry was still working at the time he had his little spree, it won't cost society anything to sober him up. Harry can be ordered to pay for it himself. He may not like that idea. But it will cost him much less to participate in the "Sober Forever" Program than he used to spend on dope and booze. He won't be buying dope and booze anymore. He will begin making restitution payments. He'll pay for the stolen gas, the lighter and his girlfriend's doctor bills. If we lock him up nobody gets paid. If he's sober, he and his girlfriend will probably get back together and get a life.

Drugs destroy the conscience of a substance abuser. Drugs cause many physical, mental and emotional changes. Drugs turn law abiding citizens into criminals.

Many people say, "A substance abuser has to hit bottom before treatment will do him any good." Then they say, "Bottom is different for different people. For some, bottom is their first arrest. For others, bottom is when they've lost everything." **This isn't true.** Involuntary drug rehabilitation programs are more effective than voluntary drug treatment programs. In some voluntary drug rehabilitation programs, the success rate has occasionally been reported to be as high as 70%. I believe that the success rate could be moved up to 98% by simply adding a determined "tail," "tracking" or closely monitored "follow-up."

How hard is it to get sober? Many (but not all) people thrown in jail get sober. People hospitalized for a thirty-day intensive rehabilitation program get sober. **Staying sober** is the hard part. There are people who have repeatedly gone through thirty-day intensive rehabilitation programs, at a cost that can reach $35,000 each time. Typical programs can easily cost $1,000 a day. I have seen individuals who have spent, on an off and on basis, half of the last fifteen years of their life in a variety of live-in drug rehabilitation programs. Sometimes they managed to get back to using illegal drugs **while still in** these programs. Sometimes they had to wait until they got out of the program to begin using illegal drugs. It is easy to get sober. Staying sober **permanently** is more difficult. But it can be done.

LESS VEGETABLES TO TEND IN THE NURSING HOMES

Do we have the right to tell people that they can no longer take drugs? Californians decided they had the right to force motorcycle riders to wear a helmet. If their brains are badly injured in an accident, motorcycle riders often sit around in a vegetative state for the rest of their lives. The costs of long-term after-care programs amount to a minimum of $1,000 a month of public monies. The totally disabled, brain damaged motorcycle accident survivor rarely has his own resources. Taxpayers pay for his lifelong care.

Californians decided that they had the right to insist that motorcyclists wear helmets. Research has since proven that helmets reduce the risk of death and disabling injuries to the motorcycle rider.

In the first six months after the passing of the mandatory helmet law in California (January to June,

1992) 148 people died in motorcycle accidents. In the first six months of 1991, 225 people died. Seventy seven less people died in the six months after the helmet law was passed. Injuries dropped by 1121, from 7,787 for the first half of 1991 to 5,666 for the first six months of 1992.[95]

Yet the motorcyclists still whine about their loss of freedom. They complain that they no longer have the wind in their hair. The helmets have reduced the number of permanent disabilities due to serious brain damage. Therefore, Californians are paying less to house the vegetable by-products of many motorcycle injuries.

There are those who say taking drugs to "feel good" is their God given right. I would agree, if it wasn't shredding our society and scuttling the American dream. What is the American dream I have often referred to? In many parts of the world owning or even renting your own home or apartment, having enough food to eat, having your children live till they grow up, are all very unlikely. This can and until recently did happen regularly in America. But it rarely happens to the druggie. He very often can't work, thus he can't get that home with the white picket fence. He can't keep a family because of mood swings, violence and irresponsibility. We have seen the American dream slipping away for all of us. Our children can't get the same help getting an education that was available a few years back. State funded college tuitions have been doubling every year or so. Courts and jails suck the money out of our schools and parks.

Do we have the right to tell a woman she can't take drugs? Her robberies cost us money. Each of her crack babies cost taxpayers incredible amounts of money. Some women have had as many as ten crack babies. To just keep these babies alive for the first few months costs a fortune. When these crack babies are a little older they are hyperactive, inconsolable, aggressive, and slow learners. They are also angry.

As these crack babies grow a little older still, they are angry delinquents. Older still, many become heavily involved in illegal drug use and crime. Then they fill our jails. The cycle repeats itself. Do we have the right to tell a drug-addicted woman who is HIV infected she can't earn her drug money anymore by selling sex and spreading AIDS? If she's sober, she won't sell her body for drugs. She won't be making crack babies. If she does get pregnant while sober, her children will have a chance of growing up to be healthy and happy Americans.

DRUNKS COVERED WITH THEIR OWN VOMIT

Homeless substance abusing males have an average life span of forty-one years. That is thirty years less than the life of the average male.[8] Substance abusing males are murdered and die of drug overdoses and related illness, such as AIDS. They contract AIDS from shooting up with needles used by an AIDS infected addict. Why should we sober them up? Why not let them die at the age of forty-one?

We need to sober them up for humanitarian reasons. Not saving someone's endangered life when we have the ability to do so is not very humanitarian. We need to sober them up for aesthetic reasons. A drunk passed out in a shopkeeper's doorway covered with his own vomit is not a pretty sight. We need to sober them up for financial reasons. After a couple years of being sober at a cost of about $4,000 a year, about half will have gone back to work. In another five years, they will have paid back in taxes all the money spent by taxpayers to sober them up.

Can we reduce illegal drug demand? The answer is: **Yes we can!** How will we do it? This involves giving a very strong and consistent message to people using illegal drugs. The message is, "You can't do drugs anymore!" Of the freedoms guaranteed by the Constitution there is no mention of the right to destroy their own lives and the lives of those around them through the use of illegal drugs. The Health and Safety Codes of California and all other states have specific regulations regarding the use of illegal drugs. Can we stop someone on the street and ask them to submit to a drug test to decide whether they are addicted to drugs? No, not unless we obtain their permission to do so.

Not many substance abusers are going to sign a permission slip to let us find out whether they are addicted to illegal drugs.

But if there is probable cause to believe that an individual may be **under the influence** of an illegal drug, it is **not** necessary to obtain their permission. You can conduct an examination against their will to determine whether or not they are under the influence of an illegal drug. This is covered in the California Health and Safety Code Statute 11552. What is probable cause? Dilated pupils, slurred speech or erratic behavior suggest the possibility that an individual may be under the influence of an illegal substance. The laws are there which give society the right to determine whether an individual is under the influence or not. For the most part, the laws are not being used.

The California Criminal Code has laws governing alcohol abuse. One such law governs simple drunk-in-public behavior without any other accompanying crime. An arrest for drunkenness with two priors in twelve months can result in ninety days in jail. The Criminal Code also outlines an alternate sentencing which could be up to sixty days in an alcohol treatment program. In actuality, multiple arrests for drunk-in-public behavior results in no consequences whatsoever in San Diego, and in most major cities in the United States. Most cities and states across the nation have similar laws on their books allowing for the rehabilitation of substance abusers and alcoholics early in their substance abuse careers. What the law says can be done is rarely being done.

In San Diego County there are about 300 (of 17,000 probationers) involved in a rehabilitation treatment program which has a good chance of leading to sobriety (see Chapter Eight). That only leaves 16,700 probationers whose needs are either not being met or are being met in only a marginal fashion.

An initial arrest gains the substance abuser entry into the legal system. But it can be several years before the system really intrudes significantly on their lives. In the meantime, there are years of legal hassles, lawyers and court appearances. While all that is going on, there are no measures being undertaken which are truly effective in helping our addicted lick their substance abuse problems.

"I WAS SO STRESSED OUT BY COURT I GOT LOADED"

The substance abusers become locked into a struggle with the law and society. They experience increasing levels of stress, fear, and hatred of the criminal justice system. To help them handle this additional "stress" the substance abuser often increases his consumption of 'feel good' chemicals.

By the time the drug abuser finally goes to jail, he has often slipped deep into an abuse/addiction/crime pattern. Substance abusers do not usually start off being under the influence twenty-four hours a day. It typically takes time to get to that point. On their way to addiction and heavy drug use the substance abuser's behavior deteriorates. The number of crimes they commit gradually increases. An involuntary sobriety program should start at the time of the first arrest in which substance abuse is involved (which is almost every arrest).

We don't have to prowl the streets asking "suspicious" people to urinate in a bottle to find out who needs help with their substance abuse problem. Most of the people arrested for **anything** in America today are under the influence. We don't have to look for people to sober up. They are on the corners selling dope, they are shoplifting. They are abusing their children. They are selling sex for drugs. They have hundreds of ways of saying "Here I am! Please help me!"

Do we have the right to demand that if someone commits a crime while under the influence that they must refrain from any further use of alcohol or drugs? Isn't that infringing on people's freedom? This issue has been debated at length. Long ago our society decided we do have the right to demand that substance abusers sober up. Though society has reaffirmed this right many times, that right has not yet been exercised except inconsistently and sporadically. If the reason for that is because we thought it would cost too much or we didn't know how to do it, this book tells how to do it. Sobering up the substance abusers who become even peripherally involved in the criminal justice system can be done at a much cheaper cost than anything else we have done or can do to control violence and crime in America.

THE LEGALIZATION DEBATE

Those who back drug legalization maintain that if drugs were legal the drug dealers would be gone. They would have to get job training and find work or settle for welfare. This is because drug dealing, the high paying and glamorous career of choice for the ghetto dweller, would cease to exist. The thousands of addicts stealing to supply their habit would quit crime. They now commit four million crimes a year to steal over seven billion dollars of property.[104]

They say that if we legalize drugs there wouldn't be turf wars and drive-by shootings. One thousand six hundred innocent people a year are killed by druggies in robberies. Many thousands more are beaten and injured. Organized crime would take a pay cut of $80 billion a year. Drugs available legally will cost only a tenth as much as they do now on the black market. Taxes will be collected on the sale of drugs providing income to help pay off the national debt.[104]

Those who want drugs legalized say that in spite of massive efforts to stop the incoming drugs, cocaine is cheaper than ever. Efforts to reduce supply don't work and are a waste of time and money. FBI agents, prison guards, custom officials and police have all been corrupted by the large amounts of money to be made for looking the other way or even dealing in drugs.[43, 102]

If drugs were legal, some liberals say, there would be no drug money corrupting officials. Once drugs were legal, drug users would not have to come into contact with criminal elements. Often the drug user is robbed. This doesn't happen if he buys a bottle of liquor, but did when liquor was illegal. The thousands of AIDS deaths every year which result from sharing needles will go way down. The government could save the billions it now spends each year to wage its drug wars.

I have promised throughout this book that a sobriety program such as the "Sober Forever" Program described in Chapter 11 would reap incredible rewards to society. These rewards would come at a fraction of the price our drug wars now cost. Above, it was claimed by backers of drug legalization that many benefits would result from easy and cheap drug availability. If these promises sound familiar it might be because I have promised that all of these same benefits will occur as a result of sobering up America's substance abusers.

If no one is buying drugs, there are no dealers, no drive by shootings over turf wars, no officials corrupted with drug money. Sobered up addicts will stop committing crime and levels of violence will go way down. We will be able to spend most of the billions now going into jails and law enforcement on roads, parks, schools or on a rapid transit system that people will use. We will be able to spend those billions on job training and seed money to create new businesses to create new jobs.

Some of those trying to sell drug legalization say drug use will probably stay the same, or increase just slightly. They maintain that all the above-described benefits are worth a few more addicts. Let's ask a simple question: If one out of ten births nation-wide, and four out of ten in some parts of the country are crack babies, what will drug legalization do? Will we have less crack babies when you can buy a month's supply of crack cocaine at 7-Eleven for $20? Could it possibly be that we would end up with double, quadruple or even twenty times the number of crack babies born now? And who will pay to take care of that new, greatly enlarged crop of crack babies? As it is now, many crack babies spend eighteen years in foster homes at a cost of around $1,000 per month per child.

When only a portion of the astronomical amounts of money going into reducing supply begins to be spent on sobering up America, the drug wars will be over.

PRESCRIPTION FOR DISASTER: LEGALIZED DRUGS

In 1975 Italy liberalized its drug laws and in 1992 had one of the highest heroin-related death rates in Western Europe.[13] In 1983, after heroin had been legalized for some time in The Netherlands, Amsterdam reported the highest per capita murder rate in the world.[116] In Alaska marijuana was decriminalized in 1975. The easy atmosphere resulted in increased usage of the drug, particularly among children. Some Alaskan school children were using "Coca Puffs," marijuana cigarettes laced with cocaine.[13] Alaska has given up its experiment in the legalization of illegal drugs.   The Alaskans became aware of the problems that marijuana was causing in their state.[153]

There have been predictions that legalization might cause a five to six fold increase in illegal drug use. The United States is already on the edge of national disaster because of illegal drugs and their results: higher crimes, destroyed families, lost lives, human potential never realized, economic resources squandered. There is ample evidence that these social ills are the by-products of substance abuse. The idea that legalization of illegal drugs will reduce crime is false.[13, 116]

With easy access to drugs, those inclined toward criminal behavior are made more violent and unpredictable. The fact is that under the influence of drugs, normal people do not act normally, and abnormal people behave in "chilling and horrible ways."[13]

Drugs are an equal opportunity killer. I have heard in treatment circles the story of one doctor who became addicted to cocaine. Cardiac arrests are possible with large doses. When your heart stops for more than a couple of minutes, you die. This doctor, one might say, 'lived on the edge.' He shot up massive doses of cocaine to get a massive rush. If his heart stopped (which it did a few times) he always had his defibrillator handy. That's the device used to deliver a powerful electric shock to the heart to get it started again. Any vidiot (avid TV watcher) has seen thousands of doctors grab the two defibrillator paddles by the handles and put them on the chest of a patient whose heart had stopped. Then the doctor shouted **"CLEAR!"** And the patient's body jumped. On TV, the patient's heart almost always started beating again. But one time the cocaine-addicted doctor went to restart his heart after a massive dose of cocaine. Even after several jolts, one after the other, nothing happened. The story goes that the doctor had quite a look of surprise and disbelief on his face as he gradually lost consciousness and died.

If ready accessibility to drugs reduced crime, why is it that the crime rates are highest where drugs are the cheapest and used the most?

Should the now illegal drugs be made legal because drug use is a victimless crime? Those who maintain that drug abusers only harm themselves are not well informed. The chaos and devastation wreaked on society by the drug addict means that everyone is a victim. To the drug addict looking for a way of getting high, any behavior is acceptable. This includes stealing from and lying to their families, borrowing money they know they will never pay back, writing checks they know they can't cover.

We, the members of society pay for this in many ways. Just one example is through higher insurance premiums. Losses from accidents caused by substance abusers drives up all our rates. Promising careers are never fulfilled. Former drug Czar William Bennett also noted, "A citizen in a drug-induced haze, whether in his own back yard or on a mattress in a ghetto crack house, is not what the founding father's meant by the 'pursuit of happiness.'" And "helpless wrecks in treatment centers, men chained by their noses to cocaine - these people are slaves."[13]

Stealing to get drug money is a major cause of most crime in America today. We have seen that drugs destroy the conscience. Human life has no value to the druggie. Past societies which legalized drugs suffered. Among them were the hashish users in the medieval Moslem empire, Peruvian laborers in the 16th century and opium addicts of 19th century China. Whenever addictive drugs are socially accepted and easily available, there is a high incidence of individual and social damage.[116]

Marijuana comes from the hemp plant. So does hashish, which is a powerful narcotic drug derived from hemp (cannabis sativa). It is smoked, chewed or drunk for its intoxicating effects. Everyone knows that an assassin is a killer. An assassin murders others for money or because of fanatical motives. Those first described as assassins were members of a secret order of Muslims. At the time of the crusades these Muslims terrorized Christians and their other enemies with their secret murders committed while under the influence of hashish. Centuries ago they were first called hashishians which finally ended up in the English language as assassins. Drugs have been connected to murder for centuries. They still are. Legalizing drugs will not result in a decrease in crime and violence but an increase.

"GIVE ME THE HOLY WEED"

When we talk about dangerous drugs, we're not talking about marijuana, right? Marijuana is harmless, isn't it? We can't interfere with Lawrence Ferlenghetti and his friends' right to pot as proclaimed by this beat generation poet's cry "Give me the Holy Weed." Or can we? We know a lot about marijuana. It creates a feeling of calm euphoria. Time seems to pass more slowly. There is enhancement of the senses. Ideas flow easily.

But short term memory suffers. Reaction time and coordination are impaired. Operating automobiles and other equipment after smoking marijuana results in more accidents. Hours after the smoker no longer feels 'high' impairment continues. Long-term effects can include psychotic reactions, even hallucinations. Schizophrenics in remission (those displaying no current symptoms of psychosis) can easily relapse into a full blown psychosis after smoking the "Holy Weed."[9]

For years, it has been known that students using marijuana receive low grades. A drop in grades from B's or C's to F's has been documented in thousands of cases. This drop in the students' grades started at the same time they began using marijuana. Laboratory studies show that small dosages of THC (the main mood-altering ingredient in marijuana) lowers alertness and retards learning and memory. The higher the dose of marijuana, the worse the marijuana users' memories become. They may remember something briefly, but after five seconds, they forget. Marijuana smokers often believe they are very alert.[114]

Marijuana smokers feel that they have a heightened sense of reality. In actuality, they miss a great deal of what is going on around them. Even if a student comprehends what is being said at the time, it is likely that the information will not make it to the student's long-term memory. That information is likely to not be there at the time of the exam, even if they are drug free when they take the exam. Extensive research shows that many physical changes accompany marijuana use. There is a very high probability that some of these physical changes are permanent.

Even moderate doses of THC (the main mood altering ingredient in marijuana) over an eight month period destroyed brain cells in laboratory animals and caused premature aging of the brain. Marijuana shrinks the brain. After smoking heavily for a few years, marijuana users' brains resembled brains of octogenarians, in terms of size. In both the smokers and elders, sinus cavities had grown larger relative to the brains of young non-smokers. Marijuana has been found to hinder speaking and concentration in humans. Marijuana use slows reaction time and causes difficulty in solving math problems. Marijuana impairs motivation or the desire to learn, as well as learning itself. Heavy marijuana users and former marijuana users are less motivated to succeed than nonusers.

In a Virginia study it was discovered that before marijuana use only one student in twenty-five had experienced serious school failure.   After regular marijuana use, three out of five students were failing in school and more than half of the marijuana using students were ditching at least one class a day.   Nearly three quarters of the pot smoking students had been suspended from school. Yet, most of those students didn't believe that Marijuana was affecting their lives.[114]

Substance abusers engage in the heavy use of denial.   They refuse to accept the devastation their substance abuse is causing even if substance abuse is tearing their lives to shreds. If they do admit to problems in their lives, they almost invariably blame their problems on something or someone else.

Marijuana seems to dull the substance abuser's conscience, which is perhaps why it is used.   That little voice that comes from somewhere behind our shoulder and tells us to not do this or that can be quieted by marijuana. That little voice that used to say "It's time to do your homework" is stilled. If the thought of homework comes up, the response is, "Oh, well." How does the marijuana smoker react to criticism or anger from others?   Their angry critics are labeled as rigid and up-tight. People who smoke marijuana **used to** have problems, but believe that marijuana has solved their problems.   Those little nagging feelings of failure, worry about passing through the milestones of life, are all gone, silenced by marijuana. The D's and F's and other signs of failure begin to lower self-esteem.   The students begin to see themselves as losers. Getting high then becomes a way to escape from the feelings of failure.   A vicious cycle has begun.[114]

Marijuana damages the brain, the immune system, the reproductive system and the lungs. It increases heart rate and blood pressure. Marijuana users are more likely than non smokers to get bronchitis, emphysema and lung cancer.   Because the immune system is impaired, marijuana smokers are more likely to contract cancer, AIDS and other diseases. Long-term marijuana users lack ambition and direction. They are passive and apathetic.

Mental and physical health is impaired.   Work, family life and friendships suffer.   Off his pot, the ex-smoker can experience anxiety, insomnia, tremors and chills.   Withdrawal can take several days.[9]

Cocaine can cause a loss of appetite, weakness, brain damage, high blood pressure, strokes and birth defects.[116]

Alcoholism leads to an early death.   Alcoholics who sobered up and stayed sober had death rates which returned to normal.   However, those who relapse die at a rate five times that of Americans of similar age, sex and race.[33]   The study by UCSD (University of California at San Diego) scientists concluded that sobriety, once established among long-term alcoholics, is likely to not only lead to better day-to-day functioning, but to a longer life as well.

AMERICA LOVES ITS JAILS

The Sentencing Project reviewed incarceration trends and pointed out that on a per capita basis the United States had more of its citizens locked up than any country in the world in 1990.   There were 1.1 million Americans in federal or state prisons or local jails, costing taxpayers 203 billion dollars a year.   The United States surpassed South Africa, whose incarceration rate was 311 prisoners per 100,000 in population.   The United States imprisoned 3,370 blacks per 100,000, five times greater than South Africa's rate of 681 per 100,000.

In The Netherlands there were 36 prisoners per 100,00 inhabitants.   Iceland had 41; Norway, 47; The Netherlands, 36; Sweden, 61; Denmark, 69; Germany, 86; France, 92; Great Britain, 100; Northern Ireland, 125.   In the United States, there were 455 prisoners per 100,000, double the rate of ten years ago.   We lock up ten times as many people as Iceland and four times as many as England.   One of every four young black men in the Unites States is behind bars or on probation or parole.   This disgrace is happening in a nation supposedly so enlightened we shout **"BIGOT!"** at the Serbs, the Russians, etc.

The Sentencing Project recommended greater use of alternative punishments such as community service and **supervised probation**. They recommended more crime prevention efforts and **drug treatment**. They recommended repeal of mandatory sentencing laws and studies to find other ways of reducing the prison and jail population.[148]

In response to this report, the Justice Department cried "foul," saying the report was partial and misleading. The Justice Department claimed that imprisonment policies had stemmed the rapidly growing rate of violent crime. Attorney General William Barr claimed that because of longer sentences, the violent crime rate leveled off and held relatively steady. But most other statistics seemed to indicate a continued rise.

The Justice Department reported on felons in seventeen states who had been placed on probation in 1986. Within three years, 43% had been rearrested on other felony charges. Federal prisoners have a lower rearrest rate than those released from state and local prisons. Even so, a 43% rearrest rate suggests that whatever rehabilitation was tried was relatively ineffective. There certainly was not a fail-safe method of guaranteeing sobriety as has been outlined in Chapter 11 of this book. In fact, 46% of the drug traffickers were rearrested for the same crime. Thirty-four percent of the 12,370 felons studied who were on probation were convicted of drug crimes.[7]

EUROPE AHEAD OF U.S. IN DRUG POLICIES

Even though European countries have a much smaller percentage of their citizens locked up than the United States, the number of addicts in Europe is lower than in the U. S. Why is that? 'Bad seeds' in the U.S.? Weak minded people? The answer is that European countries approach the drug/crime problem in ways close to the solutions recommended in Chapter 11 of this book. The focus in Europe is on treatment and rehabilitation and not on punishment.[43]

European countries have drug laws. But European judges don't have mandatory sentences. They can decide whether or not they want to send people to jail or treatment. Since 1990 those caught in possession of small amounts of drugs (100 mg. heroin, 150 mg cocaine) are given treatment and sanctions. These include suspension of driver's license, curfews and fines. A third offense may result in jail.

In The Netherlands marijuana is sold at coffee shops but selling cocaine or heroin will get a coffee shop closed down. Drug use in Holland has decreased in the last few years. The Dutch policy keeps the goal in mind of reducing the harm of drugs. They try to prevent users from sliding to the fringes of society. Treatment and health care are made accessible. As we know, addicts in the U.S must often wait months for treatment. By the time their names come up on the list many are too loaded or too dead to go. The Europeans don't lose track of their dopers. They make concerted efforts to get people into treatment. Jail is a last resource. In the U.S. jail is the only resource. Only 200 of California's 100,000 prisoners were receiving in-jail therapeutic community drug rehabilitation in 1992. Only 364 of the 41,000 federal prisoners with serious drug problems were receiving in-jail drug rehabilitation in 1991.[43]

In 1989 Zurich, Switzerland began to make clean needles, medical care and social services available to drug users. They created a "zone of tolerance" for illegal drugs in the Platspitz Park. Unfortunately, addicts were attracted from all over Europe. In spite of easy access to drugs, the Platspitz degenerated into a cesspool of crime, violence and degenerate behavior. The park was closed in February, 1992.[43]

In Europe in 1991 there was relative economic prosperity and ready drug availability. In spite of this, usage of the big three, heroin, cocaine and marijuana, was far lower than in the U.S. Criminal laws in Europe do prohibit drug possession and sales. But, prevention, treatment and education were priority interventions with incarceration used only as a last resort.[43]

Some people feel that being born in the ghetto is the same as a life sentence to poverty and misery. They will maintain that the only solace for a horrible life can be found by staying under the influence of drugs or alcohol. The complaint is that we must provide job training, jobs and housing to encourage the substance abuser to turn his life around. But a substance abuser often cannot keep a job, he cannot follow through on job training and he often cannot live in a house without tearing it up. For failing to pay the rent he often gets evicted.

DRUGS: THE EQUAL OPPORTUNITY PATH TO RUIN

What has been accomplished for blacks by equal opportunity policies and by making education available? One study seemed to question the assumption that liberal social programs can reduce crime by reducing social and economic injustices. Rising pay and education did not result in a reduction in the black crime rate. At the time blacks were making dramatic educational strides in the sixties and seventies, the crime rate among blacks was also rising. Rising income and educational levels since World War Two were accompanied by a drop in crime rates by whites in the sixties and seventies but not among blacks.[121]

What the study does not address is the fact that many blacks who were born in the ghetto **have** taken advantage of the opportunities offered to them. They went to the Job Corps and learned a trade or they found a way to go to college. They entered mainstream American society and do earn decent wages. But they left behind a large group of their black brothers and sisters who did not take advantage of these opportunities. This growing disparity in the black population between those who succeed and those who fail is strongly tied to substance abuse.

Five out of six criminals who sober up stop committing crimes. Substance abuse is directly related to crime. Not all blacks are committing crimes. Some got an education and are doing very well. Others are committing crimes and abusing substances at a higher rate than ever. Percentage-wise, blacks are getting locked up at a higher rate than whites. The media has focused on this fact and on the problems in the ghetto. But the drug addiction/crime rate in white and middle class America is also out of control. Blacks are the ones getting locked up.

The social programs must continue. The Job Corps and other ways of getting a career or an education must continue to be made available. But the blacks, as the rest of those who are abusing substances, must first become sober in order to be able to take advantage of these opportunities.

In an episode of "Cops," a woman in Portland, Oregon, was pleading with a police officer to take her paint-sniffing son to a treatment program. She complained that her daughter had died of a drug overdose a few weeks before. The police officer talked to a bleary-eyed youth he had just pulled out from under some dirty blankets in a back shed. All over America our druggie children are living in filthy squalor in or near their own homes. Sometimes they take up residence in the garage after they have been "kicked out." They had been told to leave because they had been acting like an animal. They were stealing from their homes and trashing their rooms and maybe the whole house. They seem to have forgotten everything they were taught about basic hygiene. Their teeth are rotting from neglect.

To the mumbling youth dragged from under the filthy blankets the police officer on "Cops" gave the suggestion that he volunteer himself for treatment. When the boy refused and staggered off, the boy's mother pleaded with the police officer to do something. The officer explained that he couldn't force the boy into a treatment program. At the conclusion of that episode the announcer said that three weeks after that episode was filmed the paint sniffing boy had killed himself. In a few weeks that mother had lost all of her children to substance abuse.

The officer was wrong. The laws **are** there to force somebody into treatment. They are not being used. The crime and violence rate in America is out of control. The Criminal Justice System is unable to stem the tide of addiction, crime and violence. That's because the money is being spent for all the wrong reasons and in all the wrong places. Four thousand dollars a year can keep an addict **alive and sober.** Instead, money is wasted on expensive court appearances, defense and prosecuting attorneys and on very expensive jails where no rehabilitation is provided. Most jails are places where normal people who got high and then got into a little trouble are turned into hardened career criminals and vicious animals.

Newly recognized is the "false memory" phenomena. The unconscious mind can be comforted and solaced, as noted in Chapter Ten, by imagining 'new endings' to unhappy experiences. But highly emotional "memory searches" done in cults, therapists' offices, etc., are producing false memories of molest, abuse and satanic rituals. Children and adults going through these emotionally intense inquisition sessions end up believing that the information produced reflects events which really happened. Bobby Fijnje in Florida and Dale Akiki in San Diego were accused of and tried for child molests that never occurred.

CHAPTER SEVEN

INTERVIEW WITH VICKI MARKEY, DEPUTY CHIEF PROBATION OFFICER OF SAN DIEGO COUNTY

THE PAPER CHASE

Vicki: San Diego is the only County that has a truly bifurcated custody situation in that the sheriff runs the maximum security institutions and the Probation Officer runs the minimum security institutions. We've been closing our minimum security units to save money. Now we have three minimum security jails and a work furlough center.

Whoever is booked in the jail and is going to do some time, we do a check to see what warrants are there. Let's say all of a sudden the judge puts him in custody. Then you would pull all of these warrants and they may be from all different courts. We book a court hearing for each felony warrant so that when they leave, we have gotten all their felony warrants cleaned up.

Don: You mean if there's twenty warrants, there may be twenty appearances?

Vicki: There could be. A single judge may not handle them all. You may have one in South Bay, you may have one in Vista.

Don: So he has to be driven back and forth, all over the place?

Vicki: That's right, and he has to be in custody. We used to also process all misdemeanor warrants. Our goal was that when a prisoner was released, we had all warrants cleaned out of the system. We stopped doing that. The sheriff stopped a year or so before us. We just didn't have the manpower to do it anymore.

My guess is that if you found the time that the Sheriff and probation stopped cleaning out misdemeanor warrants you'll probably find that that is when there was a real escalation in outstanding warrants. Usually the worst that happens in misdemeanor warrant cases is that they get credit for time served or they serve the time on the warrant. Or they are sentenced on their misdemeanor warrant concurrent with the sentence being executed. Now a felony warrant is a different issue. Both probation and the sheriff's department act immediately on a felony warrant. We set a court hearing.

Don: I had heard that you have to have fifteen warrants before they do anything. Ten or eleven of them have to be under the influence and one of them has to have some violence associated with it. There is strict criteria before they even take them in, and when they do, you said that thirty days is the most that they are going to do.

THE WARRANT BANK: LIMBO OF THE ABSCONDED

Vicki: We've got about 17,000 people who are under probation supervision, active to us. Those are people who have gone before the court, they've been sentenced. They have either been placed on probation in lieu of the jail or they serve jail time and then they are under probation supervision. I have probably another 5,000 cases to investigate and another 2,000 cases that are in our warrant bank. These are people who are in violation of the terms of their probation who we can't find in order to get them back to court to be processed.

Don: You mean you've actually gone out and looked for them, checked their homes?

Vicki: No. Probation, adult supervision, has been cut tremendously. About six or seven years ago we had to get out of supervising misdemeanors. We don't supervise misdemeanors at all any more and if they get probation, it's probation to the court. All that means is that if they're arrested again on a misdemeanor and it goes to court, his punishment is that he's on probation to the court. That means he's in a file somewhere in the court. If he gets arrested again, and convicted of a felony we will be asked to do a pre-sentencing investigation report after his conviction. They want to know what we think we ought to do with him and what does the law say we have to do with him.

When we search our files and do a record check, we'll find out whether or not he was already on probation from the courts. If so, we will revoke their probation. Then we will escalate the punishment. That's all that means. If he's arrested again on a misdemeanor, we do not do a report. In that case, the court would take a look. A court clerk would search the records and find whether he's already on probation to the court for something else. Then he'd likely get a grant of probation to the court and/or custody. There will be some escalation of punishment but it still won't be probation supervision.

On the felony side we have to provide supervision. But we don't have the manpower so seventy percent of our cases of those 17,000 people are in the banks. So to answer your question, 'Do we go out and look for them,' the answer is 'No.' Being in the bank means they mail us something every month to tell us what they are doing to comply with probation. They give us a sign-off sheet if they've been going to A.A. (Alcoholic's Anonymous) meetings or if they've been going to treatment. If they have been ordered to pay restitution, we know through the computer program if they haven't been paying.

Most of the violations by people in the probation bank are failure to report and showing up positive for drugs on their urine samples. We have a random notification system of people who need to be urine tested for drugs/alcohol as part of the bank caseload. They have to come in and be tested. So the violations are primarily positive urines and failure to notify us of their whereabouts. On the whereabouts issue, we will follow through and call telephone numbers that they gave us.

Nothing happens to the warrant until the person is rearrested for something. While he's being booked the sheriff's department will run a record check. They'll find out if there's a warrant for probation violation. Then he'll be automatically incarcerated and we will be notified. If it's a misdemeanor offense, the street officer knows that the jail typically is not going to book him and so he generally hands out a citation.

Don: The beat officer doesn't always check so they can miss some.

Vicki: The officer on the street may be suspicious about something. Let's say they've gone through a briefing. So now they're looking for this six foot, white guy with a mustache. Let's say they have stopped somebody for speeding and the guy is six feet tall and has a mustache. If the officer on the street remembers all that, he might think "Something is not right here." Then they can use the radio to call the dispatcher and say, "I want a record check on driver's license number such and such." They just don't do it for all their citations. We're real worried about our warrant bank, and it keeps getting bigger. The bank means about 600 people per probation officer, that's 600 felonies for each probation officer.

Don: There's no way a probation officer can really follow that many people.

Vicki: That's true. Every once in a while, somebody will get arrested and they'll say, "Well, I was at home I don't know why nobody got hold of me." We go back through the file and sometimes we know we should have done a better job. We should have tried to look for them. I wish I had a couple officers just to go out in the field and do that because these felony probationers are generally not transients.

Don: So when you say you can't find those 2,000 people who have violated probation, you haven't really looked.

Vicki: We've done what we can. We don't allow anything to go to the warrant bank until we have made an effort to find or contact them. We also have to do an ex parte court report and describe in that report what we have done to look for this person. For example, I might report that I called the number I had on file and it was disconnected. Or I might report that I sent a warning letter to the last name and address on file but it was returned to the office. Or I might report that I called the girlfriend who the man had when he first came into custody. Those are the sorts of things we do from our desk quickly. It's not that I went out into the community to check.

We don't know much about these people. We might have a probation report that was done a year or so ago. When I say these people aren't transient, what I meant by that is that they don't live on the street. Generally they've lived with one girlfriend, then she kicks them out. So they live with somebody else or a doper buddy. What I just said is in reference to the 6,000 plus probationers in the bank caseloads. We do closer checks on our clients who are in our intensive caseloads.

Don: I guess if you had someone more closely tied in with these people, then someone could say, "Oh, yea, I know where Joe is."

Vicki: We have a special unit that runs under the assistant chief's jurisdiction. It's called the Gang Suppression Unit. It's a group of probation officers who are located downstairs with D.A.'s and San Diego police officers. They target a group of about 12,000 active gang members who are involved with drugs. Each of the officers carry about fifty cases and they share intelligence. One of the Probation Officers might say "I know Susan Smith hasn't been to court." Or they might say, "Joe Brown hasn't been reporting to me for three weeks. I can't find him. I've called his home. His mother says she doesn't know where he is."

THEY CAN BE FOUND IF SOMEBODY LOOKS FOR THEM

That shared intelligence alerts everybody in the unit including the probation and police officers who work in the evenings. They're out there with the gangs on the pavement. They're doing surveillance work, they're building cases. They will be on the lookout for Joe Brown. And they find him because he's hanging out with his buddies. You don't have to issue a warrant. What you do is you pick him up, put cuffs on him and take him to jail. So it's very easy. These gang members hang out with each other. If you sight one you'll say to him, "Where's Joe, we're looking for Joe." He'll probably say, "I saw him down at the liquor store awhile back." It's very easy to find them if you're working the streets.

Don: You were saying that to involuntarily incarcerate somebody, a facility has to meet a lot of standards. What about SB 38?

Vicki: SB 38 (Senate Bill 38) is a drunk driving diversion program for second time offenders. If they don't participate in the program that triggers court action. They set a court hearing, they bring the person back to court, and ask them to show cause why they didn't participate.

SENATE BILL 38 FOR DRIVING UNDER THE INFLUENCE

Vicki: If they can't show cause the District Attorney pursues filing on the underlying case. SB 38 is a year long diversion program. Actually it's post-adjudication diversion. They usually spend a few hours a week in meetings and counseling.

Don: So that person could end up doing some time if they didn't follow through?

Vicki: Yes, but SB 38 isn't necessarily a residential treatment program. Residential facilities are generally very, very expensive. If you have a little money you can go into a thirty day drug detox and rehab center run by Southwood Hospital or some other place. Those kind of treatment programs are extremely expensive.

Don: A thousand dollars a day.

Vicki: Some of them. The Betty Ford Center is a lot less than that. It's also an excellent one. It's probably the cheapest one in the nation and that's because of the endowments she's able to bring in to offset the cost. But few people can afford that. The ones who can are generally not the people in the warrant bank.

Don: The people in the warrant bank usually don't have insurance that will help out.

Vicki: Right.   Under SB 38 they can agree to a treatment program. That's generally something a court would be looking at if the District Attorney makes a case that they are addicted as opposed to simply using.

Don: Addicted to alcohol, you mean.

Vicki: Or drugs, yes. The court might look at the option of residential treatment as opposed to going to a therapist. Another option is going to one of the community based agencies which will provide treatment on an outpatient basis on a sliding scale. That way those who can't afford it can still get treatment. The court wouldn't insist on residential treatment unless they felt that the person was addicted. Or the court might feel that they were so strung out, so involved with alcohol or drugs, that they could not overcome their addiction on an outpatient basis. Some of the research suggests that maybe outpatient treatment is as effective as inpatient treatment and it is a lot less expensive.

Don: My thoughts were that maybe even just two weeks of some residential program or in a detox center would let you saturate them with a lot of video tapes on sobriety. They could attend a lot of group meetings, to start the reprogramming for sobriety. The most powerful urges to get high would be fading because the first few days are really the hardest.

Vicki: But it takes at least thirty days. It takes about a week for people to get enough of the drugs or alcohol out of their system for them to start thinking clearly. It takes another week to start really processing what's happening in the group, what's happening with themselves. It isn't until about the third week that they begin to develop a good plan. A plan that makes sense in terms of where they want to go with themselves.

Don: So it might not work to arrest someone and tell them they can keep out of going to jail by showing up the next day to start the program. You think some are so strung out that they are going to go home and use alcohol and drugs and forget about showing up because they're hurting. Even if we threatened to come get them and put them in jail if they didn't show up?

Vicki: You'd get a good sense of how strung out they are just by asking how many times a week they used, how many times a day they used. Some of these guys use several times a day.

Don: So there are certain people who are infrequent enough users that if you arrest them and say, "Show up tomorrow for your ten hours a week meetings and urine testing or go to jail," they would show up. But then others are so far along that if you said that, they'd walk out of there. Then you wouldn't see them again until you went to get them.

DWINDLING SUPPORT SERVICES

Vicki: That's right.   They need support services once
they're back in the community.   This is true whether they
are getting out of jail or getting out of the treatment
center.   That's another real challenge for us that's
beginning to defeat us.   Not only do we not have enough
support mechanisms now, but the ones we do have are
drying up badly.

I don't know if you've ever talked to Judge Coates,
he's been a real activist for the homeless.   He believes that
there are what he calls "the infamous one hundred"
homeless downtown.   These are the guys who get arrested
and cited over and over again.

They are a public nuisance and if you pull their
names, they're known to the police, they're known to the
detox center on Island Avenue.   In fact they're on a "We
don't want you anymore" list at the detox center because
it's hopeless.   They probably contribute significantly to
the number of those unserved warrants because they never
show up for their court hearings.   If the police saw them
and cited them again, they just turn around and do it again.
They're not harming anybody, they are just an irritant.

What do you do with the homeless?   The homeless
group has grown.   I think we make a great deal of headway
with some of our drug addicts and alcoholics while they are
in custody, both in the jail and in the honor camp.   We
have a really good drug and alcohol education program.   We
have an excellent self-esteem course they go through.   We
get them into vocational programs.   We get them seed
money so they can get started in the process of learning a
vocation and earn their high school diploma.

A lot of good things happen if you can hold onto a
person for about six months in custody.   But then release
time comes and they don't have anywhere to live.   They
don't have any money.   We pay them sixty-five cents a day,
five days a week, and that's what they use to buy shaving
cream, cigarettes, whatever.   They have to call friends a
week before they leave and their friends generally are into
drugs and into the drug scene.   That's where they came
from.   That's where they were arrested.   And that's where
they go to live when they get out.

They get back into drugs all too quickly. Gangs form a support network for gang members coming out of jail. No matter how proud they feel about themselves, no matter how committed they are to the life of sobriety as they go through the program. As soon as they get out of jail the temptation is right there.

Don: So the real problem then is that there is no tail or long term follow up. You've expended huge amounts of work, money and effort. A lot of professional time is spent working with them. But it's wasted if they go right back to their old buddies and drugs. They really need some kind of pressure to get them to show up the next day for a follow-up program if we want to keep them from sliding back. Is the SB 38 program for second conviction drunk drivers run by a private group?

Vicki: There are a number of private groups that have SB 38 funding and are certified. I believe the State certifies the provider agency. After they meet certain standards clients are brokered out to them. The clients are given a list of the SB 38 providers and pick which provider program they will attend.

Don: Do they also work with people involved in drugs?

Vicki: I believe SB 38 is also for drugs. It's for driving under the influence, but driving under the influence is not just alcohol. If they are convicted of a DUI (Driving under the Influence) and they go SB 38, I think we expunge the record after they have completed the SB 38 program.

P.C. (PENAL CODE) 1000 DIVERSION PROGRAM

Vicki: P.C. 1000 is a pre-adjudication program. It is a diversion program for somebody picked up for a second time for possession of drugs or for using drugs. Rather than the DA prosecuting for those infractions they can be diverted into a P.C. 1000 program for drug and alcohol rehab and treatment. If they complete that program the DA does not prosecute. Then it would show on your criminal history information as an arrest with no conviction, no prosecution. The P.C. 1000 program primarily involves treatment. You go to a treatment program as directed by your Probation Officer. In our P.C. 1000 bank now, we probably have 3,000 who are in the process of going through the program. They are being given the opportunity to complete a program of treatment in lieu of prosecution.

Don: What's the success rate on that?

Vicki: I have no idea. I have three probation officers handling 3,000 cases. It's very difficult to keep up with them.

Don: I was wondering about VisionQuest.

Vicki: VisionQuest is a twenty-four hour school. It's headquarters are outside of California. There are strict standards they have to meet relative to education, care, medical care and all sorts of things. It's a "for profit" school as opposed to a nonprofit organization.

Don: You know that on a percentage basis we have something like ten times the number of people locked up in this country and in this city than are locked up in England. Most other places in the world have fewer people locked up then we do in the United States. While people are in custody you have pretty good control over them. But an hour after their release it can all go down the drain. If more effort was shifted to the "tail," keeping better contact with them when they're out, I think we would be putting a lot less people back in jail. The studies I've looked at show that when the substance abuser knows for certain that something is going to happen when he messes up, they are more likely to stay sober. When they're sober, they only commit about one-sixth the crime as they do when they are getting loaded all the time.

You probably have a lot of people who say, "Well, you didn't have a job for me, so that's why I got loaded to hide the pain of my failures." The problem with that kind of thinking is that if you're loaded, you can't work anyway. I think sobriety has to be a priority ahead of any other services you can provide.

THE PIR PROGRAM: PROBATIONERS IN RECOVERY

Vicki: Absolutely. We've got to find a more effective way of dealing with the underlying drug problem. In my service we have 17,000 probationers. We have a special program in which we're targeting approximately 300 probationers with serious drug problems. It's called the PIR program, or Probationers in Recovery. They are not mentally ill. We put them through a day treatment program where they have their own residence and a place to stay. We try to get them jobs. They have group therapy three times a week. They meet individually with counselors and their probation officers who supervise their case. It's really an interesting model. We are conducting research on the project with SANDAG (San Diego Association of Governments).

I went to some of the PIR program graduation ceremonies. They talked about what had happened in their life as a result of the program. I think we're looking at some tremendous benefits from the program. We had one white woman who wore tight leather jeans and looked like she had just gotten off the back of a motorcycle. She had really been through the school of hard knocks. She was a meth addict in her forties. We got her into the program and she is now employed doing repairs on motorcycles. We catch them as they come out of the institutions and jails so they are still on probation. We find them a place to live if they need it. I think that's the kind of program we need.

Don: In the PIR Program, what keeps them sober after they graduate?

Vicki: We have an after-care group for them. There's also a group for those who feel that they are failing. They can come back to that group.

Don: Is that voluntary?

Vicki: Yes. To pick people for that program we identified the profile of the offender. We basically wanted offenders for this program who have noteworthy drug problems. We also wanted people who were not mentally impaired. Once we had picked our sample, we randomly selected one group who went into traditional probation. Another group was randomly assigned to our Probationers In Recovery or the PIR program.

We're going to look at those who stay with the program and graduate and those who failed. Some of them complete the program but don't graduate. That's the group who went through the paces but never committed themselves. We'll be taking a look at the outcomes for those four groups of offenders. From our preliminary data it looks like we have a recidivism rate of about five percent every six months. The success rate seems good.

Don: The 300 people in the PIR program are not in custody?

Vicki: No. They could have been. Some were identified as PIR candidates when we did the pre-sentence investigation. Some were identified at sentencing just before they went into custody for a period of time. Once we have selected a candidate for the program they go on a waiting list and we track the release date. As soon as they're released we assign them to the PIR program as soon as possible.

Don: They live outside of jail someplace and come in during the day?

Vicki: Yes, it's day treatment. We have evening treatment programs for those who are employed. We worked really hard to try to get them employed within sixty days of release but it's beginning to be really tough because of the economy.

DRAGGING THE LOST SHEEP BACK TO THE FOLD

Don: What kind of follow-up program do you have for those three hundred to keep them sober?

Vicki: We work hard with them. We test them twice a week. If they're trying to sober up but they slip and come up with a positive urinalysis we sit down with them and we may do a sanction. We wouldn't revoke their probation or send them to jail. But we might say, "Okay, we want you to go to sixty A.A. or N.A. (Narcotics Anonymous) meetings in sixty days. That's one meeting a day for sixty days. That will be in addition to your regular day care treatment." Then we'll track and follow them. For those who slip a little bit, that usually is enough of a net. Or we may have them go into residential treatment for thirty days and then put them back into our program when they come out of residential treatment.

MITE (McAlister Institute for Training) has a residential treatment program. For a few of them we've used MITE. After they have been through MITE's program we pick them up again and they return to the PIR program. Even those who slip, after they return to the PIR program they generally graduate. But the third time they slip they go back to the court and back to jail or to prison.

Don: How long do you keep track of them after they graduate?

Vicki: The PIR program lasts six to eight months. It takes some people a little bit longer to get through it. Once they graduate or have completed the program, they move back to a regular supervision caseload. If they are a predatory offender they'll move back to our intensive supervision officer. If they are predatory but have been stabilized for about nine months, they'll go into level two probation supervision. At that level, they will see a probation officer once a month at most. If they're on a lower list, they'll go into our bank and report by mail once a month. SANDAG will probably follow these individuals for, I would say, two years.

Don: Do you know what the success rate is, or how many of them slip back to substance abuse after graduating from your program?

Vicki: No, but we will get some really good data in about twelve more months. We've got some good preliminary data so far.

Don: That program sounds really good. It sounds close to the ideal, and still isn't real expensive. But with just a little bit more money and a little bit closer and longer follow-up, you might push the success rate a lot higher.

Vicki: Absolutely.

Don: It's about four or five thousand dollars a year to follow somebody with a really good tail to keep them sober and out of jail and it costs thirty-five thousand dollars a year to keep them in jail.

Vicki: Oh, I'd say twenty thousand dollars to sixty thousand dollars a year to keep them in jail. That after-care is so important. We do so much for people when they're in custody or in some program. We raise their expectations and hopes, then they go back to the streets and reality sets in.

Don: Do you think it would help to keep them sober if there was a really tight follow-up that started the moment they left jail or the treatment program? It wouldn't be a month or a year before they were seen again. They would be expected to initiate compliance with a sobriety program starting the very next day after their release.

Vicki: The swiftness with which we can respond with graduated sanctions is one of the great things about the PIR program. To get some people's attention we need a more drastic approach. Some of the referrals to the PIR program are people who were in the warrant bank and came up with a dirty urine test. The probation officer might try to send them to the PIR program if there are any openings. It is best if we can act swiftly. If somebody comes up with a positive urine test while they are in the PIR program we might take them back to court. Then we might give them a couple days of custody and give them some time in a work project where they pick up trash on the highway.

PREDATORY OFFENDERS WALK A THIN LINE

Don: What if they start using again even after you've done all that?

Vicki: If their urine is being tested and we pick up another dirty urine test then they go back to court. They can end up with jail or prison time. That seems kind of harsh, getting a prison sentence just for coming up with a positive urine test. But we've given these people the benefit of getting probation instead of jail after committing a really serious criminal offense. Because of the seriousness of the offense, we've drawn a really thin line there and we really don't want some of these guys who are real predators to step over it.

Don: You mean like burglars?

Vicki: No, by predatory, I mean somebody who may have molested two or three kids in the neighborhood.

Don: While he was on drugs?

Vicki: Maybe he's on drugs, usually there's an underlying alcohol or drug problem. Sometimes they're just sick, real sick. Let's say you molested a couple kids and you got a plea bargain that allows a little bit of local time and probation supervision. If you test positive, we're not likely to take a risk of that kind. If that guy is somebody we sent to the PIR program, we're not going to give him a second chance. The court may give a lot of people a second chance, but not a real predatory type, like rapists.

Don: Even with those people, if there was some way of really guaranteeing their sobriety from the day of their first arrest, the probability of them reengaging in that behavior goes way, way down.

Vicki: Oh yes, oh yes.

Don: I think we'd have a good deterrent system if they did ten days the first time they test positive. The next time they test positive, even if it's just a month later, they do another ten days, or maybe fifteen days. If 85% of all people arrested in San Diego County are loaded at the time of their arrest, we know substance abuse is really behind most crimes, even predatory kinds.

BRAIN BLOCKERS FOR CRACK COCAINE

Vicki: Something else has to happen besides doing the time. I went to a seminar about the future. They talked about what kinds of innovative programs are being developed now that will help us in the criminal justice system. The new ideas will provide some challenges to us ethically. One thing that has been successful in research is a brain blocker specific for crack cocaine.

The technology is there to provide an implant. For example, Norplant, the birth control chemical you stick under your skin. The technology is there to find inhibitors. They could put it in a capsule and stick it under your skin. Then, for five years you would have this chemical released into your body that would inhibit any reaction to crack cocaine. You could spend your last dollar, but you're not going to get high. Taking crack cocaine would have no more effect on you than having a drink of water. Now the ethical challenge would be if you made that a condition of probation. Is that what we want to do in this country?

Don: But crack cocaine isn't the only drug available. What if they switch to something else?

Vicki: I guess you could keep putting a different inhibitor in their arm for each new chemical they become involved with on the street. Ethically, I don't think we'd ever want to do that. But I'm hoping we will find something to help those people who really want to be clean and are struggling so hard to sober up. It's a terrible addiction to get over, terrible. It would be wonderful if there was something for them to help them in their struggle to get sober. With these brain specific drugs you will not have the negative ramifications of a lot of the drugs that we've used over the years like methadone.

Methadone impacts every part of the body including the liver, the kidneys and the lungs. That's in addition to the massive impact methadone has on the brain. The speaker at that symposium talked about a variety of different vehicles which are being explored. They're hoping to find more effective ways to deal with drug addicted clients.

Don: If these people sobered up they would be capable of getting more education and job training. We could reprogram these people with a good set of values. We could teach them the laws of the land. We have the technology to change people's behavior and their attitudes. China claims that only five percent of their criminals get rearrested after spending time in jail. In America we have a 65% or higher recidivism rate. What are they doing in China that we aren't doing? They also have less people, percentage-wise, locked up in jail than we do.

Unless the Chinese are lying about the number, I don't think we can legitimately keep saying, "Well, it's easy for them to do because they have a totalitarian society. In America, we don't want to sacrifice our precious freedom. We can't suspend the Bill of Rights just to get people off dope." The Chinese claim they use education and treatment to get and keep people off drugs. Of course, they use some reprogramming techniques for which they are famous. We called it brainwashing when they tried it on our troops. They have people write out what behaviors and attitudes they need to change and how they are going to go about doing that. There are some powerful reprogramming techniques which are not being fully utilized in America.

CUBANS AND AIDS

Vicki: Maybe we can't do some of those things due to political reasons. There are ways to go about changing one's behavior which would be very offensive in this society. I was reading a recent article in the Sunday newspaper that there is only one nation in the world which has contained the AIDS epidemic. The only country which has not had an escalation of AIDS cases is Cuba. The reason Cuba hasn't had an escalation is that they lock up all the people who test positive, in relatively decent housing. They give them food that others in Cuba have to stand in line to get if there is any. They test them all through their lives. They test them for AIDS when they begin to be sexually active in their teens. If they come up positive, they are swooped up and put into segregated housing.

It's interesting that from what the newspaper article said there has been no public outcry in Cuba about this. People pretty much accept it. In this country if any politician suggested that solution to the AIDS epidemic it would be political suicide. In terms of what we do with the incarcerated population and how far we go, these are very fragile issues in this country.

Don: What about six to eight hours a day of educational experience. Nobody should object to that. The 15% of the prisoners who do get some kind of rehabilitation while they are in jail have a much lower rate of returning to crime and drugs when they get out. The 85% who get nothing in the way of therapy or rehab when they're in jail are the highest repeat offenders.

In the few in-jail drug rehab programs they do have, they usually take a look at their feelings. They are asked to find answers to questions, such as what pains were they covering up with drugs. There are a lot of intervention techniques, a lot of different approaches to therapy. There is reality therapy and cognitive therapy. The in-jail rehab programs would work even better with a very tight follow-up that started the same day they are released. Otherwise, like you said, they go back out with their friends and get high almost immediately.

Maybe they shouldn't even be allowed to go back home after they have been arrested or get out of jail.

Maybe they need to go to a drug-free residential environment. Maybe they should leave jail in groups of two or three at a time. They would have a buddy system. They would be checking up on each other. If one of them slipped, but the others were really convinced about the value of sobriety, his buddies would call. They'd say, "Look, we're really concerned about John, he's starting to shoot up. Maybe you need to come have a talk with him."

When A.A. first started they used to go around dragging each other out of bars. If somebody did that now the ACLU would probably jump in and say, "You're violating people's civil liberty by getting them to narc on each other." But they're violating our civil liberties with all the crime they do while they're under the influence.

SOBER LIVING HOUSES

Vicki: Different things work for different people. One of the things that seems to work best is a concept developed in A.A. Namely, the importance of recognizing that a tendency or habit of substance abuse is a lifelong problem. Another part of that concept is the recognition that substance abusers need a support group to be able to deal with their addictive tendencies. They have to realize they can't handle it alone.

I have a friend who has opened up a number of sober living units in Northern California. She has a dozen or so now. They are houses. People leaving thirty day drug programs move in there. They pay for their room and board either with their Social Security disability income, or maybe they work. They pay her something like $350 a month to live there. They work together to form a cohesive group. Also they can live there forever if they so desire.

She has one client living in one of the houses who is a very wealthy business man. He owns a mansion in Palo Alto. But he knows that whenever he goes home and lives in his house he gets lonely and he drinks. He is an older man. Alcohol is his problem. He knows he has to live in a group home. He knows that he needs a support system. He knows that he needs that for the rest of his life. In San

Diego, we don't have many facilities like that. We have seven-day recovery homes and thirty-day recovery homes.

We use some of those for people coming out of the adult institutions who are committed to recovery but don't have a place to go. If they go to live there the costs are on a sliding scale. But nobody else is paying for it. No money has to come out of County funds. As soon as they get their unemployment benefits they begin paying their share. But the problem with these programs is that after either seven to thirty days they're out and don't have a place to go again. We need to have sober living settings where people can stay as long as it is needed.

There are some neat things about the concept of sober living units. First, as long as you have a number of adults living in the same place together and you don't provide treatment, you don't have to have special use permits. Providers can rent houses or even apartments in a residential area and open up these facilities. They can go in on a lease. It takes forever to get a conditional use permit. Neighborhoods get all upset.

A group of people committed to a life of sobriety living together are good neighbors. They take care of themselves and it's not a burden on the taxpayers. They're paying for it themselves in one way or another. If you can open up one of those sorts of facilities and get those people out of the system, you could take the resources you have left to deal with the real problem people. These problem people are the ones who carry dual diagnoses who need a more intensive kind of care.

Don: So for as little as $350 a month you could provide room and board for these people and even some other services beyond that. They could be involved in a lot of peer counseling. There are people who would jump at the chance of going to a place like that instead of jail. But a lot of them would have no intention of abiding by the rules. They basically want a place to keep getting loaded. I've talked to a lot of them who started using again while they were living in what was supposed to be a sober living setting.

We need to reduce their options, and be able to tell them "You choose: you can be sober outside or sober in jail." I think that the only thing that is going to work is to completely remove from them the choice of getting high. The $350 a month housing sounds like the cheapest way to go as far as a place to live is concerned. With their sober living housing as a home base, they could be going to school, working on their GED or learning a trade.

I ran a halfway house for schizophrenics. It was called "Independent Living" which means unlicensed board and care. That really means room and board with a peer support system. The schizophrenics help each other out. I had first worked with schizophrenics in 1958, and I liked working with that population. But the ones who ended up in my program were all dope fiends and/or alcoholic schizophrenics. The cops were there every night because of their yelling all night. My blood pressure went up and we got evicted from the place we were renting.

I finally realized that if those people had been sober, probably half of them wouldn't have become schizophrenic in the first place. In many cases mental illness was really produced because of chemical abuse. I've seen many of cases where they were forced to sober up in jail. After they had been sober for awhile, they were no longer psychotic, no longer schizophrenic. They didn't need haldol, prolixin or thorazine anymore. But as soon as they got out of jail they started back on alcohol and drugs.

In three or four months they were hallucinating again and needed their haldol and thorazine again. There have been studies showing that schizophrenics in remission, who have had no psychotic symptoms for a time, can trigger another psychosis by just smoking marijuana. It was very frustrating for me trying to work with those people. Alcohol and drugs ruined my program.

HOMELESS SCHIZOPHRENIC SUBSTANCE ABUSERS

Don: At least 50% of the homeless problem is related to alcohol and drugs. Some people have broken it down to 35% of homelessness is alcohol related and 15% is drug related. Some researchers say as much as 70% of homelessness is drug or alcohol related.

Vicki: A lot of the homeless are mentally ill.

Don: Some of the homeless are dual diagnosed. They abuse alcohol and/or drugs and they are also schizophrenic. There is another large percentage of the homeless, about 15% to 20%, who are not alcoholics or drug addicts but are only schizophrenic. If an involuntary sobriety program was implemented, think of the huge reduction in the homeless population. As for crime, we should experience an 85% reduction in crime by sobering up criminals. That's because 85% of all crimes are committed by people under the influence. Once they are sobered up five-sixths of the criminals quit committing crimes.

My guess is that when a lot of those dual diagnosed people are free of drugs and alcohol for a period of time they are not going to be raging problems. Their schizophrenia will disappear. I've seen it happen. Not to all of them, of course. Some will stay psychotic even if they never touched a drop of alcohol or another illegal drug again.

Vicki: Exactly, but right now, we don't have any money to care for them at all. We try to care for this big group of very needy people with all kinds of problems. We need to start taking whoever we can out of the system. If we could place a lot of people in sober living houses, we could use the limited resources we have to deal more effectively with the mental health cases. Now, we don't really deal with them.

I have probation officers who have mental health cases. These are people on probation who live in the street. They come by to see us every once in a while. They're living out of dumpsters. They don't make sense when they come into the office to talk to us. Sometimes they present a danger to people in our office.

Don: These are substance abusers?

Vicki: They drink, oh yes, they drink and they use drugs. If you look at the files, generally it's somebody we might have known in juvenile probation years ago. A lot of times there is a history of growing up in a dysfunctional family. Sometimes they've been incarcerated and we have some information about their mental health state. And also information about how their mental health state may have changed after they sobered up in jail.

Their needs are beyond the capacity of our probation department to deal with. And, unfortunately, we don't have the time for them. Our specialty is not providing counseling services for the mentally ill. What's happening in San Diego is that we're losing even more mental health beds. You can't get them into treatment facilities. In terms of the substance abusers, I'd like to see the county provide some seed money for any reputable vendor who wants to open sober living units. I'd like to see help provided for these people who would like to be committed to a life of sobriety. The population I'm referring to are substance abusers. We need to process more and more people through these sober living units. We need to get them off probation and out of the criminal justice system and into a self-supporting type of system.

Don: Can sobriety still come about if these substance abusers have the option of leaving that sober living unit anytime they want?

Vicki: The way this particular vendor friend of mine up north operates is that if you get loaded, you're gone. If you have a thirst for drugs or alcohol there are other people living with you who have gone through the same thing. They can help you deal with your cravings. Most of these people, by the way, have insurance, and they have treatment resources. They just have to reach out to them. They have a support group there to reach out to and to be with.

NO DRUNKS OR DOPE FIENDS ALLOWED

Vicki: If they don't want to take advantage of the help that is there, if they want to get loaded, they get kicked out. Then they're on the street. They are the problem of the criminal justice system from that day forward. Somebody else comes in and takes the bed in the sober living unit.

Some say we should deal with this guy who is not committed to getting sober because there are so many sanctions we can use to convince him that sober is best. Like send him back to jail for awhile, for a thirty day detox experience. Some say we should do whatever it requires to try to deal with them and get their attention, and get them sober.

Don: I've heard many people who are running a rehab program tell their clients "One slip and you're out of here, we don't want drunks and drug addicts." It makes me think "What are you in business for if it isn't to deal with drunks and drug addicts?" I think that's why a lot of these people fall through the cracks. They haven't really made the choice to be sober. They think a lot about getting sober. Sober sounds good to them. They've all heard how people's lives were turned around after they got sober. They talk about it but don't do it. When they do get high and get kicked out of whatever program they're in they have succeeded in getting rejected one more time. They think that rejection has brought them a ticket or an excuse for a good drunk or a good high.

Vicki: That's okay, and then the criminal justice system picks them up and we'll reprocess them.

Don: But that system is overloaded and doesn't have a very good success rate of sobering up the people processed through it.

Vicki: At our PIR program graduations, generally three graduates of the class speak. They are in their 30's or 40's, sometimes a little bit younger. Most of them say they've gone through A.A., they've gone through long and short periods of sober living. Yet they kept falling on their face. It's a repeat pattern. They are addicted, down and out, then they generally get arrested, incarcerated. Then they get clean for a time. They get released from jail, then addicted, and down and out again. They've gone through that whole cycle over and over. But most of them say that the PIR program is different. After going through it they feel a high level of commitment to sobriety. They're proud of themselves. It's a little different than a lot of other programs.

Don: I think if you do a good, tight follow-up on them, you wouldn't be wasting all that money you spent on them. Can you follow them for three years or five if you want?

Vicki: SANDAG is going to follow them.

Don: Your success rate will stay high on a long-term basis if the first time they slip you take them in for five or ten days. Then you give them a choice: "Sober in jail or out here, take your pick." I've seen many people who must have had a half million dollars spent on them over the years in various drug rehab programs. Their graduation from each one was followed by a return to substance abuse and another dive to the bottom.

Think of the huge amounts of money we would save if they weren't recycling through these very expensive programs over and over. You say you closed down some of your honor camps?

THE NEW RAGE: BOOT CAMPS FOR DOPE FIENDS

Vicki: Yes, it's sad. We've closed down two. There's a different crowd out there and we were forced to close. We were in partnership with the California Department of Forestry. Our able-bodied inmates would go there and learn to be firefighters. It was really regimented.

Supervisor Susan Golding (elected mayor 1992) has rediscovered the boot camp. She's looking for grant money to start one. I hate to say this, but I don't think boot camps do much when you're talking about the average length of stay being about eighty days of a sentence. We cut people loose so early in their sentence. A boot camp is expensive, you're not going to accomplish much with a boot camp type program.

Our forestry camps were very much military regimented but they were regimented for a purpose. The purpose was to discipline your crew to handle an emergency. They knew how important it was to march in line, carry their tools and maintain such and such a distance from each other. They learned to appreciate how important it was to know who was in front of them, who was in back of them, and how to cut brush. In the fire season they would be dispatched throughout the State.

They were just wonderful crews, they took such a pride in what they were doing. They were learning a trade. They were on the front line during emergencies. They were thinking clearly and doing something that was very important. Unfortunately, we closed those camps and now Supervisor Golding wants to open a boot camp.

Don: A lot of people keep saying "Just lock up all the drug addicts and dope dealers." But even if we wanted to, we can't. You said that there just isn't room in jail. I'd like to see a program where they spend eight hours a day digging inside themselves, hunting down their pain and discovering what they have been trying to fix or numb with drugs and alcohol.

I think that approach would lead to sobriety and less crime a lot sooner than learning how to march in a circle. A lot of the politicians and lay public have an idea of what they think is needed. They are not experts in the field. They generally have not researched what really works. Studies on boot camps for drug rehabilitation shows that they have a very low success rate.

People are angry at what's going on, angry at the danger that drug addiction has put into everyone's lives. In the back of their mind they want to get even. They have a punishment orientation. I think boot camps look enough like punishment to be appealing. They seem to think "We're going to toughen them up, so they'll sober up." But toughening up these people won't sober them up. These people are already tough, they're pretty hard. I think they need to soften up and get more in touch with their feelings.

That way, when they start to feel bad, they can ask themselves, "What's going on with me today, where is this pain coming from?" You have to be sober and softer, not harder, in order to look inside yourself. Boot camps can turn out some people who are in good physical condition. But as soon as they go outside again and start to feel bad, they think of getting loaded to feel better. That's because they didn't learn that there are other ways to deal with pain and have fun besides getting loaded. "Finding where I hurt" certainly isn't one of the courses taught in your average boot camp. I think we can do better than a boot camp.

Vicki: One thing about boot camps is that the public likes the idea. They think it's a remarkable idea. There's no research on the boot camps, their effectiveness is not proven. But the public likes the idea of taking somebody and shaping them up. It has that taint, and so politically it's a very high profile kind of effort. That's why we're going in that direction. I think the forestry model was an excellent one and I'm real sorry we closed it down.

Don: In the forestry program they had a feeling of camaraderie and a feeling "I am important, I'm doing something worthwhile."

Vicki: And they had a real involvement in a team. They had to be part of the team in the forestry work. They couldn't go off on their own because somebody would die. That's the consequences, somebody would die. It was very impressive watching them work and change and feel good about themselves.

It was real sad to see those two facilities close. The reason those two camps closed is because they were small facilities. They were not economical to run. We can't afford it. The State of California can afford that. They have taken them on. Local government can't afford small facilities.

TEACHING CONVICTS TO READ AND WRITE

Vicki: We class alcohol and drug addiction as some sort of a generic thing, but it really isn't. You know that from your work. These people are all very different in terms of what leads them down the bad road to alcoholism or drug addiction. With most of the people I've dealt with, self-esteem is a big issue. I used to be the director of Camp Barrett. That's where we put our education program.

Some of those grown men at Camp Barrett couldn't read a menu if they took their girlfriend out to dinner. They had to rely on someone else to read the menu. It was very painful for them. One guy one night was working with the night officer on probably what would be a fourth grade spelling test. He finally got most of them right and he cried. As he cried, this guy said, "I never thought in my whole life that I could learn this stuff." The guy was twenty five years old. We got him to the tenth grade level before he left us. We saw that so often.

Half of our honor camp inmates don't have a high school diploma. About 25% scored at about the fifth grade level or below in reading and academic skills. They have a very hard time making it in the world. They believe that they never will. That's what the school system has done for them, not much. They got lost so quickly in the school system. Most of the inmates who test out at the third grade level had horrible failure experiences at a very young age. They end up thinking "I'm stupid, I'm never going to make it."

They go out on the street and they find out that if they live in the ghetto, nobody there is going to run them down for their lack of academic success. That's the value the street system has. In going to the street and getting involved with a gang, it gives them self-esteem like no other system can do for them. And then all of a sudden they learn that selling drugs is pretty darn lucrative. As long as they don't get caught. Then they become the first male in the family who is able to buy the family a new TV set and a new car. If they are real successful in the drug trade world, all of a sudden, they become a very important person.

Don: And you have to be arrested fifteen times before anybody does anything to you to really mess up your business.

Vicki: Exactly, exactly.

Don: So you can go on for years using and selling dope.

Vicki: That street gang is a very important support system. We end up with a lot of them in custody. How on earth are we going to help them believe there's something out there that's better than what they were doing and something better than the money they can make selling dope? What can we do to convince them that "Yes it may take a few years to get there, but you can do it?" We try. We teach them to read and try to point them toward a job and a career. But then they go out the door and who's waiting for them? Their gang. The gang says "Hi, we missed you, you're important to us." So which direction do you think they are going to take?

HIDING PROBLEMS AND PAIN WITH DRUGS

Don: Most people see drugs as this huge problem in our society. But to substance abusers, drugs are a solution to huge problems. Drugs solve that self-esteem problem, drugs solve that unemployment problem. That's because if you're loaded, all of these problems, even the food problem, go away.

They might be getting high on crystal meth and lose weight. When they lose fifty pounds, down from 170 to 120, they say to themselves "Well, I'm kind of skinny but oh well." The drugs let them say, "Oh well" to everything. I'm sure you've seen them. They're emaciated and they're not concerned about it because they've solved the self-esteem problem. When they stay high on drugs for three days running, they talk constantly. They think they are saying all these brilliant things.

I used to watch them in my halfway house. They'd be high on drugs, and up talking all night. I'd go to bed, because I lived there too. When I'd get up in the morning, they'd still be talking. That would go on for three days. No sleep, just having what they thought were these brilliant conversations. About the third day their voices became garbled and slurred. By that time they made no sense at all. From the expressions on their faces, you knew they thought they were saying these terribly important things. Then they would crash (sleep) for three days. And finally they would wake up angry and with a terrible headache.

I've called the police and told them "Take this guy away." They'd say, "Did he pay you rent?" I'd say, "Yes, but that was months ago. He's been loaded for weeks and hasn't paid for months." The police would say "If he's ever paid you any rent, you have to evict him." It took me $100 and forty days to evict that guy. We had to put up with his craziness for forty days. Unless you're loaded yourself, drug addicts are no fun to be with. They drive you crazy with their mood swings and temper tantrums. I had no way to even begin to sober those people up and I received no help from the police. I had to close down the program to save my own sanity.

As far as those problems with the low self-esteem, the lack of jobs, or the need for training, none of those problems can get fixed while they're loaded. If you offer therapy, jobs or training it won't do any good as long as they're loaded. This is what we have to tell them: "I know how bad you feel because you read at only a third grade level. But you're not going to learn to read at the fourth or fifth grade level while you're loaded." We need to tell them, "I know how bad you feel about not having a job, but you're not going to be able to get training for a job or hold a job as long as you're loaded." I think sobriety has to be the first priority.

Vicki: The other good thing about living in sober homes is that you can locate them in neighborhoods that don't have a high crime rate or high gang activity. All you have to do is go in and lease or if you can do it, go in and buy a house. Nobody can stop you from putting adults in that home, six non-related adults can live together by law. You can't really be kicked out, though you may want to leave because you can't get along with your neighbors. But that's a different story.

Don: We managed to get evicted from the place where I was operating my halfway house program. But then we were renting.

SOBER LIVING HOUSES MAKE GOOD NEIGHBORS

Vicki: Many years ago we had females on work furloughs from the jail living in Golden Hills in a couple of houses adjacent to each other. The County bought them and we got our conditional use permit. But the neighbors were up in arms. There was a really bloody battle, but within six months, they found out that we were better neighbors than the ones who had been there before. And within a year, the neighbors were coming to our annual Christmas party, and some of them were volunteering at the center.

Don: You had the tools to enforce sobriety. If they are sober, most of these people are all right. It's when they're drunk, screaming all night long and beating up on each other that everybody else is driven crazy.

Vicki: That's the advantage of the jail. If they came back from furlough loaded we had the authority to put cuffs on them and off they go to a maximum security jail. It's that simple. In a voluntary residential setting like you were operating, it's a little bit more difficult to get them removed and get them to stay away. And sometimes the taking away is more dramatic because a police car comes up and the lights are blinking. In our program we just drove a van to the back door and put them in cuffs. The neighbors thought it was a regular van. We can do a lot of things with a low profile that you couldn't do. Ours was a multi-dimensional program.

I guess where we are in corrections, we work real hard to give people the opportunity to make them fit for the job market. We want to make them competitive in the job market. That way, when they reach a decision that they really want to stay sober, they have the competitive edge to go out there and get a job. They're just not able to compete for jobs very well when they can't read and write, have low self-esteem and if they don't know where the A.A. groups are meeting and all the rest of that. When we have a chance to work with them, I think we do a pretty good job. At least we have some research in progress now. If it shows that we aren't doing as good a job as we think, hopefully, it will head us in a good direction.

In terms of models, I was talking to a friend of mine last night who is the Vice President of a YMCA program. It's for kids who are homeless, drug addicted and who have been molested. These are kids who later on in life would be our clients in the adult arena if nothing good happens to them before they grow up. My friend has one outdoor program where they go and climb mountains. They do all kinds of challenging things. The participants are really proud of themselves when they finish.

Her people just finished an outing at Camp Marston. They took leaders from rival gangs and put them all in the same room to give them an orientation to the program. Then they all signed a pact that they wouldn't beat each other up or kill each other while they were in the program. After they finished the wilderness outing they came back as a different group. That was the first time we've tried anything like that. It had a really wonderful outcome.

My friend said, "You know, Vicki, if my people had told me ahead of time what they intended to do with these gangs, I probably would have been very hesitant to approve their activity. That's because it's a high risk thing. If one of these gang members gets offended, goes off, something could have happened. But they all got together, it was a wonderful cohesive group at the end." I wonder if maybe that's one of the things we should be doing with gangs.

Don: I've seen it many times that as a condition of probation people are ordered to keep away from any former associates who are still involved in alcohol or drug use. Gang members could be environmentally relocated as they come out of juvenile hall or jail. As the whole gang was sobered up one by one, they would be allowed to reconstitute into their old gang. But by then, they all would be sober and working on sobriety together.

Vicki: Corrections has had big jumps in budget support in the past few years, in the area of incarceration, in the area of prosecution. But there has been no increases in the area of treatment. The knowledge and budget support have fallen woefully behind in the area of treatment and recovery. They need to rediscover treatment and recovery.

If the two million homeless and mostly drug-addicted teenagers living on the streets in the United states are not sobered up and taught to work, those surviving to adulthood will unleash new terror as they prey on a citizenry already held hostage to drug violence.

CHAPTER EIGHT

INTERVIEWING ART FAYER AT MITE

Art: I know you were interested in the P.C. 1000 (Penal Code 1000) drug diversion program. But let me start by giving you an overview of MITE (McAlister Institute for Training and Education). That will help you see the P.C. 1000 program as it fits into our overall program. We have a two million dollar a year budget and 75 employees at MITE. Our main offices are in El Cajon. Our office in Oceanside provides the same services. There is another satellite office in Carlsbad.

The first thing we do at MITE for people with serious drug problems is put them through a two week detox program. Once they've gone through withdrawal, reentry is the next step for people who are motivated to get their life back. This is through what we call our Phase Houses. They are more than a halfway house. With six people or less living together you don't have to go through any licensing procedures.

The Phase houses program is very important. It provides an environment that supports sober living. We have rented about 20 houses. MITE doesn't own anything. We rent everything, all our facilities. The Phase Houses are self supporting. The clients pay. There is usually money available from somewhere. Some of them work, some get unemployment. The cost per person only runs about $250 a month, or $280 with food.

TOOLS FOR SOBRIETY

Art: These Phase Houses are one of MITE's most powerful tools for getting and keeping people sober. The people in this program have a buddy system. They watch each other, they help each other to maintain their sobriety. You might say Big Brother is watching you because they are required to monitor each other's behavior and report any slips or problems that come up to MITE staff members. A MITE counselor is assigned to each of the phase houses and oversees the basic operation of each of the houses.

We do have licensing for KIVA. That's our program which involves 35 women living sober together. KIVA is designed to be a nine to twelve month program. Women can come live there with children, if they meet certain criteria. They have to have been a resident for 90 days, making good progress, and, children's beds have to be available. It's a twelve step program.

KIVA is an intervention operated by MITE which has many aspects of a therapeutic community. It's real strict. There are a lot of rules which apply 24 hours a day. I think it's a marvelous program. About five of our employees are graduates of KIVA. They are now counselors. After graduating from the KIVA program they went to counselor training and then got jobs working for MITE.

We were supposed to have only a two week waiting list for people who wanted to sober up to get into our detox program. Because of all the people applying for detox, our waiting list started to get too long. At the same time, we didn't have sufficient funds to open up more detox houses. Rather than have people waiting forever out there for a chance to sober up, we decided to try something no other agency around here is doing. We have opened up an outpatient detox program.

That program just started this week, in fact, just two days ago. It's brand new. We told them "Come in and hang around with us." But it's a madhouse. We are still doing all the other things we did before. But now, we have these six people who have come in to hang around with us to try to get sober. They are here from nine in the morning until eight at night. They don't know how to stop using. They're waiting to go into detox to stop using. But this is a new experiment, an interim program. We're afraid we'll lose people who want to sober up if we leave them out there too long. Some could even die.

The money is always the big question. With more money, we could do a lot more things, serve a lot more people. We could have a lot more programs. A lot of our money comes from our own fund raising. We do most of our fund raising through bingo games on Friday night, Saturday, Sunday and Monday. In fact, we just added Thursday.

Don: You get people coming to play bingo from all over town?

Art: We have two or three hundred people at a time coming to our bingo games. We are run like a church, a non-profit organization. The maximum prize is around $100 or $200. I've only gone to the bingo games once. I brought my wife and my mother-in-law last Sunday, we played. It scared me, the 300 women with white hair playing with me and my wife. Elderly people tend to play it, and they're really serious. It's electronic. It's a fancy setup. It has to be in order to handle that many people at once. The bingo players come in part because they know the bingo helps support our organization which is dedicated to helping people get sober.

All the profits from the bingo games are plowed back into the organization to help pay for the services we provide. County funding doesn't pay for even half of our budget. Client fees which are supposed to support the rest of the services don't begin to cover our costs. We not only have bingo games, but we have other fund raising events such as dances.

NO MONEY FOR A HAMBURGER AT MCDONALDS

Art: What else do we do? We have a lot of programs underway, and a lot of others we're thinking about developing. We've got thirty to forty people here just today involved in one way or another with our various programs. One of the things we do is operate what we call a drop in center. That means that if someone feels scared or lonely, they can come over here and hang out with somebody. There's always someone here to talk to. We provide free coffee. We have an on-duty floor counselor at all times. The duty counselor listens to people and to their problems.

These people always have more than their share of problems. The duty counselor makes referrals to places they might go to find a job. Some families with no place to go might not fit into a phase house, so they will be told about places they can go to get housing. The duty counselor tries to line people up with whatever services they need. Even emergency food. Some people's substance abuse life style has left them with zero resources. Not even enough money to go to McDonald's for a hamburger. Another one of our counselors does nothing but out-patient counseling. That is done by appointment.

There are meetings going on all the time, that's what a lot of the people are doing here today. One of the groups meeting today is an all women's group. They come three days a week with their kids. The ones who say "I'd like to come get sober but I can't get a baby sitter" don't have that excuse. We have child care available for the mothers attending the groups. That's a new program we started fairly recently. I feel real excited about it. I'd like to see that child care program grow. It's so important for these mothers to have this support available to them to get sober and to stay sober. It's so important for their children. Loaded mothers are usually not good mothers. Or at least not as good as they could be at mothering if they are sober.

BREAKING THE JAIL CYCLE WITH A SAFETY NET

Art: You know that most of the time people are going to jail because of substance abuse. Either because they were busted and sentenced on a drug charge or because they did something crazy while they were loaded. When these people have done their time where are they going to go? Some of them go back to where they were before, which usually means with or near people who were using. Some of them end up on the streets trying to find some way to stay high.

Something is needed to break that cycle. We have a couple of programs designed for men and women coming out of jail. We try to provide them with some sort of safety net so they don't just fall out of the jail and back into substance abuse. Our counselors go into the jail and meet with these people before they are released. We let them know that we are here and what we can do for them. We invite them to come live in one of our phase houses. We reach out to them. That way, when they leave the jail, they know they have some place to go. We're waiting for them. We tell them that we're going to help them stay sober. They're amazed to find that there is something different than drugs out there waiting for them.

In order to keep as much employee time as possible available for direct services, we have volunteers answering our phones.

We had a fight last week. Once every three months or so there will be a little outbreak or a tussle among our clients. Considering all the violence that surrounded a lot of these people before they came to us, that is a very low rate of violence. And when something breaks out, nobody really get hurt. It seems that once they are in a setting like this, everything calms down. Even if they are still using but trying to get sober, everything calms down.

Don: Counselors are authority figures to the clients who come in. If they were going to cause trouble, they don't want to do it right in front of mom and pop. They usually wait until they get around the corner.

Art: Now that I've given you an overview of MITE, we can get into the diversion program I was hired by San Diego County to rewrite the P.C. (Penal Code) 1000 drug diversion program, which I did based on my contracting and experience in the program. I have a Masters in counseling and a law degree. I was given the chance to create a new program for drug diversion which isn't in place yet. They're still talking.

The new program will be more extensive than the current program. In San Diego County there are six providers for diversion county-wide, of which McAlister Institute is one. MITE runs P.C. 1000 programs here in El Cajon and in Oceanside. MITE is the largest provider. I manage the program. Last year we had approximately 1,250 people go through the program between the two offices. County-wide, 4,000 to 5,000 people went through it in a year's time.

ELIGIBILITY FOR DIVERSION

Who participates in the program depends on the referrals from the judge. The judges make up their minds whether they want people to go through this program or not. Interestingly enough, the number of referrals from the judges has gone down a bit. Not the number of arrests, but the number of referrals to drug diversion. We're trying to talk the judges into increasing their referrals. We're not sure what happened in that area. Upon successful completion of the diversion program records of the participants arrest, their charges and even the record of their participation in the diversion program are all quashed. That information is then not available to the general public.

Don: They are actually arrested and charged?

Art: Yes.

Don: But they don't go to trial?

Art: They have a diversion hearing in the initial phases of their arrest and involvement in the legal system. Some judges extract a guilty plea and they hold that guilty plea in abeyance. Not everyone can go to diversion after an arrest for drug involvement. There are certain criteria which must be met. After an arrest they do a check to see if the defendant has had any other felony or drug convictions or if he or she has been through the diversion program in the last five years. If they meet the criteria, they will often be granted diversion. By doing that, a lot of time is saved in the courts.

There usually is an officer of the court who is a diversion counselor. Or there is a clerk who specializes in the diversion program and does the checking on the defendant's background in conjunction with the Probation Department. Then a recommendation is made to the judge, who doesn't even see the client, except very briefly.

Don: The court part of it is a very fast process?

Art: Yes, but not fast enough. The defendant could be arrested December 1st, and could actually be enrolled in the program January 1st. It can be that fast. The court part could take just a half hour. That part could happen somewhere in the middle of the month. What happens to quite a few of them is that they are charged, they see the judge and are referred to the diversion program. Then they are released and they wander off. But 80% of those referred do eventually turn up in the drug diversion program. About 20% never show up again. They are listed as failures to appear, and warrants are issued for their arrest.

When I say 80% show up, I mean they **eventually** show up. Sometimes they don't come in for a year and a half or not until they have been arrested again for a minor traffic violation. If the arresting officer checks they find that there is a warrant out for failure to appear in the diversion program. They may take them to jail. After they are brought back in the judge may regrant them diversion after they have done a night in jail. I would say roughly 75% to 82% of the people granted diversion actually enter the program. The percentages depend on what year we're referring to. Of the number who do finally show up, about 85% complete the diversion program. The program is basically ten hours, although the new program will be twenty hours.

SPEEDY DIVERSION

Art: The new program has a component called Speedy Diversion, which is going to require funding and cooperation from the court. What it means is that as soon as the judge assigns a defendant to diversion, he becomes a client. He immediately goes from the judge's chambers to a diversion counselor. He is in a diversion program the next morning, in a group or in a class. If we hit them immediately, there isn't this buffer period when they have to go find a program somewhere out there in the streets. Instead, they can come over here and find us and sign up for the next month's round of classes. They immediately come into the group. It's an open enrollment kind of thing. It's a new concept which I call Speedy Diversion.

They immediately become a part of the program. That way we get them right away when they're willing, when they're scared. I think that will change that 80% show up rate to 100% or at least 98%. They can get lost walking down a corridor from the judge's office to the diversion office. When they are immediately brought into the program it's an intervention technique in addition. There is no intervention as such in this program now.

Don: These people really need to be almost hand-carried from one spot to the next.

Art: In most P.C. 1000 programs it's five two-hour sessions, for a total of ten hours. In the State Statute for P.C. 1000 it doesn't specify what the program must be. It's up to each county to decide. In San Diego County there are two programs. One is the ten hour program but one is eighteen hours. The eighteen hour program is only in Oceanside. It's sort of a pilot program in North County. In that program, they do urine testing. It's a more intense program. All the other providers do the ten hour program. McAlister does both the ten hour and the eighteen hour programs. The eighteen hour program is supposedly designed for Level Two defendants. These are people who have been assessed as having a greater risk for higher levels of substance use. From my own experience, I think every single defendant qualifies for the second level program. I think that is true even if their use is really minimal. There's absolutely nothing wrong with getting them into a twenty hour program. That way they can spread the information to their children, to their wives and friends.

"NOPE, THAT'S NOT MY DOPE"

Art: Somebody may get pulled over while they are driving a borrowed car. In checking the car the cops may just find scrapings of dope, less than a line of crystal. This is a very minor offense. The people being charged say "It's not my dope." Sometimes it's true, it wasn't theirs.

Although they do lie, of course. They'll say "I don't do drugs," or "I hardly drink." It is rare when that really is the case. Even those folks know it. They're hanging out with folks who are doing drugs. They're all mixed together. They're all into the same use. Instead of hassling ourselves with Level A and Level B programs, I decided to create a Level B program for everybody. That will be the 20 hour program.

The ten-hour program consists of some information about psychopharmacology, or the effects of drugs and alcohol. Most use alcohol too. There is no alcohol program. That's the second thing that I've been working on with some of the county people. There is a drunken driver program. But there is no alcohol diversion program for alcohol related crimes such as committing acts of violence while under the influence. There are a lot of crimes in which being under the influence of alcohol is a major factor in the commission of the crime. **In other words, if they had been sober, the crime probably wouldn't have been committed at all.**

There is no recovery program for alcohol abuse as such, unless you're caught driving under the influence. We have been talking about creating a program for people who commit crimes while under the influence of alcohol. It may not be a diversion program, but it could be part of their probation. With crimes committed while under the influence of alcohol, there may have to be a guilty plea and a conviction. They can still require an alcohol rehab program similar to the drug diversion program. I think that would be real useful.

Don: Eighty-five percent of all people who were arrested for anything are under the influence of something. Being under the influence of drugs or alcohol eliminates your conscience.

Art: That's right. Drugs or alcohol are a major component in those problem behaviors. These other offenses all bear down on these same issues over and over again. Spousal abuse, child abuse, and so forth.

Don: Do you have any idea about follow-up? What is the success rate of the P.C .1000 diversion program a year later, two years later?

Art: There's no information on that.

Don: There should be intense, long term follow-up to keep these people sober.

TO TEST OR NOT TO TEST

Art: There's a lot of debate on that issue. One question is should we require urine testing on these people because they were not really convicted. Those of us working on the new program are fairly evenly divided on the issue of whether we should require urine testing.

Follow-up **is** important. Miami, Florida has a major follow-up component to their diversion program. We do follow-up with our outpatient counseling clients who have been referred through the courts. Follow-up hasn't been made a part of our diversion program yet. There's no money for it. So far we've just talked about it.

Don: Right now you don't know how many of the people who went through your program have stayed out of the criminal justice system? You don't know if that diversion program fixed them up? How about five years after the program. Did half of those people who went through the program stay off chemicals? Or did they keep using and keep going downhill?

Art: We don't know.

Don: Ten hours is a light tap on the shoulder. It may take a lot more than that to get their attention.

Art: Yes. Los Angeles County's diversion program consists of 40 hours. Orange County's program is about thirty hours.

Don: Do they have any follow-up there, do you know?

Art: I don't know.

Don: This seems to be the area where every program I've looked at is weak.

Art: It's hard to do follow-up, it's real hard to do.

Don: They'll spend $100,000 to convict somebody and put them away for a year and a half. Then they won't spend

$4,000 a year to keep track of them to make sure they stay sober when they get out. Even though sober usually means they stay out of crime.

Art: The El Cajon P.C. 1000 diversion program is conducted in these rooms. I have two groups starting today at 4:00 p.m. and 6:30 p.m. We schedule like that each month. We do the same sort of thing in Oceanside. The most exciting part of the new drug diversion program is the idea of Speedy Diversion. Coupled with an enlarged curriculum, I think we would have a powerful one-two punch. The problem will be to get the clients to pay for it.

Are you familiar with the drinking driver program?

Don: Yes, doesn't that cost about $800 for SB 38?

Art: SB 38 is $980 and the program lasts over a year-and-a-half period of time for each participant. They can't pay for it all at once. Part of the behavior modification is that they have to pay a certain amount each time they come. They have to have the money ready and available as they come in. That's for their second drunk driving conviction.

The first conviction program used to be ten hours in length. It's been changed, now it's thirty hours and it lasts two months. It's actually six months, but the class work can be finished in two months, depending on the program. Some have classes all day Saturdays. It varies. On the average, the first drunk driving conviction program lasts about two months and costs $285 or $290. It used to be $75 or $80. It changed as of the first of 1991. The clients in that program pay for it also. The current fee for the P.C. 1000 program is about $130.

A P.C. 1000 task force was meeting in the County. It was an interlocking network. The different providers would meet and talk about different problems. Like how to deal with clients, fees, agreements on service, and the referral system. The new program will cost more because it's double the length of time and provides more services. It's not up to me to say how much it should be. I thought the price might range from a minimum $190 up to $260. I don't know what is appropriate.

We turn no one away for lack of funds. If you came in here to register and you didn't have any money, I would do everything I could to get money out of you. I would shake you upside down and see what comes out. I interview the clients to see how they are living today, what's going on.

Don: You mean you might ask, "Where did you sleep last night?"

SOBERING UP THE HOMELESS

Art: That's right. Sometimes there really is no money. They're homeless, still trying to take care of their court requirements. But still homeless, and without any funds. If that's the case we try to get them involved doing some kind of volunteer service. That way they work off the fee at about five dollars an hour.

Don: Where?

Art: Right here in our facility. Jean McAlister, the Director, and the namesake of this place, started the diversion program in 1973. That's when they first started diversion in this County. She's been involved in working with substance abusers for a long time. We have about 70 employees who work in 15 different programs. The diversion program is just one of them. Our primary focus is on drugs.

San Diego County had a separate drug department and an alcohol department. They just merged. At MITE, we're going to change too. It used to be a strict requirement that we would only deal with people whose primary problem was drugs. Meaning other drugs than alcohol. But what we found, of course was that the secondary drug is always alcohol.

Don: You can do crazy things if you're under the influence of just alcohol, or just drugs, or both.

Art: Right.

Don: What if the first time they got a 911 violence call and found that the guy is loaded they put him in a sobriety program right away? Sobering up that guy...

Art: Or girl, her, too.

Don: Could save all kinds of money over the next few years.   For example, hospital bills, court costs, foster care costs if the family breaks up. We could easily spend a half million dollars in five years on one family.   By sobering that guy or girl up, we could save it all.   The thing is the tail. The tail is missing. Everywhere you look there is no tail, no follow-up. If they finish this program, they go on their way.

You were saying that the judges aren't sending people to P.C. 1000 as much. There might be a reason for that.   Maybe the judges are seeing too many P.C. 1000 graduates back in court on new charges. Maybe the judges are thinking "What's the use of sending people to P.C. 1000. They keep coming back." With good follow-up that could all change. Good follow-up might only add another $200 to the cost of the program.

THE FCP OR FIRST CONVICTION PROGRAM

Art: That's what's happening with the new FCP or First Conviction Program.   That is for people who have been caught drinking and driving for the first time. After they complete the program they have to come in once a month. They continue going to A.A. meetings once a week and show proof that they attended.   That's exactly what you're talking about.   In East San Diego County, the FCP program is right across the parking lot from us.   The Episcopal Community Services runs it.   They are the largest provider in town for various services including drug services.   They also provide alcohol services, including the drinking driving program.

We at MITE bid on that program.   By the way, I wrote the proposal for that. I used to teach the drinking driver program at U.C.S.D. (University of California San Diego) when they were offering the program. They retired the program voluntarily.   When I worked there I was the program manager. U.C.S.D. got out of the business. But by then, I was already working here at MITE. We at MITE only bid half-heartedly on the program.

The drinking driver program is big. I think 2,000 people a year go through that program. That's an enormous number. It's a much bigger program than P.C. 1000 in terms of the hours they have to spend and the overall level of involvement. It's a six month program. Only six to eight weeks of the program is classroom experience. The rest is follow-up, tapering off. I believe that after the initial couple months of classroom experience, they continue to come for another four months, for about one to two hours once a month.

Don: Do they have any statistics on the success rate of that program?

Art: It's new so I wouldn't know. The same thing is true for SB 38, the second conviction program, the one you mentioned. That was a year program but now its been expanded to an 18 month program. The additional half year is basically for after-care or follow-up. The clients keep coming in periodically to help them work on long term sobriety, for at least 18 months.

Don: Drugs will show up in testing longer than alcohol.

Art: Oh, gosh, yes.

Don: Drugs still will show up maybe a week, two weeks, some maybe three weeks later?

Art: Exactly.

Don: But alcohol, 24 hours would be longest.

Art: Depending on how much they drank. If they drank a case of beer, and they were a small person, it could show up for up to 28 hours. It could also vary depending on whether we're talking about a male or a female.

Don: In the drinking driver program they could still be drinking but manage to get sober one day a month. That is when they only have to show up once a month, toward the end of the program.

Art: Sure, if they were inclined to cheat, there's no way to stop it.

CHEATING ON URINE TESTS

Don: I've heard people say, "I can blow these tests."

Art: They talk about golden seal, vinegar, salt. Golden seal is available at the health food stores. The health food stores have a number of purifying agents. Golden seal is the most popular. What happens is that the stories are being put out by people who are testing for probation and parole. They normally test twice a week. They go in for a urine test. But a lot of times they've used the night before, crystal typically. That's methamphetamine.

Out here in El Cajon it's the main drug of choice. Then they drink a bunch of golden seal or niacin which is also a favorite, and come up clean on their tests. What happened was that probation and parole do not test every sample. They take a urine sample, but they don't always send it in to the lab. That way they save money. Only about 40% of the urine samples which are produced by people who are on parole are actually sent in for testing. Less than that on probation. Only a third of the urine samples collected from probationers are actually tested.

When we test them here at MITE, they actually are tested. The urine samples go to a lab and the first thing the lab does is analyze the nature of the urine sample. If the person has drunk a lot of water, they can literally leach their system clean. It takes an enormous amount of water, but they'll do it. If they drank huge amounts of water, nothing but water comes out for awhile in the urine test. One of the first things they do at the lab is check for specific gravity. That will indicate whether or not the guy is urinating water. At the lab they know right away if somebody has been messing with the test. It comes back as a "no test." They can't get around the test, as far as I know.

KEEPING UP WITH PROGRESS

Art: The cops are now using instant-on radar. That way, the guy driving along with his radar detector on isn't detecting anything. So they got him. Also, the police are using lasers which aren't really radar at all. I believe that the same thing is happening with drug testing. Every time the people getting tested get a little smarter the people doing the testing get a little smarter.

Our clients may do just a line of crystal which is methamphetamine. That will be out of their bodies in as little as 24 to 38 hours, if they haven't been doing it regularly. If they test today, they'll get high tonight. They know they're not going to be tested again until at least Monday. If they always do that, they can keep using, maybe at lower levels. I mentioned that there was a debate about the diversion program, whether or not to make urine testing a requirement. If they did, that would cost more money.

Don: What does urine testing cost?

Art: If you brought a urine sample in just for testing, and you are not a client at MITE, it's $25 for a complete test. But if you're an ongoing client at MITE we charge what we pay, which is $12.50. It's cheap at $12.50. In most private labs and doctors' offices, it's at least $40.

We do urine testing of the clients enrolled in that nine week Oceanside program I mentioned. We charge them $12.50 for the two testings we do. We do it once at the initial entry or beginning of the nine week program. If they're dirty, they're out right away. There is one more mandatory random testing sometime while they are in the class. That class runs like five to six people a month. With that small number of people, it's not cumbersome. We had this big discussion about whether to do testing, and as I said all the providers were split pretty even. About half were in favor and half against it. I didn't gather the County's sentiment one way or the other. The providers each had a representative. I vary on it as far as my own personal feelings. I'm basically against it, for the reasons that we just described. Unless you're testing them every other day it really doesn't work.

WORKING WITH TRUST

Art: When I am conducting the P.C. 1000 classes, I talk about testing at our first class meeting. First of all, I tell them, "If I want to, I will test you." I don't tell them I really am not empowered to do that. If I suspect deviant behavior, I'll just tell them, "You're out of the program, you're going back to court." If they complain, and try to maintain that they haven't used anything then I say, "Let's go test." Or if I smell or observe something that makes me strongly suspect the use of drugs or alcohol I say, "You're loaded and you're out."

If they object, then I say, "Well, let's go test." So I do test them. And if they refuse, I say it's a condition of staying in the class. But I don't have a legal right to do that. But it doesn't come up as an issue. In every case, they say, "Never mind, I'm loaded." They admit it. Then I refer them back to court because they violated the terms of their probation. Although I'm in the helping profession, I'm not a cop or a probation officer. But my basic attitude is that they're court referred, and if you play, you pay.

If they can't stay sober enough so that I can't detect it, then they need more help than I can give them. They need the court for more enforcement. So I let them know that right away that if they are using and coming to class, they may very well lose the diversion option. Then they go back to court. And court might make them do some time. They know that this possibility is hanging over their heads. But the advantage to not generally testing is that I'm trusting them. I'm not really trusting them, but I put it out there to them that I am.

Don: Does that work?

Art: I have to throw someone out of the program about once every three months. That means that most of them are cooperating with the program. They're motivated to appear normal, because this program is so good for them. Especially when compared to the alternative, which is basically a minimum of ninety days of jail time. Yes, they are motivated.

Don: If the courts did what the law says they could do, they could get ninety days in jail. But in reality they have to have fifteen warrants before they even get hauled into court. Then they do five days of jail time because the jails are full. They can make them do ninety days jail time, but they never do.

Art: It rarely happens, yes. But it does happen sometimes. Our clients don't want to do any jail time. When they get convicted for being under the influence, normally the judges will give them some jail time, plus a fine, plus work service. Added together, it mounts up to more than what they would have to do here, much more.

I start off each class telling them that I am going to trust them and that the group is going to work together on sobriety. As time goes by, by the end of the month-and-a-half that we're here, that trusting sometimes works. If they don't choose to get sober, if they don't choose to stop using drugs, they're going to do drugs anyway. There's nothing that I can do to stop them from doing it. I make it as attractive as possible to choose sobriety. I start off the classes by telling them that "I accept you for who you are right now." I tell them, "Let's see if we can talk about why you should choose to get better."

MAKING SOBRIETY LOOK GOOD

Art: Instead of threatening them with all the things that can happen to them legally if they don't sober up, I try to make sobriety look attractive. I try to give them the tools they need to change their behavior if they so desire. I even tell them that if they are determined to do it, they can cheat on the testing by simply using drugs or alcohol only once a week. So the question might be asked, what good is the testing? Testing will turn up "dirties," especially if they smoke Marijuana. That can show up on a test a month after their last joint.

I would guess at least a third of the P.C. 1000 participants smoke marijuana. We spend a lot of time talking about that. They all say, "Well, it never killed anybody, unless you are trying to save your roach in the ashtray while driving and you crash into a car." That has happened. But as far as dying from an overdose of marijuana, that's pretty unusual. I've never heard of it. The literature says no one has ever died from an overdose of marijuana. But it sure has changed a lot of lives. We get into marijuana in some detail, both medically and in terms of social behavior.

Don: It does some brain damage and reduces memory capability.

Art: I myself am a recovering addict. I will have been clean and sober for eight years in four more days. Who's counting, right? When they do the EEG (electroencephalogram) you can see the difference in the brain wave behavior of someone under the influence of marijuana and someone who is not. There is a very real effect on the brain behavior. I'm sure there's an effect on the immune system in terms of fighting off infection.

Don: They get more colds.

MARIJUANA KILLS THE DESIRE TO ACHIEVE

Art: They get sick much more often. I've worked with these people for a long time. I've seen them coughing all winter like they had constant pneumonia. Even so, they never seem to connect their constant colds to their marijuana smoking. Sometimes after they've been sober for awhile, and if they think about it, they'll remember how sick they were all the time. But more than anything else, they just can't seem to get going.

With marijuana I tend to stress a motivational syndrome as the prime consequence. They lose interest in trying to achieve anything. We talk about that in detail. I use my own personal experience and numerous case histories to let them know what can happen to people from just from smoking marijuana. That's the one drug they have the hardest time quitting even though that isn't the drug that brought them in here. Mostly it's crystal in this area.

Don: My guess is that the ones who slip through the cracks and get loaded while they're in the P.C. 1000 program are the ones who really need help the most. They are the ones who are further along in their addiction. There needs to be some way to seal up those cracks to catch those people who are falling through.

Art: Yes, that would be great.

Don: We need to go out and get those people who didn't show up. We shouldn't be waiting five years until they get in big trouble. By that time, they've gone so much further into their addiction.

Art: That's right. That's where that Speedy Diversion Program comes in.

Don: But if they **still** don't show up?

Art: They can still walk down the hallway, and not show up.

Don: Right. Then the Probation Department still ends up with a warrant bank. The wrong people, the worst ones, the ones that need it the most, are slipping through the cracks. You're getting the people...

Art: Who are motivated.

Don: Yes, the ones who want to keep straight with the law. The other guys know the game. They know that if they do get arrested they can still go five more years of doing everything they want as long as they want. If they do get arrested they might end up going to jail for five days. Then the sheriff kicks them out. The judge may say six months, but the sheriff says five days because the jails are full.

YUPPIE AMERICA AND THE DOPE DEALER ON THE CORNER

Art: I've always been fascinated how drug use has evolved over the past ten years. For example, the dope dealers on the corner. They stand out there on the corner with their dope in their pocket waiting for their customers to come by. Ten years ago everyone I knew was still doing cocaine. Then, it was inconceivable that someone would be selling dope on the corner. You would have gotten busted in a heartbeat.

We did all our dope deals behind closed doors. It was much harder to find connections then, to keep supplied. Maybe it's because of the numbers, the sheer weight of numbers of people involved in illegal substances now. It's like the old French saying, if enough people break the law, then there is no law to be broken. Maybe that's what's happening.

There is something that I do know. The whole dope game has gotten vicious and violent. Yesterday there was a drive-by shooting in Oakland. A lady and her two children were killed in their own home. She had testified against some drug dealers. They retaliate. There's a lot of danger in taking that pro-active stance. And like you say busting a bunch of dope dealers is really just a temporary palliative. If you have big sweeps and they all seem to disappear for a time, in reality they are just hiding and they'll be back. Like Arnold said.

Don: I heard about the dope dealers on the corner. People in cars drive up to make buys. Someone was brave enough to stand there and take down license plate numbers of the buyers. A lot of the cars were registered to people living in the wealthy sections of Escondido, Poway and Rancho Bernardo. There were Mercedes and Porsches from very rich areas stopping at this ghetto corner down on Imperial Avenue in East San Diego.

That is that guy's corner. He fought for that corner and will kill to keep any other dealers off his corner. He is on that same corner every day. If they chase him off that corner with a megaphone and a parade of outraged citizens, this guy will give up his corner. He moves two blocks away and calls all his customers to tell them where his new corner is. Yuppie America is doing an awful lot to help support the bad guys in the drug wars. Their huge purchasing power fuels territorial drug wars.

Art: That's for sure. A lot of people say the crack thing is a black problem. But when you look at arrests and research, the facts say there are still more white people doing crack than blacks. It doesn't show up that way in terms of convictions: Ninety percent of the convictions are of black people. In terms of cocaine use, the majority of the users are still white.

Los Angeles did an interesting experiment in the area of neighborhood control similar to what you have been talking about. They've stopped doing it now, but for awhile they manned barricades in certain areas of high levels of dope activity.   No traffic was allowed in except bona fide traffic.   That included residents, business people, whatever was normal. It was quite successful. That screening of who went in and out of that area cut down on a lot of the drug activity. But they're not doing it anymore.

The neighborhood loved it. The residents loved it. But they stopped doing it. I guess they didn't have the policemen to keep doing it. It helped one neighborhood, but hurt the others. Like in the downtown shopping mall, Horton Plaza. They took out the part that used to be in front of the fountain in Robinsons. They planted it with striking flowers. It's very beautiful now. There's no bums there anymore. But walk 100 yards in any direction and they're everywhere else.

RUNNING FROM THE PROBLEM

Art: We work here at MITE with people who are addicted. They are drug addicts. But they want to get well. A lot of them think "All I've got to do is leave El Cajon and move away from this bad environment. I'll go to Chula Vista or Montana." They think of all kinds of places they can run to and they think their problem will go away when they reach this new place. They think they will be clean and sober, free of drugs, and their lives will start to really work for them. We call this "Doing the Geographic." In other words, by making a geographic move, they will have solved all their problems.

One group I work with is called Intro-Groups. The clients involved in that program are really a great group of people. It's similar to diversion, but they're not court-referred. They are referred to us by Child Protective Services or by the probation department. These are post-conviction people. It's an eight-week long program of group involvement in addition to individual counseling sessions with me. In addition, I do after-care with them. We have quite a few clients in that program. One day we had a large group meeting here, a houseful of people.

One couple began talking about what they wanted to do when Child Protective Services releases their child to them. The baby was born toxic, with drugs in its system. Of course that means the mother was using drugs right up to the time of delivery. There is a legal process that kicks in after it is discovered that a baby was born addicted or with drugs in their system. You know how all that works.

The parents have to get involved in parenting classes, drug education, counseling, and so forth.

They were saying that when they had completed all the requirements they were going to move to Tennessee. As if there's no drugs in Tennessee. As if they are not going to bring the drugs with them if there aren't any drugs where they are going. They can have drugs mailed to them.

Maybe it was a nostalgia thing. Like "We're going home." Those magic words: home, family. Their plan is to return to their family. Home and family will fix everything. They want to go back to a time when they were young and pure. Long ago one of them came from Tennessee. As I said, they are doing what we call a geographic. It's a palliative measure.

In the group yesterday, they talked about their plan. I said, "Anybody have any comments about that?" The group grabbed that and ran with it. They got a lot of comments. Some people started joking with them. They said "What's your address, we'll mail you some crystal." Some other people told them why that running away wasn't going to work. Those people in the group saw what was happening. They may have all loved to take dope but they were not dummies. They knew what was inside of themselves and inside of that couple. They knew about that feeling that something is wrong. They knew how those people think that they need to party, meaning, use drugs, to have a good time. Or they think "I just need a little dope to fix how rotten I feel now."

The group was able to see through that quick fix as a solution. They confronted this couple with everything that was going on with them. They knew. They had the answers. It was very powerful. I didn't have to do anything. They were their own therapists. They were forcing each other to face their cop-out thinking. They kept pointing out how the quick fix was probably not going to work.

It got very hot. The couple felt like they were being attacked because they were new. They had only been in the group for two weeks. They felt like they were being singled out. They got really angry. The guy got red in the face and he's a very, very physical guy. I thought for a little while that he might explode.

But finally we were able to give him the message that we were sharing all these thoughts with him out of love and concern. We let him know that it wasn't that they were being picked on and that everybody in the group had the same problem. Most of the people in the group had thought at some time or another "I'll move away and all this bad stuff happening in my life will go away."

It was a real good session. We asked the couple to deal with the idea of changing their behavior instead of running away from it. The basic approach in these Intro-Groups is the same as in the diversion class. We try to help them realize why it might be a good idea to actually change their behavior. Then we try to get them to see that changing their behavior could be very positive for them instead of boring them. They're so afraid of being bored. What they see or feel as bored, when they are not loaded, is a vague or sometimes very intense feeling of uneasiness. Being loaded makes that go away. We try to teach them that they can sober up and start to face all the things that they are afraid of.

LEARNING TO HAVE FUN WHILE SOBER

Don: For so many of them, and for so many years of their lives, the idea of any kind of fun is always connected with chemistry.

Art: Absolutely.

Don: They have no idea that you can have fun without it.

Art: Sexual or otherwise. Having fun without drugs is inconceivable to them. All these people in MITE's Intro-Groups program have been referred here because of drug-related problems. They get confronted with the facts of how they got sent here to the group. Like having crack babies, spousal abuse. They confront each other with the fact that drugs were probably behind most of the trouble they were having with the law. After this confrontation by the group, a lot of them will finally admit, "Yes, I've got to stop doing drugs, my life is out of control." That sounds so good to hear. But here's the catch. Almost immediately a very high percentage of the ones coming to that conclusion turn to alcohol. Alcohol is legal and no one stops them. No one says you can't do alcohol. **Except me**.

So they realize drugs were ruining their lives and they quit. But then we see them coming in hung over or talking about drinking. They'll admit that all of a sudden they are drinking alcohol a lot more. They may be drinking a case of beer or more on the weekend. So when the miracle of quitting drugs has happened that's still just the beginning. There are still so many issues to deal with, including their desire for immediate gratification. And their need to use some kind of chemical to change their mood, to change how they feel.

At MITE we don't really get into a lot of core issues such as the molest and parenting issues, or childhood issues. So many of our drug addict clients grew up in dysfunctional families where they were abused by substance abusing parents. I don't usually get into that. I mostly don't do psychotherapy. I refer people out for psychotherapy. I may at times get into the origins of their fears, the poor models they had from their parents. I have a degree in counseling. But the major constraint against digging into the possible childhood origins of their addiction is that there is no time. Also, that basically isn't our function or purpose here at MITE.

Sometimes I'll work with a family, doing some family counseling. But even in that setting I'll focus on behavior and the here-and-now. I want to know what they are doing **today**. I try to show them that who they are depends on what they do. I tell them that if they take dope and scream at each other all night then they are drug abusing, spouse abusing and family abusing people. I tell them that if they don't like who they are or who they have become, they can change. Then I try to show them how to change those behaviors. Sometimes its something simple. Like first, quit dope. Second, remember two things when you talk to each other. Don't raise your voice and always let the other person finish because they'll give you your turn. I've seen marriages turn around with those simple behavior changes.

DIGGING INTO THE PAIN

Art: Sometimes we're talking and someone starts crying when we talk about poor parental models.   Something simple, like talking about them being better models to their children than their parents were to them.   That would mean there are some deprivation issues there, maybe some A.C.A. (Adult Children of Alcoholics) issues. It may look like they need to get into some program that will help them to dig deeper.   Some of those people I try to refer out if I can.

What they need is someone to help them dig deeper and find out what the core issues are.   There is one group called Double Trouble.   It's a local CMH (Community Mental Health) group for our dual diagnosed people (substance abusers with a diagnosable emotional problem, e.g., schizophrenia).   We have a fair number of our clients in those groups.   In fact, I have one coming in today at 2:30.   The guy has been trying to get clean for literally seven years.   He's known to everybody, every drug treatment facility.

I haven't talked to him yet but I've seen him here getting coffee and socializing.   People can come here and hang around if they need a place to be and someone to be with to keep from using.   He's just starting up with MITE. I know he comes from a background history of molest.   I already know there are serious issues of low self-esteem with him.   All the standard stuff.   The way he slinks around makes it look like he's always ready to ward off a blow that doesn't come.

Don: A guy like that needs some very close supervision to stay sober.   He might not like being sober.   Without the drugs, without the alcohol, he's going to be miserable.   If he can, he should get some help and support while he's facing life sober.   But if the help isn't available and the only thing that happens to someone is that they are getting sober, there will still be some natural healing things that will go on.   The body and mind can start to heal by themselves when the toxic chemicals are no longer tearing things up.

When they first get sober these people may have nightmares and horrible dreams. But finally their bodies will start to heal. While they are under the influence, any healing is put on hold. Their lives are put on hold. Nothing happens. Health-wise, it's better for these people to be sober even if they can't get any help in digging into their old pains. Of course, help with the pain as well as the sober support group makes getting sober a lot easier and more likely to happen.

Art: Sure, certainly. When we get them sober, we don't leave them hanging out there just being sober and nothing else. We're not a twelve-step based program. But we promote twelve step programs and the concept. A lot of twelve step meetings take place here at MITE. We have had as many as 20 meetings a week in our three units right at this little shopping center.

When folks work the twelve steps it's like free psychoanalysis. One of the first things they need to do in the twelve step programs is to find a sponsor. Hopefully, it will be somebody they can work with. Number four of the twelve steps is when they make this personal inventory of all their resentments, their fears, their angers. The fifth step is when they share that with somebody and pray about it. There's a lot of deep inside healing that can take place for free, without paying for expensive psychotherapy, while they are getting sober. **They can't do that healing when they are using.** Like you say, they have to be clean. Nothing happens if you're high. They can't learn anything about themselves if they're high. So we get them clean first and then we begin working the steps.

You were suggesting short trips to the jail to get their attention. I'm wondering what would happen if we told our clients "Because you had a dirty test you've got five days in jail ahead of you." I think they would say "Well, save my room for me." Five days in jail poses absolutely no threat to them. I'm thinking, what if we were to tell someone "You messed up. Now you have five years of jail ahead of you." Some of our clients are 30 years old and have already spent 17 years of their lives in jail. They are institutionalized. Five years in jail is no big deal. We're doing a project with a program called Partners in Parole.

PROTECTING PRIVACY VS. SAVING LIVES

Don: Well, in that case, if the guy can't even walk out the door without getting drunk or loaded, you don't let him walk out the door. At least not alone. If he goes anywhere, he should have three sober buddies with him. Years ago A.A. used to work that way. They'd go drag guys out of bars.

Art: Absolutely. That's what being a sponsor meant in those days. They would literally drag them out of the bar and tell them, "I'm your sponsor, you're coming with me!" Bill W. was the founder of A.A. Some of the first people he worked with he took out of the bars and carried them home to his own house. They slept on his couch.

Don: I think we need to get back to some sort of buddy system. My brother's keeper, so to speak. That may be viewed as an invasion of privacy. But, if we don't sober them up they **are** going to die at 40. Sobering them up is going to save their lives. Maybe we need to tell them that they can't even walk out the door without two sober buddies going with them. If they reach for a drink or a needle or a pill their sober buddies will take it out of their hands.

Art: Big deal, invasion of privacy. It's proliferation of life.

Don: Right.

Art: You know, the Supreme Court weighs those factors all the time. Is this a violation of the Bill of Rights or is this for the greater good of a society? And there's no doubt that what you're talking about, sobering people up, is for the greater good of society.

Don: Let's say that these three guys had to be together 24 hours a day. They would never let each other out of their sight. Maybe they would do nothing but sit around and keep making sure they stayed sober. It would cost four thousand dollars each for a year to house them and feed them. That would still be ten times cheaper than the $20 to $40 thousand it costs to keep somebody in jail for a year. And apparently MITE can house and feed people for under three thousand a year from what you said. That's even cheaper.

Myopia seems epidemic when people argue about collecting or not collecting fines from the 700,000 warrant holders in San Diego County because they will or won't get a big enough share of the money.[84] We know that most of the outstanding warrants belong to substance abusers. Getting to the heart of the problem and sobering up the people who have outstanding warrants doesn't seem to have occurred to anyone yet. Not only would collecting that money not pay the County very much, but enough of the owners of those warrants probably have their lives in so much of a shambles they couldn't pay anyway. They wouldn't even show up for a community service program such as picking up trash on the freeways to work off their fine. The jails are too full to go get them and hunt them down. After a time the police may be instructed to only arrest people who look like they have the money to pay their fines since we know alcoholics and dope fiends do not bother with such matters. 'When all else fails, read directions,' which are given in Chapter 11.

CHAPTER NINE

THE LOST BATTLES: AMERICA'S DISGRACE

Why should America be ashamed of its treatment of its drug crazed and still growing criminal population? Because America is engaging in a witch hunt and locking up its addicted with little concern for treatment and rehabilitation. "We do care," our nation's leaders say, but then they ration treatment across the land. For example, in San Diego County three thousand times the dollars spent on substance abuse services go toward arresting, prosecuting and locking up our sick puppies, the substance abusers.

In the 91-92 San Diego County Alcohol and Drug Services plan, the list of **unmet** needs far outweighed the list of drug and alcohol needs being met. One of these unmet needs was, "Incarcerated juveniles are at a very high risk for drug abuse. Drug use is frequently related to the offense for which they are incarcerated. **They could benefit from an early intervention program.**" To this author, such a statement is akin to saying "5,000 children were accidentally pushed off the cliff into the canyon 500 feet below during the games at the Labor Day picnic. Children could benefit from a fence built along the canyon rim."

These children are our future! We whine that we don't have the money to sober them up and keep them sober. So we wait until their addiction has gotten so out of control they end up going to jail for years for increasingly more violent juvenile crimes. San Diego County and most counties in America aren't even scratching the surface of the substance abuse problem.

In 1992 San Diego County spent **no** money on alcohol rehabilitation. They administered $13 million in "matching funds" on drug programs and including that amount, administered $12 million of federal and state money. The total alcohol and drug budget was $25 million.

The over one billion dollars San Diego County spends for law enforcement/courts is 40 times the drug/alcohol treatment budget. Considering the county's share of the treatment budget, the county spent 3,000 times more for law enforcement than on treatment/prevention of substance abuse.

BINGO PLAYERS HELP SOBER UP SAN DIEGO

MITE (McAlister Institute for Treatment and Education) conducts a wide variety of drug and alcohol rehabilitation programs. They have contracted with the county to provide drug rehabilitation services and thus they receive some of the funds administered by the county. Some funds come from participants in the P.C. 1000 Drug Diversion Program who can afford to pay for some of MITE's services. All this money pays for only a part of the services provided by MITE.

MITE hosts huge crowds of mostly elderly bingo players several times a week to bring in money to help sober up San Diego County. In Chapter Eight, Art Fayer discussed the P.C. 1000 first time offender drug diversion program. Five thousand people went through the P.C. 1000 diversion program in 1991, but court referrals were down. This was perhaps because judges were beginning to feel that the program was not truly effective.

THE MOST ADDICTED SLIP THROUGH THE CRACKS

Of every 1,000 people referred to P.C. 1000, 80% or 800 people (some a year later) arrived at the program. Eighty percent of those arriving graduate. Thus, only 64%, or 640 of every 1,000 people referred actually completed the ten-hour program. Nobody has any data to indicate how many P.C. 1000 graduates successfully stayed sober, stopped crime, and stayed out of the criminal justice system. Judges are seeing many people referred to P.C. 1000 show up in court again. Ten hours of drug education classes, if follow-up data is ever obtained, is likely to not prove to be a powerful deterrent to drug use.

Also, the worst offenders, the ones deepest into their addiction, are completely by-passed by P.C. 1000. They are the ones who don't meet the criteria because it isn't their first offense. Many of those arrested for drug offenses don't show up for their court appearance at all and end up in the Probation Department's warrant bank. Also in the warrant bank are about 360 of every 1,000 those who **are** court referred to P.C. 1000 but either don't go at all or don't finish. We have seen that the San Diego County warrant bank is a sort of limbo or maybe purgatory. People are put there and ignored for a few years while they are on their way to a living hell.

SPEEDIER PROCESSING PLEASE

The plan for speedier processing of offenders into the P.C. 1000 program is a step in the right direction. Each individual who has gotten into legal problems because of substance abuse must be known to be sober at all times. Until this happens, the mayhem will continue. The spouse/significant other beatings will continue. Crime rates will continue to rise.

A system designed to not let **anyone** slip through the cracks is imperative. That is, if we are serious about a solution to the substance abuse problem which is destroying our nation.

Plans in San Diego to expand the California State Drug Diversion Program (P.C. 1000) include more hours of education, more urine testing and follow-up. The program will still be grossly inadequate because of the still existing massive potential for the most addicted to fall through the cracks. Those using while in the program are sent back to the limbo of the warrant banks and the courts. When they fail the P.C. 1000 program they should immediately be moved to a more intense level of intervention: A level which would **guarantee** sobriety.

Three hundred sixty out of every 1,000 referred to P.C. 1000 don't finish the program. Those are the ones we should go get and monitor very closely even if it means involuntary detox. Even the ones who do finish need to be periodically checked for at least three years. At this time, once they finish the few hours of classes, they're done - until they show back up in the courts for something else. And how many that happens to, nobody knows.

Chapter 11 describes the "Sober Forever" Program. This far reaching involuntary sobriety program is designed to seal the cracks and close the loop holes and thus guarantee sobriety. Numerous interventions are described in Chapter 11 which make the proposed program "fail-safe." Art Fayer (Chapter Eight) said that there are many substance abusers who will get high even if they know they will spend five days or five years in jail. He felt they had acclimated to jail.

These hard core addicted individuals need to be placed in sober living houses. Ten to 20 people can live in sober living houses (six to a house) at the same cost of keeping just one person in jail. Sober living houses approximate the outside world. The move from a sober living house to normal living is a much smaller step than the move from the jail to normal living.

KEEPING HELP WITHIN ARM'S LENGTH

The high risk substance abuser who gets loaded whenever and however he can will not be able to go **anywhere** alone. He must be accompanied by two sober buddies at all times. If he tries to get high his two buddies will place him under citizen's arrest for breaking the sobriety conditions of his probation. Then they'll take him back home to watch more "staying sober" videos and to face the group. And to get courage from the group so he will eventually be able to say "No" to substance abuse all by himself.

The rapidly advancing technology in electronic monitoring will give us new tools. In the near future, devices will most likely be available which will not only tell where you are, but whether you're high on something and if so, what substance it is that you have taken.

The Japanese have guidance systems for their cars. They enter a destination in their in-car computer. Their movements are tracked by satellite. When it comes time to change directions a voice tells them "Please turn right (or left) at the next corner." In the U. S., many trucks are equipped with satellite dishes which hook into the same global system of satellites used by the Japanese. The truck drivers' bosses know where that truck is at all times. This is the same satellite system we use to fire our missiles with an accuracy that beats our pretty good strike ratio in the Gulf War. It is the same satellite system that almost all the nations in the world with missiles can use to fire their missiles with similar accuracy. This is thanks to equipment sold by U.S. companies which always includes the secret codes needed to enter and use the system. It will not be long before we will be able to keep even better track of our addicted and literally guide them on their path to sobriety.

When the right equipment is developed, the following will occur in the near future: An ex-druggie on his way to a job interview decides instead to go get high. A voice starts coming from his interesting looking bracelet. The voice starts saying, louder and louder, "No, no, no, you took the wrong turn back there. Better go back unless you want another ten days in detox. If you don't, the cops will be waiting for you on the next corner."

Each time a substance abuser's joust with the law results in some jail time he often makes some resolutions to go straight. But within a few days or sometimes as long as a few months, the released substance abuser almost invariably returns to his old addictions. Why is this? For awhile, getting high feels good. Everybody else he knows is doing it. Also, it seems that nobody is really watching. Probation and parole supervision are generally ineffective. Those who even bother to show up for their court ordered urine tests often fail them. But in San Diego County and most big cities across the United States they still generally stay free and uninvolved in rehabilitation.[22]

FEELING GOOD FAST

Getting out of jail with no job waiting is not the same as graduating from Harvard. The ex-con's feeling of self worth is often very low. Getting a job would help him start feeling good about himself again. But that could take weeks, maybe years. Anyone who has gotten high knows there are ways to feel good in just a few seconds to a half hour, depending on the choice of substances. After a pleasant high and when they start to sober up, the substance abuser feels worse. The solution: get high again, stay high all the time if possible. But sometime or another, if he doesn't die first, he may temporarily run out of drugs and have to sober up. And each time he does sober up, there is less of his life left. If he had a family, they will be gone. If he had a house, it will be gone.

Each time he uses a substance, he goes further down and the journey back becomes longer. Why do people engage in such illogical and destructive behavior? To avoid the pain. For example, many substance abusing mothers have lost all their children to the foster care system. Their own families won't allow them into the house because they steal. As soon as they sober up, they have to face the loss of everything that could conceivably be of value. This includes their family of origin and their own immediate family, their husband and children.

With some years of effort at rebuilding their lives and sobriety, these females can eventually regain some measure of self-esteem. They have to spend months or years of living sober with the help of support groups. If they do that they may begin to have short periods of time off and on when they begin to feel good about themselves. This feeling good can occur in spite of the past, in spite of their losses.

What if they don't want to wait those many months or years to feel good again? What if they don't want to spend those years working through the grief, sadness and losses? What if they want to feel good right away? There are many substances designed to produce an instant feeling of "I'm okay." When substance abusers are given the choice of drug rehab (with the chance to feel good some time later) or to keep using and feel good now, what happens? Studies show that the feel good now option is almost always preferred to the long, hard road to sobriety. That future 'feel good' while sober will only come after a lot of hard work and suffering. To go through that period of grief and the slow rebuilding of self-esteem is best for that abuser, for his family, for society.   There is incontrovertible proof of that fact.

The sobered up substance abuser often can stay with and support, his family.   That prevents the heartbreak of family break-ups, foster homes, crime, jails and death. The sobered up substance abuser is not stealing, crashing into other people's cars. He is not draining the resources of the local hospitals. He is working, paying taxes, buying goods. He is not sending large amounts of money to Colombia or Peru. We can no longer wait for the substance abuser to make the decision to be sober. We must make it for him.

PREVENTING THE DESCENT INTO HELL

A foolproof sobriety program in which the substance abuser becomes involuntarily involved from the time of his first offense would prevent that descent into hell. It would prevent a long series of crimes which are usually committed on the way to this Hell. In the "Sober Forever" Program they will start back through detox within minutes or hours after their "slip."   Not six months or six years later after their lives have completely fallen apart again. Whereas the punishment for a slip now is usually nothing, it can be very drastic. The punishment can include a return to prison and completion of a lengthy prison sentence.

Many violators of their probation are serving out extensive jail sentences. One man was stopped for a broken tail light. A driver's license check revealed that he was on probation and subject to search at any time. He had been ordered to not drink as a condition of probation. He had been in jail only briefly after his arrest. A six pack of beer was found in his trunk. He was sent back to jail for

five years for "violating probation." Many slips are
overlooked, because of under-staffing or perhaps pity,
until the substance abuser does something horrible and is
finally reincarcerated. Or in the above case, a six pack of
beer got him five years. That return to jail ended his job
and his tax paying.

A system in which the first slip has not gone by
unnoticed, but results in immediate sanctions (such as a
short time in jail/detox), is absolutely necessary to make
sobriety stick. A series of graduated sanctions (or
punishments) is a much more effective deterrent than
doing nothing for years except making threats then
overreacting. The certainty of even minor punishment is
much more of a deterrent to continued substance abuse and
crime than long and high intensity punishment which is
sporadic.

FIRING PAROLE OFFICERS WHILE BUILDING MORE JAILS

Francis Valenzuela was one of the 231 Los Angeles
parole officers who lost her job in 1992 because of budget
cuts. Her caseload was distributed to the 1197 officers
remaining. That jumped their caseloads from around 65
each to around 85. It was impossible to keep track of their
parolees even before the 20% increase in their
caseloads.[63]

Before she lost her job, Francis was looking for
"Albert." He was released from prison in July of 1990
with $200. He was one of 65,420 parolees in California
in l990. By 1992 there were 85,000. Albert had served
over a year of a three year sentence for selling cocaine.
Most California parolees have a substance abuse problem.
Albert was a cocaine addict with few skills. Even so, he did
well for a time after his release. He got a factory job and
lived with a girlfriend. But drugs and jobs don't usually
mix. It wasn't long after he started using again and
hanging with his old buddies that the job was gone.

In the summer of 1991 he was arrested for
assaulting his girlfriend and went back to prison for

5-1/2 months. He got out in January, 1992. Again, he did okay for awhile. By April, Valenzuela couldn't find him, meaning he was using.

In May 1992, Valenzuela caught up with Albert at his girlfriend's house. He tested dirty. She talked him into trying a substance abuse program. He left the program after a month. He got a construction job that didn't last. Even so, he tested clean in July and August 1992. September's test was dirty. He wasn't keeping appointments. His girlfriend locked him out. He broke in and stole her VCR. Last word: Albert was using and missing.[63]

THE RIGHT HAND DOESN'T KNOW WHAT THE LEFT HAND IS DOING

Those providing treatment and those in the criminal justice system usually ignore each other. Each goes their own way. Not only that, different law enforcement agencies ignore each other, having no idea what their fellow agencies are doing. Martin Edward Walters was on an out of control drug/crime spree. He had been arrested by several different agencies, including the San Diego police, the county sheriff's department, the U.S. Drug Enforcement Administration (D.E.A.) and the federal Bureau of Alcohol, Tobacco and Firearms. None of the agencies knew he had been arrested by several other agencies, and Walters didn't tell them. Each capture was treated as a first arrest and was followed by release. In 1988 he killed Kristy Reyes during a desperate search for drugs.[53]

Obviously, each of the different criminal justice/law enforcement agencies need to know what the others are doing. If they had been aware of the multiple arrests of Martin Edward Walters, would they have done the right thing? Not the right thing as it is spelled out in this book. Even after being arrested and locked up, he would not have received any treatment for his drug addiction. Few do. If these agencies had compared notes about his multiple arrests, Walters would have been locked up for a long time. He wouldn't have murdered Kristy Reyes because he would have been locked up.

But after doing his time he would have come out of prison and gone right back to drugs and crime. Without treatment, most do. Almost any A.T.M. (automatic teller machine) in the U. S. can tell you how much money you have in your account. The technology is obviously there. The local sheriff's department should immediately know if the D.E.A. agency down the street or across town has arrested the same out of control criminal/drug addict in the last few days or weeks.

Chapter 11 provides the details on the computer linkage system which must be implemented between the different law enforcement agencies.

THE SHOTGUN WEDDING

Once the different law enforcement agencies know what each other are doing then there will be a wedding. Treatment and the criminal justice system need to be married. They must be dragged, kicking and screaming to the altar. They don't like each other. That's why a shotgun wedding will be needed.

Why must they wed? Because American society has given birth to a social disaster created by substance abuse. Two parents are needed to take care of this sick baby. Both treatment and law enforcement have their own contributions to make. One cannot function or do even a passing job without the other. Treatment alone of substance abusers is virtually useless. Arrest, jail and incarceration alone of substance abusers is virtually useless. When the criminal justice system backs up treatment and forces a substance abuser into a treatment program that keeps him sober he stops doing drugs and crime.

Treatment providers are horrified at the brutality that substance abusers must endure in the criminal justice system and in jail. Many are raped in jail. Many get their first exposure to drugs and become addicts in jail. But law enforcement in turn is disgusted with what they see as the namby pamby approach that treatment takes. For this reason the Bureau of Justice Administration in the Federal Justice Department has waged a war on drug rehabilitation.[27] They have cut treatment to the bone or eliminated it entirely wherever possible. They want more jails. They say rehab doesn't work. They are wrong. If you don't do rehab (which they aren't) it doesn't work. If you do rehab, it works.

Treatment and law enforcement must marry. They must get in bed together. They must give birth to a new program that uses the best talents of both. Only such a program can save America from further decay. The nuts and bolts of the treatment/law enforcement shotgun wedding are presented in Chapter 11. After the marriage, each can go their own way, as long as they 'keep in touch' for the sake of their offspring, the "Sober Forever" Program.

Whatever treating agency the substance abuser signs with must enter a periodic "all clear" into the central computer criminal/substance abuse tracking system. This means "He/she is still doing okay and we have recent proof of their sobriety." If this message is **not** received by the law enforcement/criminal justice system they go get the lost sheep and herd him/her back to the fold. The only time the law enforcement/criminal justice system will get involved is to go get the strays. When that is all they have left to do, they should be able to do this very well.

Jeff Dahmer got drunk every day and killed bunches of people while he was on parole. He also had a dedicated and concerned parole officer. But also just as ineffective as Albert's. If Francis Valenzuela had the tools of the "Sober Forever" Program outlined in Chapter 11, Albert would be sober, and most likely working today. Albert should have gone directly from jail to a sober living house. Any "slips" should have immediately resulted in a move, perhaps temporary, to a higher security facility. Maybe like the one in the desert proposed in Chapter 11. It wouldn't be wise to try to leave that one before someone said you were ready. It would be a long walk to the city.

NOWHERE TO GO AFTER JAIL

Valenzuela said that three out of four prisoners have no place to stay when they are released from prison. In order to save the $3,000 to $4,000 a year it would cost to put these guys in sober living houses, we all wait until they get in big trouble. Then we pay their $20,000 to $40,000 a year rent in jail for the next few years.

Valenzuela said few services are available. There are long waiting lists for drug rehab programs. By the time their name comes up, the doper has usually lost interest and can't be found anyway. Valenzuela tried to get her parolees to a program called "Jobs Plus" which helps parolees find work. Most wouldn't make the trip to Santa Monica (a few miles from Los Angeles) to sign up. Obviously, they were busy doing something else, namely, drugs and crime.

Valenzuela's supervisor discouraged parole revocation for testing dirty, even though the druggie was usually supporting his habit with crime. The reason: The jails were full. Even so, California revokes more paroles than any other state.

Within two years of leaving prison nearly 40% of parolees are sent back to prison for a parole violation. Another 26% are returned for a new criminal conviction. That means that 66% of everyone released from jail is back in jail in California within two years. Why do we love to pay that $40,000 a year rent for these people? We are talking about billions of dollars spent just in California every year to lock these people up **again**. We have seen over and over that we can feed and house them outside of jail, in sober living houses for ten percent of the cost of jail. And sober, 85% quit crime.

My estimate is that half of these ex-cons are getting G.R., or General Relief. In California, this amounts to about $400 a month. That is more than enough to pay their room **and** board in a sober living house. Once the "Sober Forever" Program is implemented, this will happen: Any ex-con with a drug history who receives any kind of state support, social security, or welfare money will be able to pick from a list of sober living programs.

His money will be sent to the one he picks. Why will the ex-con object to that? Because he feels that his state or federal pension/relief money is for him to get loaded, not to pay rent or buy food. He can get those at the homeless shelters.

PARENTS' RIGHTS TO SOBER KIDS

An involuntary sobriety program should respond to the cries of distraught parents. Other programs have done so in the past.[64] When the police are called by a parent who says their son or daughter is high, loaded and causing problems, what do the police do? If they come at all, they say, "If you are having a problem with your son or daughter, we suggest that you obtain a restraining order. Then you can force him or her to leave the premises." They may promise that if he/she violates the restraining order, the police will make an intervention. That doesn't usually happen either.

The parent might ask, "Isn't it illegal to be under the influence of a drug and to be screaming all night, to be stealing from your parents?" The response from the police would be, "But we don't arrest people for that, that's a domestic matter." America's parents deserve sober kids and when they ask for help in getting their children sober they should get it. When you give love to a sober kid he gives you love back, not hate. Sober kids can live at home. Sober kids can go to school and get jobs. Sober kids can have a life. Sober kids don't have to join the ranks of the other homeless teenagers.

Most of the two million homeless teenagers are on the streets because of their substance abuse. Their irrational behavior, tantrums, stealing, was destroying the whole family. They were finally ejected from the home so that the remaining family members could survive. Others ended up on the streets because their home disappeared, thanks to substance abusing parents.

Parents are usually on their own in dealing with their drug/alcohol addicted children until their children break enough of society's rules to get the attention of the criminal justice System. They usually have to do some big-time crime to do this. Then, as noted elsewhere in this book, the criminal justice system often brutally overreacts.

Parents must be able to ask for help in bringing their children back from the living hell of substance abuse. If we aim to sober up all the substance abusers, then parents can help by letting us know when their children need help in getting sober. There are millions of Americans who desperately need help in sobering up. That is the only thing which will stop their descent into a living hell. More and more, they are dragging the rest of America down with them.

NO SHORTAGE OF PEOPLE NEEDING HELP

We don't have to go look for the people who need help in sobering up. They are everywhere. They are staggering down our streets. They stand around in parks putting needles in their arm. They shoot up dope a few feet away from roving police patrols. In San Diego County we could start with the 17,000 people in the "probation bank." Only a small percentage of them are sober enough to begin rebuilding their lives.

In New York City we could start by picking up the many thousands of customers after they make their purchases at the 300 known street drug markets.[25] Not to lock them up but to enroll them in the "Sober Forever" Program at whatever the appropriate intervention level would be for that individual.

Don't take his B.M.W. from the rich yuppie who bought dope on a ghetto corner. If you do he'll get mad and spend a lot of money fighting you. Instead, tell him "The jig is up. You can keep your B.M.W. but it's time to get sober." Chapter 11 tells how.

San Diego Union Tribune writer Joe Cantlupe said that there is "An undermining of life in a community hapless against a growing band of petty criminals - many influenced by drugs - who know they won't be arrested, fined, or jailed!" Violent crime increased by 18.9% in

1991, and "today, law enforcement agencies are dealing with a different kind of defendant who is on drugs. They are fearless and don't react to police as they used to." Drugs kill the conscience and make the druggie feel invincible.[20]

Just how much of our economic problems are caused by the out of control drug problem? There are billions of dollars going into the drug economy to help Colombians have a better standard of living. Think what would happen if those many billions were spent on goods and services instead of on drugs. Sobering up America would jump-start our economy in a way that would shock even the most optimistic forecasters. We would have a financial boom beyond their wildest dreams.

Beware, the thousands of Colombians making their living in the drug trade will **not** be happy with America's financial recovery. They will have to look for different work when America's financial resources are not being sucked into foreign countries to buy drugs. Our national budget deficit has run around $300 billion a year. Some estimates are that dope fiends steal around $600 billion a year in goods to feed their habits.[117] We have seen that money that stays in the economy is invested, spent, and in one way or another ends up getting taxed. Just cutting theft by 50% to 80% (easy to do if we sober up the thieves, who then stop stealing) might by itself help balance our national budget.

Why does Europe, with a focus on drug treatment and use of jails as only a last resource, have only a small fraction of the murders and thefts that we do in America? Prison is the only solution currently used in America to solve our social/drug addiction problems. Could it possibly be that locking more and more people up as long as there is a couple feet of space left in a jail somewhere doesn't work? Don't tell that to the politicians or to anyone in the Department of Justice or to anyone in the Criminal Justice system. They don't want to hear it.

The same tired solutions are often trotted out. The naive say we should root out the underlying cause of crime. We should clear out crack houses and our parks which are loaded with drug dealers. A particular neighborhood may profit by vigorously forcing out drug dealers. But hard data shows that the overall drug activity level is not influenced by this "root them out" strategy. Dealers may have moved a few blocks or miles away.

CRIPS AND BLOODS: AMERICA'S NEW OWNERS

The Los Angeles Crips and Bloods gangs have spread out across America. They have made drugs available to our most remote states, cities and counties.

Another popular notion: "Save our Streets." The media loves the idea. That approach is like turning the light on in the garage at night. Have you ever noticed the cockroaches running for cover? To speed up the process, take a big stick, bang it on the floor. Almost immediately, all the cockroaches disappear, at least until the light goes off.

When we "take back a neighborhood" the drug activity moves a couple blocks north or south until we stop banging the big stick up and down the block.[131] Then the illegal drug activity comes right back. If we lived in Singapore, we could line up all of the drug dealers in the neighborhood and shoot them instead of chasing them two blocks away. We don't live in Singapore, we live in America. These are our fellow citizens. There is proof that we can rescue them from the hell of using and selling. Most drug dealers sell drugs to support their own habit.

It is admirable for a neighborhood to "take back the streets." But why stop at such a limited goal? Why merely shove the illegal drug problem two blocks, two counties, or two jails away? They have to be let out of jail some time. And again, they'll be back. Most will do the same thing they did before: Deal, steal and take dope.

Since most dope dealers are dope users, why not sober up all the substance abusers? They are the ones making those streets so dangerous. If we sober up whole neighborhoods, the substance abusing youth, as soon as they are sober, can return to their old neighborhoods, homes and families. We need to bring our lost sheep back from their living hell of drug and alcohol addiction. We have the technology. We can rebuild America.

Our leaders across the nation keep saying we need more jails. As far as the drug crisis goes, our leaders are like the blind men looking at the elephant. The one holding the trunk says an elephant is like a vine. San Diego Police Chief Burgreen knew the law and jails. Therefore, law and jails are the solution.[20] Our leaders are holding onto the wrong part of the elephant. If they weren't blind they could see the **whole** drug problem. They could see that most criminals quit crime when they are sobered up. They don't see that sobering up America would cost somewhere between a tenth to a fiftieth of what fighting the drug wars is costing now.

REHABILITATION WORKS: FOR THE FEW WHO GET IT

Another reason for America's disgrace is that 85% of all prisoners are locked up with no hope. Only 15% or less of America's prisoners are lucky enough to get drug rehabilitation and job training while they are in jail. For the most part, they come out of jail less prepared to earn a legal sober living than when they went in. They come out hardened, having learned more from other inmates about the dark side of life than about how to live and cope in normal society. The disgrace is that, in the few cases in which prison rehabilitation was tried, it worked. Most graduates of in-prison job training/rehab programs left jail to go to **work** instead of back to crime and drugs.[45, 48, 115, 152]

It is clear that sobering up substance abusers is going to be cheaper for everyone than what we are doing now. Early intervention will keep most people from going to jail, which costs taxpayers $20 to $60 thousand a year per person. During incarceration, the individual often develops more criminal skills. They scheme on how to not get caught so soon the next time. In jail they earn their C. A. (Criminal Arts) degree[133]

In the involuntary sobriety program proposed in Chapter 11, there will be little or no time in custody in most cases. And that time which is spent by the substance abuser in custody will involve several hours a day of work on sobriety. Release from jail in the current criminal justice system is usually followed quickly by reinvolvement in old behaviors and drugs. The recidivism rate (percentage of people who end up in jail a second time) is 65% and climbing.

THE LEGAL SYSTEM AT A BREAKING POINT

The whole legal/law enforcement system all across the United States is close to a breaking point. San Diego is no exception. The San Diego Police Department budget is $162 million a year. The Sheriff's budget is $137 million a year. These figures do not include several other smaller town police department budgets in San Diego County. Most police department budgets have doubled in the past few years,

The increase in budgets and police officers still has not kept up with crime, which has quadrupled in the last few years. This is the direct result of increases in substance abuse. The minimum drop in the crime rate if we sober up America would be at least 50%. Doesn't it make sense that if crime levels were cut in half, we could reduce the many billions of dollars we spend on law enforcement across the nation by at least twenty-five percent? In San Diego County the combined budgets of the public defenders ($18.5 million), superior court ($35.3 million), District Attorney ($39.6 million), probation ($46.7 million) added up to $135 million dollars in 1992. Doesn't it make sense that all those budgets could be reduced by at least 25% if crime was reduced by 50%?

San Diego could be sobered up for under a tenth of what its judicial system budget of over a billion dollars is costing now. It's a disgrace that we spend twenty-five million dollars on prevention. But forty times that, or over a billion dollars a year, on catching and locking up our citizens who need help. That means that over 70% of San Diego County's total budget is spent playing cops and robbers. Sobering up San Diego would result in a surface savings of several hundred millions of dollars. I say "surface" because the total cost of drug abuse has to include the cost of foster care for the children of druggies, goods stolen to fence for drugs, etc.

UNCLE SAM'S SHARE OF THE DOPE MONEY: ZERO

Many additional millions of dollars are lost in other indirect ways because of the druggies who don't work and don't pay taxes. Plus there is a gigantic underground multi-billion dollar drug economy, on which not one cent is paid in taxes. We know that the financial costs to America of substance abuse is astronomical. Adding up all the monetary costs still leaves untold the many other ways drugs sap the emotional lifeblood out of our citizens. Every drug-driven criminal who goes to jail leaves behind a loved one with a broken heart, a mother, a sister, children or a girlfriend. The money saved in a sober America could be recycled into job training, a library, a sewer system. The energy and emotions not wasted in mourning and grief over losses caused by drugs could be channeled into achievements.

Services and hours are constantly being cut back or eliminated in our schools, public libraries, parks and recreation centers. We are closing schools and shutting down prenatal care clinics because we are out of money. All the money goes for law enforcement and to build and operate jails, jails and more jails. One out of six people who are civil service employees in the State of California work for the Department of Corrections.

Hospitals could go back to quality care if such huge amounts of medical resources were not spent on drug emergencies and crack babies (one out of ten births nationwide is a crack baby). The crack crisis has turned the Oakland Hospital into a "zoo" and a "nightmare."[131] Substance abuse is draining the emotional/financial resources of this nation in virtually every area of existence.

BUYING OLYMPIC SIZE SWIMMING POOLS FOR COLOMBIANS

Many Americans are worried about the unequal balance of trade. They regret that many more goods are being shipped into the United States than out. They should be delighted at a plan to stop the importation of many billions of dollars of very expensive illegal chemicals each year. That money, now spent on marijuana, cocaine and heroin would stay in the United States. It would be spent for goods and services here instead of paying for Olympic size swimming pools for members of the Medellin Cartel in Colombia. When that money is spent on goods in the United States, it will create jobs. Taxes will be paid on the goods. Taxes will be paid on the money earned.

As it is, millions of dollars leaves the United States daily. This money spent on drugs results in the poisoning of our citizens' minds and bodies with toxic substances. Illegal drugs are shredding the fabric of our existence in America, crumbling the family, ripping apart the legal system. Illegal drugs are creating second and third generations of mind crippled people who have lost so much. They have been left unwilling and often unable to compete in the job market.

Someone proposed a plan in Washington to pay Peruvian farmers to **not** grow the poppy plant, from which heroin comes. We were going to send people down there to show them how to raise other crops to make money. Perhaps we should pay all the marijuana growers in Northern California to raise potatoes instead of pot. What about all the people in the Pacific rim countries growing poppies to ship heroin to the United States. Maybe we can teach them to grow squash. We give methadone to heroin addicts. Many I have seen love this arrangement. They don't need as much real heroin to stay high. The poppy grower can have his subsidized squash crop on one side of the mountain and his poppy crop in a bit more seclusive valley on the other side of the mountain. Wouldn't it be easier to just stop people from buying dope?

WE CAN'T TREAT YOUR COLD YET: LET'S WAIT UNTIL IT TURNS INTO PNEUMONIA

What we are doing now is like telling someone who has a cold that there is no money to treat them. We can't afford the antibiotics which could quickly cure the problem. We tell them they have to wait until they are almost dead with pneumonia before we can do anything. Then we will take them to a hospital and fix them up for $20 to $30 thousand at the taxpayer's expense. This cost is several thousand times the cost of the penicillin shot which would have cured them in the first stages of their illness. Lucky for us medicine is not practiced like that.

But the criminal justice system does practice justice like that. They claim that we can't afford to act early in the career of the substance abuser. Yet when the substance abuser is five to ten years into his addiction and substance abuse pattern, each addict can easily cost the taxpayers up to a million dollars apiece per year. Let's not forget the costs of jail time, court time, judge time, prosecution and defense attorney time, foster home time, etc. Let's not forget all the television sets which were stolen and pawned before the substance abuser got to jail.

These addicts can be sobered up in about two years for about $4,000 each per year. Addicts early in their substance abuse careers can be sobered up for a small fraction of what it costs to run them through the criminal justice system.

This estimate of savings does not take into account the money these sobered-up ex-substance abusers will be paying in taxes. Research shows that at least half of them will be working once they have been sober for awhile. Will the "Sober Forever" Program really work? Multiple studies prove that involuntary sobriety programs are the only interventions which do work most of the time.

PREGNANT AND ON DRUGS? LOCK THEM UP AND TAKE THEIR BABIES

The Bush administration's response to women's drug use during pregnancy was to place massive political and budgetary emphasis on law enforcement. There has been an inadequate emphasis on prevention and treatment for drug/alcohol use. The law enforcement approach was to lock up pregnant women and put their drug addicted infants in foster homes. This approach swamped the legal and foster home systems.[124]

Some writers said that these substance abusing mothers, many of whom were homeless, needed drug-free residential treatment programs. They needed to keep their children with them. Sober, they can be good mothers. Who are we to think we can do a better job than all these natural mothers in raising their children? We do have to sober up these mothers first. Once we do that, they will beat the care provided by virtually any foster home in the system.[124]

We keep reinventing the wheel. We are finding in this case that natural mothers (once sober) do the best job of raising their children, and at the lowest cost to society. America found out many years ago that orphanages turned out severely emotionally damaged people. We turned to foster homes for the answer. Now we're finding that children do more poorly in their foster home system than in their own sobered up homes.[68, 135]

Vicki K. Markey, Deputy Chief Probation Officer of San Diego County, described several county-run in-prison drug/alcohol rehabilitation programs (Chapter Seven). These were very successful in turning people's lives around, at least temporarily. Prisoners were generally sober while they were incarcerated and many received education and job training in jail. These new skills helped them restore self-esteem. However, after release from incarceration most of these substance abusers usually had nowhere to go except back to living in the streets or with their doper buddies. Their sobriety resolve was usually short-lived.

SOBER LIVING FOR ONE TENTH THE COST OF JAIL

Instead of spending a year in a very expensive residential treatment program, alternatives are available. After an overnight stay in detox, the substance abuser would be asked where he intends to live. If he plans to live someplace where sobriety would be tough or impossible, he will not be allowed to live there. Instead, he will be given the option of going to jail or going to a low cost (as little as $250 per month) sober living house. We may escort him there. If he promises to go on his own to the sober living house but doesn't show up we will go get him. He **will** be sober.

Ms. Markey knew what substance abusers needed, probably on a lifelong basis: An environment to support sober living. She eloquently described such an environment in Chapter Seven which an older millionaire found critical for survival. He realized he couldn't live in his own home without getting drunk.

But the drug/alcohol recovery programs Ms. Markey described were mostly voluntary programs. Of her friend's sober living homes she noted, "If they don't want to (sober up), they're kicked out on the streets. They are the problem of the criminal justice system from that day forward and somebody else comes in and takes the bed." Art Fayer said the same thing (Chapter Eight). Those caught using are kicked out of the P.C. 1000 program and referred back to court (but usually don't show up there).

That's the problem! We **don't** want the substance abuser/criminal back in the criminal justice system because they were caught using. The system is too crowded, it does not work, it does not rehabilitate people, it is very expensive to run. With few exceptions, incarceration/jail experiences are very stressful and very demeaning. Some of those excellent voluntary recovery programs Ms. Markey described are available to a small minority of prisoners upon their release. These programs need to be made involuntary recovery programs with determined tracking and follow-up. They need to be available for every single person released from jail. The rehabilitation **must** start before they even leave the jail.

A STITCH IN TIME SAVES NINE

It's best to treat a disease early in its course. The sooner cancer is diagnosed and treated the higher the cure rate. This is true in virtually any disease. The disease of substance abuse is no exception. The newly addicted are more likely to be doing misdemeanor crimes. If they are sobered up early in their substance abuse career, they don't go on to felony crimes.

The P.C. 1000 diversion program is moving in that direction. Many people advocate traditional handling of drug criminals. They say, "That's the law." But if that is the law and we don't like it, we can change it. All kinds of diversion programs are also the law. By using a "Sober Forever" type of diversion program we can by-pass lawyers and courts in at least 50% of the cases. We can have summary hearings over closed circuit TV and have the addict in their first recovery meeting within hours of their arrest.

There are now laws on the books that allow us to do much more than we are doing now. The California code spells out a 90 day sentence for the first drug offense. This never happens. Getting the legal right to implement an involuntary sobriety program is the least of the problem. Most important is to do what we have learned works best with the substance abuser. We have found that rapid intervention at the time of the substance abuser's first appearance in the legal system is critical.

Letting an out-of-control substance abuse pattern drag on for months or years teaches disrespect and results in the abuser diving even deeper into their abuse pattern. Once in a Diversion program, the substance abuser must be guaranteed that the legal system will leave him alone as long as he is sober (and of course commits no more crimes). The agency he has contracted with to guarantee his sobriety will send very brief sobriety confirmation reports periodically to the probation department. The probation department can stay completely out of the picture until the contracting agency says they need help to keep somebody sober.

Some of our leaders are convinced that a generation of hardened criminals has been lost. This is not true. The fact is that sobering up a substance abusing criminal, in almost every case, does turn them into human beings again.

TEETERING ON THE EDGE OF A SOCIOLOGICAL ABYSS

The proposed "Sober Forever" Program **will** guarantee sobriety, and all that comes with sobriety. There **will be** a reduction in violence, crime and broken families. We will see a drastic reduction in all the sociological ailments which have been escalating at an incredible rate in the last ten years. Has mankind suddenly deteriorated? Was man okay for the first few millennia of his existence? And now, has man suddenly turned bad at the end of the 20th century?

What has happened in America in the past few years is a constant escalation in the use and abuse of intoxicating substances. Along with this abuse has come all of the deteriorations we have noted in society. These include the increases in crime, violence and the splintering of the family. These sad truths have been documented in this book over and over.

Has man been teetering on the edge of a sociological abyss all along? But just now he has been pushed into that abyss? And as a result of this sociological plummeting, he has now started taking drugs? This author believes that the increase in drug usage has caused the plummeting. Why this point is understood by some but is not universally understood is a mystery. There is overwhelming research proving that wherever this fall into the abyss occurs, it is almost always accompanied by substance abuse. This abyss can consist of homelessness, prostitution, foster home placements, crime, violence, etc.

I have maintained throughout this book that America's social ailments are caused by substance abuse. What I am about to say may seem at first to contradict this statement. It won't. Sobering up America still needs to be done. But it is time in this book to start recognizing the complexity of the problem and the complexity of the solution.

We have a massive and growing very alienated underclass. They are completely outside the American dream, American law and American morality. This underclass exists in a state of siege. At the same time, they hold the rest of America hostage. They are robbing America and sucking up all our resources because this underclass places tremendous extra burdens on our health care system, on the foster home system, etc. Many are born on welfare and raised on welfare.

We taxpayers are now raising their babies either through direct subsidy or in foster homes. I have said they got there because of substance abuse. This is at least half true. Even closer to the truth is that drug addiction is both a **symptom and a cause** of the alienation of the underclass. Drugs are both symptoms **and** causes of America's social difficulties.

WATER BUFFALO HEROIN ADDICTS

During the vietnam war B-52 bombers made many raids. They roared low over the Asian countryside and produced great booming claps of thunder as they dropped their bombs. The water buffalo grazing below were all "stressed out" by these strange and frightening events. They would gallop over to the poppy fields and calm themselves down with heroin. When the bombings stopped the water buffalo stopped their treks to the poppy fields.

Poverty causes stress. Many people educated and worked themselves out of poverty and out of the ghetto. Others, like the water buffalo, comforted themselves through their stress with chemicals. Unlike the water buffalo, a time to stop chemicals when the stress stopped did not occur. This is because the poverty did not go away like the B-52 bombers. Being on drugs had resulted in bad judgment and in an even further decay in their quality of life. Using chemicals to feel better rots morality and allows addicts to commit unspeakable acts that make sense to them in their conscienceless state. Crack addicts in crack cocaine houses have given their crying infants heroin to quiet them down. Crack addicts have killed their children to collect insurance money.

This book has talked about rehabilitation. The prefix "re" means "again, anew, back." Rehabilitate means to restore to former capacity, health and constructive energy. Unfortunately, we are now talking about millions of people to whom this term does not apply. Millions of Americans cannot be rehabilitated because they have never been habilitated in the first place. For millions of Americans, we will have to begin at the beginning and teach basic social skills, attitudes and morality that not only don't exist, but never existed.

WE MUST PASS CIVILIZATION ON TO OUR CHILDREN

Drug treatment works. The longer the addict is in drug treatment the better it works. We cannot just say "Here is treatment." There are millions of Americans who have no idea how to be a parent. This skill has been lost in some groups and some families for three generations. There are people who for three generations have lost the concept of work. Job training was either ignored or unavailable. Even more important, what was missing is an attitude that "I can earn money by doing things that are legal." Also missing is the attitude that "I will get up every morning and make an effort every day." This has to be learned. We usually learn this by seeing our parents get up every day to go to work. People who have not seen that for three generations know nothing of work. We are not passing civilization on to our children.

In many cases, the town must be the client, the community must be the client. We will have to go in and change the way whole communities function. We will have to teach moral development. We must pass civilization on to our children. We seem to love to talk about the high rate of single parents in certain communities and populations, 60% in some groups. But when we have locked up all their men, who are they to marry?

Within a few months of publication of this book, estimates are that 40% of all non-white males between the age of 18 and 30 will be incarcerated or under criminal justice supervision. United States is the first industrialized nation to try to solve its social problems with prisons and jails. Sixteen percent of San Diego's population is Mexican American, but 47% of the incarcerated juveniles in San Diego are Mexican American.[86]

Large segments of our sub-cultures are falling apart. The parents of these incarcerated juveniles, many of whom grew up in Mexico, were not locked up as teenagers. Whatever values kept these parents from being locked up in their youth have not been passed on to their incarcerated children. We must pass civilization on to our children.

People are disconnected, from each other and from a sense of community. Children have little contact with adults. If we live in isolation and selfishness, we have no connection with others. With the breakdown of community, neighborhood and family, we have seen the loss of the places where the values we recognize as human are formed and grow. A gang member was asked what might lead to murder. He said "I might kill someone if I'm mad at them or if I'm bored."[97]

There is an African saying, "It takes an entire village to raise a child." When there is real community there is not as much drug use because there is not as much pain. When there is real community people's needs are being met, people feel safe, cared for and comforted. We have to teach people how to start taking care of each other. We need to find ways to turn our underclass neighborhoods into healthy communities. We must pass civilization on to our children.

HUMAN TOXIC WASTE

Rod Mullen and Naya Arbiter have developed effective in-prison treatment programs. They recalled the time the New York barges, full of garbage, roamed the seas looking for a dumping ground. Like the ports that refused entry no neighborhood or community wants drug addicts or offenders near it.

Drug addicts are considered toxic - like garbage, never to be brought back into the home. "As with toxic waste, drug users attract little community attention when they are out of sight." Locked up is one way they are temporarily out of sight. "They are forgotten until their toxic properties begin to cause harm.... Homeless children grow into gang members then become violent adults. I.V. drug users spread AIDS. As with toxic waste, they all bring harm. We begin to comprehend the true cost when we follow drug users through their wasted lives and through their criminal activities." Looking even closer we can see "their lost productivity, their arrests, trials, and incarcerations, their illegitimate, abandoned and abused children."[97]

We need to find out what the gangs do, how they provide a feeling of community and belonging, and do it better.[99]

In cases where someone keeps committing crimes whether under the influence or not, more extensive rehabilitation programs need to be implemented. Currently, most jails/prison situations are warehousing prisoners. But there is concrete proof that doing an in-prison rehabilitation program, counseling, job training, greatly reduces the recidivism rate. Combining the in-prison rehabilitation/job training programs with a guarantee of sobriety after release from jail, would be an unbeatable combination. The implementation one simple therapeutic technique, the teaching of T.M. (transcendental meditation) to prisoners so they could relax and not get so stressed out when things go bad, resulted in reducing repeat offenses by 40%.[126] If a band-aid does that much, think what we can do if we really treat the wound.

GIVE ME YOUR HUNGRY, YOUR POOR - AND I'LL LOCK THEM UP

Jerome Miller is the director of the Alexandria, Virginia based National Center on Institutions and Corrections.[110, 111] He said that our jails are filled mostly with homeless vagrants, petty thieves, domestic abusers. Many inmates are alcoholic or mentally ill. Miller referred to the Clarke County Nevada criminal justice system excess. Excesses which are repeated in jails across the nation.

Miller maintained that the jail populations could be reduced by a third to a half by halting harassment arrests of the homeless, by lowering bail and/or releasing more people from jail on their own recognizance. He said we lock up many people the criminologists call America's truly disadvantaged "rabble class." This is a group that turns out to be predominantly black males, and poor. Some say the jails are a modern day version of the 18th century poorhouse. We are slipping back through the centuries to our lowest, worst times. Shame on America!

When Jerome Miller was Director of Youth Services in Massachusetts twenty years ago, he closed the juvenile detention centers. Then he spent the money that had been used to run the centers on alternative, community-based care programs. He reduced the number of youths locked up in institutions from 2,000 to 40. The result, a few years later, was a huge drop in the adult prison population. Many adult offenders had previously come from the alumni of the juvenile justice system.[111]

When the young hoodlums were rehabilitated, they didn't graduate to adult crime. Miller said that if moves were made "to unwind" the juvenile incarceration system, the results would be that "we divert future crime waves and soon dampen the nation's prison-building boom, and the incarceration craze in which we now imprison young black males at four times the rate of South Africa."

Miller speculated that there probably are going to be 10% to 15% of the kids in juvenile facilities who have committed violent crimes who will need a secure facility, and a hard focus on their long-term rehabilitation.

NOT EVERYONE NEEDS LONG TERM REHABILITATION

Programs that work are those that provide structured social support. It is necessary for these youths to learn discipline, but this is best done through mentors, counselors, big brothers and peers. Young people also need a supportive, nurturing, disciplined physical setting - an 'extended family' sanctuary off the street.[111]

"The bottom line is that we know with certainty that these personalized, decentralized but systemic approaches increase young people's self-esteem, help them stay in school, get employable, avoid drugs and crime. They don't work for every youth, but they work for enough to make a stunning difference if we tried them comprehensively."

The article concluded, "Compared with America's prevailing approach to these young people - indifference, fear, then incarceration and criminalization - there really ought to be no contest."[111]

Jerome Miller's program was proven to work in Massachusetts. That program should be combined with a long, hard follow-up or long "tail," to guarantee sobriety. If that were done, the result would be an intervention combination which would be guaranteed success.

Evidence shows that even the hard-core addicted can be sobered up. There may be more residual damage to their bodies and to their brains. Recovery time may be longer. Their attempts at recidivism will be more concerted. They may require a few more cycles through the initial detox process. They may require a lengthy group based educational anti-drug awareness program before their denial/resistance is finally broken down.

They may have to be constantly watched by their sober buddies for quite awhile before they realize that their fellow citizens really want them to be sober. After awhile, they themselves will also recognize that it is the best thing for them to be sober. The person under the influence does not feel it is in anybody's best interest, not his or society's, for him to stop taking these wonderful substances that make him feel so good.

SANCTUARY TRAUMA

We can't afford to **not** sober up our substance abusing citizens. Our whole world is becoming more dangerous. Most people know that drugs are almost always involved in the violence. Most people don't see the direct connection, that drugs and the changes they cause in people actually fuel the violence in gangs, random killings and drive-by shootings.

Soon, there won't be enough people to fix the cars, nobody will go to trade school, or their work will be too sloppy to hold up. We need to make a firm commitment to pass on civilization to the next generation. The increasing ruthlessness in America's streets and in America's homes proves our efforts to do so now are woefully inadequate.

The most dangerous place for the American child today is in the American family. Sanctuary trauma must stop. Sanctuary trauma is when children suffer trauma in a place that should have been safe. These are places like their own home, sometimes their church and more and more frequently, their school. As we have seen, most of the abusers of these children were drunk or loaded at the time of the commission of the abuse.

Any costs for an involuntary sobriety program will quickly be refunded to society in many ways. As higher numbers of sober people walk the streets, there will be less need for costly jails, heavy law enforcement and funerals of the innocent. Psychologists have proven that we can change attitudes, we can change behavior. Advertisers are also well aware of that fact. But you can't talk a drug addict into getting sober with a thirty-second television spot.

The "Sober Forever" involuntary sobriety program will use many standard therapeutic intervention/rehabilitation techniques. The already available voluntary sobriety programs will need to be used just once for each participant. The same people will not have to be recycled through expensive programs over and over. They will **not** slide back into drugs. We won't let them. We'll be watching them too closely. They will not be allowed to relapse.

The "Sober Forever" Program's foundation is intense follow-up. Lack of this intense follow-up is the primary weakness of almost all existing sobriety programs as extensive research has documented (see Chapter Two). The laws to run such a program are already in place. Even so, there may be tremendous opposition to such a program. Opposition may come from very unexpected sources. If everybody were sober, many people whose living depends on illegal drugs in one way or another would not favor this program. For example, the economies of whole counties in Northern California are fueled by their cannabis crops.[94]

The first of the twelve steps in the Alcoholics Anonymous and Narcotics Anonymous programs is to recognize that one's life has become unmanageable because of substance abuse. It is recognized by these organizations that, without substance abuse, one's life can become manageable again. Perhaps still very difficult, but manageable. Part of the "manageable" means, as has been mentioned repeatedly in this book, that illegal and violent acts virtually cease once the substance abuser is sober. The vast majority of illegal and violent acts today, in the adult and juvenile population, are committed by substance abusers.

"WE HAVE MET THE ENEMY AND THEY IS US"

These substance abusers committing crimes are our children, brothers or sisters, our husbands or wives and sometimes our parents. That's the whole point of this book. Already quoted in Chapter One was Walt Kelly's Pogo who said, "We have met the enemy and they is us." This is more true now than ever before. If the enemy is not ourself looking at a dope fiend in the mirror very often it is someone we dearly love.

Many of these loved ones we tried to stop loving because loving them hurt too much and cost too much. There are groups to help with this process called "Tough Love." Parents at the end of their rope, with out of control children, have their children taken in by other group members. But if that still doesn't work, the group backs you up and gives you moral support if you have to throw your substance abusing children out into the streets. Many parents have had to take that drastic step because their children's substance abuse had made their life unmanageable.

Let's stop getting tough with our children. Let's stop throwing them into the street. There are over two million homeless teenagers already. Let's sober them up instead. We can have our babies back. But we have to take them back. Sometimes kicking and screaming on their way to sobriety.

Some people say "Yes, we wish that we could put the drug addict and substance abusers into treatment programs, if only there was money to do it." They want to shoot the drug dealers or at least lock them up for the rest of their lives. But the dealers, especially at the middle levels of the drug cycle, are almost all addicted themselves. They get money from their sales to supply their own habits.

Guess what is the most rapidly developing multi-level marketing plan in America today. Hint: It isn't Amway. It's drug dealing. By signing up or addicting ten friends or neighbors in your sales network, your own drugs are paid for. When they in turn each sign up ten more, their drugs are paid for. Then your profits go up because you have moved more "product." Of course, you get a percentage (as in all multi-level marketing programs) of the sales of all those in the marketing tiers below you.

Drug dealers at the highest echelons are smarter and fewer of them are substance abusers. They justifiably should be punished. But for each one now being locked up, another drug dealer takes his place. The dealers highest in the hierarchy get the least time in jail because they can turn in somebody else and cut a deal. There is very little difference between the middlemen dealers and their clients. Once sober, these middlemen will stop dealing illegal drugs. If nobody is using and dealing drugs, the higher echelon drug suppliers will be out of business.

DOPE DEALER NEEDED: APPLY IMMEDIATELY

The monetary rewards of dealing drugs are so great there will always be someone ready to take the risk of dealing drugs no matter how many people we lock up. Those street sweeps of drug addicts and dealers that so impress the public and make flashy lead stories on the 10 O'clock news flood the criminal justice system and clog the courts and jails. But others also watch the 10 O'clock news and to them, news that 81,000 dope dealers were taken off the streets was like seeing a big sign saying [47] **"HELP WANTED! DOPE DEALER NEEDED. SHORT HOURS, HIGH PAY, EXCITING WORK BUT SOME RISKS. APPLY IMMEDIATELY."** The best way, no, the **only** way to put the dope dealers out of business is to steal their customers from them. We will do this by sobering up America. The only way to keep our law enforcement personnel honest is to have no one buying drugs. That way, the astronomical amounts of money now tempting our policemen will not exist. Some officers in the Coast Guard, F.B.I., C.I.A., and most other law enforcement agencies have been bought off or have gone bad because of the monetary temptations.[43, 102]

Those whose lives have been ruined by substance abuse and who have been turned into monsters weren't born that way. If drugs turned our children and the boy next door into monsters, once we rescue them from dope they will be monsters no more.

The proposed involuntary sobriety program is **not** a program of alcohol prohibition. No plans are being made to usher in a rebirth of prohibition. No plans are being made to limit alcohol sales, to close down bars and liquor stores. Drugs should remain illegal. But as far as the consumers of alcohol are concerned, only the people who have gotten into trouble because of their alcohol abuse will be enrolled in involuntary sobriety programs. Who are these people? They are the ones who have exhibited their inability to consume alcohol without engaging in problematic, destructive behavior. They are the drunks we have seen in countless episodes of "Cops," slurring in the doorway while their wives stand in the background wiping blood from their noses. The usual advice from the police officer: "Calm down, go sleep it off. We don't want to have to come back out here tonight."

No more! It will become: "Congratulations, you have just enrolled yourself in our 'Sober Forever" Program. You get a free night of lodging and you get to go to your first meeting in the morning. And if you come back sober to your next meeting tomorrow night and to the other meetings every night after that for awhile you won't have to go to jail."

7-ELEVEN SELLING COCAINE AND VITAMINS

There has been a great deal of talk about decriminalization of drugs as a means of easing the burden on the criminal justice system. This author is strongly in support of decriminalization of drugs and alcohol. This doesn't mean "legalization" or easy access to drugs. Marijuana cigarettes should not be available at your corner liquor store, nor should you be able to buy cocaine along with vitamin pills at the 7-Eleven stores. Should we legalize a drug that has caused fathers to rape their daughters and has resulted in parents giving heroin to their crying babies to shut them up? Crack addicts have done these things.

What I mean by decriminalization of drugs and alcohol is that people who are arrested for a minor crime while under the influence should **not** go to jail. Instead, as soon as they have come to the attention of the judicial system they should immediately be enrolled in the "Sober Forever" Program which will guarantee sobriety. They need not proceed any further through the criminal justice system. If kept sober most stop doing crime.

There is ample evidence that even marijuana, which many people believe is relatively harmless, is extremely destructive. Marijuana kills brain cells, kills motivation to succeed and causes failure in school and in life.[9, 114] Marijuana must not be legalized. Alaska has reversed its once liberal stand on marijuana as Alaskans realized that a whole generation of failures was being created.[154]

There are various opinions about methadone maintenance programs. I oppose the use of methadone. In my experience, methadone seems to allow the addicted individual a bit more freedom in his addiction. On methadone, he doesn't need quite as much heroin to achieve the high he desires. I believe that the technology is available to provide current methadone maintenance users with other programs. Visualization procedures, self-hypnosis techniques, relaxation/biofeedback training, are only a few. There are many ways of teaching addicts to help themselves to feel better without chemicals.

Methadone is not "free" as far as bodily damage and mental functions are concerned. For some addicts, methadone has allowed them to reduce or eliminate the consumption of illegal drugs and reduce or stop criminal activity. Methadone users are less likely to spread AIDS through needle sharing. But methadone is not supposed to be used for nonopiate drug users, and the largest proportion of addicts are now addicted to drugs other than opiates. Methadone does not promote individual psychological development or community integration. However, it does stabilize some people and reduces criminal behavior.[97.]

60 MINUTES ON METHADONE

On February 21, 1993, the TV show "60 Minutes" did a show on methadone, focusing on Texas. They reported that addicts are awarded at methadone clinics with a free week's supply of methadone if they recruit another methadone user as a customer. Methadone deaths are on the increase. People who asked the doctors working at the methadone clinics if they could get off methadone were told "No." They were told they would never be able to get off methadone.

It is unknown how many methadone addicts ever got off methadone. It is known that some addicts recognized the methadone trap and did manage to get off. They tried to pick up what was left of their lives but found that their bodies and minds had been badly damaged. Addicts claimed it had ruined their lives and left them with twitches. Methadone is more addictive than heroin. People take methadone not to feel good, but to feel normal.

People were able to go to a number of clinics and get methadone from each one. Some people wanted methadone but did not want to register at a clinic as an addict. Others would sign up at several clinics to get methadone and sell it on the streets for a mark up. Some people who wanted methadone didn't want to sign up at a clinic so they obtained their methadone through a middleman. Some recognition of the dangers and dead end to life that methadone often creates is beginning to occur. A group of worried mothers banded together. They called themselves "Mothers against Methadone." They fought methadone usage because of the damage and deaths it had caused in their children.

Governments across the land are in denial about the realities of the job market. They want to keep doing quick and cheap training for jobs that aren't there. How many "medical receptionists" will fit in a doctor's office? The world of work has become much more complex in the past few years but the government doesn't want to train people for the two years they need to get the jobs that are there.

CHAPTER TEN

MEMORY HEALING

A variety of therapeutic intervention techniques have been referred to or discussed in this book. In Chapter Eight Art Fayer suggested that working through childhood trauma may need in-depth interventions. The fact is that that many different approaches work to help people sober up and stay sober. Numerous studies reviewed and referred to in other parts of this book confirm that this is true **provided** there is a very determined long-term close follow-up.

For those who feel that past traumas need to be fixed/worked through/resolved, there are techniques available for that purpose. One is called "memory healing." What follows is a description of this technique in practice.

CONGRESSIONAL MEDAL OF HONOR WINNER

Tom was 72 years old when I first met him. He had just been discharged, after a ten-day stay, from a hospital where he had almost died. There had been serious problems with his liver, which had stopped working. Tom had retired from the United States Marines somewhere in the 1960's. He was in the Infantry in World War II and in Korea. He had been awarded the Congressional Medal of Honor, two Silver Stars, two Gold Stars and three Purple Hearts.

For the two months just before he had been admitted to the hospital, his days were spent as follows: He would awaken in the morning about 6:00 a.m. Leaning on the walls for support, he would go down to the corner liquor store and purchase a half gallon of vodka. By the end of the day, the vodka would be gone. Those two months had brought him closer to death than any of his other periodic binges, which had occurred for at least thirty years.

One event which could trigger a binge was when someone from the media interviewed him about his Congressional Medal of Honor. Each time they asked him what he had done to earn the Congressional Medal of Honor he would go on a binge because of the old painful memories which were resurrected.

Here's what Tom did to earn the Medal of Honor: In World War II and in Korea he had been attached to units of 200 men who were in the thick of combat. Three different times, twice in World War II and once in Korea, he and his unit were completely cut off. There were four to six survivors during each of these episodes. Tom was always one of the survivors. All three times hordes of enemy troops had continued to attack his position.

He had kept firing his high caliber machine gun. In all three battles the enemy finally retreated. Tom's unit was left decimated. Each of the three times, when the battle was over, there were piles of bodies all around, the bodies of both his fellow soldiers and the enemy. He had seen friends blown apart. Hundreds of people had been cut or blown to pieces in front of his eyes. These were the horrible memories which would periodically reemerge. These were the painful memories that Tom would numb with alcohol, sometimes for weeks at a time, sometimes for months at a time. Then, broken in body, he would try to limp back to some kind of job.

I talked Tom into a relaxed state. First, I had him pay attention to his breathing. Then I suggested that he let different parts of his body relax. I had him take an imaginary walk to his favorite quiet spot. He was in a boat on a lake. He was fishing. When he was ready, I told him that the scene would gradually change to the worst battle he could remember.

In the midst of watching his best friend being blown apart, I suggested he stop all of the action of the battlefield, freeze everybody in position, except himself. Then, I suggested that in this special state of frozen time, he would be able to witness events which he had not seen or perceived at the time the battles had occurred. I suggested that he could now see an angel come down to his friend's mutilated body. The angel lifted his friend's soul out of the body and began to carry his friend's soul upward.

SAYING GOODBYE

I suggested that all over the battlefield, the souls of his other fallen comrades were being lifted by angels. Then, as the angel carrying his friend proceeded upward, his friend looked over at Tom. Tom was standing by his machine gun. Tom motioned so that the angel would carry his friend closer to where Tom stood. The angel stopped briefly. I suggested that though his friend's body was mangled, his friend's soul was still in perfect condition. Everything was there.

I suggested that Tom would have a conversation with this friend. I asked him to tell me what they said to each other. I thought that if he saw his friend's soul leaving his body in good condition, this could act as a memory healing event. I was trying to help Tom superimpose new memories over the old, horrible memories. These new memories were designed to create a 'happy ending' to those horrible events. These new memories were to be superimposed over the old brutally painful memories in order to soften them.

Since Tom had never had a chance to say goodbye to many of these close friends he'd lost on the battlefield, I thought that perhaps this saying goodbye could help. I was surprised at the conversation Tom reported. As his friend's soul stopped in front of him, still in the angel's arms, his friend said, "Goodbye, Tom. I stood beside you as long as I could. Semper fi. We gave it the best we could. I'm sorry to leave you alone. I don't want to leave you alone, but my time is up. I'll see you some day."

Then, his friend was carried off by the angel. Tom was crying. He said he had never cried about those many times he lost all his comrades except when he had been drunk. This was the first time he had ever cried about those tragic events when he was sober.

ALONE IN THE FIELD OF BATTLE

I was surprised at Tom's conversation with his dead buddies. I knew that he had felt a terrible loss over their deaths. It turned out that what had been even more traumatic for Tom in those battles was his feeling that, as his buddies died, he was abandoned and was facing the enemy alone. This feeling of being abandoned in the face of overwhelming odds and danger left more inner terror/trauma than the loss of his buddies. Of course, their loss was also highly traumatic.

I asked Tom how his buddy looked as he floated off with the angel. Tom said, "He seems to be at peace. He seems serene. So did Paul. So did the First Sergeant. I guess they were on their way to soldiers' heaven or something."

I waited while Tom said goodbye to many of his fallen comrades. He talked briefly with them as they were wafted up to heaven. I suggested that Tom follow them to see where they were now, to see what they were doing. I suggested that he make a quick trip to wherever they might be. He said he found them, all 600, with their wives and children at a picnic.

He said, "They've got lots of candy, hot food, a case of beer. I see a Corporal. I can't remember his name. All the lost faces, ice cold cans of beer, women, home. That's why I kept on firing, to defend the home." He talked to a few of the guys at the picnic. They were still young. They invited him to play baseball. He told them he didn't feel up to a game now. But he told them, "I'm getting pretty old. I'll be joining you soon."

I saw Tom for just three more sessions after that. I called him two years later. He had not had anything to drink for over two years. He said he had a different feeling about those horrible war experiences. He said it was still sad, but now he had a feeling of inner peace and serenity about those past events.

Memory healing can be done in a group setting. The individual can take whomever he wants back with him to a traumatic event. Some of my patients have chosen Christ, a guardian angel, or sometimes a good friend. Variations on this "memory healing" method have been utilized in cases of molest and other traumas from childhood.

Laura had been divorced for three years. She came to me because of her drug problem and also because she was having anxiety attacks. She said she could not understand why she was so frightened all the time. I guided her with a series of images into a state of relaxation. Then I suggested that she allow her unconscious mind to take her back to a time when something had happened to produce her fear. She found herself back four years in time when she had been seven months pregnant and still married. She was trying to escape a beating from her husband. He was screaming that he hoped his blows to her stomach would cause a miscarriage. She couldn't get out the door.

TURNING INTO THE HULK

I told her that I was right outside the door and that I had managed to crack the door open slightly. Then I handed her a vial. She was to quickly drink it down. As soon as she did she would undergo a transformation. She would become seven feet tall and weigh 400 pounds. As soon as she had visualized that she had grown that big I asked her what she wanted to do. She looked down at her now small and frightened husband. She didn't answer at first but finally said, "I killed him. I threw him across the room. He bounced off the wall and landed on the couch. He's bleeding."

Her fear went away after that but she still had to do other things to turn her life around. She had to find a support system, some Narcotics Anonymous buddies to help her stay sober. The memory healing that had reduced her fear was an important part of the healing process.

CHOOSING CHRIST TO MUFFLE THE BLOWS

Marion had a dependence on prescription medications: tranquilizers and sleeping pills. She was sixty-eight and said, "I feel like I'm in limbo now, drifting along, just waiting to die." Marion was depressed. She had been so badly abused by her mother at the age of fourteen that a pall had been cast over her whole life. She had her first boyfriend at the age of fourteen. Sometimes they had kissed. Her mother saw them kiss one day and when Marion came into the house her mother greeted her with a coat hanger beating. That beating left her body covered with bloody welts. This was in 1938, before vigorous prosecution for such abuse was more likely.

Marion later married and had children, but she would be forty before her body would first experience sexual or erotic feelings. The beating had taught her that those desires she had begun experiencing at age fourteen were forbidden. There had also been other beatings, until Marion was sixteen. Those beatings taught her to be afraid the rest of her life.

Constant fear had led to constant uncertainty and a feeling that she could never do anything right. That self doubt and self criticism had led to her life long depression. Many people who were verbally and/or physically abused as children continue to be verbally abusive to themselves their whole adult lives. Being put down or insulted constantly, by others or by oneself, is very depressing.

I told Marion she needed to go back to the time of the beating, but this time she wouldn't be alone. I asked her to pick someone to take back with her. She chose Christ to accompany her. I told her that while He was getting her ready to face the beating, Christ was explaining to her the reason she had been given to her mother to raise. "It was your time to come. I made the best match I could. I knew she would not be a perfect mother. But I knew I would always be there with you, to protect you from serious harm."

Then the beating was begun, but this time Christ opened his robe and covered Marion. Though the blows passed through the robe and made contact, they were muffled, the sting was gone, and Christ's presence meant that the healing would be quick.

A week after that memory healing session Marion was driving down the street and saw a young girl near a school.   Marion burst into tears.   She realized that the young girl reminded her of herself at the age of fourteen, and of all that she had lost.   By forcing her to live in terror, Marion's mother had robbed her of her childhood. You can't enjoy growing up, you can't experience all the wonders of life as it unfolds, when you are terrified. Facing her pain, and with Christ there to ease it, Marion had finally let grief and sadness emerge.

She had never cried about those beatings and her lost childhood before. Her tears were the beginning of the healing process. When we are depressed, and finally find out what we are depressed about, then we can start grieving, then we can move on. Marion's depression began to lift. She did learn to sleep and live without her pills.

TANKS BUT NO TANKS

Joyce had been sober for eight years. She worked at a drug rehabilitation center. When the budget was cut they asked her if she could somehow fill in for the people who were let go. She said she would do her best. Her father, like the father of many alcoholics, was almost impossible to please. But Joyce had never stopped trying. Long after her father was dead she kept working hard, hoping that someone, somewhere, would give her the approval she could not get from her father. But for many years she had drank and drugged because that numbed her feelings of failure.

The budget was cut again. Joyce was the only one left at the center. There used to be a staff of five. They asked her if she could somehow fill in some more. One day there were ten people at the reception desk asking for help. Two homeless women with their children needed housing. The phone was ringing again but three people were already on hold. A rough draft of page two of the newsletter appeared on the computer screen in front of her.

Joyce began shaking. She couldn't think. She suddenly felt very frightened. She had to leave. One might say Joyce had a problem saying **No**. She had learned to say **No** to drugs and alcohol, but not to much else.

If you are driving up a mountain on a hot day and the red idiot light comes on saying your car is too hot what do you do? Reaching under the dash and disconnecting the light is not advised. Yet, I meet many people like Joyce who do just that. They ignore all the signals of exhaustion and overload and work until their 'engine' seizes.

"Tell your boss 'I won't do it!' " I ordered Joyce as I banged on the chair.

"I can't!" She said. "I'm afraid!" She had never been able to confront her father either. He was too powerful.

I was taking her back to her job, in fantasy visualizations and role playing, to "fix" or "heal" the memories. Getting her to do now, even in fantasy, what she should have done then, was going to plant new memories. These would replace or at least modify the memories of helplessness. It was unlikely she would ever return to that same job. But someday there would probably be another job. And it was time she learned she didn't need to either drink, drug, or go crazy trying to please people. She could say no. She managed to keep her appointments with me. But she was afraid to even leave her house, let alone go confront her old boss, a man who reminded her of her father.

I asked her to close her eyes. I said, "You are at your home now. You hear a strange rumbling sound outside your window. You go to look. Your best friend is standing there. She beckons for you to come out. Beyond her, in your driveway, is a Sherman Tank. You and your friend go get in the tank. (Joyce was afraid to go out alone). You are driving down the street. The cars get out of your way. You are arriving at your place of work. You demand over the tank loudspeaker that your boss come out. He refuses. You begin to drive the tank into the building.

"The walls collapse, the roof starts to cave in. There he is, on the second floor, hiding behind his desk. Only a small piece of floor is left up there. The rest has collapsed. You rumbled right over it. You aim the tank's cannon at him. He is shaking. You tell him 'I won't do it anymore. I won't take your crap anymore.' You fire a burst of 50 caliber rounds just over his head. He has an accident. His pants are wet. I think he got your message. You can drive home now."

At our next session Joyce said, "I'm not afraid anymore. Oh, maybe sometimes a little. But I have the tank idling in the driveway all the time. The little background rumbling noise it makes is very reassuring. I can get in it and go tell anyone whatever I need to tell them."

Joyce knew there wasn't really a tank there. But the unconscious mind isn't always real bright. You can feed it strange stories and it will believe them. Even if the unconscious mind doesn't really believe them all the way, the effect is the same. You can end up with a feeling of mastery about a past failure situation.

The memory healing technique can also be a way of doing rehearsal for the future. As painful as it was at first, I asked Joyce to spend a few minutes each day visualizing what she would do with that job if she returned. In doing this homework, she prioritized the jobs, did what she could, farmed out as much as she could to volunteers, and **let the rest go**. Letting the rest go, even in her imagination, was the hard part. That involved saying **No** to the newsletter, to the bookkeeping and many other aspects of that job.

Not everyone can jump into this method and use these powerful visualization tools. But when they can, the results and speed of recovery can be incredible. Joyce said that though she had been involved in counseling for years, she felt that this time there was a deep inside healing going on. Healing that went all the way back to her childhood.

GETTING RID OF NIGHTMARES

A variation of memory healing can get rid of nightmares.[72] People suffering with emotional problems seem to have a higher rate of nightmares. Substance abusers who have squelched their bad dreams for years with drugs or alcohol often experience horrible nightmares when they sober up. The growing and healing and pain they put on hold while loaded for all those years comes back with a vengeance.

In a research study 28 people suffering from recurrent nightmares were instructed to 'redream' their nightmares while they were awake. Whenever they got to a scary part of the nightmare, they were to imagine or visualize a completely different outcome. In these new endings to the nightmares, they mastered the situation in one way or another. These new 'dreams' were then rehearsed for several minutes a day. The bad dreams disappeared. Not only that, the subjects felt better overall. Their levels of anxiety and depression decreased markedly. They slept much better.

I have found that the 'waking dreams' technique is especially effective with children who have night terrors. They are good subjects. I start by having them imagine that they are watching their favorite cartoon. Every time a nightmare comes on they are instructed to switch the imaginary channel back to the cartoon. Or, they can enlist the help of anybody they want, from the Ninja turtles to Batman, in their battle against their adversaries. Often, by the second session, the nightmares are gone.

Sometimes after a session or two these children were able to remember that a nightmare had started. But then they had either used a variety of powerful weapons or their super friends had come to their rescue. The result was that the tide of the battle instantly turned and victorious, they quickly returned to sleep. By the third session, the nightmares were usually squelched before they got scary enough to wake up the children.

TALKING TO THE DEAD

Where does psychotherapy end and voodoo begin? What is the dividing line between seances and carrying on a dialogue with the departed? Is one role playing and the other occult? If so, which is which?

Richard wouldn't have been classified by most people as an alcoholic. But there were times, maybe just twice a year, when he had to cancel his whole caseload of patient's because of a nasty hangover. His sister had died 22 years before when he was 18. Without realizing it, he had been experiencing a mild to moderate depression ever since. Such a depression may not prevent you from preparing for an advanced career. Such a depression may not prevent success and recognition.

But depression can cast a pall over everything. Richard always had a feeling he was going to lose something. He drove his wife half crazy checking up on her. He was afraid she would leave him for someone else. She finally did. His wife's leaving increased his levels of depression so much that his work was affected. He was listless, apathetic, and couldn't get going. His thought of ending it all frightened him and brought him into therapy.

His parents were on the cold side. He and his sister had been constant companions and best friends before she died. The grief work over her loss had never been done. People recognize the pain that loss of a child, spouse, or parent can bring. Long term grief over sibling loss as a cause of chronic depression is often over-looked. Even though somewhere in the case file of a patient under treatment a note might read "20 year old female sibling deceased when the patient was age 18."

THE REUNION

I asked Richard to close his eyes. There are thousands of "induction" or relaxation techniques. Some involve breathing. I asked him to listen to his breathing and notice whether the air going in and out made a little whistle. I asked him to pay attention to his chest moving. And to let the air go down deep into the lungs. To use the diaphragm muscle to breathe. Effortless breathing. Then, a walk in the woods to a quiet spot by a stream. A figure approaches from a distance. He can finally see that it is a female. When she is closer he recognizes his sister. He greets her. He hugs her. He tells her he has missed her. By now he is crying. The long pent up tears finally flow.

His sister wipes his tears and comforts him. She tells him she is here. She promises she won't leave him again.

His sister became his guide. He talked to her every day. She gave him advice, about his parents, about the new lady he had started dating, about his practice. In a few months he found new energy. He used some of it to improve his practice. He was seeing more patients. The patients he had were referring more patients to him. They were responding to his new aura of confidence. He used some of his new earnings to buy new updated office equipment. He had meant to do that years ago but just now finally got around to it. How was his sister able to advise him as to what modern pieces of equipment he should buy? She had been dead for many years when this new equipment was invented.

Here is the question: Was he actually in touch with the spirit of his departed sister? Or, did he know his sister well enough to create a wide variety of conversations from his memory bank? And yet, in his visualization sessions, he could hear her voice talking inside his head.

We know visualizations can be startlingly real. Everyone can do it. Unless they've forgotten. The young story teller 'sees' the saloon doors swing open and 'hears' the sheriff say "Black Bart, your days of Crime are over!" He 'hears' the gunshots which follow in his story.

That still doesn't answer the question. Was Richard, and anyone else who talks to their departed loved ones, recreating conversations? Were they making up new dialogues out of their memory banks? Or were they really in touch with that person's spirit? I have never tried to answer that question. A decision as to whether or not they are truly in contact with the spirit of the deceased is not necessary for the technique to work.

Richard had his sister back. His depression lifted. He remarried. This time he wasn't constantly afraid of being abandoned. After three years he found himself carrying on a dialogue with his sister on a very infrequent basis. But he knew she would still be there whenever he needed her. After three years, he was finally able to say goodbye, but a goodbye that left the door open.

THE DOUBLE TECHNIQUE

Psychotherapists are always telling people "Get in touch with your feelings!" You have to know what you are feeling in order to start helping yourself to feel better. But therapists don't always tell you **how** to get in touch with those elusive feelings.   People will often ask themselves "Why do I feel so sad?" Or "Why am I so angry?" Sometimes they will get an answer. But if they don't, there is another way to see behind the many upsetting murmurings of the mind. You start by stopping the search for an answer to the question "Why do I feel so (sad, angry, etc.). **The search is not for the right answer, but for the right question.   When you ask the right question, you will know the answer.**

Imagine there are two of you (The Double). The other you, perhaps the one sitting in the other chair, begins asking you a series of questions. You listen carefully to each question. If nothing happens, you go to the next question. Your body will tell you when your double asked the right question. Then you will have the answer.

I taught a 16 year old girl this technique. One day she had no energy and was "bummed out." Following my instructions, she visualized that her double was asking her questions. The double started with "Are you upset about getting a D on your algebra test?" She felt a little twinge inside. "Are you upset because your mom yelled at you when you came in fifteen minutes late last night?" Another little twinge, this emotional twinge had an angry feeling to it, not depression. More questions.

Finally her double asked her "Are you upset that your older brother is going off to college?" She knew this was a long shot. Lots of times she didn't even like him. He treated her like a little kid. But why did she suddenly start crying? She couldn't stop for ten minutes. She sobbed. Her chest hurt. Suddenly there was peace. The depression was gone. It surprised her to realize that she loved her brother so much and would miss him. Knowledge will set you free. She was now free to write him more than she would have without the dialogue with her 'Double.' She was free to heal the pain of loss by keeping in touch, by talking to him on the phone. She looked forward to his visits home.

ALL ALONE WITH NO ONE TO LOVE YOU

What do you do when you find the answer? That depends, of course, on what you found. In one variation of the 'Double' technique, when you locate the pain and find out what is hurting, you play out a worst case scenario. Once you have faced the very worst you can face reality much easier.

Jerry had left his wife for the sweet young thing who was great in bed but turned out to be a paranoid psychotic. Now all alone, he was waking up at two each morning in a cold sweat. There was fear, and he usually couldn't get back to sleep. I taught him to ask the questions. "Are you worried about money?" That got a strong twinge. Alimony, child support and rent on his little apartment kept him strapped. "Are you worried that your career isn't progressing as well as you like? Are you upset that you got passed by on that last promotion?" That question produced a strong twinge. But it was a twinge of disappointment with some anger. It still didn't tap into the raw fear that was jolting him awake.

How can you dig in deep enough to find the right question? I told Jerry "Get wild. Pick stupid questions out of the blue. Absurd things. Even if they are a million miles off." So finally one early morning he asked himself the stupid question, the one he knew could not be true: "Are you afraid that you will be alone forever and no one will ever love you again?" What a stupid question. But why was it that Jerry couldn't stop crying for a half hour after he asked that question? Then he fell asleep. He had his first good night of sleep in months.

Is it just by chance that you almost always come up with the right question if you keep asking questions for awhile? Of course not. But if you are persistent, your unconscious mind, which already knew the answer, will finally let you ask the right question. It can help if you let yourself get a little wild or absurd. You have to let go a little to let the right question emerge.

THERE IS NO FATE BUT THAT WHICH WE MAKE

No matter how great is the fear that keeps you awake it is almost always better to face that fear than to keep it hidden. Behind many fears is the big question: "Am I loved? Will I be loved?" Facing that pain of past losses and fear of future abandonments turns the fear into sadness and grief. Once the grieving is done you can rest. That doesn't mean the grieving is permanently over. You may have to do more grieving the next night. But each time the process goes more quickly. Sleep comes more quickly.

The next night Jerry tried my advice and did a 'worst case scenario.' This was after the same question about being alone had caused another burst of tears. He told me at his next session "There I was, 92 years old, in a wheelchair, in a nursing home. I was sitting in the hall by the phone. The phone rang. I struggled to rise up out of my wheelchair to reach the phone. I was old. I couldn't stand up. I couldn't reach the phone. My whole body was shaking. An attendant came along and answered the phone. He talked for a second then looked down at me as I was groping toward the phone. The attendant said, 'It isn't for you.' I sank back into my wheelchair destroyed."

"How did that make you feel?" I asked.

"At first, horrible," Jerry answered. "But then I realized that I'm not 92. I'm not in a wheelchair. I'm not in a nursing home. I might be someday. But now, I'm 42. I don't have to be alone. I can do something about it. After that I slept good again. And the next day when I got up I called up my kids and sort of badgered them into going camping with me. Then I called up and put an add in the singles column. I realized I didn't have to be alone."

In "Terminator Two: Judgment Day" the phrase "There is no fate except that which we make" figures heavily. This may not always be true. But identifying what is behind our unhappy or scary feelings, however we do it, is the beginning. From there we can start taking whatever action is necessary to feel better. The nice thing is that we have done all of this without numbing substances.

We need to teach Americans how to love their children so we don't have a society full of hurting, lonely, lost people. The average family has eleven minutes of conversation a day. Seven minutes of that is instructions. This is the average family. In the substance abusing family we get more loneliness, isolation, and terror. Children early in life learn to medicate that deep feeling of longing and abandonment. These are the feelings that came from the times mom or dad got drunk or loaded and weren't there to respond to them and make them feel like people.

Recovery is waking up from a long sleep and becoming aware of your world, your body, your different body parts. Recovery is tuning into yourself. An Ojibwa prayer: "I step into the day. I step into myself. I step into the mystery."

The search is not for the right answer, but for the right question. When you ask the right question, you will know the answer.

CHAPTER ELEVEN

THE RETURN FROM HELL: THE SOBER FOREVER PROGRAM

It is time to begin a drug rehabilitation program that will reverse the bad American habit of locking up more of its citizens than any country in the world. The involuntary sobriety program proposed here will cost a tenth to a fiftieth of the cost of using jail to solve America's drug/crime problem. It is time to begin taking an enlightened humanitarian and workable approach to the substance abuse problem. It is time to stop being the only nation in the world that is trying to solve its mental health and social problems with jails.

It is time to start an all encompassing program and prove that sobering up substance abusing criminals reduces crime, saves lives, saves families, boosts the economy and will save the inner cities from decay. It is time to help each member of our great nation to become the best that they can be. Across the nation, between 50% to 85% of all people arrested for **anything** are under the influence of alcohol or drugs at the time of their arrest. As more people have become substance abusers, the crime rate has escalated across the land.

DRUGS ARE ROTTING THE AMERICAN DREAM

Sobering up substance abusing criminals stops five out of six of them from committing further crimes. This assumes, of course, that once they are sober, we keep them sober. As a nation, we are poised to launch into a new spiral of prison building. It is time to prove to the nation and to the world that an involuntary sobriety program can reverse most of the horrors that have been rotting the soft underbelly of the American dream.

The first state or county in the United States to accept the challenge and put into practice this involuntary sobriety program will have implemented the final solution to the drug wars. That city or county will be the first to reap the inevitable rewards of such a program. Remember? If nobody is buying drugs, nobody is selling drugs. And the drug wars will be over. And we will have won that final battle. We will have won back the hearts and souls of our addicted brothers.

If we do not control this plague that has beset our nation, where are we headed? Movie buffs know what many film-makers predict our future to be. They picture a bleak and dangerous world filled with substance abuse and crime. One such movie was "Future Kick" starring Don "The Dragon" Wilson. In most of these movies depicting a future drug-crazed lawless society, people are usually eating okay. The movie makers are wrong because when things get that out of control the food chain will be disrupted. People will be starving. The water will be polluted. The sewers will no longer work. Those not murdered will die of starvation or disease.

"SOBER FOREVER" OPENS FOR BUSINESS

Let's conjure up another future. One with a happy ending. A county somewhere in America has overcome all the detractors. The program is a **"GO."** Somehow the voices of those who said it would never work, and that it would cost too much, have been temporarily stilled. This state or county has decided to call their involuntary sobriety program the "Sober Forever" Program.

The "Sober Forever" Program has managed to win out against many competitors for the use of a phased-out military base. The base won't be turned into a condominium development, a camping ground or even a new university. At least not right now. Everything is already in place: the pool, the shops, the theater, the chapel. Yes, the chapel, too. It might help if we can teach some of these substance abusers to pray. Or at least get in touch with their higher power, whatever form they envision that to be.

Many special interest groups have proposed new usages for the military bases being phased out. These bases would make excellent locations for a nation-wide network or "Sober Forever" Centers. If we are going to really get serious about our drug problem, we need facilities to house and treat very large numbers of people. The barracks can house hundreds to thousands, depending on the size of the base. We have to teach our addicts how to have fun without drugs. For that purpose there are bowling alleys, a gym, pool, theater, hobby shops, auto repair shops for career training. And again, a chapel for prayer.

Our first clients are arriving. There's Harry. Remember the fellow from Chapter Three who beat up his girlfriend and ran off without paying for his gas? He'll eventually have to pay all that back, including his girlfriend's medical bills. He couldn't do that if he had gone to jail. He can if he sobers up. He has chosen to take part in the "Sober Forever" Program as a diversion. That means that if he participates in this program he will be "diverted" from the usual series of legal steps: He will not have to face prosecution and jail.

THE FIRST ANGUISHED HOWL AFTER GETTING SOBER

It's been said before in this book that getting sober is easy, staying sober is the hard part. I might have lied just a little bit because getting sober isn't always easy either. It will take about seven to ten days for Harry and our first guests to get the drugs or alcohol out of their system. After another week, their ability to process information about themselves and their surroundings will begin to return. By the third week they can begin helping with a plan to keep themselves sober. By this time there are probably at least a few minutes each day when they are not thinking about how nice it would be to get loaded. During this recovery period they won't have to waste time thinking about lawyers and how to beat the rap. As long as they are sober and keep out of trouble there won't be any rap.

They'll spend several hours a day learning about addictions and about themselves. There will be no heavy confrontations about denial or how they screwed up their

lives.   They will be helped through the detox process.
That's the time when the body and the mind are both
screaming because of having to face life without the
numbing chemicals.   There is a powerful rebound effect
that can go on for a long time during and after withdrawal.
When substance abusers give up their drugs and alcohol
they go from "everything is cool" to "everything hurts
and is too loud!"

The body's sensory system has been cranked up to
the highest possible volume to compensate for the numbing
caused by the drugs. It is like yelling at someone at the top
of your lungs in order to be heard over a passing train. If
you're still yelling after the train passes your voice is
deafening.   The drugs and alcohol muffled the body so it
began to shout louder and louder.   When the drugs and
alcohol were gone the body was still shouting.   Off
chemicals, every sound, sensation and feeling becomes
magnified a thousandfold.   This is the time the substance
abuser in withdrawal needs support from others who can
guarantee that this emotional roller coaster won't last
forever.   They can promise this because they have already
gone through it.   Quite often most of the staff at
drug/alcohol rehabilitation centers are substance abuse
addicts in recovery.

LEARNING NEW SOLUTIONS TO OLD PROBLEMS

There will be some easy-to-watch videos that give
a thousand reasons and a hundred ways to stay sober.
Newly sober brains can't process a lot of information.
Newly sober brains are crying "Numb me again, knock me
out."   They will have to hear the "Sober is better"
message more than a few times before they believe it in
their hearts.

They will learn how to relax their bodies.   They
will have fear and anger. These emotions can be tamed -
with practice. And with the practice, comes growth. They
will be taught to feel better without using drugs.   They
will learn to have fun without drugs or alcohol.   The
'enlightened sober' are those who were never addicted to
drugs or alcohol. They are convinced that anyone with an

ounce of will power could quit anytime they see that addiction and substance abuse causes problems. They often see substance abuse as this terribly destructive experience that wastes people's lives.

But to our clients, drugs were a problem only when they couldn't get them. Drugs were a solution to all their other problems. Poor? Get loaded. Got a broken heart? Get loaded. Drugs can make all the other problems go away, at least for awhile.

Our clients used drugs to feel good. When they accidentally sobered up long enough to see how bad things had gotten, what did they do? They got loaded, and quickly. The more drugs they took the less they took care of themselves. The more drugs they took the worse things got around them. They did not want to face the disasters their lives had become. The first thing the junkie wants to do when he gets sober is to quickly get high so he can forget.

Others who have sobered up and gotten their lives back will share their experiences. Our clients will listen to their new buddies talk about why they wanted to get sober. There are Bradshaw videos on the dysfunctional family. It is good to understand your roots. Our clients will go to group meetings. There they will be encouraged to face themselves and their fears.

Alcoholics Anonymous has a saying, "Go to ninety meetings in ninety days and if you are not satisfied, your misery will be cheerfully refunded." Narcotics Anonymous and Alcoholics Anonymous are good programs but they are voluntary. Few people stick with those programs. Those who do get their lives back. The "Sober Forever" Program is designed to give back the lives of substance abusers who haven't even asked for them back.

I DON'T HAVE A PROBLEM

We can anticipate that almost everyone in our program will tell everyone else they don't really belong there - they don't have a problem. They could quit drinking and drugging any time they wanted. Besides, they could handle the drugs, though they admit that sometimes others can't. Substance abusers live and die in denial of their addictions.

I often find just cause to tell my clients, "You're still floating down that river in Egypt."

"What river is that?" They ask, unsuspectingly.

"De Nile," I chortle.

Our clients will learn rage reduction techniques. Substance abuser's tempers flare over minor issues. Over half the homicides are committed by people who are loaded at the time. They beat up on their wives and children for no reason. They might have thought they had a reason but it is not a reason that we can see or understand. They will learn guided imagery and relaxation techniques. When they get angry, nervous and frightened, they will be able to calm their bodies down instead of looking for a needle or a bottle. Eventually, they will learn to let their mind drift into and through the old pains. The sting of the old traumas, the old beatings, the abandonments will gradually fade away. Chapter Ten on Memory Healing elaborated on this technique.

Many of our clients have already been through one or more substance abuse rehab programs. These programs can vary in length from three days to three years. On their graduation day, this usually happened: "Adios amigo, good luck, come and see us if you have a problem!" But most of the graduates were high within a week or so because there was no follow-up and they could see no reason to stay sober when they hurt so much.

LIFE MEMBERSHIP IN THE "SOBER FOREVER' PROGRAM

Everyone has heard of organizations like the Mafia in which, once you join, you are a member for life. Some street gangs are like that. "Sober Forever" is also that kind of club. We love you! We want to keep in touch! After you have tested clean for a couple of years, maybe we'll only need to see you once a year for a few more years. If you decide to quit our "Sober Forever" club you will be in for a surprise. We will come find you and explain that you joined up for life. If you have a problem understanding this and are under the influence when we find you this will happen: We will take you to a quiet place for a few days so you can think about it. We're not going to revoke your probation and lock you up for five years because you slipped once or even twice.

Unfortunately, locking people up for a long time after one slip is a common practice in many parts of our current legal system. At what point do we say "This one is hopeless. All our efforts have failed." This is common in almost all programs. In the "Sober Forever" Program we will **never** say that and we will **never** give up. Not once. There is no one we cannot save. Some will just take longer than others.

In the "Sober Forever" program the detox time will vary with each individual.   Some of those just arrested for a first offense who are not too strung out on drugs may be able to go home and detox. They will come back the next day for their first meeting and testing. Others may only require a 24 hour detox experience. Still others, deep into drugs for many years, may need a good 30 days before their minds begin to clear. Then we may be able to start helping them to think of a place to live where they can stay sober.

Someone who can return to a sober environment, a wife, a job, may not need to go to detox at all. They just need to show up the next day. Someone from a ghetto gang may not be able to go home at all. Maybe never. Or at least not until his whole neighborhood is supportive of sobriety.

If our ghetto gang member doesn't like our barracks and he can arrange it, he can move out and rent a place with some sober buddies. He and his buddies will still have to come back to the sober center several times a week to talk and to test.

The days following the initial detox experience in the "Sober Forever" Program will be a lot different than most detox programs. Usually you come back for a post-graduate "staying sober" meeting in a week or so, **if you feel like it**. After graduation from the detox portion of the "Sober Forever" program, the conversation will go something like this: "You're going back to work tomorrow, is that right? You'll be at work from 7:00 a.m. until 5:00 p.m.   Then we'll see you at 6:00 p.m. for your first meeting. If you don't show up to give us a urine sample and to learn more about why you should stay sober, we'll come and get you.

"We'll keep looking for you until we find you. When we do find you, you'll have to come spend a few more days with us before we can let you go the next time. We will keep you until we feel good about the chances of your coming back. All we want is about ten hours a week of your time. You'll go to group meetings and give us a urine sample a couple times a week. The other 158 hours a week are yours. You can do just about anything legal that you want to as long as you stay sober during your 158 hours.

"When you leave here sober, you may want to get loaded the minute you walk out the door. If it turns out that you can't be sober out there, that means you'll have to be sober in here. Your freedom will be limited until you decide, in one of your trips outside, that sober is the way to go. We certainly hope it doesn't come to that. What you must understand is that you can no longer choose whether you want to be sober or not. Your only choice is to decide **where** you are going to be sober, in here or out there."

NO MORE WAITING LISTS FOR TREATMENT

There are waiting lists all across America to get into drug treatment. The people who are most in need of sobering up haven't even thought of putting themselves on a waiting list. By the time their name comes up, the ones who are on the waiting list have often changed their minds. They have decided to get loaded. Usually they think, "just one more time." Many thousands of clients could be processed through just one military base-turned-sobriety center each year. The waiting lists for treatment to get sober will be a thing of the past.

There are National Guard Armories in most cities. With federal approval, these armories could be meeting places for program participants. Just how committed is the federal government to the war on drugs? Enough to provide program space to save our money-strapped local governments the expense of meeting space rental? Even if the abandoned military bases are used for the initial detox phase of the program, they might not be as accessible as the armories for near daily meetings. So far, about 95 out of every 100 dollars our government spends on the war on drugs has been thrown away on attempts to eliminate the supply and a pittance on reducing demand.

The "Sober Forever" Program is voluntary in this way: Our clients can voluntarily stay out of jail by meeting the conditions of their probation. These conditions specify, first of all, that they cannot hang around with substance abusers. People who get sober and stay sober almost always have to 'change their playmates and their playgrounds.' They cannot live with or near people who are abusing substances. They cannot have any kind of intoxicating substance, drugs or alcohol, in their systems at any time. They have to go to meetings to work on their sobriety. They cannot be alone. Man is not meant to be alone. People getting sober need a "community," a support system, a place to live and hang out that includes other people. And everyone there must be sober. They have to test to prove their sobriety.

If they refuse to abide by these conditions, that is when the program is no longer voluntary. That's when the short stay in involuntary incarceration begins. Higher legal standards of housing must be maintained in involuntary incarceration, which makes it much more expensive. It can cost as little as $3,000 a year to house someone with some sober roommates. It can cost up to $60,000 a year to lock them up in prison.

Again, here is the choice: "Give us ten hours a week and stay sober. If you can't do that, you will give us **all** 168 hours a week of your time in a high security facility. This will go on until you to decide that you are ready to be sober outside."

A variety of living arrangements will be permissible for those who are staying sober, coming to meetings, and working the program. They might live in barracks, at home, or with some sober buddies. It's when the "voluntary" involvement doesn't work, when they don't show up for meetings and testing, that the involuntary, high security system of jail or prison kicks in. Hopefully, this phase of involuntary custody will be brief: a week, ten days. Not the one to five years substance abusers now often face for getting loaded.

A FEW GOOD MEN

It would be nice to keep a few Marines at our sobriety center, a couple watching the front gate. Not necessarily to keep people in, but to keep unwanted visitors out. We don't want five or fifty gang members hanging around trying to entice one of their buddies to come back to their gang. We don't want people trying to sell drugs to our clients. We don't want to cut out visitation from families. If they earned them, our clients will be able to go out on passes. If they don't come back, we will go get them. If they come back loaded, the next pass will take longer to earn. If they leave without a pass, we will go get them and then they spend a little time in a higher security facility.

We'll tell our clients "If you really want to see your old buddies from the gang, have them come join you in the "Sober Forever" Program. And when you are all sober, you can rent a house together. You can work on your sobriety together. You can get a life. And if you think that selling and using dope and running the streets and dying young is a life, you won't think that anymore after you have been with us for awhile."

DRUGS IN THE SOBRIETY CENTER

Why will all the program participants and all the staff be given periodic drug screenings? Because we want to be sure. Most of the staff will be ex-substance abusers. We don't want them slipping back under pressure. Brand new clients will test twice a week. The frequency of testing will decrease with time in the program. The less frequent testings will be on a random basis. Not even the staff will ever know when they are to be tested. That way they can't just sober up periodically for their test. Strange behavior, mood swings, jaw twitches, or other signs of possible substance abuse can trigger a test.

What are we going to do to make absolutely sure nobody ever smuggles a single drug into our program - not even a microdot of LSD on page 425 of the bible their mother brings them? To be truthful, we're not going to even try to do much to keep drugs out. We will have some standard security measures. There will be at least a cursory screening of visitors. But there is no way, in virtually any institution in the United States, to keep drugs out.

Are we going to inspect the anal and vaginal cavities of every female visitor? If we don't, some drugs will get in. Will we inspect every anal cavity of every male visitor? If we don't, some drugs will get in. Will we make every male or female visitor vomit or in some other way empty their stomach on the way in? If we don't, some drugs will get in.

Loving mother birds regurgitate food for their babies. Once they get inside, loved ones of our clients will vomit up the little plastic baggies of dope which they swallowed just outside the front door to bring in to their sick puppies. They have been told how bad their loved one inside is "hurting."

We can't stop the dope coming into our prisons or even into the "Sober Forever" Program any more than we can stop the dope coming across our borders. We shouldn't entirely stop trying to catch those smuggling dope into America, or into our "Sober Forever" Program. But the effort should be minimal, tokenistic. Why? Because, as we have found out over and over, reducing supply doesn't work. It doesn't really matter how much dope is smuggled into America or into our "Sober Forever" Program. What matters is how much dope is used. If nobody is using dope, nobody will smuggle in dope. People stopped making button hooks and buggy whips when people stopped buying button hooks and buggy whips.

We will know when our clients or staff have taken some dope because they will test positive. When that happens, any number of actions could occur. There might be a move to a high security facility. There might be an intense 24 hour marathon meeting to explore the pain that caused the relapse. There will not be a big inquisition to find out how the dope got in. That's a waste of time.

Staff members who slip become clients again until the relapse is worked through. When they go back to staff they will continue for months to test twice a week on a random basis.

Our "Sober Forever" Program will monitor our client's moves. One no-show, one failed urine test, triggers action. This action still might not involve the courts, police, or probation officers. Ten sober buddies might be able to talk to the guy who slipped into coming back into the program. They might all go to the desert for a soul searching survival weekend to study the ancient ways of becoming a warrior.

THE RIGHT TO PRIVACY

We must guarantee the right to privacy when people are giving their urine samples, right? It's a violation of the law to have someone actually watch the urine leave the body, right? One of the problems with this line of thinking is the D.F.F. or Dope Fiend's Friend. This device is marketed in underground circles under various names. It is a simple contraption, all plastic, so it doesn't show up on metal detectors. It consists of a plastic bag you fill with "clean" or drug-free urine donated by someone who does not abuse substances. You strap it to your chest or underarm. A plastic tube exits the bag and, in the case of males, is routed under the penis. There it is held in position by clear, easy-off tape. With females, the D.F.F. is even less detectable.

Somewhere on the line, by the bag, or perhaps at the end of the plastic tube, is a petcock or valve that releases the urine flow. A dope fiend can stand in open view with his penis in his hand and appear to be giving a urine sample. This sample appears to come from his penis. In actuality, the urine flows from a clear plastic tube a fraction of an inch from the tip of his penis.

One lab became suspicious once that a D.F.F. was involved when a male's urine sample showed that he was pregnant.

Should mirrors be installed in the sample collection area so that same sex observers can make sure that the urine comes from the client? Perhaps not in all cases.   But it must be remembered that every possible loophole will be used by substance abusers to get high. Remember that pain they are trying to numb? Remember that their idea of fun is nodding out and being barely aware of what's going on?

Program participants will have to sign a consent form allowing for this close visual monitoring of their donation of a urine sample. Also, we don't want their clean and sober buddy taking the test for them. So, the people giving the test need to know the people taking the test. We don't want a clean sample that had been brought to the test in a small one shot whiskey bottle. When the tests are private this is the standard device drug abusers use to test clean. They haven't had to rely very heavily yet on the D.F.F. In most cases, they can simply remove the little one shot bottle from their mouth or some other hiding place and pour the contents into the collection cup. They are seldom watched.

What if someone refuses to have even a same sex observer watching their privates during the collection of the urine sample? No problem! We'll go for a blood test instead.   The program participant will have to somehow pay the higher cost of a blood test. He/she cannot just bring us a blood sample. It has to come out of their arms.

What if they refuse to do either? What if they say that one procedure invades privacy and the other causes panic because they have this irrational fear of needles? That means that they are very determined to get high. It also means that they have violated probation. They must now go to a higher security situation or facility where the chances of getting high are lower, or hopefully, nonexistent.

DRUGS IN JAIL

Why will there be urine or blood testing of our clients even as they are rotating through our most secure prisons or jails? The sad truth is that in most of our supposedly secure prisons drugs are easily available for a price. The sad truth is that some guards make four times their guard salary in their drug business. The only way to stop people from selling drugs, even in our prisons, is to stop people from taking drugs.

Why will it be necessary to have an independent lab, with no contacts with the prison or guards, to enter the prison to do drug tests? Not all guards are crooked and running dope rings, obviously. But those who are will guarantee clean tests for their 'clients.' The prisoner's file and photograph will be matched with the prisoner being tested. This will prevent substitution of a sober prisoner for a user. Direct observation will prevent the use of the D.F.F. (The Dope Fiend's Friend) or other devices used to produce a clean sample. Samples collected in the prison will go directly into a case. This case is to be held at all times by the lab technician from the time of his entry into and exit from the prison. Those producing 'dirty' samples will be transferred either within the prison or to another facility where clean tests are almost always obtained.

Drastic changes must occur in the jails. The jails must become civilized. They can be. The therapeutic programs such as "Stay'n Out" cost only $4,000 a year per inmate but save millions of dollars in other costs **per prisoner**. Every prisoner must have access to this rehabilitation. We know it works. Wardens need to be given leeway on the length of sentences. They need to be given rewards for graduating people back into society who sober up, go to work and do not get rearrested.

Wardens need to have the freedom to cut ten year sentences to two years. They need to provide intensive drug rehabilitation during those last two years using the "Stay'n Out" model. They need to be able to use the savings on guards and jail space to launch massive follow-up programs for their graduates. They need to keep a very close watch on each and every man who leaves prison. They need to have teams who will quickly bring back to prison those who have slipped. Additional brief episodes of in-prison treatment will be provided for those who wavered in their determination to be sober.

If the wardens we now have are unable or unwilling to make these drastic changes, the whole prison system needs to be put out to bid to private contractors. These contractors will run "for profit" prisons.   Their contracts will either be renewed or taken over by others depending on who rehabilitates the highest percentage of prisoners. That means who succeeds in producing the most clean and sober, law abiding, working Americans.   Sorry, the drinking days of those joining the "Sober Forever" Program are over.   They will not be allowed to simply substitute a legal drug for an illegal drug.   Alcoholics are perfectly capable of extreme acts of violence and of ruining their lives and the lives of everyone around them just as are drug addicts.   Clients enrolled in the "Sober Forever" Program will be monitored closely for drugs **and** alcohol.

'VOLUNTARY'   CLIENTS

Many addicts and substance abusers may want to join the "Sober Forever" Program on a voluntary basis. They are welcome! At last there will be no waiting list for those who want help. When they walk in the door we ask them to give us a brief history of their substance abuse. A few minutes after their arrival, their urine is tested. If it is positive for an illegal substance, they are eligible for the program.   But, we want to avoid the problems of an 80% to 95% dropout rate most voluntary programs experience.   So, in just a few minutes after they test positive, the voluntary clients are arrested, booked, and appear before a judge. They plead guilty and are sentenced to probation.

Their first condition of probation is that they participate in, and graduate from, the "Sober Forever" Program. All this will be done through a closed circuit TV system wired into the courtroom. Necessary papers are filled out and faxed back and forth. Only a couple minutes or less of judge time is required for each case. The clogged courts will experience immediate and dramatic relief. The courts and probation officers may never hear of the case again.   Or not until they receive notification somewhere down the road that all the conditions for release from probation have been met. Each voluntary enrollee, as soon as he tests positive, immediately becomes involuntarily enrolled. There is no place in the United States where being under the influence of an illegal substance is not against the law.

The probation departments across the land will **not** monitor "Sober Forever" clients except under certain circumstances. Some 70% to 95% of all people on probation or parole in America are under-monitored even in the very tightest of systems. Most can get loaded and stay loaded for months at a time before anyone does anything. Jeff Dahmer stayed drunk for several years while on probation during his most active killing phase. When the system does finally react, it is often an over-reaction resulting in several years in jail.

THE HAND IN THE COOKIE JAR

If you don't remember Joan and the worst case parenting scenario see Chapter Five. Here is another variation: Mom says, "Keep out of the cookie jar." But she leaves it on the kitchen table, in plain sight, bulging with cookies. We try just one. Nothing happens. We try another. Still nothing happens. We stuff ourselves with them. Still nothing. Until finally one day the order to keep out of the cookie jar has been completely forgotten. We're sitting on the couch munching down cookies and watching TV. Mom comes in. We say "Hi, Mom" and go on munching.

Suddenly we are snatched up off the couch and locked up in our room for five years. If we are 12, we'll be 17 when we get out. We can't go to school, food is brought to us. We'll miss five years of growth experiences. We'll certainly have learned our lesson about keeping out of the cookie jar, right? Probably not. That's not how people change their behavior. In reality, mom would be locked up for child abuse. She would be told that she should have tried a number of different interventions before she went to such drastic measures. She would be told that she could have checked our breath every day for cookies.

There are certain "laws" of learning. This means we learn things in a certain way. If we do something that feels good for years, being brutally punished one time will not be likely to change that behavior. The child should be caught **every time** he does something wrong and then be given a mild punishment. This works much better to change behavior than infrequent strong and vicious punishments. The best way of all to change behavior is to reward the child when he is doing what you want. Why punish him for having a dirty room when praising him for a clean room works so much better? What makes you feel better, doing something you'll get punished for if you don't do it, or praised for something when you do? Obviously, praise feels better than punishment. Children exposed to these techniques start enjoying having a clean room instead of being afraid when it's dirty. Besides, being afraid doesn't mean they will clean that dirty room.

Most of the people employed in some aspect of the criminal justice system operate in the same fashion as our crazy mom. They tell people "Say no to dope." But they don't really do anything to guarantee that people really will say no to dope. Not until they are ready to lock them up for as long as they can. When that time comes they use whatever corner of the jail where there is two feet of room left to bunk down another lost soul on a foam mattress.

We have seen that being locked up for five years doesn't guarantee saying nope to dope. In fact, many petty criminals didn't really get introduced to heavy drugs **until** they went to jail. If mom locked up junior from age 12 to 17 for getting in the cookie jar that's insane. Those are junior's years to learn about the world, to grow into a man. Is there any difference if we lock up someone from age 18 to 23? Aren't those important years when people are supposed to be learning something about love and life? And unfortunately, we know all too well the kind of love that goes on in the prisons. We know all too well what kind of preparation for life prisoners receive. They are raped, hardened, embittered, turned into animals and receive advanced training in the criminal arts.

RETURNING THE LOST SHEEP TO THE FOLD

When all else fails, and a higher level of security is required to guarantee sobriety, we finally call the probation officer. Since we have been doing most of his work, he now has enough time to really do his job. He calls on all his resources, special squads, and in 24 hours or less he has brought the lost sheep back into the fold. Back into custody. Not for five years for violating probation, but in most cases for as little as five days.

Now, because of crowded jails, five year sentences often end up being eighteen months or less. When people hear that they scream "More jails! Let them do their full time!" Our whole society is fixated on trying the same stupid solution over and over. Why stupid? Anything that has been proven conclusively over and over to not work but is still being used over and over **is** stupid.

The eighteen month rotations back through the jails are welcomed by the homeboys. They need these times in the joint for networking, making new connections and new business contacts. They learn a lot in the joint about what is the new good dope and who has it. Snitches and traitors can be killed, vendettas arranged.

As it is, only 15% or less of all prison inmates known to have serious drug abuse problems are bothered with the inconvenience of having to go to meetings while in jail to try to get sober. Such meetings would interfere with body building and other 'business as usual' inside the joint.

"Sober Forever" Program participants will be deprived of the opportunity to network and establish new 'business' contacts in the joint. We won't be putting them back in jail long enough for them to build up new networks. They'll go in for five days the first time, then ten days and thirty days if they still don't get the picture. In jail they will spend some eight to twelve hours a day working on their sobriety. While in jail they will be watching videos, rapping in groups. They will be enrolled in a therapeutic community type of in-prison rehabilitation. This will be modeled after the "Stay'n Out" Program which has a very high success rate. If they don't have one, they will learn a trade. The one weakness in the

"Stay'n Out" Program, lack of adequate follow-up after release from prison, will be corrected in the "Sober Forever" Program.

KEEPING OUR PROMISE

We will be turning "voluntary" program participants into "involuntary" participants from the start. That way, their request for help in achieving sobriety will be honored. We will keep our promise even if they change their minds later. What happens if they change their mind after a few days in the program, as most addicts do. What if they decide that the pull of drugs and their old way of life is too strong to resist?

Since we have made a contract with them, a promise that we will help them fight these urges, we will honor our contract. We will make it possible for them to honor **their** contract. Once enrolled in the "Sober Forever" Program, if people change their minds about getting sober or even being in the program, it won't make any difference. They are still going to get sober.

Sometime in the future, after a few days, months, or perhaps even years later, they will be grateful. When they have a life and they are still sober and still alive, at some time in the future, they will thank us. Probably not at first, maybe not for months or years. They may call us every name in the book as their bodies and minds scream out for the instant relief that they know is available from chemicals. They will finally, one day, be grateful that their new friends helped them face their fears without chemistry. One day they will be glad we didn't let them slip back. But there will be many struggles on the way to sobriety and this new life. They will often fight like hell to get back to the hell their life had become on drugs.

Is the "Sober Forever" Program that different from many programs now in existence? Yes, in one very important way. There is virtually no tracking of the substance abuser in almost all other programs as soon as he leaves or graduates. No one knows where most of the drug offenders on probation are, or what they are doing. The goal of the "Sober Forever" Program will be to know where our clients are almost all the time. Our clients' health and safety, which can only be assured if they are sober, is worth the effort of 'keeping in touch.' This is the "long tail" discussed earlier. Multiple strategies will be used to guarantee that we 'keep in touch.' If a program participant gets high or gets drunk this will be known, ideally in minutes.

YOU CAN'T GO HOME AGAIN

Risk factors will be evaluated. Long term and heavy users are least likely to return to participate in the "Sober Forever" Program once released from detox. High risk clients will not be able to go out on their own. For example, gang members with a long history of drug involvement won't be allowed to go back to their old haunts. Some people may be at such high risk that they can't be left alone even for a few minutes. They may be required to live with and be with three to six sober buddies at all times. These sober buddies would be clients who have been in the program for awhile and are further along in their sobriety. If this high risk client still slips away from his sober buddies, we know he has gone to get high, drunk, or loaded.

That's when he should be tracked down within minutes, or at least hours. He might succeed in getting high once before being brought back. He might get one snort of cocaine, one joint, one chance to shoot up. But then, he would be back in detox, perhaps for double the time on this trip through detox. If it becomes obvious that the message given to him didn't take, then he needs to hear it all over again.

He will be watching more video tapes on sobriety. He will be working on his own plan for getting and staying sober. He will make his own video tape which will be titled "I want to be sober because...." He will fill in the blanks. Then he will watch his own tape over and over. Research shows that you can act as a model for yourself to change your own attitudes, thoughts, and behaviors. Our reluctantly sober client will learn about his choices: to be locked up someplace where sobriety is guaranteed, or to be sober on the outside. He can make the choice of where he will be sober but he cannot make the choice whether or not he will be sober.

Our clients will be organized into groups of six to ten. These groups will sleep together, eat together and study together. They will make "I want to be sober because...." videos together. They will work together. They may have problems getting along with each other. Drug addicts often missed out on the development of basic social skills.

When the time is right, the whole group may move out of the detox center or the barracks together into rental housing. They will have meetings in their new quarters. They will return to the "Sober Forever" Center for testing and meetings. The longer they have been on drugs the less skill in getting along with people they will have. They may not even be able to make up a shopping list without a fight.

LEARNING TO WORK TOGETHER

These groups will watch videos on how to plan a meal, how to shop for groceries. They will even be given guidelines on how to set up a rotating dishwashing roster. They will learn how to solve problems through discussion, without wrangling or shouting at each other. Whenever they have a fight, they can watch a video showing people resolving conflict through discussion.

There are basic social skills necessary to survive in the sober world of play and work. People under the influence do not acquire much in the way of new knowledge. Chemicals blunt the ability to absorb new information. Many stages of growth and development are by-passed in the years under the influence. Once sober, growth can begin. But, even sober, a 30 year old who has been on drugs for fifteen years will act, in many ways, like a teenager. In about a year of sobriety he can grow five years. In just three years he'll start looking and acting like a 30 year old. Since he'll be 33 then, he'll only be three years behind.

The law allows six unrelated individuals to live in a rented home or apartment. This can amount to less than $200 a month for rent and utilities per person. Food could cost as little as $100 a month per person. Thousands could live in barracks if we get one or more of those phased out military bases rent free. That way, $l00 a month per person would provide basic support and a sober living setting.

There are many ways of providing room and board for under $4,000 a year. Giving our addicts a place away from their old drug haunts to sober up won't be expensive. This is especially true when we compare these costs with the cost of putting just one person in a hospital ($1,000 a day), jail ($20 to $60 thousand a year) or a live-in drug rehab program.

Many of the lower risk substance abusers can live at home while they sober up. If they are still 'early' in their substance abusing 'career' their lives are probably not in the shambles we find typical of long-term abusers. Maybe they haven't yet completely destroyed or been ejected from their home and family. They may still have homes, wives, children, even jobs. Of course, all these generally go as their substance abusing "career" progresses. The longer they are abusing substances, the easier it is to end up homeless.

Talk to the homeless. You'll see that many had jobs, homes and families just a few months or years ago. That was when they were still 'early' in their substance abuse 'careers.' Estimates vary, but substance abuse is behind homelessness in about 70 percent or more of the cases.

We'd love it if everyone, once enrolled in our program, really did stay sober forever. This is not going to happen. But 'slips' will trigger various interventions. Someone who slips while living with six to ten sober buddies may not have to go anywhere. A marathon meeting might be all that is needed to get him/her back on the sober trail. Maybe that has already been tried on this person and didn't work. If the client who slipped is ranting, raving, and causing a neighborhood disturbance, the 'pick-up patrol' will be called. This would consist of plain clothes police or probation officers in unmarked cars. They would quietly remove the offender to another level of security. Not necessarily to jail at this point. Perhaps back to the ex-military base "Sober Forever" Center. A high intensity detox experience awaits them. There, they can still leave, it is still "voluntary." But they know that if they do leave or start to leave, the next highest level of security (probably our desert facility or jail) will be invoked.

TRACKING THE STRAYS

How long does it take to track down someone who has decided to go off and get loaded? In San Diego County and in cities all across America there are thousands of "lost" probationers who haven't drug tested as ordered. Nor have they gotten into treatment as ordered. Though they are in violation of probation, the Probation Department says they can't find them. Many of them live in their own homes. When probation officers called their number and someone said they weren't there that was the end of the search.

The Probation Department says they don't have the resources to track down "absconded" or "on the lam" criminal dopers to get them sober. But, special units working gangs knew how to locate anyone they want within an hour. Every large city in America has unserved felony warrants in the thousands. Denver has 10,000 loose felons who haven't been tried yet for crimes such as rape, murder, etc. Los Angeles has 20,000. Law enforcement is so busy handling each new crisis they don't have time to track down these felons.

It turns out that a lot of different approaches work in treating addictions. Getting sober is hard, staying sober is even harder. Creativity in utilizing a wide variety of different methods to keep track of people and keep people sober on a long term basis is critical. Our drug addicts are truly our "lost sheep," and we, the shepherds, must leave the flock of 99 to track down and return the strays. The certain knowledge of the consequences of getting loaded, that is, jail or a higher security setting, will help. Add to that the absolute determination of a powerful peer group to do whatever they can to enforce sobriety. Those efforts will make jail and courts unnecessary in most cases.

It can be done. Here and there across America it is being done, in one way or another. In a town in Georgia the local police handle the diversion program for substance abuse offenders. Once arrested and placed in the program, the police show up, unannounced, at the homes or place of work of probationers in the program. They politely request a urine sample. If it is dirty, the probationers may have to watch an autopsy of someone whose death was related to alcohol or drugs.[1]

The Georgia program called for educational and support group meetings. Traditional in-depth counseling was minimal. The focus was educational with lectures, rather than getting deep into the psyches of participants. Liberals are going to hate this, but the most powerful and effective part of the program was a variant of "Big Brother is watching you." The 'punch line' of the program was "And he'll come get you if you get loaded."

It works best if we catch them every time the hand goes in the cookie jar. No, we don't cut the hand off, but we do let them know for certain **"No more cookies!"** The program in Georgia claimed a 90% success rate. The ones we don't watch, the ones we allow to continue taking drugs, destroy their lives and the lives of everyone around them on their descent into hell.

Stories about the effectiveness of A.A. (Alcoholics Anonymous) are legion. Unfortunately, of those referred to A.A., less than 20% show up even once. Of those who do show up, the percentage who actually follow through with regular, long term attendance and work a good A.A. based program is smaller still. Even so, we have learned a lot from A.A. That is because very important long term attitude changes occur in those who do make A.A. a way of life. Sometimes these dramatic changes don't occur until months or years after achieving sobriety. We have found that the drop-out rate from most voluntary programs runs between 50% and 95%.

After substance abusers finally quit all the denial, they can recognize how endangered their lives had been. The addict who is involuntarily pried away from his favorite form of chemical happiness can also gradually absorb the knowledge that his/her life was out of control and that death was near.

The average life span of the homeless alcohol/drug addict is 41 years. This is 30 years less than the average American male.[143] The sobered up addict has to be reminded frequently how much his quality of life has improved since he became substance free. It is rare that sober doesn't mean a longer and better life.

Though our clients will watch video tapes to learn about all aspects of the addiction process, a heavy emphasis will be placed on relapse prevention. There will be speakers and tapes to show the pitfalls that lead to relapse, and what to do when you feel like you want to drink or drug. A.A. has a word, **HALT**, to remind members that states of **HUNGRY ANGRY LONELY TIRED** can place them at higher risk than usual of relapse. Other tapes will teach relaxation so that feelings of tension don't need to mean they will start looking for a bottle or a needle. There will be tapes teaching coping skills and social skills.

THE POSSE

Five or six members of a ten person support system will track down their missing buddy who didn't show up for a meeting. Having worked on sobriety together, they'll be more likely than anyone to know where he/she might have gone to get loaded. When they find him/her, they will try to talk him/her into coming back into the program. If that doesn't work, they will perform a citizen's arrest. Their buddy is violating the conditions of his/her probation by using an intoxicating substance and therefore is breaking the law.

The citizen's arrest procedure allows them to avoid kidnap charges when they physically take him/her back to the "Sober Forever" Program. If that doesn't work, if he or she is too big or too feisty to drag off without anyone getting hurt, go to plan "B": Make a phone call and keep him/her in sight until the specially trained pick-up unit arrives to reaffirm the creed of the "Sober Forever"

Program: "You can choose where you want to be sober, you cannot choose whether or not you will be sober."

Plan "B" might also be necessary if others who want someone loaded are guarding him or her, defending his or her right to get loaded. Drunks and dopers know that each time one of their own sobers up, they have lost a friend or a customer or both. Once sober, substance abusers almost always have to 'change their playmates and their playgrounds.'

Someone in prison for his third set of drug charges might have gotten a ten year sentence. But with early release due to crowding and good behavior, he still might have three more years to waste/serve. If we let him out now we'll save $150,000 in jail costs, provided we keep him sober. Since we don't want to throw him out on the streets or back with his doper buddies, we will put him in a sober living setting with a bunch of guys who are working on sobriety.

For the first few days, or with high risk of relapse clients, they will be equipped with an electronic monitor. They can't leave the premises without permission. Even when they do leave the premises, they'll be escorted by a sober buddy. They'll still have a lot more freedom than they had in jail. They can start developing a bridge to the outside world. Besides saving jail costs by letting them out three years early, it is very likely that within two years after their release they'll be working and paying taxes.

Another alternative, discussed in greater detail elsewhere in this book, is to cut the druggie's sentence from whatever it was down to two years. That last two years in jail would be spent in a therapeutic community drug rehab program like Stay'n Out.

FOR WANT OF A NAIL....

Remember that little ditty, "For want of a nail the shoe was lost, for want of a shoe the horse was lost...." To make a short story even shorter, the battle was lost because the rider couldn't get there to warn the troops.

Camden house in Camden, New Jersey was in a similar position.

They had taken tough, mostly drug-involved teenagers with at least one major conviction and run them through a program that has been copied by several states. Groups of ten teens worked, played, studied and slept together. For several hours a week they helped each other face their denial, pain and anger in group sessions. Eighty percent of the graduates quit drugs and crime until the funding for follow-up was cut. In 1992 the success rate had dropped to 50%.

To avoid spending only one tenth on follow-up of what their whole year long program cost for one individual, New Jersey had dropped their success rate for Camden house by 30%. Half, instead of only 20 out of every 100 graduates, was returning to drugs and crime. Those 30 per 100 more failures would steal more in a month than it would cost to follow-up 50 graduates for a year.

Camden house was an expensive program. Less costly alternatives must be utilized to justify a program that is to bring about universal sobriety. This is where barracks or group living settings come in. The participants themselves will finance whatever portion of the program they can afford. Part of the financing might be through a variation of the student loan program. Perhaps in this case they would be redesignated as "Sober-up loans," to be repaid when the sober graduate is back to work.

Providing jobs, either real jobs or made up jobs, will be important. Camden house residents were cleaning up abandoned row houses to make them livable again. They were reclaiming real estate which had been abandoned to drugs and crime. They got into the habit of engaging in that four letter word activity called "WORK" for a few hours each day. These basic work skills cannot be developed in someone who is under the influence of chemical substances. Concentration, memory and patience are too impaired in the substance abuser for them to learn much in the way of new skills.

They not only can't learn basic job skills while they are under the influence, they are not interested.

Money earned in the standard work force is often seen as "chump change" by the sixteen year old who can make $1,000 a day selling drugs. But if nobody is buying drugs, nobody will be selling drugs. When that happens, the "job" of dope dealer will no longer be a career option.

THE JOB LADDER

What will the sobered up substance abusing dope dealers do when drugs are no longer a source of income? What will they do when drugs aren't used any more to feel good and numb pain? There will come a time when they will be getting high on waking up and seeing the sun. They will be getting high on their new lives and new loves. There will come a time when they have finished job training and have jobs. Eventually, acceptance of the job market reality will come.

The job market reality usually means 'paying your dues.' They will probably have to get training and start low then work their way up. That path is rarely followed by the substance abuser. Some of the reasons why this is so: He is too angry, he can't get up in the morning, he can't concentrate. Also, he can make lots more money in the drug world than he can working a regular job. "You won't catch me slinging hash at McDonalds" even twelve year old dope dealers say. But even at McDonald's someone is the assistant manager, the manager, the district manager. And most of them started out "slinging hash" (not hashish).

Studies show that when there is good, tight follow-up, within two years of getting sober, about 50% of the former criminal addicts were working at legitimate jobs and 85% had stopped crime. Once we have sobered up our criminals they stop doing crime. As soon as we can guarantee that they will be sober after release we can safely empty 85% of our current inmates out of our prisons. That's about the percentage who are there as a direct result of substance abuse. Going to jail now is no guarantee that someone will get sober. We have discovered that you can get anything you want in a lot of jails.

THE ELECTRONIC 'BIG BROTHER'

The age of electronic monitoring is still in its infancy. As soon as implementation begins, the "Sober Forever" Program will explore the development of electronic monitoring and transmitting devices. These devices will tell us not only where our client is but what he has in his system. The miniaturization technology is advancing rapidly. It may be possible in the near future to have a miniature lab in an ankle bracelet which will analyze perspiration for drugs.

We will know within seconds when our client is 'testing positive.' We will know what they have taken. We will know if they are where they were supposed to be. If they aren't, we will know where to go get them. Will this be an invasion of privacy? Any drug addicted criminal who thinks so can serve out their years in prison instead of walking around outside with some minor limitations on their freedom.

In Japan, you can punch a destination into those cars equipped with computers. Your location is monitored via satellite and a voice tells you when you need to turn a corner. In the near future we will know where our sobering up addicts are. We will know if that is where they are supposed to be.

Until this device is perfected, every other method available for intensive follow-up and tracking must be used. A client who has trouble remembering his first follow-up appointment with us the day after he leaves detox could be sent to a sober living halfway house. This setting is still much cheaper than jail and still "voluntary." Work in therapy and the development of a feeling of community in the halfway house will be intense.

If our client who "forgets" to show up for his treatment refuses to agree to stay in a "voluntary" setting, the next highest level of security, which could be jail, would be implemented. We will find a way to be assured that our clients will return on schedule to their education, therapy, and affirmation of sobriety meetings. If the only sure way to guarantee that they will be there tomorrow is to not let them go home tonight, that is the course that will be taken.

THE ROAD BACK GETS LONGER

We need to round up and hold in a guaranteed sobriety program all the substance abusers who are currently falling through the cracks of the existing diversion programs such as the P.C. 1000 program in California. Only 60% of those referred actually complete the program. Nobody knows what happens to even that 60% just a few weeks after they finish the program.

The ones who fail to follow through on P.C. 1000 end up in the "warrant bank" limbo on their way to hell. The ones too angry and/or too loaded to even do that easy diversion program are the same ones most in need of sobering up. Every day that they are out there doing drugs they go further into their personal hell and the road back gets longer.

Court referrals to California's P.C. 1000 diversion program decreased in 1992. This was most likely because the same drug offenders previously referred to P.C. 1000 kept showing up back in the courtroom. The judges began shifting to sentences they thought might work. The P.C. 1000 program is apparently not a powerful deterrent to further drug abuse. Nobody seems to have any real follow-up data on the program. We do know that of every 1,000 people referred to the P.C. 1000 program about 640 complete it. The other 360 disappear into the "warrant bank." This is the limbo into which thousands have disappeared after not showing up for court, treatments, testing, etc.

Will the 10 or 20 hours of educational experience given in a beefed up P.C. 1000 Program cure a dope fiend? Probably not. Real follow-up data would probably reveal that some first time offenders new into the drug scene did get the message. The P.C. 1000 experience may well have helped some to give up drugging. The substance abusers further along in their drug usage career are most likely the ones who never showed up at all. Unfortunately, even a goodly number of the P.C. 1000 graduates who do learn to say "no" to drugs started saying "yes" to alcohol.

Beefed up P.C. 1000 type diversion programs must include urine testing. They must include periodic, unannounced breathalyzer tests, with an added prohibition against alcohol. Substituting one addiction for another has accomplished little or nothing. These diversion programs need to include **long term monitoring,** which would be less and less frequent over a period of five years or more. As it is now, after the four to six weeks in most of these diversion programs, no further contact is mandated.

Any kind of hard follow-up data would likely show that most of the graduates of P.C. 1000 type of diversion programs are back into the legal system in a year or two. These programs must have plans to quickly track down the ones who don't show up. These are the ones who need it the most. They must be forced to participate in a fail-safe drug rehab program. The 1992 slightly beefed up P.C. 1000 program still had no determined plans to track those not showing up at all. Their fate in San Diego: just one more admission to the three-fourths of a million member "warrant bank."

NOT ONE CENT FOR TRIBUTE

P.C. 1000 type diversion programs barely scratch the surface. The "Sober Forever" Program envisioned here is designed to be all encompassing in order to guarantee sobriety at all levels and with all substance abusers. In a city of a couple million the "Sober Forever" Program could have up to fifty thousand participants at any one time. Who will pay for this program? In 1992 San Diego County paid over a billion dollars for jails, courts, lawyers and law enforcement. That was 70% of the total budget. Everything else, buildings, roads, parks, etc. had to come out of the other 30%.

San Diego County spent virtually nothing in 1992 on drug treatment and rehabilitation. The $29 million dollars of drug and alcohol treatment money they **administered** was almost all state and federal money. "Not one cent for tribute (treatment) but millions for defense (arrest them, try them lock them up)" seems to be the working philosophy. The $29 million dollar treatment budget is only one-fortieth of the local judicial system budget. The Chief Probation Officer Cecil Steppe said his department couldn't get more help, and had even been reduced in budget and staff because he lacked "advocacy."

Lawyers and judges, who often become politicians, are wonderful advocates for what they know most which is the judicial system. They apparently know very little about treatment, rehabilitation, or that sober people quit crime. Lawyers, judges and politicians keep doing more of what they do know, which is arresting, trying, defending, and locking up substance abusing people. Because our jails are so stuffed, our leaders claim we can't afford to give America's prisoners the drug rehabilitation they desperately need while they are in prison.

Is it too cynical to say that perhaps the current approach to our drug crisis is a way of guaranteeing the continuance of the jobs of those working in the legal system? It is a well documented fact that the large majority of untreated substance abusers go right back to crime as soon as they are released from prison. Are judges, cops and lawyers afraid of being out of work if we really sober up our criminals and they stop doing crime? Let's not accuse them of that. Let's blame it on a lack of information. But, after this book, there will be no excuse to continue the same travesty.

There are exceptions here and there to the 'Rehab doesn't work lock them up' mentality. Fifty federal judges refused to hear drug cases because they maintained that the mandatory, extremely long sentences constituted cruel and unusual punishment.[30]

Judge David Admire in Seattle, Washington, recognized that our judicial system is in crisis because of substance abuse. He said we must cast aside the band-aid approach. He has been a one-man rehabilitation force, bucking the system, imposing graduated sanctions. He has been accused of being a softie because he gives people many chances to sober up. When they don't follow through on his assignment to a sobriety program he gives them five days in jail. The second time it's thirty days. Prosecution is deferred and if people finish the two year program the slate is wiped clean.[2]

For driving under the influence, since there was never a guilty plea, insurance rates don't sky-rocket. Judge Admire lets them keep their license because if he takes it away they only drive without it, and without insurance, because their rates had quadrupled. With convictions for drunk driving on their record, they are forced to exist outside the system. Then, everyone they crash into pays since they have no insurance. Judge Admire often orders them to have a Guardian lock installed which takes a sober breath to activate the ignition lock.[2]

Judge Admire involved the abused spouses and girlfriends in treatment so they could understand: (1) They were being abused (some really didn't know). (2) That whatever they did did not justify the abuse and it wasn't their fault, and (3) They did not have to put up with ever being hit again.[2]

DOUBLING THE PUNISHMENT

At the bottom of the sophistication ladder are parents who spank a child because he forgot to do something such as hanging up his coat. When he forgets again they figure, "One spanking didn't make him remember, I better give him two spankings." Or they spank him twice as hard or twice as long. When the poor frightened child keeps forgetting to hang up his coat, he can end up a bloody mess. Even though the first beating and all of the following beatings didn't change his behavior, his parents got locked into escalating the usage of the same punishment. The same punishment which had already been proven to not work.

One quick look at any "How to Raise Children" book will provide multiple alternative discipline strategies that do work! For example, when the child throws his coat on the couch, have him put his coat back on and go back outside. With the parent talking him through the motions, he now walks back into the house and hangs up his coat. This should be done two more times to reinforce the new behavior. Now, entering the front door becomes the reminder to hang up his coat, instead of mom's scream. By using such methods parents can obtain desirable behaviors from their children without ever having to raise their voices.

The child should be praised for each step toward mastery of these simple behavioral sequences. The child is praised for practicing the behavior the parent wants to see more of instead of being beaten when they forget to do something. If we use a lot of praise, it will not take long for the child not only to remember to hang up their coat but also to feel good about it. Is the parent who keeps beating their child for making the same mistakes a horrible parent? No, just horribly misinformed. If they are substance abusers, this misinformation is coupled with mood swings, irrational anger and has resulted in Sanctuary Trauma. This misinformation about how to discipline children has killed children and gotten parents locked up for child abuse.

CRUEL AND UNUSUAL PUNISHMENT

What excuse does our judicial system have for being locked into the same escalation of vicious punishments? Standard judicial procedures often dictate a doubling of sentences with each new offense. Would you call ten years in jail for getting sucked into the hell of drug addiction a vicious punishment? I would. So do a lot of judges. We already know that only 15% of drug abusing criminals do get drug rehabilitation while in prison.

Drug rehabilitation programs in jail are the equivalent to having a child practicing hanging up their coat, which is the behavior we want. We need to teach sober behavior. We need to stop brutally punishing people for engaging in junkie/crime behavior. That's like beating the child for dropping his coat on the floor. The few lucky prisoners who get in-jail rehab, such as those in the "Stay'n Out" program, learn the new behaviors of living sober and work. And that's what most of them do when they get out.

Our national judicial system, like the abusing parent, is slow to explore the alternative interventions such as those outlined here. Those in leadership positions who read proposals like this often say "We can't afford it, we are already stretched too thin."   Secretly, they don't believe in this rehabilitation crap and feel that not only punishment, but **hard punishment**, is the only thing these stupid dope fiends will ever understand.

That 'vendetta' attitude may have some emotional catharsis value to it as our prosecuting attorneys brag "I put that sucker away for life."   But our attorneys' emotional catharsis does not sober people up, nor does it stop criminals from committing more crime. It does not protect our children from unprecedented dangers in their own homes, in their neighborhoods, and in their schools.

When our public officials whine about the money it would cost to sober up America, they still don't get it. The new jails they want to build and the new cops they want to hire to lock up criminals are going to cost a hundred times more than sobering up those same criminals. Besides, the new jails and new cops won't begin to make a dent in the problem of a decaying America. Some people's initiation into substance abuse began in jail!

Since everyone in control of the budget now thinks that all the resources available must be spent on courts, cops, jails and lawyers, financing for the "Sober Forever" Program may have to come from other sources. After the "Sober Forever" Program has been in effect for a few years the jails and courts will be almost empty. Maybe then some of the money now thrown away in the judicial system can be used to build parks or roads or jobs. But don't count on it. Lawyers do not like to wait in line for unemployment checks.

FINANCING THE 'SOBER FOREVER' PROGRAM

If those in power will not crank even another dime loose to sober up America, where will the money come from to implement the "Sober Forever" Program? The people who will benefit most from the program will have to pay for it. That is, the program participants or "Sober

Forever" clients themselves. There are many privately run programs which are financed from a variety of sources. The California P.C. 1000 drug diversion program is paid for by the participants, as is the SB 38 drunk driving program in California.

Not everyone going into the "Sober Forever" Program will have the money to pay for it. We will be going after, treating and rehabilitating the bottom line drug addict who has no money. Alternatives include:

(1) The drug offenders with money may have to be charged a bit more than the program actually costs to help pay for those without money. The two year SB 38 drunk driving program charges fees on a sliding scale but the private providers of this program still manage to stay in business.

(2) Funding sources, city and county governments, may have to be talked into reallocating resources.

(3) Make the cost of the program a loan to the druggie who has no money. Collect from him later when he is working and sober. Instead of a student loan, it could be called a "Sober Loan."

(4) Open up more bingo games as MITE operates (see Chapter Eight) and let the bingo fans subsidize the drug rehab programs. When we as Americans become convinced that the "Sober Forever" Program is the way to go, we **will** find the money to run it. Or, let agencies like MITE run gambling casinos with **all** the profits to go for treatment for drug and alcohol addiction.

(5) Law enforcement agencies have made a lot of money fighting the war on drugs. The DEA (Drug Enforcement Administration) has boasted for years that it is the only U.S. Agency besides the IRS that operates at a profit. In 1989 the DEA seized $1.1 billion in cash on a budget of $500 million. Antidrug enforcement, like the cocaine traffic business itself, pays well.[136, p119]

All law enforcement agencies should be forced to funnel half of all money from seizures, sales of confiscated boats, vehicles, cash money, into a treatment fund. The monies should then be dispensed to fund those treatment programs with the best track record. Another criteria would be that the program, if it is an outpatient one, would have had to incorporate the "Sober Forever" Program principles. That means the "never give up" approach and long follow-up. We have proven that supply curtailment does nothing to stop the problem. We have proven that treatment can and does stop the problem. Doesn't it make sense that more money needs to go to treatment instead of more jails and cops and robbers?

(6) We are facing a national crisis, a failure in morality, a decay of our cities and of our moral values perhaps not seen since the legendary Sodom and Gomorrah were destroyed by God's wrath. Not looking back might have saved Lot, but our ignoring the problem and the right solution is disastrous. We don't need God to rain hell-fire down on us. It turns out we are perfectly capable of totally destroying ourselves without His help.

When the German peoples faced the gigantic task of reuniting the two Germanies, they rallied round the cause. East Germany was a disaster area of antique equipment and hazardous, highly polluted working conditions. The Germans were willing to do whatever it would take to make the unification successful. They knew it would take money. They cheerfully accepted a 50 cent a gallon increase in the cost of gasoline to help fund the reunification costs. Gas in Europe already costs two to four times what we in the U.S. pay for gas.

We have a crisis of much greater proportion than was facing the German people. They wanted to bring their people together under one rule. We have a nation in decay. We could provide treatment for the millions of Americans who need it with a 50 cents a gallon price increase. We could provide treatment for the three million alcoholic teenagers and the seven million adult alcoholics. We could provide treatment for people in prison so they will stay sober when they get out.

We must take the two million homeless teenagers off the street. Most of them are there because of substance abuse. They may have been kicked out of their homes because they were loaded all the time. Some left home because their parents were loaded all the time and the streets were safer than home. We must feed them, house them, educate them, give them job training, teach them

values, and sober them up.   And finally, we must love
them. Which no one is doing now.

ABANDONING OUR YOUTH

If we want our younger generation to take care of
us after we grow older, we better get them off drugs and
teach them to work.   It is not only the two million
homeless teenagers we have abandoned. We neglect our
youth in general and treat them worse in many ways than
any other industrialized nation.   This brutal attitude
toward our youth is only matched by our supreme gall of
foisting upon them the task of providing us with wonderful
old age benefits. Not only that, we have left them the task
of paying off the bills we ran up in our massive 1980's
spending/credit   binges   now   totaling $4.5   trillion
dollars.[109]
We are discarding the population of over two
million homeless teenagers and the many more millions of
homeless adult Americans (many if not most of them
substance abusers) as though they were toxic waste. We
just don't know where to dump them. When we do try to
dump them, they don't stay dumped. They keep coming
back to rob us or shoot us or each other. We need to regard
the existence of these millions of substance abusers as
untapped resources and as opportunities to add to
America's productivity. We need to be moving them
toward maximizing and fulfilling their now unfulfilled
capabilities and promise as human beings. If we don't do
that, nobody will be there to pay for all these wonderful
social security benefits Americans have so generously
voted for themselves over the years.[109]
If we choose number six to raise money to pay for
sobering up America (increase the gas tax by 50 cents)
who will have the power to demand that the money be used
for the reason it was collected? Advocates of treatment and
the "Sober Forever" type of program will have to fight
hard to make sure that money, if it is ever voted in,
actually goes to where it was intended.

The Justice Department is full of very powerful and influential people who snatch every dime they can away from treatment to spend on more cops and robbers games. They love their expensive toys. Just $10 million for this wonderful helicopter that will catch maybe two airplanes full of pot next year. We could have sobered up 2,500 drug addicts next year with that $10 million.

We must be very careful. In Latin and South America all the major cities each have thousands of homeless teenagers. The total comes to millions. These are the lands of the poppy, the coca plant and hemp. Even so, these children don't seem to have good access to cocaine, heroin and marijuana. Their drug of choice? Airplane glue. Hungry and high, robbing people, snatching purses from tourists, they have become a threat.

In Brazil there are death squads, paid for by local merchants, who hunt these problematic teenagers down and kill them for a few dollars each. "They are bad for business" the merchants complain. So far, prosecutions for these murders has been nil. We must never let this happen in America. We must take action now while there is still time. Unless we rescue and rehabilitate the two million homeless teenagers from the streets of America we will soon be viewing them as toxic waste. They are now perceived as that by Brazil's merchants. Our homeless youth are already disappearing off America's streets and the face of the earth at a frightening rate. But nobody really has any statistics on that. Just how many of those "missing" American teenagers are really still alive? Nobody knows. How many of those lonely, desperate, drug addicted homeless teenagers were viciously sodomized, murdered, and lie in shallow graves somewhere? Nobody knows. I don't think America wants to know. We have a whole nation floating down that river in Egypt called 'De Nile.' Those homeless teenagers who do survive in the streets very often grow up to be dangerous and violent adults.

As we have seen, America's adult homeless are basically in the same dilemma. Substance abuse put most of them on the streets and keeps most of them there. San Francisco tried a grand experiment a couple years back, a tent city for the homeless, with portable toilets spread liberally around the compound. The residents of this tent city were too drunk or too loaded to walk the few yards to the portable johns. Soon the place reeked with a stench that carried for blocks. Another failed experiment. It never occurred to anyone to make sure the residents of this tent city were sober. If they had, the outcome would have been considerably different.

San Diego County recently dropped a couple of very expensive lawyers from the usual bevy of attorneys at each child custody hearing. They took that money and used it to fund more in-home preventive services. They realized that what they were doing wasn't working. They decided to try to keep families intact instead of spending so much money fighting over the pieces these families had become in court.[4]

SOBER FIRST, THEN BASKETBALL

Whatever monies are raised to run the "Sober Forever" Program, must be kept out of the hands of those currently controlling the judicial system budgets. Every time somebody pours money into the criminal justice system it is immediately grabbed and then poured into the same bottomless pit of more cops, jails, judges, courts. The high profile "Weed and Seed" program of the Justice Department is no exception. The idea was to "weed" out criminal elements and "seed" alternative programs such as recreation centers.[103]

An incredible 90% of all the millions going into that program was for curtailing supply, a minuscule 10% was for "prevention," meaning youth activities, basketball courts, etc. Virtually none of it was directly aimed at sobering up users. The Justice Department wanted it all to go for more law enforcement. Congress had to pass a special bill to let cities have some discretionary use of the funds. But the Justice Department, still waging their own personal war on Drug Treatment, didn't have to worry. The cities were smart. They were not going to throw the money down the black hole of treatment. The small percentage of the money not going to more cop and robber games is going to develop parks, basketball courts and after school recreation.[103]

That's nice, and necessary, but how many drug abusers will it sober up? My estimate: not many. Prevention? Maybe. But lots of kids who had all kinds of healthy activities available no longer could find time to do them when they got on drugs. Let's get them off drugs first, **then** ask them if they want to play basketball.

How many years will it take America to stop spending the billions of dollars we do each year in the criminal justice system? Not until the courts are empty and the nation has been sobered up will major budget shifts be possible. When substance abusing parents are sobered up they will stop abusing their children. Then, the foster child population will drop to just 30% of what it is today. Some of those billions going into the foster home system might finally end up in new parks. We may even be able to build a non-polluting rapid transit system so good everyone will want to ride it. Seventy percent of all children now in foster care are there because their parents were failing as parents because of substance abuse.

With the money we save by quitting playing cops and robbers we might be able to help pay for our children's education again. Now, we are raising their tuition every year in even the state supported schools. As a result, many of our children have to either forget about college or mortgage the first ten years of their working career to obtain student loans. The last 20 years of their working career is already mortgaged to pay the worthy retirees a nice pension and to pay off the money we borrowed because we needed it for our 1980's spending binge. We won't even help our children get the education they need to get the jobs and money they must find to provide us with the cushy future we demand. Why? Because we want to spend it on more jails, that's why. Now that's a real investment in America's future. Ask our lawyers and politicians. That's what they'll tell you. The best possible way to spend the taxpayers dollars to fight the drug wars is to invest in more cops, courts and jails.

Whatever government or social system currently in power will always resist change. The lawyers who will lose their jobs if America sobers up may not be eager to back a program that will guarantee their unemployment. They may ignore all the facts and figures and insist that we can't let criminals get away with crime. They may insist that we can't put criminals into diversion programs without going through lengthy court hearings. They are likely to claim that not doing so would either be coddling criminals or violating their civil rights. The judicial system is locked onto the concept of a "fair trial" followed by a long, brutal, dehumanizing experience in jail. Never mind that it doesn't work to stop crime, drug abuse, or the decay of the American dream. Never mind that the current judicial system is the biggest contributor to the decay of America's values. When you systematically lock up huge numbers of Americans in places where they learn to take dope and become vicious animals and then release them back into society, guess what happens.

MULTIPLE INTERVENTIONS AT MITE

MITE (McAlister Institute for Training) in El Cajon, California, is an excellent model of the kind of **non-governmental** organization needed to carry out a "Sober Forever" Program. They provide multiple services to substance abusers including detox and sober living centers. That's where ex-addicts live together in rented homes or apartments and work on getting sober together. They can collect urine samples on site and send them to a lab for analysis at a cost of $12 per sample. MITE's workers are sent into the jails to conduct group sessions and to recruit prisoners near release into their sober living program.

MITE's biggest drawbacks are the same as in most programs. The truly problematic and most addicted, the substance abusers who have used the longest, are the least likely to become involved in or stay involved in their program. If these hard core addicts go to MITE at all, they have a good chance of being ejected from the program. This can happen as a result of failure to cooperate, failure to show up, failing urine tests, or just having a very bad, even obnoxious attitude problem.

Hard-core addicts work hard to get rejected and they succeed admirably. Years of addiction have decayed their social skills and turned them into conscienceless animals. Yet many drug rehab centers make high demands on even these most disturbed and long using addicts. These people generally are not capable of meeting these demands. Thus, the substance abusers most in need of help are also the ones most likely to slip or be pushed through the cracks.

MITE, and all the other drug rehab centers need to make this tough population a high priority. That doesn't mean they should stop providing any of the services they are offering now. They desperately need to find ways of holding onto the highest risk abusers. These are the ones doing the most damage to themselves and their world. Instead of dropping some important aspects of their programs to make room for this new priority, MITE and other drug rehab programs need to add the goal of sobering up anyone who enrolls in their program.

THE CLUB YOU CAN'T QUIT

Holding onto the high risk substance abuser will have to be done by using the series of steps outlined in this book. Failure to comply with rules, failure to attend meetings, testing dirty, hanging out with users, will result in an intervention. **This intervention will never be ejection from the program.** Remember? This is the club you can't quit. If a sobering up junkie gets loaded or wants to keep picking fights with everyone, maybe he needs to be moved to a higher security facility. He hopes that if he's obnoxious enough he will be sent home where he can then get loaded. This is now often done with the truly problematic client.

Another possibility is a 24 hour marathon to find out what anger or pain caused the fighting or the relapse. If none of these things work, the probation department may finally have to get involved. This won't occur five years down the road, after five years of having slipped back into the world of substance abuse. A special task force must be ready to reacquire offenders within 24 hours after their names are called in to probation by the contracting rehab agency.

Ninety-five percent of the probation department's work must be shifted to agencies like MITE. That way, with only five percent of their work left to do, the probation department should be able to do it very well. Their job will be to chase and bring back the lost sheep. If they can't even do that then the wardens of the prisons must do it. If the wardens refuse to do it the whole prison system must be put out to bid. Contract renewals will be based on how many people they have rehabilitated back into society and back into jobs.

Finally, we will be able to rip the bars off the nearly empty jails and turn them into places where our homeless teenagers or adults will go to sober up. There, they will learn to become human beings, learn a trade and how to work.

The primary job which will be left for the probation department will be to pull back into the system anyone involved with drugs within 24 hours of their first no show. Then, brief (five days, not five years) of incarceration will be followed by cycling back into the treatment system. Maybe we would reenter them into the program at a remote desert facility until they earn their way back to civilization by acting civilized. This desert center could be fifty miles from nowhere.

High risk cases might be given their choice of this desert center placement, for perhaps thirty days of detox, or jail. All the high tech, legally required and very expensive aspects of an "involuntary" prison program need not be in place, since this would still be a "voluntary" placement. Even "home arrest" with electronic monitoring is "voluntary" in that the individual is given his choice between jail or home arrest.

In a program located in the middle of the desert, access to drugs would be minimal to nonexistent. Escape on foot would not be smart. A few hours in the desert sun without water can be lethal.

Anytime the client is a captive audience and forced to participate, there is a danger that the attitude of the providing agency will become obnoxious and abusive. To prevent this, clients who enroll in the program will be able to make two changes to other providers, other organizations offering rehabilitation services. The primary goal and demand will be the same in all providing organizations: Sobriety. But how this is done may vary. Abusive and excessively confrontational approaches need not be tolerated by the clients.

As I've said repeatedly in this book, "Sober Forever" Program participants will be able to pick where they will be sober, not **if** they will be sober. This reference has generally been to "in jail sober" or "outside sober" but will also apply to a choice of agencies. The agencies who contract to provide the "Sober Forever" Program services will also have wide discretion in their approach. They will be able to decide who needs to go to a sober living house with sober buddies for two years and who can go back home an hour after their arrest. They must, however, test them all, and frequently, and on a random basis. As time goes on, drug testing can become less frequent, but still will remain random and unpredictable.

The agencies like MITE will decide who needs what services. They might decide that if someone works, has a wife and children, and was just smoking a little pot, they can be trusted to come back for a few hours a week for a few weeks or months to talk in groups and take urine tests. With these clients, by the second to fifth year, perhaps only four to six randomly scheduled urine tests a year might be all that is needed to guarantee sobriety.

If the agency miscalculated and sent someone home who couldn't seem to make it to the meetings and urine sample donations, a higher level of involvement will be invoked. This could be anything from 90 meetings in 90 days plus urine tests, two weeks of detox, or 30 days in a jail program where **ALL** the time there will be spent on drug rehab.

We will go to visit people like Ruth (see Chapter Three) who couldn't give up her beer. Besides that, Ruth said she just couldn't make it to those "stupid meetings!"

We will say to Ruth and the others like her, "You don't live here anymore."

The first time the therapeutic community approach was used with addicts was in Synanon. There, a tough, confrontational approach to sobriety was used. That approach must give way to loving people back to sobriety. Very apologetically we will invoke the next level of security needed to guarantee sobriety for those resisting sobriety. Speak softly but carry a big stick, Teddy Roosevelt said.

BRING YOUR BABY WITH YOU

By accommodating female program participants, an Amity therapeutic community program doubled the average length of time their participants stayed in the program. This accommodation was allowing the women to bring their children to live with them in the therapeutic community. Those who did so successfully completed the program. Three years later, almost all were employed. They were free from criminal activity and drug use. Their children were functioning normally.[97, 99]
These were women who before treatment at Amity were having crack babies and had averaged more than ten years of serious substance abuse. They had averaged five years of prostitution each with over two hundred sexual partners per year. Three-fourths of them had been molested or raped before age eighteen. The average number of times each had been raped was six. It is important to look after the special needs of program participants whenever possible.
Man is very clever. Here in the Amity program, he has succeeded once again in reinventing the wheel. If you take drugs out of women who have had children they start remembering that they are mothers. If you let their babies be with them they don't mind hanging around this new place where people are working together to get their lives back. Kind of like a tribe. Get it? A tribe. Man's first few million years was in a tribe. Lots of people to love and to care for you as you cared for them. Remember the African saying "It takes a whole village to raise a single child."

The therapeutic community has reinvented the tribe, or village. Now they have discovered that if the babies are there that helps. Watch closely, next they will discover that it works even better if the women can have their men there with them. And, of course the reverse is that the men will do better with their women there. But one step at a time. We do know that giving their babies back to moms who are sobering up works well.

Different agencies will bid to participate in the "Sober Forever" Program. When it comes time to renew the bids, the agencies with the best track records will get more of the business. Not every client will need two years of intense therapeutic community experience to sober up. It may be that some clients will only need a ten hour educational program on the dangers of drugs accompanied by periodic random testing to guarantee sobriety.

Others may need two weeks of detox then be allowed to go home and back to their regular jobs. This near total freedom will continue as long as they report to the required periodic meetings and drug testings to prove continued sobriety. Yet others will need the gamut, a minimum of two years in a live-in therapeutic community. For some, it will take that long for their destroyed lives to gradually be pieced back together with the aid of a loving support system.

For those in jail, the last two years of their jail term will be in a "Stay'n Out" type of in-jail therapeutic community drug rehabilitation program. Most people's time in jail can be cut to two years because we know that when given the "Stay'n Out" therapeutic community treatment program for two years, most quit crime and drugs. Job training needs to be provided during those last two years for those with no salable work/career skills. Upon release they will be provided a place to stay, food to eat, sober buddies and drug testing. If they still have a family waiting for them, that home must be supportive of sobriety.

All participation levels will involve periodic testing. Failure at one level or attempts to disappear will immediately result in being brought back into the program. This return will be at a higher level of treatment intensity and security. Some may need to do the whole two years of therapeutic community experience in jail if their resistance to sobering up is as intense as in some cases I have seen. The trick will be to never let go and never give up on even one addict.

CENTRALIZED STATE LEVEL TRACKING

We have more information in America on the level of unburned carbons coming out of our muffler than we do on where are addicts are, what they are doing, who has arrested them lately, and the current poisons they are putting in their body.

Smog certification centers in California have direct computer links to the Department of Motor Vehicles. As soon as a car tests clean or dirty, these results are registered in the State computer files. The "Sober Forever" Program will need to get such a system on line. Dates on which the program participants were tested for drugs, once entered in the treating agency files, will be automatically entered into the State computer system. Proof of continued sobriety will result in no action. Dirty tests, failure to attend meetings, will trigger a query from the central computer to the agency. A response from the agency, such as "We're doing an intervention," or "Weekend retreat to reaffirm sobriety" will result in no action.

If the agency has lost the person, or the ex-user addict is refusing to come to meetings, the agency can still have up to 48 hours to track down that client and remotivate him to get back into the program. If this fails, when the time runs out, local probation officers finally get to work. They will track down the lost sheep before they stray too far from the fold. But, they will know where to look.

Earlier in this book the Japanese satellite guidance system was mentioned. They program a destination into their in-car computer and a voice guides them, street by street, to where they want to go. With modification of existing tracking/guidance systems via satellite, the probation department will be able to quickly find anyone they want to find.

In the future, such a homing device may be built into an ankle or wrist bracelet which only the probation department can remove.   Removal without permission would trigger an intense hunt and return to the fold.   More invasion of privacy?   Those who object can serve out their lengthy prison sentences and forego freedom.   Freedom will never mean free to get high.   People invariably prefer the much more limited "home arrest" electronic monitoring units now in existence over jail.

With tracking down strays as their only job, probation officers can perfect this to a high tech science. Europe already does this.   I was in Switzerland once and had missed connecting with another couple.   It looked hopeless.   How could I possibly find them in this big city? Someone said "Just go to the police station.   They know where everyone is."   They did.

This system will also prevent the other ways people can slip through the cracks, such as "I don't like you guys anymore.   I'm going to this other drug treatment center where they have Ding Dong snacks with their coffee."   Then, they forget to show up at the Ding Dong center.   We'll know that right away.   More Big Brother is watching you?   Or a better way to treat a disease, substance addiction, before it destroys the abuser and everyone he/she loves and who love him/her.   An agency's notification of Central Tracking that a client is changing agencies triggers a "Watch."   If that client has not checked into the new agency within 24 hours, Plan "B" is implemented.   Plan "B" is "Go get them."

THE 'DOPE OPERA' MENTALITY

Many of those who have read this far in this book will no doubt have screamed "Big Brother," "1984," and "Civil liberties violations!"   They will repeat, as is done in every made for TV 'Dope Opera,' that you can't force people to sober up.   You have to wait until they've hit bottom, until they are ready.   The over-bearing 'dope opera' mother trying to railroad her pregnant daughter into some kind of treatment is made to look stupid.   She is always being chided by cops, husbands or counselors to "back off. Let your daughter decide on her own. If she sobers up for you and not for herself, it is not a good sober." That kind of thinking leads to death, crack babies, and a danger from gun toting dope fiends to every citizen trying to use an ATM machine.

Every state has laws against the use of illegal substances and laws against being under the influence. This book is not asking for a single new law. This book is a plea for the gentle rescue of substance abusers from their well documented hell. This book is a plea for America to begin the humane treatment of the addicted, with the goal of helping them to rebuild their lives as quickly as possible. This plea and this "Sober Forever" plan are in stark contrast to the do-nothing attitude now in existence. We have to stop looking at our addicted children and criminals as toxic waste to be dumped somewhere.

Society now ignores the problem of the substance abuser for years. Then society follows-up with as many years in prison as our prosecutors in the criminal justice system can manage. When you hear news announcers on TV talking about the jails being full and prisoners getting early release, on occasion they also say, "We need a completely new system, another whole set of alternatives." But mostly, they talk about how frustrating it is because we don't have enough cops and jails.

Whose privacy is being violated when a probation officer shows up at the work site of a recently sober addict's job and asks him to breathe into a portable breathalyzer to determine his blood alcohol level? Obviously, we must never endanger anyone's job. We must find ways of checking up on people without getting them fired.

How about your right to drive down the road without being run into by that same addict if he isn't reminded that we **really** don't want him to drink anymore. How about your right to shop in any area of town even at 2 a.m. if a store is open? You have lost that right. That is because we as a nation have apparently decided that people have the right to pursue their own favorite form of happiness. Even if it involves illegal chemicals which produce crazy, dangerous behaviors.

This is where our ambivalence, or even our national schizophrenia (split personality) comes in. We look the other way because people are supposed to have fun in America in their own way. Then we "throw the book at them" and lock them up for as long as we can because their "fun" went a little too far.

Why do I say America has apparently decided to allow people to 'have fun' by taking drugs? Because there are at least 300 known and well identified street markets for drugs in New York City alone. These are places throughout the city where drug dealers and users do a brisk business all day long. It is likely that a few hundred thousand or more drug transactions take place in open view in New York City each day.[25]

Suggested priority lists of whom we sober up first when the "Sober Forever" Program is implemented were given earlier in this book. The list included "absconded" addicts on probation who had failed to follow through on drug treatment and testing. It included all those in the "warrant bank" of "failures to appear" in court on various charges. Most of those people are substance abusers. It included the over a million Americans in jail and the three million more on probation or parole. Just a handful of that four million are getting the rehabilitation (or in many cases, habilitation) they need to sober up. Only a handful are on a path that will lead them to being contributors to our society. As it is, most of them are sucking up all of our precious emotional and financial resources in every area of our lives.

When we have cleaned up those lists, then we will go to the street markets. There, we will first collect all the customers and enroll them in the "Sober Forever" Program. Then we will go back and collect and enroll the now unemployed dealers so they themselves can get off drugs and get training for a new career and get a life.

EMPTY COURTROOMS, EMPTY JAILS

If the "Sober Forever" Program is implemented as designed, with no cracks left for the addicts to fall through back into addiction, what will happen? In a few years the courtrooms will be almost empty. The huge staff of prosecuting and defense lawyers and judges will have little to do. They will have to stretch out their existing work-load with longer trials. After the program has been fully operational for a few years, it might occur to someone that only a tenth of the people are being arrested and prosecuted compared to the numbers of a few years back. Maybe people will begin to realize we don't need as many cops, judges, lawyers, jails. But don't count on it.

Remember who are the highly articulate advocates of their jobs and their roles in society. Who decides when and by how much they should get a raise, recession or not? Who are the people in positions of power? Who makes the laws? Certainly not the wimpy do-good reformers who are so misguided as to think you can actually rehabilitate a criminal or a dope fiend. The rules are made by lawyers who became judges.

The rules are made by lawyers who became politicians. Being "soft on crime" means they don't get reelected so our legislators push for more jails. Some of them must know it isn't working. But they are not willing to tell the truth if that truth means they might not get reelected. Once on the bench or in the legislature most of them keep practicing the same solution to all of society's problems that they learned in law school. That solution: Arrest them, try them and lock them up! There are exceptions, such as Judge David Admire in Seattle.

The legal system can be changed in a meaningful way. But for those in charge to make these changes, it will take a huge groundswell of outrage and demand from the public. These demands for change must come from a very persistent and very vocal population of voters. These will be the voters who have been enlightened with the facts presented in this book and elsewhere which prove that sobriety works.

Nobody seems to recognize the strange truth that if you treat people like animals they act like animals. In the few places in-prison therapeutic community drug treatment programs exist and people are treated like human beings with assets whose capabilities need to be developed, they act like human beings and there is a warm, friendly, non-violent drug-free environment. Because of the availability of drugs in most jails and because prisons turn people into vicious animals, the Justice Department and all of the departments of corrections in America could be looked on as the biggest enablers in the history of mankind, since criminals are often enabled in substance abuse by first learning about or continuing substance abuse in jail. The criminal justice system in general could also be seen as the biggest contributor to the increasing levels of violence in America since they put back into society people who became much more perverted after they went to jail, people who have been turned into angry, vicious predators.

CHAPTER TWELVE

THE LAST FIELDS OF BATTLE: HOME AND WORK

The most important battlefield of all in the drug wars is the home. Our children must stop being casualties in the Drug Wars. Sanctuary trauma must stop. There are two million homeless teenagers. Most of them are on the streets because they or their parents were or are substance abusers.[74] Once the "Sober Forever" Program is implemented, there won't be a problem keeping the home sober. Everyone coming to the attention of the authorities because they need help in getting sober will get that help. Whether they want it or not.

What can parents do while they are waiting for the "Sober Forever" Program to become a reality? What if parents are not abusing substances, not using any drugs at all, but their children are? If the above isn't true, and home is not clean and sober, the parents need to focus on the whole family getting sober. Alcoholics Anonymous, Alanon and Alateen are starts. There is not much chance of parents sobering up their children until they sober up themselves.

But what if, by even the strict A.A. and N.A. standards, the parents are not abusing substances? What if, in spite of all this, their children start abusing substances? What should the parents do?

CLEAN AND SOBER AT HOME

There are lists of "Do's and Don'ts" for parents to help them in their fight in the drug wars. These lists show up in school lobbies, "Women's Day" magazines, the P.T.A. Newsletter, etc. What advice is given in these lists? Here are some samples: (1) Spend time with your kids. Establish communication. (2) Look honestly at your own alcohol or drug use. Do you drink at family and social gatherings? If so, ask what message you are giving to your children? (3) Be involved with other families, your own extended family if possible. Families that stay isolated may be headed for trouble.

Here is the list from Advanced Health Care telling what to do if you suspect your child is using drugs:[151]

(1) Get involved. Learn about drugs and drug abuse. Learn the changes and behavior that occur when adolescents abuse chemicals.

(2) Don't be in DENIAL. Open your eyes to the facts and information right around you.

(3) Set clear, firm guidelines about what is acceptable behavior. Don't give in to unreasonable demands, i.e., "It's only pot." Do not tolerate any drug use. Talk to them about their drug use. Don't lecture or holler.

(4) Talk to your adolescents' friends. Tell them you are concerned and want to help. Ask lots of questions. Listen! Find out what drugs they are using and how often.

(5) Be intrusive. Ask your children where they are going, who they will be with, when they will return, and what they will be doing. Be suspicious, check up on them. Smell their breath when they come home. Look into their eyes for redness. Check their favorite hiding places. Do it and don't feel guilty about trying to save their lives.

(6) When you actually suspect your adolescent has been recently using chemicals get a urine drug-screen test right away. Don't believe what your child tells you, believe the test.

(7) Do not rescue or protect your son or daughter from the consequences of their chemical use. Set limits. Be firm, caring and strong.

(8) Don't dwell on guilt over past failures. That only saps energy you need to engage in current positive action. Drug abusers often need professional help. Use firm and caring pressure to get your adolescent into treatment. If they refuse, contact an intervention specialist and learn what you can do. "Intervention" has come to refer to an act or series of acts in which we engage to "intervene" between the substance abuser and his substances.

One such "intervention" method for teenagers involves getting together all the family and friends who know the person in trouble. One by one, in a big meeting of perhaps 50 people (the teenager's 'tribe') they lovingly tell of their concern. They point out how they have seen him/her go downhill. They tell them they want to see them get help to get sober. Native tribes also do this, sometimes for healing or casting out demons. It is a powerful technique.

TOOLS FOR PARENTS: URINE TESTING BY MAIL

One reason I picked the Advanced Health Care list is because you can call them for more information at (619) 692-0803. Also, you can ask them to mail you a drug screening kit at a nominal cost. Your adolescent provides a urine sample. You mail it back and receive the results within a few days. You may have access to a local program where drug screening is provided at a nominal cost.

The rule is, if you suspect, test. We have reviewed study after study in this book which prove that all kinds of therapy, supervision, parole, probation, etc., without testing, is usually ineffective. Children on drugs lie to you and to themselves. To you, they say they are clean. To themselves, they say "I am just going to do this little tiny bit and I won't even show any effects from it. Nobody will know and besides I can handle it. And it's such a little amount it's really the same as if I was clean."

When should you use tough love on your child and kick them out for using drugs? The two million children to whom that has already happened are not doing well. They probably won't live long. Many are H.I.V. infected or already have AIDS. They are our toxic waste. We keep looking for some place to dump them but they keep coming back. We have not yet started to send death squads after them like Brazil. Or have we? Many disappear and are never heard from again.

While we are waiting for the "Sober Forever" Program to start you should explore every other option you can think of before you kick your children into the street. You may be able to get your child involuntarily committed to a detox program.   Psychiatrists can still commit children involuntarily.   Once they are in the hospital tell your children that they can come home if they agree to test twice a week and continue in treatment.

Tell them they have to agree to give up all their doper buddies and start hanging around with people who are sober.   These can be people who they met in treatment. They need to hang around with people who are working on sobriety to remind them that they can have fun sober.

What should be put on a list of the most important things any of us on this earth are supposed to do?   Most people would put "Be successful parents" at or near the top of the list.   The definition of a successful parent is one who has a successful child.   A successful child is one who is happy and achieves as much as they are capable of achieving in life.   Children who are substance abusers don't even come close.   They end up filling our graveyards and our prisons.

A parent's number one priority should be doing whatever they can to help their children arrive at adulthood sober and prepared to make something of themselves.   Parents should do whatever it takes to get their children sober.   In the process of sobering up their children parents should never lose their temper.   Getting angry doesn't help.

Try the things suggested here.   Keep calling people and asking for help.   Go to parent support groups to get more ideas.   Don't ever give up.   Raising sober children is a parent's most important job.   Finally, beg and plead with everyone you can think of to have the "Sober Forever" Program implemented in your town or state.   When "Sober Forever" is in place throughout the land, one phone call will do it all.   Your child will be tested at your request and enrolled in a fail safe sobriety program if he/she tests dirty.

DRUGS AND WORK

Sixty percent of the world's production of illegal drugs is consumed in America.   Drug use is not just a big-city/inner-city problem.   Drugs are just as pervasive in the suburbs, but hidden better. The New York Times in 1985 finally documented how crack caused child abuse, violence, and destroyed the family. Efforts to seal the borders are useless. Of the twenty most abused drugs in the U.S. 16 are made in the U.S.[141]

Twenty-five percent of all homicides in the U.S. are related to drug trafficking. In 1988 the National Institute of Drug Abuse found that between 54% and 82% of men arrested for serious offenses in fourteen cities were loaded at the time of their arrest. South America has 520,000 acres of land planted with coca. Colombia makes more money on cocaine than on coffee. The number of South Americans working making cocaine is 304,000. Billions have been spent confiscating drugs coming into the United States. Only a tiny fraction of the 400 tons of cocaine and heroin that comes in every year is actually confiscated. There is so much cocaine that the price of cocaine dropped to around $8,500 a kilo in 1989, one sixth of what a kilo cost in 1979.[17]

Substance abuse, including drugs and alcohol, is estimated to cost the business community $160 billion a year. Substance abuse is responsible for eroding productivity, industrial accidents, absenteeism and tardiness, and inflating health costs. Substance abuse added an average of $400 to the cost of each General Motors vehicle.[141]

Eighteen to twenty percent of all employees are substance abusers. They are 3.6 times more apt to injure themselves or others on the job, and five times more likely to be involved in an accident on the job. They incur 300% higher medical costs and benefits and are one third less productive. General Motors reported that the average substance abuser was on the job only 140 out of 240 workdays during the year prior to treatment.

Stutman[141] recommended comprehensive programs to deal with substance abuse. Such programs should include educational efforts, crisis intervention, testing and treatment for abusers and their families. Urinalysis, which too many people look to as the panacea to stop drug abuse, is not the answer by itself. It's just part of the solution.

KEEPING GOOD WORKERS SOBER

It is cheaper to treat good employees who have slipped into substance abuse than to fire them and train new ones. A sound program will put a strong emphasis on cost-effective out-patient programs to keep employees productive and on the job.

For about $60 a year each, an employer could randomly test his employees for drugs five times. Some companies immediately fire anyone testing positive. This policy costs them to train new employees and is devastating to the person fired from their job. Employers could have a signed hiring-in contract with their employees. The employer pays for the periodic and random drug screening tests until one is positive. From then on, the testing goes to twice a week on a random basis and the employee pays for it and their drug treatment. Testing could be reduced in frequency as time goes on and all tests are clean.

As it is, coming up "dirty" on pre-employment drug screen tests almost universally means you don't get hired. Substance abusers still thinking of working usually apply for jobs where they are not tested for drugs. When they can't work or when they decide not to work, what do they do? Many drift deeper into addiction then commit more crimes to pay for drugs. Offering them a job when and if they sober up could establish a whole new battlefront in the drug wars. Each person who stops buying drugs means that less drugs are being sold. When nobody is buying drugs the drug wars will be over.

Instead of the stick (jail and no job for being a doper) they would get the carrot (a job and their life back) for sobering up. However, they would have to agree to pay the costs of more frequent drug testing for a period of time to prove that their sobriety is permanent. As time goes by with continuous clean tests, the testing could be spaced further apart but is still done randomly.

America can become competitive again with other major industrial nations if 20% of our workers were not loaded. American products cost much more than they need to because of drugs and alcohol. Substance abusers take more "sick" days. They really do suffer from more physical illnesses in addition to their drug and alcohol hangovers that cause missed work days. Drugs weaken the immune system making substance abusers vulnerable to many different ailments. Their higher rate of injuries, accidents and accidental destruction of equipment all cost money. The worker under the influence produces less and costs more.

Sobering up the workers, even the job applicants, would have a very big financial ripple effect. The worker teetering on the edge, who is usually fired for flunking his urine test, will be sobered up and kept working. Putting the substance abusing job applicants to work on the condition that they sober up will save society bundles of money. Sobered up job applicants and sobered up workers won't be in the ranks of the unemployed who might start stealing or dealing when their unemployment benefits run out.

Stealing costs money. We all pay a higher price for goods to cover the costs resulting from the fact that 2% of all the merchandise on the shelves in stores gets stolen, not bought. Drug addicts who shoplift then "return" the items for cash ("I lost the receipt") don't call this stealing. They call it "boosting."

What does the substance abuser cost society on the home front? We have talked about the incredible cost of foster home placement. In foster homes, 70% of the kids are there because of substance abusing parents. Substance abuse often leads to child abuse and neglect.

THE NEW NUCLEAR FAMILY

In the past ten years in my practice I have run into a strange new kind of nuclear family. Over the years, I have counseled many young married couples. Often they were having problems with their children and their marriage. I helped them in their struggle to learn parenting and communication skills. Many of the new generation of young couples struggling to do the right thing in their marriage and with their children still come for counseling. The strange new arrangement I refer to is the drug addict and his girlfriend.

No, they are not married. However, the two or three children the couple have had together live with them. They've often been together for five or six years. He doesn't support his girlfriend or the children even though he works. His girlfriend pays the rent out of the money she receives from Welfare or Aid to Financially Dependent Children.

I get inquiry calls from the druggie's girlfriend saying that she and her boyfriend have been fighting all the time. She doesn't think it's good for the children to see all this uproar (she's right). She thinks they might need counseling.

Within the first thirty seconds of talking to this lady I know what is going on. There are a number of clues to make me realize we are dealing with a familiar pattern. No, they aren't married. Yes, they have children together. They've been arguing. The girl's voice sounds sad and scared. "Is he involved in some kind of substance abuse?" I ask. The answer is always yes.

She says her boyfriend has agreed to come in with her for counseling. She makes an appointment. He never comes. Sometimes she calls back and says her boyfriend had to work late. Something suddenly came up. Sometimes he simply refuses to come. Sometimes she comes alone and tells how things have gotten gradually worse at home. He hits her sometimes.

He used to give her a little money. Now, he tries to "borrow" from her when her welfare check comes. He's working and has an income four times greater than what welfare gives her. Yet, she buys the food and pays the rent because he never seems to have any money. Drugs are not free. His drug appetite has gotten bigger over the years. What does he do when she says she needs that money to feed the kids? He gets mad. He might hit her. He might forcibly take the money.

Why did he agree to even make the one appointment which he would never keep? He did that because she was threatening to leave. Promise them anything. Tomorrow they'll forget. These girls seem to work themselves up to a brief moment of courage then fade back into fear. Fear of his anger, fear of the loneliness they would experience if they really do leave their substance abusing boyfriend. He will probably lose his job after awhile due to his substance abuse. Anger, accidents and absenteeism plague the substance abuser at work. Then he will be completely dependent on her for food and, if he can get it from her, money. It is at this point he often starts slipping into dealing and stealing to supply his habit.

These relationships which had not even developed into marriages don't have a chance. The children have two strikes against them. With time, the live-in boyfriend will become more irrational and abusive. He is likely to eventually lose his job. His girlfriend might finally actually leave him. She and her children may be homeless for a time. Many homeless women went to the streets to escape violent and abusive men who were high all the time.

There is a good chance they will be evicted for not paying the rent or for disturbances. If he abuses the children they will go to foster homes, even if she promises to separate from him and even if she never hit them herself. Why? Failure to protect the children from abuse.

If she does leave the substance abuser after welfare has taken her children, she will still have to prove that she can be a good mother. She will have to take parenting classes and prove she can stay out of abusive relationships. If she does all that, she can get her children back in a few months. What does every relationship involving a substance abusing non-supportive male cost society? I would say that a conservative estimate would be at least $50,000 a year.

Ever hear of having your cake and eating it, too? That's what the druggie wants. And he'll work hard to get it. He wants a family, children, companionship, sex. That's what people get married for. But he also wants his drugs. So he has found a way to have both.

If he marries the girl, he has to support her. So instead he acts like she did this stupid thing and got pregnant a couple times. But if she doesn't gripe too much he'll overlook that and let her stay around. And now and then he'll swear he loves her. And he'll swear that he will change and go to counseling and do anything she wants. She is placated for the moment and tomorrow all the promises are forgotten.

The above scenario is yet another example of the many hidden costs of the drug epidemic. Sober, most of those druggies would marry the girl, support her and the children. She wouldn't be on Welfare. We, as a society, wouldn't be making it possible for him to spend all his money on dope. Sober, he will eventually develop a feeling of pride and not even want the welfare money. If this guy can be sobered up at work before he gets fired, everybody wins.

There has been an overwhelming helplessness experienced by this author in dealing with these beautiful people. They have so much potential but they are sinking into a living hell. They take their children with them. If both the man and the woman were abusing substances, the journey down into a living hell of addiction, with their children in foster homes and them in jail, is ferociously rapid.

REBUILDING NEIGHBORHOODS FROM SCRATCH

Certain neighborhoods, sometimes stretching for blocks or even miles, are in states of incredible decay. We could call it "The Inner City Blues." Taking care of a crack baby for one year can easily cost over $100,000. Special education programs for one year for a third grade child who was born addicted can cost $13,000. That is, if the money is there to provide such a program. Most school districts' budgets have been cut to pay for cops and jails. Johnny is suffering from long term intellectual deficits, the effects of being born addicted. It not only is hard for Johnny to learn to read, there usually isn't money to pay the special tutors to teach him.[145]

In 1981 twelve female cocaine users sought treatment in Philadelphia. In 1989, 3,300 sought help. One in five babies born in Philadelphia in 1990 was born with cocaine in their system. Nearly half the addicts in the city are women. Many of the adult users in the system are children whose drug addicted mothers were ignored by the system two decades ago.

Rod Mullen and Naya Arbiter are leaders in the effort to save America from drugs and the criminal justice system. They claim that the criminal justice system creates and perpetuates the very evils of drug abuse and crime in our society which it is supposed to correct. They work and write together in the Amity Therapeutic Community Program. One of their articles is "Against the Odds: Therapeutic Community Approaches to Underclass Drug Abuse." This article appeared in Peter Smith's book "Drug Policy in the Americas."[97]

They wrote "As the tide of casual drug use that crested in 1985 recedes, the United States must face what it has long ignored: the intractable and entangled wreckage of inner city social ills. Addiction-driven criminality among the urban 'underclass' is the force behind the dramatic growth of prisons, jails, probation and parole. Always marginal, this population is increasingly separate from the middle-class experience and deviant from middle-class values. It will not and cannot respond to programs designed for mainstream society. Effective interventions for urban underclass drug users must focus on methodology that is 'habilitative' rather than rehabilitative, providing the very basics of healthy living. Emphasis must shift from individual recovery to community and institutional recovery."[97]

A study of a Philadelphia inner-city neighborhood revealed the new sexual morality: Casual sex with as many women as possible. Getting as many of them pregnant as possible was the goal. For each additional woman who has his baby, the self esteem and prowess of the amoral youth was enhanced in his subculture. It was a hit and run ethic where you bragged about, but never admitted to, impregnating a woman. It was a culture where abandonment of the female is the norm. Illegitimacy rates in the inner-city Philadelphia neighborhoods studied hovered around 80%. The rate of illegitimacy in the general population is 30%, 5.5 times greater than 30 years ago.[73] This is yet another substance abuse fueled morality decay in America. Sober people do take more responsibility for themselves, their mates, and their children. Sober people are much more likely to have relationships last and to stay married than substance abusers.

CRACK HOUSES: THE NEW SODOM AND GOMORRAH?

We know that certain drugs, especially cocaine, can enhance sexual activity. Marathon sex with multiple partners is common in crack houses. The conscience is gone. The female is a victim of the predatory males and of their own drug involvement/addiction. There has been a lot of debate about the fact that most of these pregnant females immediately begin receiving welfare as soon as their pregnancy is confirmed. They are often second and third generation welfare recipients. They are much more likely to continue to receive welfare and raise their children as single mothers than they are to get off welfare through work or marriage to a wage earning male.

A lot of debaters have asked the question "By what moral logic should a taxpayer be asked to give a part of his earnings to sustain a child fathered by a young man who disappears leaving mother and child as wards of the state?"[79] Some suggest continuing charity or welfare for widows and orphans but cut off welfare to mothers of illegitimate children. Others recommend replacing welfare with an offer of a neo-WPA jobs program. President Bill Clinton suggested a "two years and out" welfare reform plan.

How much of this immorality is drug driven? My guess: Most of it. My answer: Sober these people up. How?: Through a massive effort using all the tools outlined in this book. Test every inner city youth who comes in contact with the law in any way. This is legal. Suspicion of being under the influence allows for testing. If the test is positive, and most will be, enrollment in "Sober Forever" begins.

There will likely be times, sometimes just for a few days, sometimes for a year or more, when these young men and women will have to be taken from their neighborhoods and placed in sober living centers. There they will be taught their A B Cs, parenting skills, given job training, moral development and provided with health care. Expensive? A bargain at twice the price when we add up what these people cost society by continuing to go down the inevitable and well traveled road of addiction.

We can't ask probation to follow these people. They can't and apparently won't. Organizations whose growth and continued existence depends on producing well documented success stories will be funded. They will use every trick in the book (listed in Chapter 11) to keep these people sober. When nothing works, then jail (hopefully for just a few days) will be used. But jail will come quickly and for just brief periods after failure to cooperate, refusal to attend meetings or refusal to test.

If we sober up the people on drugs who are making crack babies which the state pays for, will the illegitimacy rate go down? Sober men and women and boys and girls are more responsible, less impulsive and more cautious in their sexual activities than junkies. Sobering up America is likely to drop the illegitimacy rate to a third of what it is now.

Some couples may decide to not get married even if they are sober. But sober, they will be able to continue to operate as a couple, as a family unit. Drug addicts cannot even get along with each other. Violence and break-ups stalk their relationships. Sober, a much higher percentage of them will be willing and able to support their own children. Sober, these couples and their children will have their brains working right. Being able to think and learn will give them the chance to be all that they and their children can be. Sober, they can build for a future: Theirs, their children's, and America's.

The addicted are the people who are breaking the economic and emotional back of the American society. They are the people who make us tremble in fear that we will get shot when we go to and from the bank. At the bank we deposit our payment to the I.R.S. That money we give to the I.R.S. is then used to pay for the foster care needed because of substance abuse, the prisons needed for our addicted, and Social Security payments to the "disabled" addicted. Substance abusers rob us directly with guns or indirectly by sucking up most of our tax dollars to catch them, try them, feed them, and lock them up.

PRESCRIPTION DRUGS

We found in Chapter Two that male drug abusers typically obtained illegal substances through "street markets." The female substance abusers who chose drugs rather than alcohol were more likely to abuse prescription drugs. These were obtained through one or sometimes a whole string of doctors.[134] What can be done about these ladies who spend their days stoned and hidden away? For those wanting to break the habit, most cities have prescription drug abuse groups. Few of the prescription drug abusers seek and attend such meetings. Sometimes the few people with whom these prescription drug abusers have maintained contact in the outside world notice they slur their words, repeat themselves and often don't make much sense. But then when you are the pizza delivery boy or the drug store delivery boy, who cares?

Help must be found for these unfortunates who are destroying their lives and their brains. But that help may have to wait. Priorities must be established. Sobering up that part of the population whose substance abuse is costing the most must come first. This includes all the criminals on drugs, all the gangs on drugs, all the spousal abusers on drugs, and then all the workers on drugs. Perhaps first of all on the list of who to sober up should be all the children on drugs.

There is yet another category of substance abuse so insidious and yet so widespread I hesitate to mention it. Yet, such a book as this would not be complete without giving the reader the opportunity to look at the facts and make a decision for themselves.

Let me start by reminding the readers I have not yet recommended, anywhere in this book, that they read any other book. There is an extensive bibliography at the end of this book for those wanting to study the drug crisis in greater detail. But now, I am recommending that every reader of this book, "Drug Wars: The Final Battle" also read one other book of monumental importance.

This book depicts a nation enslaved to a major professional group, the psychiatrists. The name of the book is "Toxic Psychiatry" published by St. Martin's Press in 1991. The author is Peter R. Breggin, M.D. Yes, M.D., doctor of medicine. He is a psychiatrist. His is the most hated and feared name in the field of psychiatry and perhaps in medicine in general. He has spent his whole professional career as a psychiatrist trying to protect people from other psychiatrists. As a result, he has had to defend his right to continue practicing medicine on more than one occasion. There are many people who want to see him gone, or at least with his license to practice revoked.

Even before the table of contents, Dr. Breggin had a bold face **"WARNING. Do not abruptly stop most psychiatric drugs."** He described most psychiatric drugs as highly addictive and very likely to cause serious permanent brain damage. But he warned that abruptly stopping them "...can produce withdrawal symptoms that are emotionally and physically distressing and sometimes life-threatening." He advised gradual withdrawal from psychiatric drugs, with professional guidance.

His battle against his fellow psychiatrists began in 1954 when he was eighteen and a freshman at Harvard University. He and other volunteers went frequently to The Metropolitan State Hospital, a classic psychiatric snakepit. They found that by befriending "hopelessly mentally ill patients" he and his group of volunteers succeeded in getting many of them functioning again. By the end of the year, eleven of the fourteen patients his group had worked with were well enough to be discharged.

The reaction of the professional psychiatric community to this miracle? To warn about the damage these untrained students could do. The president of the Boston Psychoanalytic Society had never set foot in the Metropolitan State Hospital. Yet, he said that these untrained students would forever ruin these mentally ill patients. These were patients who were being raped, beaten, and were urinating on the floor before Peter Breggin and the other students arrived. These were patients who were treated like animals and thus acted like animals.

Dr. Breggin wrote "As the volunteer program grew in size and ambition, the hundreds of us passing through each year began to transform the hospital. It was no longer so easy for the aides to rape or beat patients. A Harvard or Radcliff student might stumble on the assault."

THE FIRST FLIGHT OVER THE CUCKOO'S NEST

Sixteen years before the Jack Nicholson movie Dr. Breggin and his fellow students engineered a breakout from the asylum. He said "We also proved that the so-called violent patients weren't nearly so dangerous as supposed: two of us stole the keys and took half the women's ward for a trip into town. We gave them money to buy trinkets in the local five-and-ten and returned them to the hospital without incident."

I take it back. You better not read "Toxic Psychiatry." Dr. Breggin destroys so many sacred cows that you are bound to find at least a couple of yours among them. Dr. Breggin maintained that Attention Deficit Disorder and Dyslexia, two of America's favorite new designer diseases, are myths. These myths he claimed were created to justify the abandonment of responsibility for our children.

Why can't Johnny really read, Dr. Breggin asks? The answer: "Physical, emotional and sexual abuse and neglect produce children who typically get labeled with psychiatric or school-related diagnoses. Cognitive and emotional problems in children are caused not only by direct abuse, but by witnessing violence and the typical marital discord, separation and divorce."

Other books Dr. Breggin has written: "Psychiatric Drugs: Hazards to the Brain" and "Electroshock: Its Brain-Disabling Effects." Dr. Breggin's reward for presenting the facts regarding dangers to the public from his profession? He has been labeled as a fanatic.[107.] He has had to defend his license to practice as a psychiatrist in front of the Maryland Commission on Medical Discipline.

A complaint had been lodged by the National Alliance for the Mentally Ill. That group became upset after Dr. Breggin criticized psychiatric drugs on the Oprah Winfrey national TV talk show.

Dr. Breggin claimed that Dr. Benjamin Rush, recognized as the Father of psychiatry, killed the Father of our country, George Washington, by bleeding him to death to get rid of "bad blood." Sub heads throughout Dr. Breggin's book lead into frightening facts: On ritalin (frequently used to "treat" hyperactive children) the sub head is **"COCAINE IN DISGUISE?"** Here are some others: **"BRAIN DAMAGE FROM RITALIN?"; "THE BIRTH OF CHEMICAL LOBOTOMY - REPORTS FROM THE DRUG PIONEERS";** and **"UPJOHN PAYS TOP DOLLAR FOR A PSYCHIATRIST."** Upjohn is a major manufacturer of psychiatric medications.

THE REBIRTH OF "TALK THERAPY"

Dr. Breggin did not recommend the complete elimination of all psychiatric and psychotropic drugs. In short term and limited use, he found that some can be temporarily beneficial. He listed a wide variety of alternate interventions in "mental illness," including states of anxiety, depression and even schizophrenia. He documented the greater effectiveness of non-drug treatment of mental illness by quoting many studies. These are the "talk therapies" which the practice of psychiatry has attacked as worthless.

Dr. Breggin documented distortion and falsification of the data on various drugs. He found that the Upjohn Pharmaceutical Company touted the effectiveness of Xanax over any other treatment method in reducing panic/anxiety attacks. Dr. Breggin found that the results obtained after four weeks on Xanax were proudly proclaimed.

What was not proclaimed was what Dr. Breggin found when he looked up the original research article. After eight weeks, in the same study, the placebo patients were doing as well as the patients who had received Xanax. When the study was over and the Xanax discontinued, the patients receiving Xanax suffered severe withdrawal and rebound reactions. These included an increase in anxiety and phobic responses. They experienced a 350% greater number of panic attacks than the placebo group who received the sugar pill instead of Xanax.

Anyone with a psychiatric problem, or anyone with a loved one with a psychiatric problem, should read Dr. Breggin's book "Toxic Psychiatry" before undergoing any kind of treatment. If treatment for a psychiatric condition has begun, and this treatment involves the usage of any drugs, reading Dr. Breggin's book becomes even more important.

I have referred patients to psychiatrists to obtain medications to aid in the treatment of depression or other disorders. I know that the minimum dosages necessary to 'take the edge off' my patients' upsetting symptoms will be prescribed by the psychiatrists to whom I make referrals. I tell my patients that within two months our goal will be for them to be off the medications. Our goal will be to accomplish, through meditation, self-suggestion and other techniques, whatever the medications were accomplishing. I tell them that meditation does not have the side effects of medication.

Anyone who has been prescribed psychiatric medications for two months, or who has a loved one who has been prescribed psychiatric medications for two months **MUST** read Dr. Breggin's book. The information in his book can save your life or the life of your loved ones. The information in Dr. Breggin's book can save you and your loved ones from becoming brain-damaged vegetables. Dr. Breggin's book can save you and your loved ones from the hell of addiction to psychotropic/psychiatric drugs. That addiction, though quieter than the damage done by street drugs, is still ruining millions of lives.

A series of studies which have been conducted since the early seventies have proven over and over that talk therapy of one form or another consistently out-performs therapy with psychiatric medications only. In fact, psychotherapy alone usually out-performs therapy which combines talk therapy and medications.[105.] The author warns that psychologists, in their quest for prescription privileges, may be abandoning their strong forte, which is talk psychotherapy. Instead, they may be buying into the myth that drugs are more effective in treating depression and other mental illnesses than psychotherapy.

The appeal of psychiatric medications is that there is often an immediate reduction of disturbing symptoms. Unfortunately, the medications simply mask the problem. The longer medications are used, the more difficult it is to finally face the problem later. Of the 135 million psychotropic medications prescribed in 1991, only 17.3% were prescribed by psychiatrists, 82.7% were written by physicians of various general or specialty stripes. Psychotropic medications are designed to treat mental or emotional problems. They were medical doctors who lack extensive specialized training in mental health.[127]   Medical doctors in an HMO (Health Maintenance Organization) do not receive brownie points for referring depressed people to more expensive psychotherapy especially when they can "treat" the depression with the stroke of a pen.

YOU CAN MAKE A DIFFERENCE

What if you, the reader, decide that the "Sober Forever" Program described in this book sounds good. What if you think it should be implemented. What if you take it to your congressman or senator and find that he doesn't believe in it? That means that he hasn't been informed about the research that shows such a program could work. Or, in fact, that it's probably the only program that could work.

What can be done about the criminal justice system, especially the Department of Justice? There, the belief is still strong that rehabilitation just doesn't work, and that locking people up is the only solution. They maintain this belief in spite of overwhelming evidence to the contrary. Society and the public will have to scream so loud that even the head of the Department of Justice and the rest of our leaders in Washington will have to listen.

What will you scream? "Look at the facts and start doing what works!"

GETTING YOUR BABY BACK

If any of the readers of this book have watched with horror as your babies, early in their adolescent years, were sucked into the world of drug abuse, you have felt great pain. If you have tried to pull them back from their living hell and failed, you have known the ultimate suffering of a parent. When your main mission in life, the raising of your children, has gone horribly wrong there is little solace left for you in the world. But, as long as our drug addicted children are alive somewhere, there is still time, there is still hope.

When our children are finally rescued from the living hell of drug abuse, we will still never have our babies back, the ones we held and started loving so long ago. That is because, even sober, the years of drugging will have taken a toll. The brain will never be completely normal. Our addicted children's original pre-drug potential will never be completely realized. But, with healing and time, it will be close. Close enough to definitely make it worth while. Every parent I have ever known who got their babies back sobered up were ecstatic. Most of the time, once sober, the residual damage didn't prevent work or even school.

"How will you feel, Mrs. Smith, if Johnny is a little damaged when he finally comes home sober?" All the Mrs. Smiths who ever answered that question for me always said, "I'll take it. In a heartbeat."

When I talk about "Getting your baby back" I mean babies of any age. No matter how old they get they will always be our babies because we remember those first days and those first steps. Drugs and alcohol have slowed or stopped growth so we can say that they are still our babies in more ways than one. Someone told me once that the topic of the day at their Narcotics Anonymous meeting had been "The Sick Puppies."

"Who are the sick puppies?" I asked.

"Us," he answered. "Everybody at the meeting."

Maybe you'd like a different life for your loved ones besides alternating periods of time in jail with a marginal, drugged existence outside of prison. Or worse, is there anything more painful than attending your own child"s funeral? You can demand that when you ask for help in sobering up your loved ones that it be given. Other parents have had access to this help in the past and it saved lives.[64] Why should you have to stand by helpless as the police and courts tell you "You have to wait until they decide they want help, you can't force them." Then these same people who told you you have to wait till your children are ready to sober up turn around and lock up your baby for ten years.

You are not helpless. You can do something. There is an initiative process whereby propositions can be put on the ballot. The people in the United States do have a say in how things are going to be run. People have changed the way they are taxed and what their tax dollars are spent for. They have implemented anti-tobacco educational programs.

Since the current judicial system is still maintaining that involuntary sobriety can't be done and won't work, it will be up to you to make sure it happens. Some of your loved ones may be among the lost sheep we will bring back from their living hell of substance abuse. You can demand that people be kept out of the judicial system, out of the courts. You can demand that the taxpayers' dollars not be squandered on $40,000 trials. Trials to try to lock somebody up for trying to get a job washing windows, when what he really needed was help getting sober and treatment for his mental illness. Both are hard to come by.

This is the help they will receive from the "Sober Forever" Program. You can insist that anybody doing a crime while under the influence of an illegal substances be diverted into an involuntary sobriety program, one that is guaranteed to work. Court procedures can be completely by-passed in most cases. This is not coddling criminals. As it is now, after we spend all that money convicting them they're out in a few days to go back to drinking and drugging. There's no room in the jails.

The judicial system claims we don't have the resources to track down the substance abusing petty criminals who don't bother to show up for court. We spend huge amounts of money to slowly parade our drug addicts through the judicial system while ignoring the real problem. Finally, after the drug addict's life has been torn apart at the seams, we lock them up for ten years. They should have had help in getting sober the first time anyone realized they were getting high. If that help had come when their substance abuse had first led to problem behavior, the whole tragic scenario of loss and jail could have been prevented.

THREE STRIKES AND EATEN BY THE WOLVES

Have you ever heard of the old dog sled trick? Our leaders across the nation are getting ready to use this one again. That's when you have four people on a dog sled being followed by a pack of wolves. You push the last person off the sled and it buys you a little time. Thirty states are about to pass the "Three strikes and you"re out" legislation. After three felonies you go to jail for life. The only problem is that in California stealing a bag of avocados is a felony. After stealing two bags then beating up your girlfriend you'll never see the outside of a prison again. The third felony has to involve violence. When we decide to sober up the avocado thief after he steals his first bag there will only be the one strike. This is because we know that almost everyone who is arrested for anything is drunk or loaded on drugs or both at the time of the crime and the arrest. We also know that sobered up criminals stop committing crimes.

The howling public loves the "Three strikes and you're out" idea. Already, the bodies thrown off the sled are being ripped up. But, since crime won't stop or even slow down, they will be back after the sled shortly. Then who do the politicians kick off the sled next? As we lock up the avocado thieves we either mortgage even more of our future to build more jails or we let loose the armed robbers, rapists and murderers to make room for those with these new mandatory sentences. This is what is happening now. There are people who have been locked up all over America for over ten years for selling a small amount of cocaine. This is the legacy of the mandatory sentencing laws passed in the enthusiasm of the 1980's war on drugs.

The federal government is always trying to avoid spending money on drug treatment so they can afford more jails. They decided to conduct a series of studies to see if drug treatment could be shortened and still work.[35]

Once a Mexican studying English shared experiences with an American studying Spanish. "I'm going to study Spanish for two years," the American proclaimed. "How long are you going to study English?"

"Hasta que yo lo aprenda!" The Mexican replied, which means "Until I learn it."

Our leaders in the federal government still have not learned that drug rehabilitation takes as long as it takes. Some will stay sober forever after one slap on the wrist. A few of the most addicted will have to be in a live-in drug rehab center for two years. Then they will have to go to sober living houses and be watched constantly by sober buddies for a few more years. The "Sober Forever" Center of their choice will decide how much and how long treatment and supervised housing must last in order to guarantee sobriety. Frequent urine testing, especially in the early stages of treatment, will help these "Sober Forever" Centers to make that decision.

You have the right as an American citizen to demand that the system be changed. Why should all the other countries in the world be able to get by with locking up only a fourth to a tenth of the people that we do in the United States? Why should other countries enjoy as low as a five percent recidivism rate (rate of rearrest) when ours hovers around 65 percent? Why should most of Europe, with drugs easily available, have the advantage of a much lower addiction rate than the U.S.? Most of Europe already has programs much like the "Sober Forever" Program. They prefer sobering up to locking up their druggies. As we have seen, that's the cheapest way to go. It seems that we can learn something from systems elsewhere that stress rehabilitation and education instead of courts and jails. We know jails don't work.

TELL YOUR LEADERS

If you, the reader, are convinced that the involuntary sobriety program outlined in this book should be implemented in your town and in your state, tell your legislators. Tell them you're mad and you want to sober up the dope fiends so they'll work, pay taxes, and quit doing crime. Tell them you're sick and tired of being afraid to go outside.

Tell your congressmen and senators you want all those people out of jail. Not the murderers. Leave them in jail. But tell them to let out the substance abusers whose dope and alcohol led them down the wrong path. But be prepared, because when you tell them these things they will smile at you and say, "We are studying the problem." But behind your back they'll laugh at your stupidity and say you don't understand crime. Then you'll have to show them the numbers. You'll have to show them that you are not going to just say your piece and then go away so they can get on with "business as usual" which means more cops and robbers and jails.

Tell your leaders you want those people out of jail because only a few of them are learning anything there except how to be a better criminal. And tell them that the ones they won't let out now must start getting help. Only fifteen percent or less get any help while in jail. When drug rehab and job/work training is done in jail the chance of staying out after release increases dramatically.

Tell anyone you vote for who will listen that you want the prisoners to be sober while they're in jail. But who is going to test the prisoners for drugs when the keepers, in some instances, are providing the drugs? We know that arrangements would be made for all of the prisoner-clients of a dope dealing guard to test clean. It would not be that difficult to find somebody in the jail who isn't loaded who will urinate in a bottle for them.

And tell them that prisoners need to be prepared for a crime-free life outside of prison through rehabilitation, job training and education. Demand that these programs be started while the prisoners are still in 'the joint.' And make sure all of that treatment isn't wasted when they do get it. Make sure they stay sober and have a drug-free place to live when they get out.

This safe haven from drugs will be a place where people are working on getting sober and staying sober. Give them food so they don't have to steal to eat. Give them hope by letting them see that the buddies they live with are struggling, but still happy, and making it sober. Give them their lives back. And after you have told all this to your leaders and legislators and find they are still ignoring you and laughing at you behind your back, elect new leaders. Elect leaders who understand how America is being held hostage by drugs. Elect leaders who will know what to do about it: Sober up America.

LET'S WAIT UNTIL YOU NEED A HEART TRANSPLANT

In Chapter Nine we were glad doctors treat colds before they turn into pneumonia. In most cases, we are dealing with a sickness in our addicts and in society much worse than colds. It is, as noted in Chapter One, more a matter of the heart. Let's try another analogy: What if doctors practiced medicine like this: Mrs. Jones goes to the doctor with a pain in her chest. Her doctor says, "Sorry, I don't have time to take your blood pressure. Oh, someone told you that lowering blood pressure saves people from having heart attacks? Well, they may be right. But it doesn't matter. I don't have time to take your blood pressure or to teach you anything about a low-fat diet. You see, we're very busy here doing heart transplants and open heart surgery. We have some very serious problems to deal with here. When your problem gets really serious, let me know."

That's pretty absurd. It's a good thing our doctors don't practice medicine that way. The medical profession has found that prevention, early detection and treatment of disease saves money and saves lives. The criminal justice system hasn't yet learned that lesson yet. They ignore all the small time substance abusers still in the early stages of their addiction. These are the ones who are just beginning to have skirmishes with the law. There is this freedom thing. We seem to feel that we must do anything to avoid intruding in people's lives. At least not until their addictions are so out-of-control they need the equivalent of open heart surgery. And what a surgery they get in the criminal justice system! Locked up with the world's most violent people, raped, and turned into drug addicts and animals. Rather than replace the damaged heart/soul of the drug addict we have taken their hearts forever. They become heartless predators. Even the mostly ineffective prevention steps practiced by the criminal justice system are being drastically curtailed to pay for more jails. Probation and parole officers across the nation are losing their jobs due to "funding cut-backs."

Oh, sure, we know George gets drunk every Saturday night and beats up his wife. The cops are out there at his place all the time. His wife won't press charges, so what can we do. Nothing, of course, until he kills her. Then we can lock that rotten slob up forever. If George had been put into an involuntary sobriety program the first time his wife or a neighbor called 911 his wife would be alive. And George wouldn't have required the equivalent of open heart surgery - spending the rest of his life in jail. His children wouldn't be raised in foster homes.

What will it cost to sober up George? Nothing. He'll pay for the classes, the group meetings, the breathalyzer tests. It might cost him a couple thousand dollars for all those services the first year. That's probably less than he would have spent for booze that year. If he was high on drugs when 911 was called, he'll probably save a lot more by not buying drugs than he has to pay to sober up. Drugs aren't cheap. And we'll save all the money it would have cost to lock George up and take care of his kids for him while he's in jail. We'll save another $4,000 that George will pay in taxes that first year by staying out of jail and continuing to work. Prisoners don't pay taxes. If a bunch of Georges are sobered up each of us will save another few hundred dollars a year on our auto insurance because these loaded and uninsured Georges won't be out there running into people and running up the rates for everyone.

This is just a partial list of the savings involved if we sober up George. Our hospital wards and emergency rooms are filled with people who are there because of substance abuse. Usually they have no insurance so we pay for their treatment through some kind of county medical program for indigents. If they still have jobs and medical insurance we still pay, because our insurance rates keep going up. Crack babies are very expensive and not all of them are born in the ghetto.

Is this about freedom? And trying to not be Big Brother? Or is this about a system that turns its back on people who need help. Just how free are those 1.2 million Americans in jail who we ignored and finally locked up when their addiction inevitably led to a deterioration of their behavior? Most Americans now in jail have a history of substance abuse. Substance abuse eroded their conscience and made it possible for them to try to meet their needs by preying on the rest of society.

"DRUG WARS: THE FINAL BATTLE" - THE MOVIE

There will be opposition to the implementation of the "Sober Forever" Program. Educating our leaders and Americans in general about the only solution that will really work will be critical. Otherwise, we are doomed to keep trying the same tired solutions over and over, solutions which don't work. I have written a movie script for the purpose of helping to educate America on the "Sober Forever" Program. This movie is also entitled "Drug Wars: The Final Battle." The movie is designed to let the public see the "Sober Forever" Program in action. The movie is in the pre-production stages at this writing. It is an action adventure movie focusing on sobering up our two million drug-addicted homeless teenagers. The plan is for the movie to also be produced by Speranza Productions, the publisher of this book. Speranza is the Italian word for hope.

In the last scene of the movie, the "Sober Forever" Program director, Dr. Brennan, has gone out on the streets of Detroit with his rehabilitation crew. They are in the process of picking up three drug addicted homeless teenagers who are shooting up drugs. The teenagers say, "You can't arrest us, you didn't read us our rights!"

Dr. Brennan responds, "I'm sorry, I almost forgot. You have the right to a decent, clean and sober life. If you don't have the courage to sober up on your own, the willpower will be provided to you free of charge. You have the right to pray to the God of your choice for help in getting off drugs."

This book has outlined a program to sober up America. The movie zeroes in on what will be just one aspect of that program, the sobering up of our homeless teenagers. They are our next generation and we have abandoned them to the streets. There are two million of them. One out of twenty teenagers in America has no home.

Ninety-three homeless teenagers were interviewed. They were living in abandoned buildings, parks, fast food restaurants, under freeway bridges and on roof tops. Seventy-nine percent reported using illicit drugs in the last thirty days. Most used marijuana. As a group they had turned to prostitution, pan handling and drug dealing for income. Half received some money from family, friends, or had short term jobs.[74]

Most reported having sex but only half used a condom. Seven of the 26 females who were interviewed were pregnant at the time of the interview. Forty-four percent had had one or more pregnancies. Many had serious health problems but few were able to receive medical care. Twenty percent were seriously depressed.

This is our next generation which we have relegated to the streets and to a hopeless existence. They can be salvaged. They must be salvaged. They are our future. The movie shows how. If we do nothing, many of those two million homeless teenagers who survive will grow into violent criminals who prey on society. We have voted ourselves wonderful retirement benefits. We have spent ourselves into a 4.5 trillion dollar budget deficit. If we do not rescue our youth from substance abuse and teach them to work, nobody is going to be there to foot the huge bills we have left for our next generations.

Jerome Miller, director of the National Center on Institutions and Corrections, was the director of youth services in Massachusetts in 1972. He dropped the 2,000 institutionalized youth population down to 40 by closing the juvenile detention centers. He spent the money he saved on community-based care programs. By rehabilitating the delinquents, he averted a future crime wave since the rehabilitated delinquents did not enter the adult criminal justice system. The technology is there to rescue our youth from drugs and crime.[110,111,112] We just have to put it to work.

Researchers went to study the people in a small village in Italy. They were present when a woman gave birth to an infant. Within five minutes of the birth, 50 people had kissed the newborn baby. Before the week was over all but a handful of the people in this village of a few hundred had been to see the new baby.

In America we are much more civilized and most births are in hospitals. But too often in America and **never** in that little village in Italy, women take their babies home to an empty house or apartment. There they are alone and afraid and do not know what to do about this thing that never stops crying. What should have been a blessed, joyous event is turned into a time of painful days and sleepless night. No one told this woman how to be a mother. No one is there to show her how to be a mother and no one is there to help her with the job of being a mother.

This woman is at great risk of becoming a substance abuser. Her newborn infant is at great risk of becoming a victim of child abuse.

THE FINAL EXAMINATION

You have read the book "Drug Wars: The Final Battle." Here is your final examination. It is multiple choice. There is just one question: "When is the best time to sober up a substance abuser?" You may select an answer from the following: (A) When he has hit bottom and when he's ready. (B) When he smokes his first marijuana cigarette but before he gets into the hard stuff. (C) When he's in the second grade, through prevention and education. (D) When he is in the womb, by making sure his mother is sober so a cross generation addiction cycle is broken. (E) When he's in jail so he doesn't go back to dope when he gets out. (F) All of the above.

If you picked "F," or "All of the above" you have passed your final examination and you have learned something from this book. Congratulations.

HOMEWORK ASSIGNMENT

Now, if you believe that America is worth saving, you must act quickly. You must demand an overhaul of the criminal justice system. Here is how to begin: Make several copies of the letter on the next page of this book. Fill in the names of your representatives, your mayor, your police chief and mail them off. Let everyone who you think might have any say in the matter know how angry you are about our current drug/prison policies. Let them know that you want things to change. If you are afraid that they will think you are some kind of crack-pot and will pay no attention to you, or if they simply don't know the facts, sending them a copy of this book will leave them no excuse. And, as noted earlier, if they **still** don't listen, vote yourself in a new mayor, police chief or representative who will be willing to push hard for workable drug and prison reform.

DEAR

THIS IS YOUR WAKE-UP CALL! DRUG VIOLENCE CAN BE STOPPED! BUT NOT BY LOCKING UP OUR DRUG ADDICTED CRIMINALS. MANY KEEP USING DRUGS IN JAIL! SOME FIRST BECOME ADDICTED IN JAIL! WHILE THEY ARE IN JAIL AND AFTER THEY ARE BACK OUTSIDE OF JAIL NOBODY DOES ANYTHING ABOUT THEIR DRUG PROBLEM. SO, WHEN THEY GET OUT THEY COMMIT MORE CRIMES AND GET LOCKED UP AGAIN. WE CAN GET ADDICTS OFF DRUGS, IN AND OUT OF JAIL. WHEN THEY STOP DRUGS, THEY STOP THEIR VIOLENCE AND CRIME. SOBER, THEY GET JOBS AND PAY TAXES. WE CAN SEND THREE STUDENTS TO HARVARD FOR A YEAR FOR WHAT IT COSTS TO LOCK UP ONE MAN IN PRISON FOR A YEAR. AMERICA HAS MANY TIMES MORE OF ITS CITIZENS LOCKED UP THAN ANY INDUSTRIAL NATION IN THE WORLD. EDUCATION HAS BEEN CUT TO THE BONE TO PAY FOR MORE JAILS! I'M MAD, AND I'M SICK AND TIRED OF ALL MY TAX DOLLARS GOING TO LAW ENFORCEMENT AND JAILS. THE SOLUTION IS TO GET PEOPLE OFF DRUGS. THE FAIL SAFE PLAN TO DO THAT IS PRESENTED IN COMPLETE DETAIL IN THE BOOK "DRUG WARS: THE FINAL BATTLE - RESCUING AMERICA FROM DRUG VIOLENCE." WE CAN GUARANTEE SOBRIETY FOR A SMALL FRACTION OF THE MONEY THAT WE NOW SPEND TO LOCK UP THESE ADDICTS. I WANT TO SEE THE "SOBER FOREVER" PROGRAM OUTLINED IN "DRUG WARS: THE FINAL BATTLE" IMPLEMENTED IMMEDIATELY! BEFORE IT IS TOO LATE!

SINCERELY YOURS,

REFERENCES, REVIEWS AND NOTES

1. ABC SIX O'CLOCK WORLD NEWS, 2/9/93
Two hundred sixty seven people in Georgia who were arrested for possession of illegal drugs were put into an educational/diversion program of mandatory sobriety, and mandatory testing to guarantee sobriety. A success rate of 91% was claimed, compared to success rates between 20% and 60% reported by most programs.

2. ADMIRE, DAVID "THE NUTS AND BOLTS OF ALTERNATE SENTENCING." TOMORROW'S CITIZENS "ALCOHOL, TOBACCO AND OTHER DRUG PREVENTION TRAINING." CONFERENCE HELD 10/8/93 AT THE TOWN AND COUNTRY CONVENTION CENTER IN SAN DIEGO, CALIFORNIA.

3. ALBRECHT, HANS-JORG AND ANTON VAN KALMTHOUT, Eds. *DRUG POLICIES IN WESTERN EUROPE.* FREIBURG: MAX PLANCK INSTITUTE, 1989.
Drugs are not legal in Europe. Criminal penalties can be imposed in most Western European countries for the sale and possession of illegal drugs. In the United States, especially in the Federal Court system, judges are ordered to send drug offenders to jail for mandatory, long sentences. European judges can decide on a case by case basis whether they will send offenders to treatment or to jail. Until 1990, small amounts of drugs for personal use were legal in Italy. Since then, people arrested with even small amounts of drugs are subject to criminal penalties. Typically, they are offered a choice between treatment and various penalties which can include the suspension of their driver's license, curfews and fines. After three offenses the violator may be sent to jail. Treatment, prevention and education are emphasized. Being locked up in jail is used only as a last resort. Jail is reserved for dealers or addicts who refuse to participate in treatment over and over. Drug abusers are encouraged to go seek help. They don't have to wait months or years for treatment as they do in the United States. People in Europe have money, and drugs such as heroin, cocaine and marijuana are easy to get. In

spite of this, Europeans use drugs at a lower level than U.S. citizens. The U.S. approach to the drug problem is through law enforcement. Europe has basically a treatment/prevention approach to the problem which is similar in many ways to the approach recommended in "Drug Wars: The Final Battle."

3.   "ALCOHOLICS BRAIN DAMAGE SHOWS UP DECADES EARLY." *THE SAN DIEGO UNION,* **12/4/91, Pg. E-3.**
Alcoholics had a reduced ability to metabolize glucose. The frontal lobes of their brains were smaller than normal for their age. They showed impairments in memory, coordination and other functions.

4.   ALVORE, VALERIE, "FAMILY PRESERVATION PROGRAM GETS FUNDING TAKEN FROM LAWYERS' POCKETS." *THE SAN DIEGO UNION-TRIBUNE,* **3/3/93, Pg. B-1.**
The San Diego County Board of supervisors took $5 million from the lawyers who represent children in juvenile court dependency hearings. They put the money into the family preservation program. It was common to have three lawyers and a judge in a single child custody hearing. This included a different lawyer for the mother, father, and child. Half the 7,000 children in foster care in San Diego county could be returned home if proper intervention services were provided to and for the family. The enormous cost of the state trying to raise all the babies from problem families is just beginning to be realized. Helping parents to keep their families together is much cheaper than foster homes.

5.   ANGLIN, DOUGLAS AND YIH-ING HISER, "TREATMENT OF DRUG ABUSE." IN MICHAEL TONRY AND JAMES Q. WILSON, Eds. *DRUGS AND CRIME.* **CHICAGO: UNIVERSITY OF CHICAGO PRESS, 1990.**
In therapeutic communities, a drug rehabilitation treatment approach, only one in four clients remained over three months. Less than one in six finished the one to two year course of treatment. But 75% of the therapeutic community graduates were still drug-free seven years later. (Author's note: That means that of the 16 out of 100 who finished the program, 12

out of that 16 were sober seven years later. These were voluntary programs. A healthy 75% of those who completed the programs got sober. There are massive consequences to society and to the substance abuser because of the large numbers of failures in voluntary sobriety programs. This fact calls for removal of the drug abuser's choice to accept or reject treatment).

6. ANGLIN, M.D., "THE EFFICACY OF CIVIL COMMITMENT IN TREATING NARCOTICS ADDICTION." IN LEUKENFELD, C.G., AND F. M. TIMS, (eds.), *COMPULSORY TREATMENT OF DRUG ABUSE: RESEARCH AND CLINICAL PRACTICE.* National Institute on Drug Abuse Research Monograph 86, Washington, D.C.: U.S. Government Printing Office, 1988.
The relationship between addiction and crime is well established. Civil commitment can be an effective approach for reducing drug use. Evaluation of nearly 1,000 addicts who came into the California Civil Addict Program found that civil commitment (involuntary sobriety) suppressed daily drug use, justifying the use of a "long tail" or lengthy follow-up.

7. "ARRESTS OF FELONS ON PROBATION STUDIED." *THE SAN DIEGO UNION-TRIBUNE,* 2/10/92, Pg. A-12.
Forty-three percent or more of convicted criminals commit new crimes within their first three years on probation.

8. BACKER, THOMAS E., *STRATEGIC PLANNING FOR WORKPLACE DRUG ABUSE PROGRAMS.* DEPARTMENT OF HUMAN SERVICES PUBLICATION NO. [ADM] 87-1538, 1987.
Drug use in the work place, including lost productivity, absenteeism, accidents, medical claims, and thefts, amounts to $60 billion a year. If alcohol is included, the annual total jumps to $140 billion. The postal service found that workers whose pre-employment drug tests were positive were 50% more likely to be fired, injured, disciplined, or absent than those who were drug free. The U.S. Chamber of Commerce found that employees who used drugs are one-third less productive

and three times more likely to injure themselves or another person at work.

9.   BALCH, JAMES E. AND PHYLLIS BALCH, *PRESCRIPTION FOR NUTRITIONAL HEALTH.* GARDEN CITY PARK, N.Y.: AVERY PUBLISHING GROUP, INC., 1990.
Refers to several studies showing that schizophrenics whose symptoms are in remission or partial remission can have a resurgence of psychotic symptoms, including hallucinations, upon ingesting alcohol, marijuana and a variety of illegal drugs. Lists dangerous side effects of marijuana including impairment of the immune system, reproductive system and lungs. Marijuana smokers run higher risks of bronchitis, emphysema and lung cancer. The impaired immune system leaves the marijuana smoker more susceptible to cancer, AIDS and other diseases. The user lacks ambition and direction, is passive, apathetic, and uncommunicative. Withdrawal from marijuana can result in insomnia, tremors, chills and other symptoms that can last for days.

10.   "BATTERING FAMILIES IS A MAJOR CAUSE OF HOMELESSNESS." *SAN DIEGO UNION,* 12/17/91, Pg. A-2.
Thirty-five percent of the women living in city homeless shelters were there to escape men who beat them. There are too few shelters. Eighty to ninety percent of the women seeking shelter are turned away. If they get in at all, their stay is time limited. Sometimes they can stay as long as 90 days. Every 15 seconds in America a woman is beaten. Every six hours, a woman is murdered by her husband or boyfriend. Long term programs and shelters are needed to turn these womens' lives around. This includes time to lick their own substance abuse problems which many have, and time to learn to be a mother and get a sense of self back.

11.   "BENNET TARGETS DRUG USERS." *THE SAN DIEGO TRIBUNE,* 8/5/89, Pg. A-3.
When he was the national anti-drug director William Bennett announced that drug users would be arrested, embarrassed, fined, lose their driver's licenses, cars, and that they should

be sentenced to residential treatment facilities. Upon release they would be required to participate in carefully monitored outpatient programs. He wanted to expand the idea of civil commitment to get help for the user even if they didn't want it. At the same time he made these announcements, where the new federal drug money would go was listed: Over a billion dollars for new prisons, $350 million for street enforcement, $45 million for security improvements at public housing projects. Treatment money was to be increased in 1990 from the 1989 budget of $621 million to $925 million. Treatment was still running a weak 10% or less and jails and law enforcement at 90%. Final score: Jails nine, treatment one. Bennett's 1989 promise to focus on demand reduction through help for the user was never kept.

12.   BENNETT, WILLIAM J. "DRUGS AND THE BLACK COMMUNITY."   *U.S.A. TODAY,*   7/90, Pgs. 35-37.
Written while he was still the Director of the Office of National Drug Control Policy in Washington, he talked of how drugs have ravaged families in the black community and have resulted in many emergency room admissions and deaths. He quoted Benjamin Hooks, director of the NAACP as saying "Drugs are doing to us what the Ku Klux Klan could never do - destroy our families." Many blacks are fighting the drug plague, trying to hold families and neighborhoods together, trying to teach their children to say no to drugs. Bennett said that these individuals need our support so their voices can be heard. "We need to make the invisible man visible again."

13.   BENNETT, WILLIAM J., "SHOULD DRUGS BE LEGALIZED?"   *READERS DIGEST,*   136:   90-94, 3/90.
Bennett predicted chaos, sickness, and rising crime throughout the land if drugs were legalized. Italy liberalized its drug law in 1975 and a few years later had a greatly increased heroin related death rate. Legalization will not eliminate the black market because the government will never sell the most dangerous drugs (though they are all dangerous) such as crack or PCP so there will still be black market dealers to provide what the government will not. Legalization will give us millions of new drug users and a thriving black market.

Legalization will not reduce crime because "Under the influence of drugs, normal people do not act normally, and abnormal people behave in chilling and horrible ways," including having sex with their own babies. In Philadelphia in 1987 more than 50% of child abuse deaths involved a parent on drugs. Seventy-three percent of the child abuse deaths in New York City in 1987 involved a parent on drugs. Crime rates are highest where crack is the cheapest. Our founding fathers were not talking about someone in a drug-induced haze on a mattress in a crack house when they talked about one of the inalienable rights, "pursuit of happiness."

14. BERECOCHEA, J. E., AND D. R. JAMAN, "TIME SERVED IN PRISON AND PAROLE OUTCOME: AN EXPERIMENTAL STUDY." CALIFORNIA DEPARTMENT OF CORRECTIONS, 1981. SUMMARIZED IN *CRIMINAL JUSTICE ABSTRACTS* S 30484, 1982: 370-371.
A group of prisoners was divided into experimental and control groups. The experimental group was released six months early. (Average length of time in prison for the experimental group was 31.3 months.) The control group served their full time (an average of 37.9 months). There was no difference after release between the groups in terms of their likelihood of returning to prison. Length of sentence seems to have no effect on recidivism or rearrest rate.

15. BERKOW, ROBERT (Ed.), *THE MERCK MANUAL*. 16TH EDITION. NEW JERSEY: MERCK RESEARCH LABORATORIES, 1992.
The widespread availability of methadone has established its role as an important drug of abuse in the United States. For some addicts, methadone has normalized their lives. For others, just another drug problem has been added to their use of alcohol, intermittent heroin use, and desperate lives.

Some of the claims of damage caused by smoking marijuana have been difficult to find on a consistent basis but marijuana smokers have been found to develop pulmonary damage without ever having smoked tobacco cigarettes. Several published reports have confirmed that schizophrenic symptoms (such as hallucinations and delusions) can be increased in individuals who are afflicted with the illness of schizophrenia by smoking marijuana. This occurs even in patients who are under treatment with antipsychotic medications such as haldol. Because of changes in depth perception and timing, driving an automobile while under the influence of marijuana is hazardous. Cocaine is a powerful stimulant, causing alertness, euphoria, and feelings of great power. Hallucinations and paranoid delusions may develop, as well as violent behavior. The cocaine user can be very dangerous. Deaths due to cocaine overdose are becoming more common due to arrhythmias and cardiovascular collapse or respiratory failure. Repeated high-dose use has led to serious toxic consequences, both cardiovascular and behavioral.

Amphetamine abusers are more likely to have accidents because of the excitation and grandiosity produced along with the excessive fatigue due to sleeplessness. **A paranoid psychosis almost inevitably results from long-term use of high doses.** Delusions of persecution may come along with feelings of omnipotence. After an amphetamine run, exhaustion comes, with depression and a high risk of suicide. Confusion, memory loss and some delusional ideas often last for months after total cessation of the drug.

16. BREGGIN, PETER M., *TOXIC PSYCHIATRY.* **NEW YORK, NEW YORK.: ST. MARTINS PRESS, 1991.**
Dr. Breggin introduced evidence which seems to implicate psychiatry in the suppression of complaints of women battered and raped by their husbands through the use of massive doses of tranquilizers and electroshock. Dr. Breggin wrote of what he felt was a conspiracy between drug companies and psychiatrists to treat all mental problems with drugs though studies repeatedly show that talk therapies are superior. He spoke of the disastrous, widespread results of much of current psychiatric treatment which is done almost exclusively through medications. These results include horrible addictions, brain damage, and frequent increases in the symptoms supposedly being treated.

17. BRYJAK, GEORGE J. "REDUCING DEMAND IS OUR ONLY HOPE." *U.S.A. TODAY,* **7/90, Pgs. 20-22.**
Twenty-five percent or more of all homicides are related to drug trafficking. A 1988 study by the National Institute of

Drug Abuse Forecasting found that between 54% and 82% of men arrested for serious offenses in 14 cities tested positive for the use of illicit drugs. Between 28% and 43% of Colombia's total exports are drugs, far surpassing coffee. In Colombia, 304,000 people make a living from the coca plant and cocaine. One hundred million tons of goods and over 200 million people cross into the U. S. yearly. It is impossible to stop the 400 tons of cocaine and heroin coming into the U.S. Ten years ago cocaine cost $42,000 to $60,000 a kilo but now costs between $7,000 and $10,000 a kilo. If imports could be cut off, local production, including designer drugs, will take their place. There were over a million drug arrests in 1988. Even so, ten times the number of policemen investigating and arresting those involved in the drug trade would be needed to even begin to control known drug dealers. Fifty billion dollars was spent nationwide on police, courts, and prisons. In 1985 the National Household Survey on Drugs found that 23 million Americans admitted to using an illicit drug in the last 30 days. By 1988 that figure had dropped to 14.5 million but the people using cocaine once a week or more went from 647,000 to 862,000, a 33% increase. Drug use is learned behavior. Demand reduction is the only viable long term solution to the problem. The core values of an indulgent society must be changed to bring this about.

18. BULE, JAMES "MESSAGE FOR HILL STAFF: DRUG TREATMENT WORKS." *AMERICAN PSYCHOLOGICAL ASSOCIATION MONITOR,* 2/90.
This writer has reviewed many studies on drug treatment and recommended detox, long term monitoring, and counseling with an emphasis on changing the circumstances that initiated drug use. Also important is enlisting the support of family members to bolster motivation. Preventing relapse and establishing incentives for sobriety are necessary. The writer maintained that anyone can stop using drugs. The trick is to keep them off.

19. BUTTERFIELD, FOX "U.S. EXPANDS ITS LEAD IN THE RATE OF IMPRISONMENT." *NEW YORK TIMES,* 2/11/92.

At least half the 1.1 million offenders currently behind bars have serious drug problems. The numbers of people in jail in various nations are given.

20. CANTLUPE, JOE, "PROLIFERATING CRIME RATE OVERWHELMING AGENCIES." *THE SAN DIEGO UNION TRIBUNE,* **2/3/92, Pg. A-1.**
There were 698,021 unserved warrants in San Diego County as of January, 1992. Of these, 42,000 were for driving under the influence of alcohol and drugs. One hundred twenty one were for murders, 53 for rape. Other individuals had committed crimes, were charged, arrested and released on bail, but who then disappeared (never showed up for court and thus had unserved warrants). These included: 34 for arson, 283 for robbery, 49 for assault, 1,419 for burglary, 1377 for larceny, 1060 for auto theft, 88,000 for evasion of paying trolley fees, 20,000 for vagrancy.

21. CANTLUPE, JOE, "VIOLENT CHILDREN: REHABILITATION OR PUNISHMENT?" *THE SAN DIEGO UNION-TRIBUNE,* **2/4/92, Pg. E-8.**
There has been a 90% increase in juvenile crimes in the past ten years. In 1991 60 San Diego County juvenile felons were sent to VisionQuest to go on covered-wagon excursions. VisionQuest costs $36,000 a year per child. A county probation report said 90% of another recent group of 80 VisionQuest graduates were rearrested within a year, and 95% of CYA (California Youth Authority) releasees were rearrested within a year. CYA claimed that only 50 of their released juveniles were rearrested that year. A 1987 Rand Corporation study said VisionQuest dropped rearrest rates from 71% to 39%. A 1985 Rand Corporation study claimed one third of all serious crimes in the U.S. were committed by juveniles.

22. CANTLUPE, JOE, "EVEN 'BAD PEOPLE' RARELY SEE PROBATION OFFICERS." *THE SAN DIEGO UNION-TRIBUNE,* **2/5/92, Pg. A-1.**
The Federal Probation Office in San Diego has 73 officers and 44 clerks and covers an area from San Diego to Los Angeles, from the Pacific Ocean to Arizona. Caseloads are limited to

less than 50 probationers. Federal probation officers meet with the probationers, their employers and family members and they supervise several drug tests each month. For prisoners on federal probation, recidivism rate was considered to be low. For a three month period in 1991 14% of the offenders violated probation. That was 180 out of 1,285 in San Diego County. The Federal Probation System works better and has a lower recidivism rate than the County Probation system because they have more officers relative to the number of probationers and lower caseloads.

In the county system 87 probation officers supervise 20,000 probationers, including 6,200 felons (robbers, drug dealers, child molesters, etc.) who have no face-to-face supervision. Two thousand felons on probation in San Diego County have no contact with officials because they have "absconded." Forty eight percent of the defendants on county probation violate probation and are sent back to jail or prison. More than 50% of those on probation who are required to undergo random drug testing never show up. Most must fail drug tests repeatedly before their probation is revoked. The drug tests themselves were criticized as inaccurate and doing poorly at identifying the presence of illegal drugs in urine samples. Probationers may be supervised more closely at Level One where each officer is assigned about 50 cases. Level Two means less frequent contact or being placed in the "felony bank" which means no face to face supervision. At the other levels each officer is assigned about 600 cases. One probation officer cannot even begin to impact on probationers with a caseload of 600.

In 1987 the number of felons in the "bank" (no face-to-face supervision) was 1,500 but 6,000 in 1992. In that same time period (1987-1992) the total caseload increased from 16,000 to 20,000 and the number of probation officers decreased from 100 to 88. The Police Department added 541 new officers, the district attorney added 97 since 1982. Chief Probation Officer Cecil Steppe said "There is no vocal constituency for probation." Meaning: The squeaky wheel (the police department, the district attorney's office) gets the grease.

23. **CHAIKEN, MARCIA R., "IN PRISON PROGRAMS FOR DRUG INVOLVED OFFENDERS."** *ISSUES AND PRACTICES,* **JULY 1989, Pg. 41.**
Setting up and operating in-prison drug treatment programs, but in their own area, separate from the rest of the prison and its brutality, dramatically improved the institutional management of inmates. Ex-addicts who had been trained as drug counselors were used as counselors. Follow-up data showed greatly reduced drug usage and criminal activity in the graduates of these therapeutic community treatment programs.

24. **CHEWIWLE, DAVE, "CRIME, PUNISHMENT" IN LETTERS TO THE EDITOR,** *LOS ANGELES TIMES,* **12/01/91.**
Vernon Lamar Clark's bank robbery was a cry for help and the cruel system is responsible, a "Times" article had said. Dave Chewiwle did not agree and suggested prison reform, mandatory work, counseling, rehabilitation, skills building/training and indoctrination into the effects of crime on victims. Money now being spent to house criminals could be used to help the homeless, he maintained.

25. **CONNER, ROGER AND PATRICK BURNS,** *THE WINNABLE WAR: A COMMUNITY GUIDE TO ERADICATING STREET DRUG MARKETS.* **WASHINGTON, D.C.: AMERICAN ALLIANCE FOR RIGHTS AND RESPONSIBILITIES, 1991.**
Street markets flourish in most cities. Three hundred were identified in New York. Not as many were found in small cities. In the 17 major cities studied only 7 had citizen patrols, though these patrols have been shown to reduce street dealing.

26. **COOK, L. F. AND B. A. WEINMAN, "TREATMENT ALTERNATIVES TO STREET CRIME," IN LEUKENFELD, C.G., AND F. M TIMS, (Eds.),** *COMPULSORY TREATMENT OF DRUG ABUSE: RESEARCH AND CLINICAL PRACTICE.* **NATIONAL INSTITUTE ON DRUG ABUSE RESEARCH MONOGRAPH 86, WASHINGTON, D.C. U.S. GOVERNMENT PRINTING OFFICE, 1988.**
The TASC (Treatment Alternatives to Street Crimes) program was begun in 1972. This diversion program was backed by

court authority to keep drug abusers in treatment. Some of the functions carried out by the program were identification, assessment, referral and monitoring of appropriate substance abusing, non-violent offenders. Several evaluations of the TASC programs found that the TASC linkage was cheaper than jail, and that TASC clients remained in treatment longer. One hundred sites in 18 states had TASC programs in 1987. Most important to the success of TASC was the case management aspect which meant that drug abusers were followed throughout their drug abuse careers.

27. CORN, DAVID, "JUSTICE'S WAR ON DRUG TREATMENT." *THE NATION,* **5/14/90, Pgs. 659-662.**

"Stay'n Out" is a therapeutic community in-prison treatment program which takes convicts with a history of drug abuse who are within two years of parole and places them in units segregated from the general prison population. For a period of between nine months and two years they attend seminars and counseling sessions on subjects ranging from how to find an apartment to understanding what led to their addiction. Prison perpetuates low self-esteem. If you lock a guy up and give him nothing but hard time (meaning, he gets no treatment for his addiction) he'll be back. Stay'n Out claims a success rate of 78%. Over three-fourths of its alumni stayed off drugs and were not arrested during their parole period. Seventy-five percent of those not in any treatment programs who are released from state prisons are rearrested. Only 13% of the 10.6 million Americans who need treatment are receiving it. When inmates leave Stay'n Out they get a suit, $40, and a subway token. Even so, 70% stay sober. (Author's note: Add Stay'n Out to a good after prison support system which includes providing a place to eat and sleep and sober buddies, along with tight follow-up, and the success rate could easily go to 95% or more).

28. "CRACK CRISIS TAKES ITS TOLL ON HOSPITAL EMERGENCY STAFF." *THE SAN DIEGO UNION,* **8/6/89, Pg. A-4.**

In one 72 hour period 500 patients at a medical emergency room at Highland Hospital in Oakland, California were given urine tests. Forty-five percent tested positive for cocaine. In a 12 hour period on a Saturday night when gunfire and police sirens were heard everywhere on the streets, the same Oakland Hospital said 100% of those tested in the emergency room were positive for cocaine. In the psychiatric emergency room, between 50% and 90% of the patients were cocaine abusers. Doctors and nurses described drug users as mean, narcissistic "dirt balls" when comparing them with the non-drug using patients. Crack had turned the work of the staff into an exhausting, thankless treadmill. Alameda County had a population of 1.3 million and had 127 beds in residential settings for indigent or uninsured drug addicts. The waiting lists were four months long. (Author's note: we have seen elsewhere that many drug addicts change their mind when their turn on the list finally comes up. The most addicted and most in need of help don't even put their names on the waiting lists. In addition, most of those who finally do go for treatment drop out before 90 days). Hospitals around the country have been swamped with cocaine emergencies. Hardest hit was East Oakland, Watts in Los Angeles, the South Bronx and Bedford-Stuyvesant in New York. Dr. Robert Dailey quit the Highland hospital in Oakland because the emergency room had become "a zoo" because cocaine had turned their patients into animals. He said, "Cocaine is the devil, the most savage drug that has ever come along." Cocaine overdoses came in screaming and cursing, thrashing uncontrollably. They tried to pull out of their restraints, they spit at the staff, their faces had to be covered with surgical masks while they took up costly space for up to 24 hours until they stabilized and their overdose was no longer life threatening. The same people came back over and over.

29. **"CRACK PENALTIES BIASED, COURT AGREES."** *SAN DIEGO UNION TRIBUNE,* **12/14/91, Pg. A-16.**
A law for Minnesota has been ruled unconstitutional which called for 20 years in prison for possession of up to 3 grams of crack (used more by blacks) while possession of an equal amount of cocaine powder carries a penalty of up to five years in prison. State prosecutors believed that the reaction to the ruling should have been to increase the penalties for powdered cocaine rather than lower those for crack. (Author's

comment: The lawyers and politicians talk about raising or lowering prison time but never seem to think of just getting people, black or white, to quit taking dope. We find the same tired solution in the jails where drug testing occurs. When they get a positive urine, instead of saying "Gee, fellows, we got a drug addict doing dope right here in our jail, let's sober him up!" They add on a few months of time. We know that doesn't stop people from taking dope but as a society we are fixated on that solution).

30. "CRIME AND PUNISHMENT: MORE JUDGES DISREGARD SENTENCING GUIDELINES." *THE SAN DIEGO UNION TRIBUNE,* 5/10/93, Pg. B-6.

San Diego County District Judge Harold Greene refused to impose a mandatory 30 year sentence on a 25 year old repeat offender. Federal judges whose seniority allows them to choose their cases have refused to preside over drug trials. Judge Greene said that sentences called for by the Federal Guidelines violate the fifth amendment which guarantees due process and the eighth amendment which bans cruel and unusual punishment. Since the guidelines took effect in 1987, 17,000 drug offenders have been given ten year or longer sentences. But fewer than one in ten was a management level dealer. Big drug kingpins cut a deal with federal prosecutors, trading information for reduced sentences. The small fry had no information to barter with so they ended up doing harder time than major drug traffickers. (Author's note: Most dealers, especially the small time middlemen, use drugs, and sell to feed their habit. Sober, they would look for other jobs).

31. CURRAN, MARY-DOWNEY AND JON STANDEFER, "WHEN BABIES ARE HOOKED ALL OF SOCIETY MUST PAY." *SAN DIEGO UNION,* 4/23/89, Pg. C-5.

Ten percent of the 40,000 mothers who gave birth in San Diego in 1988 used drugs, including alcohol, during their pregnancies. Five hundred were investigated by CPS (Child Protective Services) when tests showed the babies had been exposed to drugs in the womb. Crack babies are smaller, sleep fitfully, eat poorly, and sometimes suffer from tremors. They often can't go to foster homes because they require too much care.

They can't go home because everybody there is loaded. So they stay in a hospital for months.

Women who are abusing substances avoid prenatal care for fear they'll be identified as drug users. Substance abuse is a factor in 50% or more of all child abuse cases. Physical abuse is linked to alcohol, street drugs to neglect. Crack babies suffer withdrawal symptoms such as vomiting. They have a poor attention span, constant high-pitched crying, the absence of a sucking reflex, sweating, trembling, and hypersensitivity to light and sound. They are often irritable, inconsolable when upset and have problems sleeping and eating. As they grow into children, they suffer developmental delays and mental retardation. They have weakened immune systems, they learn language late. They turn aggressive for no apparent reason, then recede into an affectless or emotionless state. They have memory problems, poor attention spans and little imagination. No one knows how to care for them. A spokesman for the San Francisco General Hospital said one in five births are crack babies. Portland's Highland's Hospital, it's one in six. In Los Angeles County, it's one in ten.

32. D'AMATO, ALFONSE, "THE DRUG WARS CAN BE WON." U.S.A. TODAY, JULY, 1990, Pgs. 22-24.
This article presented a strong argument against the legalization of drugs. Every year 200,000 babies in the U.S. are born addicted to cocaine. If cocaine was legal, cheap and easily available, the number of babies born addicted to cocaine each year could jump to millions. The cost of raising and keeping these millions of born-addicted babies alive would be staggering.

33. DALTON, REX, "U.C.S.D. STUDY SAYS ALCOHOLICS HAVE A CHOICE OVER LIFE AND DEATH." THE SAN DIEGO UNION, 1/ 31/92, Pg. A-1.
Alcoholic men who quit drinking can add many years to their lives. Alcoholics die 10-15 years before non-alcoholic men. Even alcoholics who quit but later returned to supposedly controlled "social drinking" had higher death rates than the abstainers.

34. DEANGELIS, TORI, "NO ONE METHOD BETTER IN TREATING ADDICTION." *AMERICAN PSYCHOLOGICAL ASSOCIATION MONITOR,* **VOL. 22,** 10/91, **Pg. 10.**
Though some writers have found that some approaches work better than others, this reviewer found that a variety of different treatment approaches can be effective in reducing or eliminating substance abuse in clients. As has many others, this writer also pointed out that though there may be problems getting sober, staying sober is even harder. He suggested that since relapse is extremely common among people trying to overcome addiction, relapse prevention is critical. Clients in substance abuse treatment need to be trained to anticipate high risk situations for relapse and to develop coping skills to prevent relapse.

35. DEANGELIS, TORI, "DRUG TREATMENT STUDIES LAUNCHED." *AMERICAN PSYCHOLOGICAL ASSOCIATION MONITOR,* **VOL. 22, 10/91, Pg. 10**
A three year, $68 million research program was launched by the Federal Government Department of Health and Human Services to compare and evaluate the effectiveness of various drug abuse treatments. The project was called the Drug Abuse Campus Treatment Demonstration Program to be operated in Houston, Texas and Secaucus, New Jersey. Some questions to be addressed were, can the standard 12 month residential treatment program be cut and still be effective, can treatments address other problems such as depression and HIV infection. It was hoped that if effective treatment models were found, they could be replicated across the nation. Another main goal was to find better ways to convince hard-core drug users to become drug-free. (Author's note: Less than a tenth of one percent of America's addicted will be served in the studies, but the Feds can say "We're studying the problem." Also, we know that you can't talk hard core addicts into quitting drugs. When sobriety becomes their only choice they will quit drugs. See Chapter 11 of this book for details).

36. DE LEON, G, "LEGAL PRESSURE IN THERAPEUTIC COMMUNITIES." IN LEUKEFELD, C.G., AND F. M. TIMS, (eds.) *"COMPULSORY TREATMENT OF DRUG ABUSE: RESEARCH AND CLINICAL PRACTICE."*

NATIONAL INSTITUTE ON DRUG ABUSE: RESEARCH MONOGRAPH 86. WASHINGTON, D.C., U.S. GOVERNMENT PRINTING OFFICE, 1988.

37. DVORCHAK, ROBERT J. AND HOLEWA, LISA *MILWAUKEE MASSACRE.* NEW YORK: DELL/BANTAM DOUBLEDAY, 1991.

38. DRUG CONTROL: IMPACT OF DOD'S DETECTION AND MONITORING ON COCAINE FLOW. GAO/USIAD, 91-297, WASHINGTON, D.C., GENERAL ACCOUNTING OFFICE, 1991.
Since Noriega's capture cocaine shipments through Panama have increased substantially. Greater military involvement has not reduced the volume of drugs coming into America. While fighting the drug wars has given our military something to do between wars, our streets are not any safer. It is still dangerous for our children to go to school. Of 6,729 suspicious flights spotted by the military in 1990, law enforcement managed to capture only 49 planes.

39. DRUGS IN THE WORKPLACE: RESEARCH AND EVALUATION DATA. NIDA RESEARCH MONOGRAPH 91, ROCKVILLE, MD., GOVERNMENT PRINTING OFFICE, 1989.
Estimates are that 10% of the work force is drug addicted or alcoholic. Illegal drug use varies by industry, ranging from 13% in transportation, 14% in retail, to 22% in construction. Almost half of all employees with alcoholism problems are in professional fields, less than a third are manual laborers, the rest are white-collar workers.

40. "DRUG TREATMENT: STATE PRISONS FACE CHALLENGES IN PROVIDING SERVICES." GAO/HRD - 91-128, WASHINGTON, D.C., GENERAL ACCOUNTING OFFICE, 1991.
Despite new strategies, few federal inmates receive treatment. The General Accounting Office reported in 1991 that only 364 of the 41,000 Federal prison inmates who have drug problems were participating in intensive drug treatment. More than 75% of all the at least half million state prison

inmates are drug abusers. Of these, only 10% to 20% receive any help at all. Most prison treatments, which usually consists of sporadic drug education and counseling, is ineffective. However, intensive drug treatment for inmates the year prior to release can reduce subsequent substance abuse and rearrest drastically. (Author's note: You cannot throw a few video tapes on sobriety at inmates and expect any results. **Intensive** treatment works, but that involves immersion into an in-jail sobriety program for many hours each week for at least a year before release.)

41. THE EFFECTIVENESS OF DRUG ABUSE TREATMENT: IMPLICATIONS FOR CONTROLLING AIDS/HIV INFECTION. BACKGROUND PAPER NO. 6, WASHINGTON, D.C., OFFICE OF TECHNOLOGY ASSESSMENT, U.S. CONGRESS, 9/90.

In the late 1980s, treatment received 14% of the $10.5 billion of the Federal Drug budget as compared to 25% ten years earlier. Long before the cocaine epidemic created millions of new addicts U.S. policy makers were willing to spend more money on getting people sober. Later, they decided this was a waste of time and that we should just lock all the drug abusers up in prison. So now addicts often have to wait six months or longer before they can get help. Ninety five thousand of the nation's 500,000 to 700,000 heroin addicts were in methadone programs. Studies of six methadone programs in Baltimore, New York and Philadelphia in 1986 found that addicts in treatment longer than six months reported committing crimes 24 days a year compared to 307 days a year when addicted. Methadone patients are more frequently employed and pursuing education than are heroin addicts. (Author's note: Methadone is better than nothing and gives the illusion that something is being done, and done cheaply, by the stroke of a pen on a prescription pad. But treatment to eliminate all addictions is better still since methadone ravages the mind and the body. The methadone addict's life and potential is far from fulfilled.)

42. FALCO, MATHEA, *"WINNING THE DRUG WAR: A NATIONAL STRATEGY."* NEW YORK: PRIORITY PRESS PUBLICATION, TWENTIETH CENTURY FUND, 1989.

Funding for drug law enforcement more than doubled, from 800 million in 1981 to 1.9 billion in 1985. During the same time period education and treatment funds were cut from 404 million to 338 million. In spite of dumping ever larger funds into law enforcement, in 1981 a kilogram of cocaine sold for $60,000 in Miami but in 1987 a Miami kilo sold for $12,000. (Author's note: By 1990 the cost of a kilo of cocaine had dropped to around $7,000. See Reference number 17.)

43. FALCO, MATHEA, *THE MAKING OF A DRUG FREE AMERICA: PROGRAMS THAT WORK.* **NEW YORK: RANDOM HOUSE, 1992.**
Drug use is widespread in many prisons, often with the tacit knowledge of prison authorities. Drugs are smuggled in by visiting relatives as well as by guards who sell directly to the inmates or who take a percentage of the inmate dealer's profit.

Ninety-five percent of drug dealers are also addicts who have become dealers to finance their own drug dependence. The threat of arrest and imprisonment has not proved to be an effective deterrent to drug using and selling for people desperate to finance their next fix. Treatment should be available in the criminal justice system where many street dealers spend a goodly portion of their lives.

The Amity Therapeutic Community program in Arizona was asked to come to the R. J. Donovan prison in San Diego. The large majority of California's over 100,000 prisoners have serious drug problems but only the 200 enrolled in the Donovan Amity program are provided with the highly effective therapeutic community treatment approach to drug addiction. One thousand five hundred prisoners applied for the 200 treatment slots. Between 2/1/91 and 2/1/92, 4% of the inmates not in the treatment program who were tested on a random basis at Donovan had 'dirty' urines, indicating they were using drugs in prison. Though the Amity program participants at Donovan were tested more frequently than the general population of prisoners, none of the Amity participants tested positive during the same time period.

(Author's note: We have seen over and over that involvement in the criminal justice system alone or treatment alone are both ineffective. Chapter 11 of "Drug Wars: The Final Battle" describes the shot-gun wedding of these two approaches, treatment and the criminal justice system, which is the only way to guarantee sobriety.)

44.   FALKIN, GREGORY, P; HARRY K. WEXLER AND DOUGLAS S. LIPTON, "DRUG TREATMENT IN STATE PRISONS." IN DEAN R. GERSTEIN AND HENRICK J. HARWOOD, eds, *'TREATING DRUG PROBLEMS."* VOL. 2, COMMITTEE FOR THE SUBSTANCE ABUSE COVERAGE STUDY, INSTITUTE OF MEDICINE, WASHINGTON, D.C.: NATIONAL ACADEMY PRESS, 1993.
The threat of rearrest does not stop addicts from using drugs or committing crimes after they are released from prison. The criminals deepest into drug addiction are each responsible for as many as ninety robberies and burglaries a year. Without treatment, nine out of ten return to crime and drugs after prison. Most will be rearrested within three years. But three years after graduating from the New York based in-prison Stay'n Out Program, graduates of that program were arrested at just a fraction of the rate of regular prisoners who had no drug treatment in prison. The program cost $4,000 a year over and above the $35,000 a year expense to house a prisoner. Less than 15% of the 1.2 million American prisoners are lucky enough to be involved in an in-prison substance abuse treatment program.

45.   FIELD, G. "THE CORNERSTONE PROGRAM: A CLIENT OUTCOME STUDY," *FEDERAL PROBATION,* 50 1984, Pg. 50.
Describes the positive outcome (lower arrest rate, lower crime rate) of being a graduate of a therapeutic community drug treatment program conducted in a prison setting.

46.   "FIGHTING DRUG ABUSE: NEW DIRECTIONS FOR OUR NATIONAL STRATEGY."   PREPARED BY THE MAJORITY STAFFS OF THE SENATE JUDICIARY COMMITTEE AND THE INTERNATIONAL NARCOTICS CONTROL CAUCUS, FEBRUARY 1991
In the criminal justice system, where the concentration of drug addicts is the greatest, treatment for their drug addictions is hard to come by. Less than 15% of the 1.2 million criminal

offenders (at least half of whom have serious drug problems) get any kind of drug treatment while in prison. Without drug treatment these addicts continue to commit crimes to support their habits as soon as they are released from prison. They return again and again to fill our nation's courts and prisons.

47. FRANKEL, ALISON AND LISA FREELAND, "IS STREET LEVEL ENFORCEMENT A BUST?" *THE AMERICAN LAWYER,* 3/90, Pg. 101.
In 1988, the New York City Police Department began "Buy and Bust" patrols in different areas of the city for 90 days at a time. In 1990, this program accounted for 81,000 drug arrests. Drug dealing was reduced. But after the police units withdrew, dealing resumed as usual. The arrested dealers were immediately replaced by another legion of new dealers staking out the temporarily vacated territories. These street sweeps that so impress the public and make flashy lead stories on the 10 O'clock news flood the criminal justice system and clog the courts and jails.

48. FREIBERG, PETER, "REHABILITATION IS EFFECTIVE IF DONE WELL, STUDIES SAY." *THE AMERICAN PSYCHOLOGICAL ASSOCIATION MONITOR,* VOL.21, NO.9, 9/90, Pg.1.
A reduction of 53% in recidivism rates was obtained through treatment programs. Eighty studies were reviewed which contradict the general sentiment that nothing works and criminal drug addicts can't be rehabilitated. The most successful programs in reducing recidivism rates are those which employ behavior modification techniques that reward pro-social behavior and target those anti-social attitudes and values that fuel criminal behavior. Role playing is an effective tool in changing values. The families of those in treatment can help. Techniques which have failed are psychodynamic and non-directive therapy. Pharmacologic approaches (helping the addict quit drugs by giving him some other chemical), legal sanctions, and punishment have failed. There is no evidence that "boot camps" help. Halfway houses are more effective than prison. Rehab programs don't affect low risk offenders. (Low risk offenders are people who would be unlikely to violate the law again with or without treatment. These are usually

people not very far into addiction for whom 'a slap on the wrist' is enough to convince them they need to get sober.) But if you target medium to high risk offenders for intervention, you show dramatic results. Follow-up is essential, the treatment team must keep track of where those in treatment go and who they talk to. Sometimes good treatment can be undone by bad associates. The United States has 455 per 100,000 of its citizens locked up, double the rate of ten years ago. One of every four young black men is behind bars or on probation or parole. Nationwide, 75% of persons entering prison are drug users. Just serving time degenerates the prisoners and their keepers. We need to begin to view that time our criminal drug addicts spend in prison as an opportunity for change which, if we take advantage of it, will alter the quality of life for all Americans.

49.   GERSTEIN, DEAN R., AND HENDRICK J. HARWOODS, Eds, *TREATING DRUG PROBLEMS: A STUDY OF THE EVOLUTION, EFFECTIVENESS, AND FINANCING OF PUBLIC AND PRIVATE DRUG TREATMENT SYSTEMS.* Vol. 1, WASHINGTON, D.C.: NATIONAL ACADEMY PRESS, 1990.
The National Academy of Sciences Institute of Medicine estimates that 5.5 million Americans have serious drug problems that require treatment. It was discovered that even the most expensive of treatment programs more than pay for themselves by reducing the costs of loss of productivity, crime and health costs. The longer addicts stay in treatment, the more likely they are to give up drugs and crime. A study of the California civil addict program in the 60s and 70s which treated drug addicted criminal offenders found that rates of drug use and crime among program participants were only half as great over the 7 year follow-up period compared to similar addicts not in the program. Threat of sanctions can be a strong incentive to stay in treatment. The "boot camp" idea is popular, but such programs don't work to reduce crime and drug abuse. In fact, some "boot camp" programs have been **less successful** than traditional incarceration. In Oklahoma, half the boot camp graduates returned to prison within two and one-half years as compared to only a 25% return to prison of those who did not have the "advantage" of a "boot camp."

(Author's note: We have seen elsewhere in this book that "boot camps" graduates militarize their drug activities, thus improving efficiency and discipline among their "troops," or lower level drug dealers.)

50. HARWOOD, H. J., J. COLLINS, AND J.V. RACHAL, "COSTS AND POTENTIAL BENEFITS." IN LEUKEFELD, C.G., AND F. M. TIMS, (Eds)., *COMPULSORY TREATMENT OF DRUG ABUSE: RESEARCH AND CLINICAL PRACTICE.* NATIONAL INSTITUTE ON DRUG ABUSE RESEARCH MONOGRAPH 86, WASHINGTON, D.C.; U.S. GOVERNMENT PRINTING OFFICE, 1988.
Virtually all economic measures show that crime is lower after treatment than before treatment. Cost of drug abuse was estimated to be $47 billion in 1980 with crime related costs in the same year of $18.3 billion. There was a significant reduction of primary drug use among criminal justice system referrals who went through residential treatment programs. This and other studies shows major cost-benefit effects of treatment, especially residential treatment. By cost-benefit effects is meant that for each dollar spent on treatment many more dollars do not have to be spent later on victim losses, cops, jails, foster homes, etc.

51. HAVERKOS AND R. EDELMAN, "THE EPIDEMIOLOGY OF ACQUIRED IMMUNE DEFICIENCY SYNDROME AMONG HETEROSEXUALS." *JOURNAL OF THE AMERICAN MEDICAL ASSOCIATION,* 260: 1922-1929, 1988.
The number of AIDS cases has doubled every 13 months. 30% of all AIDS cases in the U.S. are related to I.V. drug use. Many I.V. drug users are sexually active. AIDS is spreading among I.V. drug abusers through needle sharing and through sexual activity. Many female drug abusers resort to prostitution to support their drug habits. This provides a pathway for the spread of AIDS to the general population.

52. HEARN, LORIE, "CRIME IS UP, PUBLIC'S CONFIDENCE DOWN." *THE SAN DIEGO UNION-TRIBUNE,* 2/2/92, Pg. A-1.

Over a billion dollars was spent in 1992 protecting the public in San Diego County, 70% of the total yearly budget. Many thousands committing "minor" crimes such as assault and battery and vandalism were given citations which most ignored, because there was no room in the jail. Of the unserved 700,000 warrants, 421,000 were for traffic violations, 42,000 were for driving under the influence. Thousands of felons on probation in San Diego disappear from the system and are not heard from again until they are arrested for committing another crime. Armed robberies were up 18.9% in 1992, compared to 1991.

53. HEARN, LORIE AND JOE CANTLUPE, "COPS, COURTS, CORRECTIONS STRUGGLE TO WORK TOGETHER." *SAN DIEGO UNION-TRIBUNE***, 2/2/92, Pg. A-1.**

If a first time offender is convicted of drug charges in Federal Court, he can be sent to prison for ten years without parole. In the State court system it can mean a few years. Martin Edward Walters was arrested many times by many different agencies, including the San Diego police, U. S. Drug Enforcement Administration, etc. The agencies had not shared information on this man. So after each arrest, because none of the agencies knew of his extensive record with all the other agencies, he was released. They all thought this must be his first crime. In 1988 he killed Kristy Reyes during a desperate search for drugs. (Author's note: If virtually any ATM in America can tell you how much you have in your account, it should be possible to make an immediate entry on any crime/arrest by any agency into a central system. See Chapter 11 for plans to implement such a system. This kind of tracking and central record bank would also guarantee sobriety and provide immediate knowledge of non-compliance with the conditions of probation which call for sobriety, following a first arrest by any agency.)

54. HEARN, LORIE, "JUSTICE SYSTEM INSTILLS LITTLE FEAR INTO SCOFFLAWS." *THE SAN DIEGO UNION TRIBUNE,***2/4/92, Pg. A-1.**

There is no room in the jail and the law violators know it.

55. HEARN, LORIE, "NEW PRISONS FAIL TO MEET DEMAND." *THE SAN DIEGO UNION,* **2/5/92, A-8.**
A 1987 National Institution of Justice report estimated the costs of crimes committed by the typical prison inmate at $430,000 per year. These costs included security costs for firearms, guard dogs, victim losses and justice system costs. A 1989 National Institute of Justice study found that 82% of the people arrested in San Diego County tested positive for drug use, the highest percentage in the 21 large U.S. cities surveyed. A special drug court was set up in 1990 in San Diego to conduct hearings on probation violations by drug offenders. In two years 1105 cases were processed. Of these, 926, or 83%, were sent to State prison for probation violations for offenses such as drug positive urinalysis tests or rearrests for new drug related crimes. Three hundred people were arrested in black gang territories in major sweeps code named Red Rag, Blue Rag and Rock 'n' Roll.

56. HEARN, LORIE AND JOE CANTLUPE, "SPECIAL REPORT: 'WHAT PRICE JUSTICE?' IT TOOK THE JURY TEN MINUTES TO DECIDE CHRISTOPHER NEEDED HELP, NOT ARREST." *THE SAN DIEGO UNION-TRIBUNE,* **2/6/92, Pg. A-1.**
Sheriff Jim Roache said his seven jails were fast becoming a warehouse for the mentally ill. Some homeless people, who are cited by police as major violators for offenses such as repeatedly drinking in public, are sometimes taken into custody for as long as two weeks. A Rand Corporation study claimed that a small percentage of criminals is responsible for a large percentage of the total crimes being committed. Eight percent of the prisoners had committed more than 60 crimes a year. As the criminal justice system expenses go up, money is cut from social services. For example, $9 million was cut from the $83 million San Diego County mental health budget. This results in the jails becoming the mental hospitals. Christopher was a drug abusing paranoid schizophrenic who had gotten sucked into the criminal justice system because he had been abandoned by the underfunded mental health system. His trial cost $2,000 a day. He was trying to get a job washing windows, but since he was a paranoid schizophrenic and on drugs, he was acting a little strange and was arrested. The

jury threw the case out after deliberating for 10 minutes, but not before the County had spent many thousands to try him. A study by the Public Defender's office of 50 North San Diego County jury trials estimated that each case cost the taxpayers between $35,000 and $50,000 to prosecute. Total cost to prosecute these 50 cases: Over $2 million. One of the "criminals" was charged with possession of an aerosol paint can. The 50 trials ended with 24 acquittals and 26 convictions. Of the 26 "criminals" who were convicted, four were sentenced to jail. Two of them served two days each in jail. It cost over two million dollars to send two people to jail for two days each. (Author's note: All 50 could have been sent on a year long world-wide cruise for what it cost to give them jury trials. The sobriety of 531 people, at $4,000 per year each, which would also include room and board, could have been guaranteed for a year for what it cost to just try the 50. We have seen over and over that 82% of the people arrested for anything are loaded. So, at least 43 of the 50 did their "crime" because of substance abuse. Also, there is nearly a 100% probability that their very expensive trials, unaccompanied by any demands for sobriety later, did not interfere with their continuing to get high.)

57.   HEARN, LORIE AND JOE CANTLUPE, "NEW CITY JAIL HAS SHERIFF DOUBTFUL." *SAN DIEGO UNION-TRIBUNE,* **2/5/92, Pg. A-8.**
A court order was issued limiting the number of prisoners in San Diego County's seven jails to 3,685. In January, 1992 3,693 criminals, mostly suspected felons, were locked up. Sheriff Roache had been refusing to book many thousands of petty criminals cited for offenses such as prostitution, battery, and drug possession. It was unlikely that any misdemeanor offenders, unless charged with drunken driving and domestic violence, would be jailed. (Author's note: Most batterers are drunk or drugged or both so the misdemeanor drunk drivers and batterers get a few hours to sober up. Without that night in jail there would be additional mayhem committed by these people before the effects of the alcohol or drugs started to wear off.) Hopes were that a new 200 bed jail would allow some of the many thousands of misdemeanor offenders with multiple outstanding arrest warrants to go to

jail. As it was, tickets or citations issued for prostitution, battery, etc., could be safely ignored. Failure to appear in court generally resulted in no action on the part of the legal system. Judges voted to refuse to hear new cases that, if sentenced, would be released from jail in a few hours.

58. HEARN, LORIE AND JOE CANTLUPE, "BLACKS: THE GROWING TRAGEDY OF THOSE LEFT OUT." *SAN DIEGO UNION-TRIBUNE,* **2/5/92, Pg. A-8.**
In 1991, 61% of all black babies were born to unwed mothers. In Atlanta, half the babies in the neonatal unit were drug addicted. The black underclass is being raked by drugs and AIDS, and an upsurge in child abuse connected to drug addiction. There was a 28% increase in the number of child abuse deaths reported between 1985 and 1988. A Boston settlement house director said child sexual abuse in black and white underclass drug-involved families was nearly 100%.

59. HORVATH, ARTHUR T., "STATE-OF-THE ART ADDICTION TREATMENT: IT'S NOT WHAT YOU THINK IT IS." *NEWSLETTER OF THE ACADEMY OF SAN DIEGO PSYCHOLOGISTS,* **9/91, Pgs. 1-4**

60. HOWARD, JOHN, "STATE STRUGGLES TO COPE WITH BURGEONING PRISON POPULATION." *SAN DIEGO UNION TRIBUNE,* **1/7/94, Pg. E-1.**
California has the nation's largest prison system. The public's fear of violent crime has resulted in a massive prison building program. There are 120,000 inmates locked up, double the number of New York State. California has 27 prisons and state-run camps from the Mexican border to the Oregon line. Fifty thousand more prisoners are expected in the next five years. California's prison system grows at the rate of 10% a year. Each prison costs about $250 million and is designed to house an average of 2,200 inmates, but usually holds 3,500 to 4,000 due to overcrowding. In his State of the State speech governor Pete Wilson proposed to build six new prisons at a cost of $2 billion. California will have 40 major prisons by the end of the century if the lawmakers and politicians have their way. Ironwood State Prison was scheduled to open in the desert in March, 1994. Five more were scheduled to open

between 1994 and 1996 in Susanville, Madera, Corcoran and Coalinga. Laws commanding longer sentences have been at least partly responsible for the increase in the number of prisoners. A new wave of hysteria fueled by the Polly Klaas' kidnap-slaying has resulted in demands to lock up more and longer. Klaas's killer had a long criminal record. (Author's note: And of course, he had never received the much cheaper drug rehabilitation years ago, earlier in his substance abuse career, that would have prevented that crime. But less than 15% of America's criminals do get the rehabilitation that has proven not only be cheaper but stops repeat criminal acts in 75% to 95% of the cases treated.) Politicians get to look tougher by giving longer sentences so the number of people locked up in California has quintupled (increased 500%) in the 1980's. One of six prisoners locked up across the nation is in California in State prisons, 700,000 total are in state prisons across the nation. (Including federal and other prisons, America's prison/jail population is around 1.2 million). The prisons in general contain 150% of the numbers for which they were designed. State prison expenditures have increased 200 percent since 1984. In spite of all this, violent crimes continue to climb. (Author's note: Remember the Peter, Paul and Mary song? "Where have all the flowers gone?...Long time passing....When will they ever learn, when will they ever learn?")

61.   HUBBARD, ROBERT, MARY ELLEN MARSDEN, J. VALLEY RACHAL, HENRICK HARWOOD, ELILZABETH CAVANDAUGH AND HAROLD GINZBURG, *DRUG ABUSE TREATMENT: A   NATIONAL   STUDY   OF EFFECTIVENESS*.   CHAPEL HILL: UNIVERSITY OF NORTH CAROLINA PRESS, 1989.

62.   HUBBARD, ROBERT, MARY ELLEN MARSDEN, J. VALLEY RACHAL, J VALLEY, HARWOOD, HENRICK, HARWOOD, *TREATING DRUG PROBLEMS: A STUDY OF THE EVOLUTION, EFFECTIVENESS, AND FINANCING OF PUBLIC AND PRIVATE DRUG TREATMENT SYSTEMS*, VOL 1.   WASHINGTON, D.C.:   NATIONAL ACADEMY PRESS, 1990.

63.   HURST, JOHN, "PAROLE AGENTS FACE HARD TIMES." *LOS ANGELES TIMES,* **11/15/92, Pg. A-3.**
Already unable to keep track of their parolees, 231 parole officers of the 1,428 working in Los Angeles lost their jobs due to budget cuts. The 1,197 left had to pick up the 14,415 parolees of the laid off officers which jumped individual parole officer caseloads from the 60 and 70 level to around 85. (Author's note: Cutting probation and supervision personnel happens across the nation whenever there is a budget crunch. Good probation and parole supervision does reduce criminal acts. Since supervision is always first to go, we thus guarantee more crimes and people to fill the prisons we can't wait to build.)

64.   INCIARDI, J.A., "SOME CONSIDERATIONS ON THE CLINICAL EFFICACY OF COMPULSORY TREATMENT: REVIEWING THE NEW YORK EXPERIENCE." IN LEUKEFELD, C.G., AND F. M. TIMS, (eds.) *COMPULSORY TREATMENT OF DRUG ABUSE: RESEARCH AND CLINICAL PRACTICE.* **NATIONAL INSTITUTE ON DRUG ABUSE RESEARCH MONOGRAPH, 86, WASHINGTON, D.C. V.5** *GOVERNMENT PRINTING OFFICE,* **1988.**
The New York State Narcotic Control Act of 1966 established The Narcotic Addiction Control Commission. Patients with substance abuse problems could be committed for three to five years. Families could petition the courts for help with their loved ones' addiction problems. In working in conjunction with law enforcement, it is best to use the drug treatment systems already in place rather than create whole new treatment systems. An overly punitive approach may have reduced the effectiveness of the New York experience.

65.   JACKSON, IRENE "CROWDING IN JAILS 'STRESSES INMATES." *THE SAN DIEGO UNION-TRIBUNE,* **2/5/92, Pg. B-1.**
Overcrowding enhances tension and violence. They come away from prison with a paranoid mental state. Prisoners are subjected to the potential for physical harm and sexual abuse. Escapes and fighting are more frequent in crowded jails. Prisons are not a healthy growth environment.

66.   JAIL INMATES, 1990, AND PRISONERS IN 1990 UNITED STATES DEPARTMENT OF JUSTICE, OFFICE OF JUSTICE PROGRAMS, BUREAU OF JUSTICE STATISTICS BULLETIN, (JUSTICE STATISTICS CLEARING HOUSE, BOX 6000, ROCKVILLE, MO., 20850).
More prison admissions nationwide now result from parole violations rather than from new criminal convictions. When parolees test positive for drugs or miss appointments with their parole officers (often because they are on drug binges), they are arrested for violating the conditions of parole and sent back to prison. (Author's note: We know that a minuscle proportion of those parolees were getting treatment for their addictions. We also know that without treatment, threat of rearrest does not stop drug use. We know that they can be sobered up outside prison at bargain rates thus saving the billions spent on their very expensive in-jail room and board.)

67. JOSEPH, H, "THE CRIMINAL JUSTICE SYSTEM AND OPIATE ADDICTION: A HISTORICAL PERSPECTIVE. IN C. G. LEUKEFELD AND F. M. TIMS, (eds.), COMPULSORY TREATMENT OF DRUG ABUSE: RESEARCH AND CLINICAL PRACTICE. NATIONAL INSTITUTE ON DRUG ABUSE RESEARCH MONOGRAPH, 86. WASHINGTON, D.C.: U.S. GOVERNMENT PRINTING OFFICE, 1988.
Research was reviewed from an evaluation study on five probation clinics operated by the New York Office of Probation in the early 1970's. Of the 1,000 people treated from 1970 to 1973, 54% were still unemployed, but only ten percent of the first 900 admissions to the program were rearrested.

68.   KLEINKNECHT, WILLIAM, "IN-HOME SOCIAL WORK AIDS FAMILIES." THE SAN DIEGO UNION, 12/31/91, Pg. E-3.
The foster home system has many drawbacks. Many see the whole system as a failure. Twenty four states are sending social workers into homes. These social workers have light caseloads, as few as two families at a time. State and Federal governments were going to spend $12 billion on foster care in 1992. Home-based therapy costs taxpayers less than foster

care. Following this kind of intensive in-home intervention, there was a reduction in the annual number of days children spent in foster care by percentages ranging from 4.8% to 34.2%. One program was "Family Approach to Crime and Treatment" or "FACT." Separation from their families and communities scars children who often end up being moved from one foster home to another. Children who are supposed to be protected from neglect and abuse end up being subjected to another form of neglect and abuse by the state. One crack addict who had social workers guide her through five gunshot wounds, a suicide attempt, hospitalization, sobriety and house hunting said, "They taught me to be a mother all over again because I had forgotten." After getting sober and getting her life back she had signed up for computer classes at an adult vocational school.

69. KLIMKO, FRANK, "GANG CRIME STATISTICS APPEAR TO AFFIRM WORTH OF DISBANDED UNIT." *THE SAN DIEGO UNION,* **1/19/93, Pg. B-2.**
A Special Enforcement Unit (SEU) was formed in 1988 to deal with gang violence in San Diego. There had been 90 drive-by shootings and 28 gang-related murders the year before. The 17 officer team would patrol troubled neighborhoods, detain and question dozens of gang members and be tipped off to upcoming gang wars. In 1989 drive-by shootings dropped to 75 and homicides to 15, about half the rate of the year before. The unit was disbanded because of budget problems in early 1992 after which attempted murder, assaults and drive by shootings jumped back to pre SEU levels. Keith Burt, chief of the District Attorney's Gang Prosecution Unit said less than one percent of the population is responsible for 30% to 40% of violent crime and that gangs commit a disproportionate amount of crime for their numbers. With urban youth unemployment around 40%, "the local gang kingpin may have the only job on the block."

70. KOHN, ALFIE, "HITTING THE BOTTLE.": HEALTH HORIZONS, PSYCHOLOGY SECTION, *LOS ANGELES TIMES,* **10/6/91, Pg. 32**
It is popular to believe that alcoholism is an inherited disease. New studies are casting doubt on this assumption. Philadelphia

researchers surveyed 83 college students and found no difference in drinking patterns between the sons of alcoholics and the sons of non-alcoholics. A University of Michigan study examined hundreds of offspring of alcoholics and found that almost 66% drank little or not at all. Fraternal twins (with a less strong genetic connection than identical twins) who were raised   together were more likely to be alcoholics than identical twins raised separately, suggesting that the environment is a stronger causative factor of alcoholism than the genes.

71.   KONDRACKE, MORTON M., "THE TWO BLACK AMERICAS: GROWING NUMBERS ARE BEING LEFT OUT OF THE DREAM." *THE SAN DIEGO UNION,* **2/19/89. Pg. C-1**
Blacks constituted 12% of the population but 46% of the inmates in U.S. prisons in 1985 and 60% of those arrested for murder in the U.S. cities in 1987.   In 1988, inner-city cocaine wars helped raise the murder rate in Washington, D.C. by 65%. Seventeen percent of black men between the ages of 20-24 didn't work at all in 1987, at least not in the regular economy. Honest work is not valued because hustling, drug dealing and theft pay better and people lack the minimal tools for employment such as punctuality, courtesy, and elementary verbal skills.   Even when the economy approached full employment, positions in fast-food restaurants went unfilled. In 1976, 34% of blacks graduating from high school went on to college but only 26%, or 15,000 less students, went on to college in 1985.   Only 42% of those who go to college graduate.

72.   KRAKOW, BARRY *CONQUERING BAD DREAMS AND NIGHTMARES.* **SAN   FRANCISCO,   CALIF: BERKELEY BOOKS, 1992.**
Subjects who experienced nightmares were instructed to visualize or imagine themselves having the same nightmare or bad dream over again, while awake.   But this time they visualized and repeatedly practiced new endings where they won out over the terrifying creatures of their nightmares.   Not only did the nightmares stop, but depression and anxiety were lifted or alleviated.   Feeding new signals into the unconscious mind can positively affect how well people feel.

73. KRAUTHAMMER, CHARLES, "WELFARE MAMA."
THE SAN DIEGO UNION TRIBUNE, 11/23/93, Pg. B-5.

Pennsylvania Professor Elijah Anderson presented a 40 page paper entitled "Sex Codes Among Inner-City Youth" at a seminar. Anderson has also written a book called "Street Wise." He described a value system of inner city youth in which the goal of males is to get as many girls as possible to have their babies. The more times they can brag that they have just become a new father results in higher levels of esteem from peers. In addition, avoidance of any commitment or responsibility for any of these babies is part of the code. The results are illegitimacy rates of 70% to 80% in some populations, intergenerational poverty, social and family breakdown. The question was raised whether the state should have to continue to pay for the rearing of children conceived in "wantonness." There were no objections to helping widows and orphans. Thirty percent of all births nation-wide are illegitimate, 5.5 times greater than 30 years ago.

74. LANDERS, SUSAN, "FOR RUNAWAY YOUTH, A HOPELESS EXISTENCE." *THE AMERICAN PSYCHOLOGICAL ASSOCIATION MONITOR,* 11/89.

There are children as young as 10 and 11 years old living on the streets. It was estimated that two million children under the age of 18 are homeless. Many of the 17 and 18 year olds living on the streets have been on the streets for six or seven years. One-half of the 93 homeless teenagers who were interviewed for this study had attempted suicide. These homeless teens live in abandoned buildings, parks, fast food restaurants, under freeway bridges and on roof tops. Seventy-nine percent had been homeless more than once. Fifty seven of the 93 had lived part of their lives in foster or group homes. Many children are falling out of the foster care system. More than half of the 93 interviewed (60% of whom were white, 61% were male) were receiving money from their families, friends, or short-term jobs. Many of the youths had also turned to prostitution, panhandling, and drug dealing for added income. Almost half the sample met the criteria for alcohol abuse or dependence but few were getting help. There were only 50 beds for homeless teens in all of Los Angeles

County in 1988. More than half of those who abused alcohol also abused drugs. Twenty percent of the 93 were experiencing a major depression. More than 77% reported using illicit drugs in the previous 30 days. Most reported having sex, but only half said they used a condom. Forty-four percent of the females reported one or more pregnancies. Only one-third of those who had ever been pregnant had ever given birth. Twenty-five percent of the female sample were pregnant at the time of the interview. Many of these homeless teens were physically ill but few received any medical care.

75. LANDERS, SUSAN, "TEEN-TAILORED TREATMENT CAN HELP DRUG ABUSERS." *THE AMERICAN PSYCHOLOGICAL ASSOCIATION MONITOR,* **12/91.**
A variety of interventions were recommended but involuntary treatment was felt to not be applicable to this population. (Author's note: The idea that substance abusers must "hit bottom" or "be ready" for sobriety in order for treatment to work is patently false and is crippling our nation.)

76. LEVIN, JACK AND FOX, JAMES ALAN *MASS MURDER: AMERICA'S GROWING MENACE.* **NEW YORK: PLENUM, 1988**

77. LEYTON, ELLIOTT, *HUNTING HUMANS: INSIDE THE MINDS OF MASS MURDERERS.* **NEW YORK: POCKET BOOK, 1986**

78. LEUKEFELD, CARL AND FRANK M. TIMS, "COMPULSORY TREATMENT FOR DRUG ABUSE." *THE INTERNATIONAL JOURNAL OF THE ADDICTIONS,* **25(6), 1990, Pgs. 621-640.**
Provides an extensive review of the drug abuse literature which leads to the inevitable conclusion that involuntary treatment is critical to even begin to impact on the drug addiction problem since as high as 98% of the participants drop out of treatment programs when their participation is voluntary. Involuntary treatment results in drastic reductions in crime and drug use. Half or more of those sobered up have legitimate jobs upon follow-up in two or three years.

79. "LOSING GROUND." *THE SAN DIEGO TRIBUNE,* **12/24/91, Pg. B-6.**
The number of Americans using cocaine at least once a month increased nearly 20% in 1991, the number of weekly users climbed nearly 30% according to the National Institute of Drug Abuse. Hard core drug use leads to other problems. Hospital emergency rooms are overwhelmed with drug cases. There are record levels of drug-related crime and violence, parental abuse of children is on the rise and poverty and welfare dependence has become endemic. Middle class suburban residents declined slightly in drug abuse but, until progress is made in curbing hard-core drug use among America's low-income, mostly urban residents, the nation will continue to lose ground in its war on drugs.

80. LYALL, SARAH "WITHOUT THE MONEY TO SUPPLY PRISON BEDS, OFFICIALS, CONSIDER REDUCING DEMAND." *NEW YORK TIMES,* **2/17/92.**
New York State spent $2.1 billion for new prisons from 1983 to 1992, while the prison population doubled. Almost half of all current inmates have been convicted of drug felonies, compared to only 11% in 1982. (Author's note: Even non-drug crimes such as assault, rape, are almost always committed while under the influence.)

81. MADDUX, J. F., *TREATMENT OF NARCOTIC ADDICTION: ISSUES AND PROBLEMS: REHABILITATING THE NARCOTIC ADDICT.* **WASHINGTON, D.C.: U.S. GOVERNMENT PRINTING OFFICE, 1967.**

82. MAGUIRE, KATHLEEN AND TIMOTHY J. FLANAGAN, (eds.) *SOURCE BOOK OF CRIMINAL JUSTICE STATISTICS 1990.* **U.S. DEPARTMENT OF JUSTICE, BUREAU OF JUSTICE STATISTICS WASHINGTON, D.C.: GOVERNMENT PRINTING OFFICE, 1991.**
Blacks constitute 12% of the total population but account for 41% of drug arrests and a third of criminal drug convictions nationwide. In the past decade, arrests for drug crimes more than doubled. Public frustration with escalating drug crime led

to tougher laws, longer sentences, and the death penalty for major traffickers.

83. MAIN FINDINGS: NATIONAL HOUSEHOLD SURVEY ON DRUG ABUSE. ROCKVILE, MD.: NATIONAL INSTITUTE OF DRUG ABUSE, 1991.

Twenty six million Americans used illegal drugs in 1991. The survey of drug users does not include transients, homeless, prisoners, or people in other institutions. Two-thirds of all adults who used illegal drugs in 1991 were employed, a total of about 15.6 million people. In 1991, more than a third of all Americans who reported using drugs at least once a month were black or hispanic. Record anti-drug expenditures of the criminal justice system, costing $40 billion in 1992, has not helped. United States has the highest rate of addiction in its history, more than at the turn of the century when opiates, cocaine and marijuana were legally marketed. U.S. also has the highest rate of imprisonment in history because of drug-related crime. Reduction in drug use was noted among the better educated and affluent. Addiction was growing among the poor, the disadvantaged and racial minorities. In 1991 more than a third of all Americans who reported using drugs at least once a month were black or hispanic as were 44% of those who admitted to using cocaine at least once a week. The weekly cocaine use among blacks jumped 65% from 1990 to 1991. Blacks accounted for 42% of all drug arrests nationwide in 1989. Florida had the highest rate of incarceration in the country; more than 75% of those convicted for drug offenses in 1989 in Florida were black.

84. "MAKE LAW BREAKERS PAY: THOUSANDS OF WARRANTS ARE OUTSTANDING." THE SAN DIEGO UNION-TRIBUNE, 6/23/93, Pg. B-8

There are 650,000 outstanding warrants in San Diego County, each one represents a law breaker who didn't pay a fine. Lawbreakers keep driving drunk, using illegal drugs, riding the trolley without paying, driving with a suspended license, assaulting their family members, selling sex and stealing property. The county says it is not cost effective to go after these lawbreakers because under state law, the county general fund gets only 3.2% of any fines collected. The rest goes to the State, to cities and to special accounts. Since the personnel costs would run higher than the 3.2% of the fines they would collect, the county doesn't bother. However, a recent change in State law says that counties can now deduct the costs of collecting outstanding warrants from the fines. Private sector investigators and collection agencies should be used to pursue delinquents on a contingency basis. Welfare recipients and other government beneficits should be withheld from those with outstanding warrants until their fines are paid. The county needs to restore respect for the law.

85.   MARLATT, G.A. AND W.M. GEORGE, "RELAPSE PREVENTION, INTRODUCTION AND OVERVIEW OF THE MODEL." *BRITISH JOURNAL OF ADDICTIONS.* **79: 1984, Pg. 261-273.**
Relapse prevention is an important component of any treatment program. The greatest risk of relapse occurs in the first 90 days of involvement in any treatment program any time those in treatment are exposed to drug-related stimuli, meaning anything that reminds them of drugs and drug use (such as old friends, feeling bummed out, etc..)

86.   MAUER, MARK, "AMERICANS BEHIND BARS: A COMPARISON OF INTERNATIONAL RATES OF INCARCERATION." *THE SENTENCING REPORT* **1/91.**
America locks up more of its citizens on a per-capita basis than any other country in the world.

87.   MAY, ROBERT L., ET AL, "THE EXTENT OF DRUG TREATMENT PROGRAMS IN JAILS: A SUMMARY REPORT." *AMERICAN JAILS,* **(SEPTEMBER-OCTOBER 1990): Pg. 32.**
One thousand six hundred eighty seven county and state jails were surveyed. Only 7% of the inmates were involved in drug treatment. That drug treatment could be as little as periodically watching a videotape on getting sober or an occasional class. Only 2% of the jails surveyed had more than ten hours a week of substance abuse teatment activities.

88. MASTERS, BRIAN, *KILLING FOR COMPANY: THE CASE OF DENNIS NILSEN.* **LONDON: HODDER AND STOUGHTON, 1991.**

89. McCARTY, MILTON ARGERION, ROBERT B. HUEBNER AND BARBARA LUBRAN, "ALCOHOLISM, DRUG ABUSE AND THE HOMELESS." *AMERICAN PSYCHOLOGIST,* **VOL. 46, NO. 11, 11/91, Pg. 1139-1148.**

Some studies have reported that 40% of the homeless are alcoholics and 15% are drug addicts, but other studies have estimated that as many as 86% of the homeless are alcoholics. Drug abuse has been estimated to be as high as 70% among the homeless. Eighty percent of a Los Angeles sample of homeless inner city adults said their alcoholism preceded their homelessness. Alcoholism has been strongly correlated with homelessness in writings from over 100 years ago. Even so, it was felt that the causes of homelessness were multiple and complex. Many of the homeless lost their shelter for various reasons, such as loss of jobs, less demands for unskilled labor, or withdrawal of federal supports for subsidized or low-income housing. "The relationship between abuse of alcohol and drugs and homelessness, however, is probably bidirectional. Although alcohol and drug abuse can increase the risk of homelessness, displacement and loss of shelter can also increase the use and abuse of alcohol and other drugs....It was generally believed that traditional treatment and recovery approaches were not effective, in isolation, with homeless individuals because they did not seek out the homeless substance abuser, provide continuity of care and support, and facilitate reentry into the community."

90. McCULLOUGH, CHARLOTTE B., *THE CHILD WELFARE RESPONSE, THE FUTURE OF CHILDREN.* **CENTER FOR THE FUTURE OF CHILDREN, THE DAVID AND LUCILLE PACKARD FOUNDATION, VOL. I, NO. 1 (SPRING, 1991).**

Foster care placements jumped by nearly a third from 1987 to 1990, mostly in communities with the most drug abuse.

91. McGRORY, BRIAN, "CHEAP, PURE HEROIN SPELLS FUTURE EPIDEMIC, SOME FEAR." *THE SAN DIEGO UNION-TRIBUNE,* **2/21/92, Pg. A-10.**

Heroin is pouring into the United States from Pacific Rim countries in record amounts. It has gotten so cheap that 50%

more users snorted rather than injected heroin in 1990 than in 1980. There was a 74% increase in first-time heroin users in 1991.

92. "METHADONE" *SIXTY MINUTES* A B C TELEVISION NETWORK, 2/21/93
Addicts are rewarded with a free week's supply of methadone if they recruit another addict to go to methadone clinics. You can go to a number of clinics and get methadone from each one. Methadone deaths are on the increase. To get a $100 supply of heroin you have to steal $500 worth of TV's, stereos, etc. People who ask their doctors if they can get off methadone are told they will never be able to get off methadone. It was unknown how many methadone addicts ever got off methadone. Methadone is more addictive than heroin. People take methadone not to feel good, but to feel normal. Addicts said that methadone had ruined their lives and left them with twitches. By signing up at several clinics anyone could obtain large supplies of methadone then go sell it on the streets at a large mark-up to people who didn't want to register as addicts. A group was formed called "Mothers Against Methadone" because so many mothers had either experienced the deaths of their children or saw the horrible, crippling effects that methadone had on their children.

93. MILLER, W.R., MOTIVATION FOR TREATMENT: A REVIEW, WITH SPECIAL EMPHASIS ON ALCOHOLISM. *PSYCHOLOGICAL BULLETIN,* 98(1) 1985, Pg. 84.
Studies seem to indicate that the old style Synanon tough confrontational approach is less likely to be effective than treatment stressing collaboration, or working with the client to help him/her to overcome their addictions. Synanon was one of the first applications of the therapeutic community concept to treat substance addiction. Synanon did appear, at the time of its founding and for a few years after, to be the only treatment approach to really help addicts kick their addiction. The technique has since been further perfected and can be much more supportive than its founders believed and still be remarkably effective.

94. MONTAGNE, MICHAEL, "THE SOCIAL EPIDEMIOLOGY OF INTERNATIONAL DRUG TRAFFICKING: COMPARISON OF SOURCE OF SUPPLY AND DISTRIBUTION NETWORKS." *THE INTERNATIONAL JOURNAL OF THE ADDICTIONS,* **25(5), 557-577, 1990.**

95. "MOTORCYCLE DEATHS DOWN DRAMATICALLY." *THE SAN DIEGO UNION TRIBUNE,* **9/25/92, Pg. A-3.**

96. MULLEN, ROD AND NAYA ARBITER, "ADOLESCENT TREATMENT IN THE CONTEXT OF SOCIAL ENTROPY, DRUGS, AND VIOLENCE." PAPER PREPARED FOR THE CSAT ADOLESCENT AND JUVENILE JUSTICE TASK FORCE (AJJ) 7/19 AND 20, WASHINGTON, D.C.)
Many factors have resulted in segregating parents and children. Once there was the tribe, where all children and all adults of all ages were in close interaction. Then came modern society. Children are typically excluded from the adult workplace. "Television is the new parent and there is a shift in the norms and values of society away from the importance of childrearing. As a society we seem to have convinced ourselves that children can raise themselves. Parents are increasingly unavailable, kin are not available, and young children are sent to day care centers where the turnover rate ranges from 40% to 300% per year, and then to school where ratios of one teacher to 30 students is common." There has been an alarm for years over society's decay as represented in one parent homes but now 10% of our children are being raised in "no parent" homes. The words "mother" and "father" are being taken out of the school curriculum in one Oakland, California school district because so many children do not have parents. Six million violent victimizations occurred in the U.S. in 1990, or 16,000 a day. The number of murders committed by youths under 18 has increased by 85% in the last five years. For the first time in U.S. history, death rates for black and white teenagers attributed to firearms exceeded death resulting from all other causes combined. A Phoenix, Arizona gang called WBP or Wetback Power has learned a lot from the Mexican Mafia about big-time drug dealing. They are heavily

armed, have lookouts for their methamphetamine (speed) production houses. Gang membership increased 600% since the 1970's. Drive-by shootings are common in low income Phoenix neighborhoods. Juvenile arrests for cocaine and heroin have increased 713% across America in the last 10 years with a 2,373% increase in the arrest rate for African-American teens in the same 10 years. Drug use has declined among the affluent/advantaged Americans but the age of initiation into drugs and alcohol keeps dropping. The percentage of sixth graders using drugs has tripled since 1975. At what point does society collapse? What percentage of a sick society can working adults support? When only 20% of able-bodied adults take on adult social and productive roles, is that the limit? There are whole neighborhoods where "going to work" or "getting paid" means stealing, drug sales or other illegal activities. Whole communities and neighborhoods must be the clients. "Therapeutic communities for drug addicts in the United States and around the world have shown that many of even the most intractable and socially impoverished members of society can be 'mainstreamed' back into society after one to three years of intensive therapeutic community experience. The social technology is not really drug treatment, it is rather social habilitation by all members of an intentional community....Scientific experiments are being conducted today to see if this technology can be used with addicted mothers and children, the homeless, residents of public housing, and mentally ill clients. In all cases, the results seem to be promising."

97. MULLEN, ROD AND NAYA ARBITER, "AGAINST THE ODDS: THERAPEUTIC APPROACHES TO UNDERCLASS DRUG ABUSE." FROM PETER SMITH, ED., *DRUG POLICY IN THE AMERICAS.* BOULDER CO/SAN FRANCISCO, CAL: WESTVIEW, 1992.

98. MULLEN, ROD, AND NAYA ARBITER, "LINKING LOCAL INITIATIVES TO CAUSES OF VIOLENCE AND DRUG ABUSE." PAPER PRESENTED FOR THE UNITED STATES SENTENCING COMMISSION'S INAUGURAL SYMPOSIUM ON CRIME AND PUNISHMENT IN THE

UNITED STATES, DRUGS AND VIOLENCE IN AMERICA. JUNE 16-18, 1993, WASHINGTON, D.C.

"Notes: In 1989 there were 4,900 cocaine-related arrests in Boston.   During that same year there were only 677 such arrests in all of France.   According to 1989 surveys of drug use among U.S. high school students the proportion trying cocaine was more than five times that of high school students in Germany, England and Italy and about twenty times higher than for students in Sweden, Holland, and Norway.   In 1990 a little over 6 million violent victimizations were attempted or completed in the United States.   Homicide rates in the U.S. are much greater than those of any other industrialized nation. Even before the Reagan administration began a deliberate assault on the welfare state, the United States already ranked lowest among advanced industrial societies in the generosity of its safety net for the disadvantaged and in the degree to which income benefits kept people from sinking into poverty."

99.   MULLEN, ROD, PRESENTER, "100 YEARS OF DRUG POLICY OF DRUG POLICY: WILHELM FLEISS TO WILLIAM BENNETT."   UNIVERSITY OF SAN DIEGO SCHOOL OF LAW AND THE SAN DIEGO PSYCH-LAW SOCIETY CONFERENCE, 11/13/93.

100.   MURRAY, MARY   "NEW WEAPONS AGAINST PAIN."   *READER"S DIGEST*, 2/91 PGS. 74-78

Doctors are hesitant to prescribe appropriate pain control medications because of their belief that they would turn people into drug addicts.   This rarely happens.   But as a result, millions of pain sufferers are left in misery.   Untreated pain can weaken the immune system and speed the growth of tumors.   The more pain is allowed to build after surgery, the more painkiller is needed to make it subside and the longer patients take to recover from surgery.   Pain in general builds more the longer it goes untreated because pain impulses traveling through nerve fibers cause the nerves to "learn" to feel more pain.   People treated with appropriate pain medications, in spite of having conditions which cause excruciating pain, can work and lead near-normal lives.   With the conservative pain treatment usually offered, many pain sufferers are trapped in their bed in constant pain.   A PCA or patient controlled analgesia system is a morphine pump. When in pain, the patient pushes a button which releases a small amount of morphine into an intravenous line into their body. The device can be programmed to allow a patient to dose themselves every eight minutes. Small doses are released. When the patient has to wait four hours for his next dose, feeling the intense pain build up, a large amount of morphine is needed to dull the pain. When the patient has control, they use a lot less of the medicine.

101. "NEEDLES FOR ADDICTS? CITY POLICY RAISES PROFOUND QUESTIONS." *THE SAN DIEGO UNION-TRIBUNE,* **2/21/92, Pg. B-6.**
Twenty-nine thousand San Diego residents were HIV infected, 25% of these through I.V. drug use. Sixty percent of all homeless persons are drug abusers. In New York State nearly 50% of all patients admitted to hospitals through emergency services are mentally ill drug abusers. In California nearly 75% of teenage runaways use drugs. Drug-abusing teens are three times as likely to commit suicide as teens who do not use drugs. Seventy percent of all foster home placements are because of parental substance abuse. Between 1987 and 1990 there was a 30% increase in the number of foster children in the U.S. because of substance abuse. In 1988 more than one of ten first time mothers used drugs during their pregnancies meaning 375,000 newborns that year had been exposed to drugs in the womb.

102. "9 DETROIT AREA COPS, 2 OTHERS INDICTED." *THE SAN DIEGO UNION,* **12/13/91, Pg. A-53.**
Police officers were indicted on a variety of drug related charges, including conspiracy, drug money laundering and theft of government property. Other charges included firearms violations, distributing cocaine, unlawful possession of a machine gun and providing police protection for persons who were major cocaine traffickers from Florida.

103. "NOT ENOUGH SEED: DRUG PROGRAM SHORTCHANGES SOCIAL SERVICES." *THE SAN DIEGO UNION TRIBUNE,* **3/25/93, Pg. B-12.**

The Federal Weed and Seed Drug Program gives grants to cities to weed out drug dealers and other criminals in targeted neighborhoods and to seed programs that help keep kids out of trouble.   In San Diego, the $1.1 million grant is going almost entirely for law enforcement and just a pittance ($95,000) for social programs.   This is a ten to one ratio of money going to law enforcement versus crime prevention.   Police chief Bob Burgreen said the ratio should be at least a 50-50 split between enforcement and prevention.   Congressional action has loosened Justice Department restrictions on how the money can be spent.   The Department of Justice wanted virtually all the money to go for the capture and prosecution of drug offenders.   The San Diego City Manager wanted to spend $202,000 on "seeding," and proposed three programs for Little League baseball, basketball, parks and crafts.   Drug dealers arrested and prosecuted will quickly be replaced by others unless there are programs to direct the lives of youngsters toward positive pursuits.   (Author's note: In the Justice Department's continuing war on Drug Treatment, noted also in reference number 27, they have successfully made sure that not a cent of the Weed and Seed money will go to sober up substance abusers.   The big debate in how to use the Weed and Seed money is not even whether to treat or not to treat, but whether to spend more on financing more cops and jails or build basketball courts so kids will play ball instead of using dope. But dope fiends, even young ones, don't play much ball but they probably would if we bothered to sober them up.)

104.   OSTROWSKI, JAMES, "HAS THE TIME COME TO LEGALIZE DRUGS?"   *U.S.A. TODAY*, 7/90, Pgs. 27-30.

Argues that organized crime would take an $80 billion a year pay cut (the amount earned yearly by criminals through drug trafficking) if drugs were legalized.   Drug addicts would no longer have to steal to feed their habit, drug battles and shoot-outs over turf would stop.   We wouldn't have to spend the 10 billion a year on drug law enforcement that we do now. Twenty million Americans smoke marijuana not because they can't get heroin, but because they prefer it to heroin, though a half million Americans do prefer heroin.   There are two million cocaine users.   The dozens of cases of drug agents, FBI agents, police officers, prison guards, U.S. Customs inspectors, who have all been faced with drug charges, corruption, taking bribes, selling drugs, would stop. The four million crimes committed per year to steal $7.5 billion to buy drugs would stop. Legal cocaine costs $20 per ounce but street cocaine costs 100 times that. (Author's note: If four out of 10 Oakland babies, and one out of ten newborns across the U.S. are born addicted, how many will be born addicted when you can get your week's supply of cocaine and cigarettes at 7-Eleven for the same price?)

105. "PAPER EXHORTS PSYCHOTHERAPY PREFERENCE OVER MEDICATION." *THE NATIONAL PSYCHOLOGIST*, **11/12/ 1993, VOL. 2, NO. 6, Pg. 6.**
Psychotherapy (or talk therapy) alone frequently out-performs treatment for mental/emotional disorders which is done with medications only. Psychotherapy alone also frequently out-performs even a combination of psychotherapy and medications. A paper by Drs. David Antonuccio, William Danton, and Garland DeNelsky was quoted. Doctors Antonuccio and Danton are psychologists at the Veterans Administration center in Reno, Nevada and Doctor DeNelsky is the chief psychologist at the Cleveland Clinic. These authors warned that in their quest for prescription privileges, psychologists may be abandoning their strong forte, which is psychotherapy. Psychologists may be buying into the myth that drugs are more effective in treating depression and anxiety than psychotherapy. Dozens of studies were reviewed, some recent and some dating back to the 1970's.

106. PARENT, P.G. *SHOCK INCARCERATION: AN OVERVIEW OF EXISTING PROGRAMS* **WASHINGTON, D.C.: U.S. DEPARTMENT OF JUSTICE, 1989.**
"Boot Camp" like programs do not reduce recidivism. Programs lacking treatment elements do not reduce recidivism rates of drug involved criminal offenders.

107. PARFREW, ADAM "ELECTROSHOCK THERAPY COMES BACK INTO VOGUE." *SAN DIEGO READER,* **10/14/93.**

108. PEARSON, GEOFFREY, "DRUG POLICY AND PROBLEMS IN BRITAIN." MICHAEL TONRY, (Ed.) CRIME AND JUSTICE: A REVIEW OF RESEARCH. CHICAGO: UNIVERSITY OF CHICAGO PRESS, 1991.
People who advocate legalization point to the British experience, which legalized heroin. But Britain abandoned that program in the mid-70's. Rather than control the growth of addicts, more addicts were created because the "legal" or doctor-prescribed heroin was diverted into the black market.

109. PETERSON, PETER G,. FACING UP: HOW TO RESCUE THE AMERICAN ECONOMY FROM CRUSHING DEPT AND RESTORE THE AMERICAN DREAM. NEW YORK: SIMON AND SHUSTER, 1993.
The average worker age 20 to 40 earns far less than his parents. He is doing poorly economically. Who is going to be there to pay for all these wonderful Social Security and retirement benefits we have voted for ourselves?

From page 319: "Sadly, America ranks near the top among major industrial countries in terms of the damage that we inflict on the young (whether through family trauma, economic poverty, or neglect of their health) - and near the bottom in terms of what we invest in them (whether measured by how long they study in school or by how prepared they are for the modern workplace when the studying is over). Yet we expect them to cope with a rapidly aging society, foot the mushrooming bill for our public retirement programs, finance a national debt of staggering proportions and pay for a health-care system whose projected costs are utterly unsustainable....Only if we remember the original promise of the American Dream - to leave behind more than we take - will we be able to restore that dream to our children."

Peterson provided some disturbing statistics: U.S. worker productivity stopped rising in 1975. Low productivity means stagnating wages creating an income gap between expected income and reality. Family incomes slowed in the 80's. We are losing the war on poverty. Compared to seven major nations, U.S. has close to double the substance abuse in the workplace, ten times the rapes, three times the murders, 15 times the murder rate in males in the 15 to 24 age range, four times the lawyers, almost six times as many people locked up in prisons and 6.5 times the AIDS cases.

In the past generation the incomes of older Americans have risen but incomes of families under age 30 with children have dropped 28.6%. Poverty is striking the young more and more. Our consumption rate of goods, etc., is greater than all industrial nations. "In the eighties we enjoyed make-believe prosperity without the bother of producing it..." thanks to going deeper into debt. The national debt had grown ten times over in 20 years, from about half a trillion to $4 trillion dollars. Three fourths of that has been added in the last 12 years, the Reagan and Bush era. The rate of Social Security recipients is mushrooming. For each benificiary there are three workers. In a few more years it will be two workers per recipient; each worker will have to pay half his salary to cover the costs. Today's adults are promised many times more in benefits than they put into Social Security and other retirement programs, especially federal workers. (Author's note: Mr. Peterson proposed a series of steps which will be needed to reverse America's dangerous slide into financial chaos and perhaps even oblivion as the nation now exists. His proposals are well thought out, enthusiastically endorsed by Ross Perot, workable, and inevitable if we are to avert disaster. Coupling his plans with the "Sober Forever" Program outlined in Chapter 11 of this book can turn around America's economic and social crises.)

110. PIERCE, NEAL R., "THE SCANDAL OF PACKED JAILS." *THE SAN DIEGO UNION,* 1/19/92, Pg. C-2.
Only a quarter or less of our jail cells hold dangerous criminals. They are filled with homeless vagrants and petty thieves, drunken driver offenders, domestic abusers who can't come up with the $500 to $700 bail to get out. Jails are serving as a modern day version of the 18th and 19th century poorhouse. County and city local jails hold 400,000 people. Police over-book, throwing multiple charges at those arrested instead of single charges. That raises the amount needed for bail. Only 38% of all Clarke County Nevada bookings resulted in convictions which is evidence of "a system gone amok." The Clarke County excesses, said Jerome Miller, director of the Alexandria, Virginia based National Center on Institutions and

Corrections, are repeated in jails across the nation. We jail high numbers of the people the criminologists call America's "Rabble class" or "truly disadvantaged." This group turns out to be preponderantly black, male and poor, and often are those who back-talked a policeman and thus "failed the attitude test." (Author's note: Add the mentally imbalanced to the rolls of the people filling our jails, since America doesn't want to spend any money on mental health. Our jails have become our new dumping grounds for the mentally disabled.) Jerome Miller maintained that big guard staffs helped sheriffs get campaign workers. They can be "tough on law and order" and can bring up horrendous incidents as justification of their actions. More workers and more jails means a bigger budget, and whose budget is biggest translates into political power.

111.   PIERCE, NEAL, "HELPING PRISON-PRONE YOUTH." *THE SAN DIEGO UNION,* **1/26/92, Pg. C-2.** Black males are imprisoned at four times the rate of South Africa. Most of the schools which the nation's juvenile detention centers operate all too often turn troubled boys into hardened criminals. Most serious adult criminals are alumni of juvenile delinquent detention facilities. Jerome Miller was the Director of Youth Services in Massachussetts in 1972. He closed the juvenile detention centers and spent the money on alternative, community-based care programs. From 2,000 institutionalized youth, the count dropped to 40. The share of the adult prison population made up of the alumni of the juvenile justice system dropped from 55% to 20% by the early 80's. What works are programs that offer more structured social support and discipline to individual youths via mentors, counselors, big brothers, and peers. Young people also need a supportive, nurturing disciplined physical setting, an "extended family" sanctuary off the streets. A personalized, decentralized systematic approach increases young people's self-esteem, helps them stay in school, helps them to become employable and to avoid drugs and crime. Thomas Massaro, a private developer of affordable housing in Philadelphia said, "Many of the same young men capable of doing such horrible things (stabbing, shooting, beating people) are also capable of doing wonderful things. Bond them into the community in an environment of rigid discipline. Make sure they have contact with family, church, mentors, supervisors that extends beyond the workday. Give them contact with successful adult black men - mentors from churches, or coaches, or businessmen - who encourage them when they're down, challenge them, believe in them." The prevailing attitudes toward, and treatment of, America's troubled youth, which are indifference, fear, incarceration and criminilization, must stop.

112.   PIERCE, NEAL, "WHY YOUTH SERVICE CAN WORK." *THE SAN DIEGO UNION-TRIBUNE*, **6/14/92, Pg. C-2.**
Inventive youth service and Conservation Corps programs have spread to 27 states. Seventy five of them have a total budget of $180 million. They enroll 25,000 young people. One such youth service program in Boston called City Year offered recruits ages 17 to 22 a $100 a week stipend and a $5,000 scholarship upon graduation. The youth enrolled work in teams of 10-12 members building playgrounds and soup kitchens, rehabilitating homeless shelters and distributing food to the hungry. They were tutoring and mentoring younger kids and assisting the sick. The program builds self-confidence and leadership skills. Congress in 1992 was going to add $60 million in expansion grants to some of the country's best youth service programs. Military bases now slated for closing could serve as youth service camps. Writer Pierce noted: "Our hopes are slim unless we move quickly to reengage our poor, our jobless, and our disillusioned and turned-off young people." Such programs "Could be one of America's best antidotes against ominous social dissolution and Los Angeles-style riots during the 1990s..If we don't (implement such programs) the country's social fabric will keep on unraveling, rendering incalculable damage not just to budgets, but to our security as a nation."

113.   PLATTE, MARK, "FELONY JUNIOR COLLEGE." *LOS ANGELES TIMES*, **7/19/92, Pg. B-1.**
San Diego's work furlough centers which are created to relieve jail over-crowding are the only three in the State that operate with no law-enforcement supervision and are not required to tell the courts if convicts violated probation. Some convicts

were rearrested later.   One avoided mandatory narcotics testing by bribing a work furlough employee.   The county run programs follow strict requirements for counseling, housing, safety, security, drug testing, recreation, construction and health standards.   The cost for a convict to stay at one of these work furlough centers is $25 a day or $750 a month for room and board.   Wright, an operator of one of the three private work furlough facilities, claimed that only 12% of his residents were returned to custody and less than 1% would leave his center in violation of their sentence and not return. Wright maintained that these work furlough centers housed 3,500 residents "with just a few problem cases."   A third of the residents had been convicted of drunk driving and another 20% for narcotics related offenses.   One man sentenced to work furlough never showed up. Instead, he went on to commit more crime.   Work furlough center operator Wright asked how can these work furlough centers be blamed for failing a client when the courts and probation could not get that client to the work furlough center or keep them there in the first place. (Authors' note: These work furlough centers prove that affordable housing is available, and those sentenced to them usually can and do pay, but costs could run as low as $400 a month for room and board as they do in many other programs. Such residential programs are the cornerstone to recovery, but other elements must be added to these programs.   Mr. Wright claimed a phenomenal success rate for a program that offered room and board, a place to hang out after work that kept his clients away from old haunts and old behaviors for awhile, and little else.   Add the therapeutic community drug treatment program and good monitoring/tracking as described in Chapter 11 and our jails will become obselete except perhaps as havens for the homeless after the bars have been removed.)

114.   PORTERFIELD, KAY MARIE, "MARIJUANA AND LEARNING: GRASS GETS AN F." *CURRENT HEALTH* 2 16:   11/89, Pgs. 24-27.
THC (the major mood altering ingredient in marijuana) lowers alertness and retards memory and learning.   The higher the dose, the worse the memory.   Students smoking marijuana feel alert but cannot comprehend, follow, or store much of

what is going on in their long term memory. They may be drug free when they take a test later, but because they were stoned in the lectures, nothing is recalled. Even moderate doses over an eight month period destroys brain cells and causes premature aging of the brain. In a 1981 study of 2,000 high school students not only was the ability to learn impaired, the desire to learn was impaired. Marijuana has long been known as a drug which kills motivation and the desire to succeed. Formerly focused and successful youth, after smoking marijuana for a time, stopped setting goals for themselves. They forgot about their formerly important career plans. Five times as many just once-a-week marijuana smokers dropped out of high school compared to students who used the drug rarely or not at all. After smoking for a few weeks or months, and as the A's, B's and C's dropped to D's and F's, the students started to feel like failures. How did they cope with these unpleasant feelings? They smoked a little more dope to forget. Before daily marijuana use, only one in 25 students in a Virginia study had experienced serious school failure. After a few months of regular use, three out of five were failing in school, half were ditching at least one class a day and three-fourths had been suspended from school. The writer concluded "In the final analysis, marijuana doesn't make the grade - and neither do students who smoke it."

115. "PRISON TRAINING SHOWS GOOD RESULTS AFTER INMATES' RELEASE." *THE SAN DIEGO UNION,* **12/20/91, Pg. A-42.**
A study of 11,000 federal prisoners released from 1984 to 1986 shows that those who were trained behind bars were more likely to hold community jobs and less likely to slide back into a life of crime. After a year of freedom, 6.6% of the prison trained group violated their paroles, compared to 10.1% of the untrained group and 20% of all released inmates. The trained ex-inmates had a 72% employment rate, compared to 63% for the untrained group. The federal prison industries are a $343 million business that employs 25% of the 58,000 federal prisoners.

116.   RANGEL, CHARLES B., "U.S.A. 1991:   ONE YEAR AFTER LEGALIZATION."   *U.S.A. TODAY,* 7/90, Pgs. 30-32.
The writer visualized a worst case scenario of a society awash in crime and addiction a year after cocaine, marijuana and heroin had been legalized.   The results: A sad and horrifying picture.   An article by Gabriel G. Nahas, a Columbia University pharmacologist which appeared in the Wall Street Journal on July 11, 1988 titled "The Decline of Drugged Nations" is referenced.   Wherever in the past drugs were widely available and used, including hashish by medieval Moslems, heroin by the 16th century Peruvian laborers for the Spaniards, 19th century Chinese opium addicts, the "British system" of supplying heroin to addicts, all resulted in a high incidence of individual and social damage.   The prediction was that crime and murder rates would soar after legalization, and that the Colombian cartel and the mafia, since they could now produce, import and market cocaine legally, would obtain a vice grip on the American economy and American citizens.

The article summarized two National Institute of Justice studies.   One found that cocaine use among men arrested for serious offenses in Washington, D.C. more than tripled from 1984 to 1988.   Another showed that criminal activity of hard-core users decreases when they even slow down on drug use.   Of course, criminal activity is likely to stop entirely if they are completely sober.

117.   RAUCH, JONATHON, "AMERICA'S CRACK UP." *LOS ANGELES TIMES MAGAZINE,* 7/26/92, Pg. 23.
Arrests for young Americans are nine times higher than it was in 1950.   In 1989 one in 11 American males aged 16 to 34 was in jail, on parole or probation.   Americans rape each other 27 times as often as the Japanese, rob each other 157 times as often as the Germans.   Theft costs American economy $600 billion a year, sapping the country's economic vigor.

118.   *REPORT AND RECOMMENDATIONS OF THE FLORIDA SUPREME COURT ETHNIC AND RACIAL BIAS STUDY COMMISION,* "WHERE THE INJURED FLY FOR JUSTICE" (TALLAHASSEE, 12/11/90).

119.   REUTER, PETER, ROBERT MACCOUN AND PATRICK MURRAY, *MONEY FROM CRIME: A STUDY OF THE ECONOMICS OF DRUG DEALING IN WASHINGTON, D.C.* **SANTA MONICA, CALIFORNIA: THE RAND CORPORATION, 6/90.**
Drug dealers earn $2,000 a month for four hours work a day. A sixth of the ninth and tenth graders in a Rand study sold drugs, less than a third of them used drugs. Ninety-five percent of adult dealers used drugs, spending at least a quarter of their income on their own drug habit.

120.   RIECHERS, L. *AN OVERVIEW OF DRUG TREATMENT PROGRAMS IN PRISON.* **CRIMINAL JUSTICE POLICY COUNCIL: RESEARCH ANALYSIS, 1/12/91   Pg.   1.**
The United States has more than four million people under criminal justice supervision, including those in prison (over a million) and those on probation or parole. The United States has far more of its citizens, on a per-capita basis, locked up or involved in the criminal justice system than any other nation in the world. The large majority of these are drug abusers whose deteriorated behavior while under the influence led them to break the law. Most of them continue to break the law in spite of this criminal justice system "supervision" (return to prison rates hover around 70%) because the reason they broke the law in the first place, substance abuse, is rarely addressed and rarely corrected.

121.   "RISING PAY, EDUCATION DID NOT CUT CRIME RATE FOR BLACKS, STUDY SAYS." *THE SAN DIEGO UNION TRIBUNE,* **2/10/92, Pg. A-12.**
An FBI study showed black homicide arrest rates in 1962 were 23.51 per 100,000 residents. In 1991 that figure rose to 52.81 per 100,000 people. This was 14 times higher than white rates of homocide for those same years.

122.   ROBERTS, OZZIE, "DRUG ABUSE BLAMED AS COUNTY CRIME RATE RISES 29% SINCE '85." *SAN DIEGO UNION,* **9/14/90, Pg.**
In a 115 page report "Crime in the San Diego Region" by the San Diego Association of Governments it was reported that

82% of all males arrested in San Diego tested positive for drug use. The arrests were not just for drug crimes (selling, possession) but for a wide variety of offenses including property offenses such as burglary, motor-vehicle theft and larceny. Half the males and 45% of the females arrested had two or more drugs in their system at the time of arrest. From 1985 to 1989 arrests for drug violations jumped 60%, from 18,899 to 30,217. (Author's note: The truth is incontrovertible that drugs change good citizens into criminals and drives violent behavior and antisocial acts. Much of the violence is related to seeking drug money but much is a simple by-product of the drastic changes drugs produce as they destroy the conscience, value system, and a basic sense of what is right and wrong in the user.)

123.   ROARK, ANNE C.   "THE SEARCH FOR RELIEF FROM PAIN."   *LOS ANGELES TIMES*, 9/22/91, Pg. A-1.

If appropriate medications are prescribed to treat real pain this rarely if ever results in addiction, unless there was a prior history of drug abuse. Less than one in 1,000 people prescribed powerful narcotics for pain, including morphine, became addicted. Doctors typically under-treat pain. Untreated pain weakens the immune system, causes drastic changes in personality, and can rip families apart because of the now very grumpy pain sufferer. Seventeen standard textbooks on surgery, medicine and cancer were surveyed and of the 22,000 pages in all of them, only 54 pages mentioned pain. Half the books didn't even discuss pain. All across America, where pain sufferers are typically under-treated, people who could be working and leading near normal lives are trapped in their beds enduring constant misery. Estimates vary, but work productivity losses from Americans who miss work because of pain is over $55 billion a year. American doctors under-treat pain for fear of causing more dangerous and feared drug addicts. Even dying cancer patients are typically under-treated and are sent to the great beyond with excruciating pain as their last memory. Morphine pumps get people out of hospitals sooner after surgery and back to work sooner because of the pain control. It is impossible to concentrate and think (or work) when in extreme pain.

124. ROBERTSON, MARJORIE J., "HOMELESS WOMEN WITH CHILDREN: THE ROLE OF ALCOHOL AND OTHER DRUG ABUSE." *AMERICAN PSYCHOLOGIST,* **VOL. 46, NO. 11, Pg. 1198-1204, 1991.**
Various studies have estimated that alcohol abuse among homeless women ranges between 12% to 68% and drug problems from 1% to 48%. Homeless women with dependent children have a lower rate of substance abuse. A homeless mother's drug or alcohol abuse often has the consequences of neglect, violent treatment of, or abandonment of, her children. Drugs that cause violent behavior and extreme mood swings or withdrawal were more likely to be associated with violence and neglect of children. More violence and neglect of children was reported for homeless crack-addicted mothers than for homeless heroin-addicted mothers. Alcohol or drug abuse may impair a woman's ability to compete for scarce resources in food and housing, thus threatening family integrity and also creating a greater chance of losing custody of their children. Treatment is scarce across the nation for drug abusers and treatment for pregnant, drug-addicted women is even scarcer. Residential treatment programs rarely make provisions for the women's children to go along. Pregnant women on drugs avoid prenatal care for fear of having their babies taken from them. Women cannot be afraid that if their drug problems surface they will face jail and loss of their children. The dealings with these homeless female substance abusers must be decriminalized to the extent that they are given treatment instead of jail. This treatment must include plans to address both their homelessness and their substance abuse problems. Such a treatment program must include "long-term, structured, and supported drug-free residential programs that maintain family integrity...and provide the stability and predictability of a drug-free environment and the comprehensive services necessary to address the multiple health, psychosocial, and financial difficulties common to some homeless females.".

125. RODRIGUEZ, RICHARD "ARE *YOU* **AFRAID TO GO TO OAKLAND?"** *LOS ANGELES TIMES,* **4/5/92, Pg. M-1.**

In a city of 372,000 there had been 56 murders in the first three months of 1992.   Joe Marshall was a math teacher at a San Francisco high school and said, "Black mothers always took care of thir children," but since crack he has seen mothers try to sell their children for drug money.   Since some mothers have stopped being mothers, Marshall organized the Omega Boy's Club to act as an extended family.   They recruit members from the jails, schools and streets.   "A handful of adults become parents to the many, and then the boys learn to parent each other."

126.   ROVNER, SANOY, "MEDITATION: INTO THE CELLS OF THE MIND."   *LOS ANGELES TIMES,* 9/22/91.
Sixty percent or more of all jail inmates will be back in jail in just 3 years.   T.M.. (transcendental meditation) was taught to 259 prisoners in San Quentin.   After their release, they had a recidivism rate of 35% to 40% compared to the typical 60% or more recidividism (return to prison) rate.   Almost two-thirds of the parolees who learned T.M. were still clean after two years but only 45% of the parolees who did not have the Transcendental Meditation training.   (Authors' note: If we see what a band-aid such as teaching T.M. can do, when the comprehensive in-and-out of prison program outlined in Chapter 11 is implemented, we will not be bragging about a 15% drop in the number of criminals going back to prison, instead we will be looking for ways to sober up and return to society that last, very stubborn 2% to 5% who will resist our best efforts, when we begin to make our best efforts.)

127.   SAEMAN, HENRY, "CAL MEDICATION SKIRMISH TRIGGERS WAR WITH PSYCHIATRY." *THE NATIONAL PSYCHOLOGIST,* 11-12, 1993, VOL. 2, NO.6., Pg. 1.
One hundred thirty five million eight hundred ninety six thousand prescriptions for psychotropic medications (medications designed to affect mood, medications used to treat mental problems or disabilities) were written in 1991. Only 17.3% of them were written by psychiatrists. Physicians who practiced in various general or speciality areas wrote 82.7% of them.   These were supposedly medical doctors who generally lacked the extensive specialized training in

mental health.   (Author's note: In their push to obtain prescription privileges, psychologists may end up downplaying their area of strength, "talk therapy," which many studies have proven to be more successful than drugs in the treatment of depression.   See reference no. 105.)

128.   SANDWIJK, J. P., P. D. COHEN, AND S. MUSTERD.   *LICIT AND ILLICIT DRUG USE IN AMSTERDAM*.   AMSTERDAM: INSTITUT VOOR SOCIALE GEORGRAFIE, 1991.
You can buy marijuana cigarettes at coffee houses in The Netherlands.   But sale and possession of heroin and marijuana any place but the coffee houses can be fined and result in two to twelve year prison sentences.   Drug use in the Netherlands has declined since the mid-1980's and is lower than most other western European countries.   The Dutch do not try to count on criminal law to solve their social problems.   Their goal is to reduce the harm caused by drugs and addiction.   They rely on enforcement to go after dealers, not users.   Intensive health education and prevention are needed to keep people away from drugs.   If they do use drugs, the Dutch try to keep them from sliding into the fringes of society where health risks increase. The addicts who are not visible are more likely to become out of control.   This is why the Dutch make treatment and health care easily accessible.

129.   SCOGNAMIGELLO, JOANNE, "HOW TO HELP ADDICTS KICK THEIR HABITS."   *U.S. TODAY*, 7/90, Pgs 32-35.
The writer noted that "It is ironic that the two drugs most abused by junior high and high school students - alcohol and marijuana - generally are perceived to be less addictive or harmful than the 'hard stuff.'"   The emotional, physical and economic costs of these highly addictive drugs must be taught to the community at large.   "The futility of attempting to self-treat an addiction to a 'hard' drug like cocaine by switching to a 'soft' one like beer must be explained not only to schoolchildren, but to their parents."   Growing up is hard and young people who experience a wide range of moods and emotions, such as anger, boredom and fear need to know that these feelings are part of growing up and part of being alive.

They need to know that these feelings need not be drugged away.   If these children do not have parents who show that stress can be managed without chemistry, then schools, other adult role models or surrogate parental institutions need to fill that void.

130.   SELLS,   S.B.,   AND   D.   D.   SIMPSON, "EVALUATION OF TREATMENT OUTCOME FOR YOUTH IN THE DRUG ABUSE REPORTING GROUP (DARP):   A FOLLOW-UP STUDY." IN G.M. BESSINGER AND A.S. FRIEDMAN, Eds., *YOUTH DRUG ABUSE: PROBLEMS, ISSUES, AND TREATMENT.*   **LEXINGTON, MASS: D.C. HEALTH,   1979.**
The writers reported on one of two large scale federally funded treatment outcome studies.   This one followed those in treatment between 1969 and 1971.   Though some methods of treatment seem to be more effective than others, the most important factor is length of time in treatment.   Those who stayed in treatment longest did the best.   Drop out rates from voluntary treatment programs was high, but even as little as two or three months in treatment before dropping out had benefits such as reducing levels of drug use and crime.   People generally did best while in treatment, but even after dropping out of treatment, they didn't go back to being as bad (doing as much drugs and crime as they were doing before treatment). The therapeutic community approach works very well but when people have the option to leave, they very often did so.   The DARP study showed that 71% of the clients had left treatment by 12 months after admission and only 5% completed their treatment plans.   (Author's note: Implementation of the plan in Chapter 11 would guarantee that virtually everyone who entered a one or two year residential program would finish the program thus guaranteeing the high success rate to everyone who enrolls.)

131.   SHAW, CAMERON, "L.A. AREA DRUG ARRESTS DROP BUT CONFISCATIONS RISE." *SAN DIEGO UNION,* **12/28/91,   Pg.   A-3.**
Cocaine overdoses accounted for 25% of the 17,000 drug related emergencies that hospitals run by the County of Los Angeles were expecting to handle in 1991.   Heroin, hashish and

a wide variety of other drugs (including alcohol) accounted for the rest. More drugs were confiscated but arrests were expected to drop by 35%. Anti-drug education programs and longer prison sentences may have accounted for the decline. Or, the lower arrest rate may reflect the migration of drug dealers to outlying areas. Ralph Lochridge of the U.S. Drug Enforcement Administration said, "The shift is to the desert area. Riverside and San Bernadino are exploding with drug crimes and drug labs." The number of casual drug users is dropping, but the population of hard core addicts (the ones who commit the most crimes and murders) remained steady.

132. SILIA, PETER, AND SUSAN TURNER, *INTENSIVE SUPERVISION FOR HIGH RISK PROBATIONERS.* SANTA MONICA, CALIF.: RAND CORPORATION, 12/90.
In some states, prison overcrowding has increased because probationers violated parole by testing positive. The writers decided that because of the higher cost of increased supervision the program did not save money. But they found that the few programs which had added intensive drug treatment to the mix of close supervision and drug testing, reduced subsequent arrests and corrections by 10-20%. But drug treatment is scarce. Community supervision programs have problems obtaining treatment for their offenders. In one Los Angeles program, only 22% of the offenders with serious drug problems received drug counseling. In Los Angeles County overall, less than 5% of all probationers with serious drug problems participated in drug treatment and without drug treatment, even intensive probation supervision programs are doomed to failure. (Author's note: Chapter 11 descibes the minimal role of probation in the "Sober Forever" Program. Probation will not become involved until the addict's agency of choice reports him missing. **All** addicts, not just 5%, will get to choose between treatment and jail. Even in jail, they will not escape treatment and sobriety, which is not the case now.)

133. SKOLNICK, JEROME H., "DRUGS: SEARCHING FOR AN ANSWER." *U.S.A. TODAY,* 7/90, Pgs.16-18.
The writer, a University of Caifornia Berkeley professor, and his students interviewed jailed California drug dealers. Prison offered a kind of "homeboy" status, especially for gang youths

for whom the institution had become an alternative neighborhood. Prison furthers crime. In jail the youths had joined gangs, used drugs, and made useful connections for buying and selling illegal substances. Today's prisons are overcrowded, filled with short term parole violators who failed drug tests. (Author's note: These prisoners were not getting treatment while they were on probation, but somehow they were expected to quit drugs before they returned to prison because they would be tested periodically to see if they were still using. Drug testing and supervision without treatment do not work to reduce drug use.) Today's prisons now serve networking functions. The new friends and connections the criminals make in jail gets them ready for business as usual as soon as they're out, with the added knowledge of what are the new drugs, how to make them and how to market them. Felix Mitchell was one of the three big Oakland, California drug dealers locked up in big crime busting operations in the 1980's. But after he was arrested and locked up (he was later murdered in Leavenworth) the price of drugs dropped and the murder rate went up as his markets were fought over by rival gang members. Four million dollars was dumped into the Oakland area between 1985 and 1987 to expand prosecution, probation, and the courts. All the law agencies, with the extra money, did what they do best. They had more prosecutions, convictions, probation violations and more people in jail. They met their goals. But crime, and especially narcotic felonies, continued to increase. (Author's note: Had that $4 million been spent on treatment, they would have seen a difference.) Focused, saturation street enforcement will clean up an area, but it is costly and inefficient. It robs other areas of their fair share of scarce resources. It does not stop drug dealers, it displaces them. Such big street sweeps focused inefficiently on the lowest level of the criminal chain. When the supply of low potency marijuana was reduced in the 70's due to efforts during the Nixon administration, Northern California growers filled the gap with sensimilla, a marijuana plant with five times the potency. The more successful law enforcement is in cutting off the supply, the more incentive drug dealers have for hardening (increasing the potency and strength) of drugs and of developing varieties of drugs that are more potent, portable, and dangerous. Ninety-nine percent of the cost of drugs sold on the streets is spread among the people who distribute it and only 1% goes to pay the grower, refiner, and smuggler of drugs. Four hundred thousand people cross into America every year from Mexico. It is no problem for a small percentage of them to bring in a kilo or two of cocaine. The borders are a sieve.

134. SMART, REGINALD G, GLENN F. MURRAY AND AWNI ARIF "PREVENTION PROGRAMS IN 29 COUNTRIES." *THE INTERNATIONAL JOURNAL OF THE ADDICTIONS,* **23(1), 1-17, 1988.**

135. SMITH, LYNN "WHAT'S BEST FOR THE CHILDREN?" *LOS ANGELES TIMES,* **10/18/92, Pg. E-1.**
Nearly half a million children in America have been removed from their homes. In 1990, 108,000 abused children were referred to the Los Angeles County Department of Children's Services, an increase of 44% since 1984. The foster care system has functioned so poorly in the past ten years it has produced high numbers of mentally ill children who have been bounced from home to home. The government spends $2.3 billion a year on foster care but only $300,000 a year for family preservation programs. There is a legislative proposal to spend $2.5 billion over the next five years for family preservation programs or $500 million a year. Poverty, substance abuse (in 70% of the cases) physical and sexual abuse have led to the removal of the children from their homes. (Author's note: If a half million children are in foster homes, and the government spent $2.3 billion a year on foster care, that is $4,600 a year per child. This may be a low estimate, especially in California, where foster parents receive between $6,000 to $7,200 a year per child. This does not cover ancillary services such as medical care, special education programs, and the greatly increased staff of social workers needed to monitor and supervise the foster home system.)

136. SMITH, PETER H., ED. *DRUG POLICIES IN THE AMERICAS.* **BOULDER CO/SAN FRANCISCO, CA.: WESTVIEW, 1992.**

137.   STERN, MARCUS, "IN INNER CITIES, THE UNDERCLASS IS ABOIL." *THE SAN DIEGO UNION,* **6/24/90,   Pg.   A-1.**
Cocaine addicts push aside the more traditional homeless clients in the soup kitchens. Crack cocaine is a very intense addiction that impairs a mother's ability to care for her child. Alcoholism has posed serious problems throughout the nation's history, but historians say there has been nothing comparable to the crack epidemic in the central cities. "Like a tornado, the crack epidemic has ripped through many neighborhoods, spawning child abuse, neglect, homelessness, crime and violence... A generation ago, if there was a mom who was a drug addict, we could give the child to the grandmother, but now the grandmothers also are crack-addicted. They're also in jail."

138.   STEVENS, SALLY, NAYA. ARBITER AND PEGGY GLIDER, "WOMEN RESIDENTS: EXPANDING THEIR ROLE TO INCREASE TREATMENT EFFECTIVENESS IN SUBSTANCE ABUSE PROGRAMS." *INTERNATIONAL JOURNAL OF THE ADDICTIONS* **24, NO.5,1989, Pg. 425.**
Women who were able to bring their children with them to a treatment program were much more likely to feel more comfortable, safe and secure in treatment, and thus they remained in treatment longer.

139.   STILES, DON, AND ROD MULLEN, "SMART SANCTIONS: PROBATION AND TC (THERAPEUTIC COMMUNITY) COLLABORATE TO IMPROVE DRUG OFFENDER OUTCOMES IN TUCSON." U.S. DEPT. OF HEALTH AND HUMAN SERVICES, GRANT #5 H87 T100088-0100.
Written with the support of the center for substance abuse treatment, Substance Abuse and Mental Health Administration.
The study provided data on an Amity Therapeutic Community program involving 197 participants which resulted in a successful outcome in terms of intervening with probationers who were at very high risk. The program cost $13.70 per day per participant but supported 15 hours per day, seven

days per week, of treatment programming and also supported most of the cost of the criminal justice supervision for the participants as well as the costs of program evaluation. "This project, like the Amity/Pima County Jail Project, provides important new evidence that criminal justice and treatment organizations that typically work in a non-collaborative manner with the same clients can, when they combine and align their resources, make significant, positive changes in the lives of their mutual clients. These changes can significantly reduce criminal justice expense and turn 'tax takers' into 'taxpayers.'" The study also proved that the therapeutic community program can be successfully "transplanted" into a non-residential setting.

140.   STOLBERG, SHERYL, "LONG-TERM STUDY GIVES GRIM PICTURE OF HEROIN ADDICTION." *LOS ANGELES TIMES,*   **10/14/93.**
Douglas Anglin was the principal investigator in a long term study on heroin addiction reported in the Archives of General Psychiatry. Five hundred eighty one male heroin addicts were committed to the California Civil Addict Program between 1962 and 1964 when their average age was 25. Eighty percent of the sample had been arrested by the age of 18 and half of the arrests were drug related. This sample of addicts have been studied and followed for 25 years. The researchers analyzed death certificates, incarceration records, urine test results and other data. They interviewed the subjects in the 1970's and again in the 1980's. At the second round of interviews in the 80's they found that the average age was now 47.5 years, and that 28% (161) of the original sample were dead. Eleven percent (64) were in jail; 7% (40) were using heroin on a daily basis; 6% (34) were in methadone programs; 10% (58) used heroin occasionally; 22% (127) were abstinent and the rest (16%, 92) could not be tracked down. Of the 161 who died, 32% were from drug overdose, 29% were from homicide, suicide, or accidents, typically involving violence. The remaining 39% of the deaths were linked to alcohol, smoking or other causes. Addicts were more likely to die if they were disabled, were frequently involved in crime, or used alcohol and tobacco to excess over long time periods. The average age of death for frequent users of heroin

is 40. Those who do not quit by their late 30's are unlikely ever to stop. The addicts still using in the 1980's said they were worried about AIDS but admitted they were sharing needles even more than they had in the past. Anglin said that the findings suggest that treatment works, for those who get it. Most addicts have such huge psychological and social problems that it is difficult for them to either seek treatment or stop using on their own. **Anglin said that treatment programs must include housing, medical care, job training and education if they are to be successful.** He said "It is not like the clap, where you can get 10 days of penicillin and cure 98% of the cases. You're talking about people who come from disadvantaged backgrounds, families with alcoholism and criminal behavior. You're talking about people who started getting involved with drugs in their adolescence. It interrupted their education, their socialization. So when these people come into treatment, it's not just a drug use problem, it's a whole person problem." Current estimates are that 600,000 to 750,000 Americans use heroin frequently. Three decades of very different policies were in existence during the study. In the 60's the approach was through the criminal justice system and programs like the Civil Addict Program. In the 70's community-based drug treatment programs were utilized, many of which were dismantled during the 80's. The 1980's then became the time when law enforcement and jails were focused on almost exclusively as the solution to the drug/crime problem.

141.   STUTMAN, ROBERT M., "CAN WE STOP DRUG ABUSE IN THE WORKPLACE?" *U.S.A. TODAY,* 7/90, Pgs. 18-20.
Sixty percent of the world's production of illegal drugs are consumed in the U.S. Fifty-eight percent of the nation's seniors graduating from high school admit they have used illegal drugs. These drug using (or drug experimenting?) seniors are the people who are entering the work place. They will be making our hamburgers, building our cars and driving our busses. They did not claim they didn't inhale. By 1985 it was recognized that crack was found to cause violence, child abuse, and the destruction of the family unit. Shutting down our borders won't help. Of the 20 most abused drugs, 16 are

manufactured or produced in the U.S. Severe effects of drug use don't happen immediately. Drugs make you feel good. Substance abuse (drugs and alcohol) costs $160 billion a year and is responsible for eroding productivity, causing industrial accidents, absenteeism and tardiness, and inflating health care costs. General Motors said that substance abuse costs them a billion dollars a year and adds $400 onto the price of each car. The rest of America pays for substance abuse in many ways. The post office found that drug users had a 41% higher absenteeism rate and a 40% greater chance of being fired.

142.   SULLIVAN, TERRY AND PETER MAIKEN, *KILLER CLOWN*. NEW YORK: GROSSER AND DUNLAP, 1983.

143.   "SURVEY SAYS HOMELESS USE DRUGS, DIE YOUNG." *THE SAN DIEGO UNION,* 12/20/91. .
In a San Francisco study by the City Health Department of 644 homeless people who died between 1985 and 1990, 503, or 78% had alcohol or drugs in their system at the time of death. One-third of them had sufficient amounts to be considered legally intoxicated at the time of death. The majority of those who died were white men and the average age at death was 41 years (compared to the age of 70 in the general population). San Francisco has a population of 723,958. Of these, between 6,000 and 18,000 are homeless. The number of homeless in the United States is variously estimated to be between 600,000 and 3 million. (Author's note: This may be a gross under-estimate because others have estimated that there are over two million homeless teenagers in the United States, see reference number 74.) The Center For Disease Control reported a high prevalence of substance abuse and high-risk sexual behaviors among homeless black men in Dade County, Florida.

144.   TAUBER, JEFFREY S. *THE IMPORTANCE OF IMMEDIATE INTERVENTION IN A COMPREHENSIVE COURT-ORDERED DRUG REHABILITATION: A PRELIMINARY EVALUATION OF THE F.I.R.S.T. DIVERSION PROJECT.* PREPARED FOR THE NATIONAL CONFERENCE ON SUBSTANCE ABUSE AND THE COURTS, WASHINGTON, D.C., 11/7/91.

Newly arrested drug offenders earn points for completing each stage of their court-ordered treatment. These points can be used to reduce the two year supervision period and their fine. Defendants have to participate in A.A. and N.A. meetings, community counseling programs, intensive drug education classes, and frequent meetings with probation officers. Defendants are given random urine tests but those who relapse get a second chance. People in crisis (which is the feeling people have just after arrest) are connected quickly to services and treatment. Treatment is provided immediately after arrest rather then several months later (or not at all, as is generally the case across the U.S.) The participants knew with certainty that they would be returned to jail for dropping out. Legal coercion can be a powerful incentive to change if it accompanied by meaningful treatment. The program costs $330,000 a year. Following participation in the program arrests of drug offenders dropped in half. The savings in arrest costs alone (not even counting what was saved by not having to send all those people to jail) paid for the program.

145.   TOUFEXIS, ANASTASIA, "INNOCENT VICTIMS," *TIME,* **5/13/91, Pg. 55.**
There are 100,000 crack babies born each year.

146.   "TREATMENT WORKS: THE TRAGIC COST OF UNDER VALUING TREATMENT IN THE "DRUG WAR": *EXECUTIVE SUMMARY AND HIGHLIGHTS.* **WASHINGTON, D.C.:   NATIONAL ASSOCIATION OF STATE ALCOHOL AND DRUG ABUSE DIRECTOR, 1989.**

147.   TREBACH, ARNOLD S., AND JAMES A. INCIARDI, *LEGALIZE IT? DEBATING AMERICAN DRUG POLICY.* **LANHAM, MD.:   UNIV. PRESS OF AMERICA, 1993.**

148.   "U.S. LEADS WORLD IN LOCKING UP CITIZENS." *THE SAN DIEGO UNION TRIBUNE,* **2/ 11/92, Pg.   A-10.**
Easily over a million Americans are in federal or state prisons or in local jails. The cost is $20.3 billion a year and rising. Three thousand three hundred seventy of every 100,000

American black males are locked up. This is five times South Africa's rate of 681 per 100,000. Four hundred fifty five of every 100,000 in the general population of America are locked up.

149. VAILLANT, G.A., "A TWELVE YEAR FOLLOW-UP OF NEW YORK NARCOTIC ADDICTS, III SOME SOCIAL AND PSYCHIATRIC CHARACTERISTICS." *ARCHIVES OF GENERAL PSYCHIATRY* 15(6): 599-609, 12/66.

150. VAN HOUSEN, CATY "TAG! GRAFFITI ARTISTS STRIKE AT BOTTOM LINE." *SAN DIEGO BUSINESS JOURNAL,* 11/8/93, Pg 1.
An estimated 1,000 taggers (people, mostly teenagers, who spread graffiti with spray cans etc. around the town) in San Diego County cost easily over a million dollars a year in clean-up. That would amount to $1,000 to clean up after each of the taggers. The trolley spends $400,000 a year and Caltrans, the freeway maintenance agency, spends another $240,000 a year to scrub or paint over freeways and roads. Business owners spend thousands on paint, floodlights and security. Two full time detectives have been assigned to the graffiti detail. Twenty-nine percent of the graffiti is done by gang members staking out their turf. Taggers leave their name and the initials of their "crew."

151. "WHAT TO DO IF YOU SUSPECT YOUR KID IS USING DRUGS." *ADVANCED HEALTH CARE NEWSLETTER,* FALL, 1993, VOL. 2, NO. 3. 2423 CAMINO DEL RIO SOUTH #111, SAN DIEGO, CALIFORNIA, 92108, (619) 692-0803. Will provide drug screening mailer kits for a nominal charge. Call or write for more information.

152. WEXLER, M.K., G. P. FALKIN, AND D. S. LIPTON, *A MODEL PRISON REHABILITATION PROGRAM: AN EVALUATION OF THE STAY'N OUT THERAPEUTIC COMMUNITY.* NEW YORK: NARCOTIC AND DRUG RESEARCH, INC., 1988.

153.   WISH, E.D.,"IDENTIFYING DRUG ABUSING CRIMINALS." IN LEUKEFELD, C.G., AND F. M. TIMS, (Eds.). *COMPULSORY TREATMENT OF DRUG ABUSE.* RESEARCH MONOGRAPH 86., U.S. GOVERNMENT PRINTING OFFICE, WASHINGTON, D.C., 1988.

154.   WOHLFORTH, CHARLES, P., "OFF THE POT." *THE NEW REPUBLIC,* 12/3/90, Pgs. 9-10.
For 15 years possession of marijuana in Alaska meant a $100 fine but after reversing their 1975 stand Alaska can now put people in jail for 90 days for possession of marijuana. Alaska citizens in 1990 were not plagued with crack houses and the drug problems of many other U.S. inner-city neighborhoods. However, there was a growing awareness of the drug problems elsewhere. Alaska's curse is alcoholism and in native villages alcohol-related accidental death, murder and suicide are leading killers. The counter-culture of the 60's which cried out for more freedom and then pushed for a mere fine for marijuana in the 70's was discredited in the 80's and 90's by AIDS and drug violence. (See also Reference number 13 in which former Drug Czar William Bennett said Alaska had decriminalized marijuana but Alaskans took a hard second look at the problem when marijuana use increased among younger and younger children, and some were found to be smoking "coca puffs," which was marujuana laced with cocaine.)

155.   ZIMRING, FRANKLIN E. AND GORDON HAWKINS, *THE SEARCH FOR RATIONAL DRUG CONTROL.* NEW YORK: CAMBRIDGE UNIVERSITY PRESS, 1992.
Seizure of the car used in drug buys, when drugs are found in the car, is a civil rather than criminal proceeding, requiring a lesser standard of proof. The $750 cost to get it back discourages a drive-through market. Law enforcement typically wants to drive up drug prices which, if successful, leads drug users to steal more to support their habit. Disrupting street markets, making it hard for drug users to find dealers, reduces property crime and drug use. Drug users who can't find dealers spend less money on drugs. (Author's note: If you take the yuppie's BMW he used to drive to the ghetto to buy drugs on the corner, he will fight you. If all he

has to do is sober up to keep his BMW we win the little drug wars skirmish with that yuppie.)

ABOUT THE AUTHOR

Dr. Don Miller was born in Detroit, Michigan January 8, 1935. He attended Compton Community College, received Bachelor's and Master's Degrees in Psychology from Long Beach State University in 1955 and 1956, respectively. After serving as a "Psy Warrior" (Psychological Warfare) for the 1st Radio And Leaflet Batallion at Fort Bragg, North Carolina, he attended U.C.L.A. (University of California, Los Angeles) from 1958-1960. He received his Ph.D. in Clinical Psychology from the University of Utah in 1966. He worked from 1966 to 1971 first at the San Diego County Community Mental Health Center, then at the South Bay Guidance Center in Chula Vista, Caliornia. Since 1971 he has engaged in the private practice of Psychology in Chula Vista, California, a city adjacent to San Diego. He is a past president of the San Diego Psychological Association.

INDEX

Admire, David, (Judge), 252 253, 271

Advanced Health Care (Advice For Parents and testing kits), 273-274

AIDS, 28,42, 104, 107, 133-134, 199, 274

Akiki, Dale, 64, 91

Alcoholics Anonymous (A.A.) 39, 80,129, 135, 173, 202, 244, 272

Amity, Therapeutic Community, 77, 82, 265

Arbiter, Naya, 198, 282

Assassins, Hashishians, and Hashish, 111

Bennett, William, 40

"Boot," 93, 140-142

Brazil Death Squads, 258

Breggin, Peter, (Psychiatrist), 93, 285-289

Budget, Balancing Of, 13

C.A.) Criminal Arts Degree, 18, 189

California Civil Drug Addict Program 29,30

California Criminal Code, Alcohol Abuse Laws, 105

California Health And Safety Codes, Drug Laws, 105

California Mems Colony (CMC), 9

Camden House (Drug Rehab Program), 246-247

Camp Barrett (Prison Honor Camp), 143

Cannabis, 1, 202

Cantlupe, Joe (San Diego Union Tribune Writer), 186

Chester, Donna, 66-68

China, Drugs in, 38, 76, 110, 133

Citizen Patrols, 37

Coates, Robert (Judge), 83, 125

Cocaine, Effects of, 113

"Coddling Criminals," 35

Colombia, 1, 186, 191, 275

"Cops" (T.V. Show), 4, 117-118

Cornerstone, Therapeutic Community, 77,

REVISED INDEX

Admire, David,(Judge) 278-279, 298

Advanced Health Care (Advice For Parents and testing kits) 301

AIDS, 26, 32, 62, 117, 121, 126, 149, 221, 301, 334, 353, 357, 377, 394, 398

Akiki, Dale, 102, 132

Alcohol Abuse Laws, 117

Alcholics Anonymous (A.A.), 44, 58, 225, 270, 300

Amity, Therapeutic Community, 86, 292, 310, 349, 392, 393

Arbiter, Naya, 221, 310

Assassins, Hashishians, and Hashish, 124

Bennett, William, 44, 123

"Boot Camp," 104-105, 156-157

Brazil Death Squads, 285

Breggin, Peter, (Psychiatrist), 104, 314-318

Budget, Balancing Of, 3

C.A.(Criminal Arts Degree,) 21, 209

California Civil Drug Addict Program, 33

California Criminal Code, 118

California Health and Safety Codes, Drug Laws, 117-118

Cal. Men's Colony (CMC), 10

Camden House (Drug Rehab Program), 273

Camp Barret (Prison Honor Camp), 158

Cannabis, 1, 225

Cantlupe, Joe (San Diego Union Tribune Writer), 206

Chester, Donna, 75

China, Drugs in, 42, 85, 124, 148

Citizen Patrols, 41

Coates, Robert (Judge), 93, 140

Cocaine, Effects of, 23, 26, 41, 183-184, 219, 228

"Coddling Criminals," 39

Colombia, 1, 4, 199, 212, 304

"Cops" (T.V. Show) 4, 131, 228

Cornerstone, Therapeutic Community, 87

Dahmer, Jeffrey, 73-75, 203

D.A.R.P. (Drug Abuse Reporting Program), 36

Decriminilization, of drugs, 38, 205

Dederich, Charles, 86

Degelder, Terry (Police Sergeant), 104

Donovan Prison, 92

Dope Dealers, 6, 183-184, 227

Drug Testing, 22, 32, 173, 177, 302

Electronic Monitoring, 196, 275, 290

European Drug Policies, 128, 129

Fayer, Art 165-192, 194, 196

Federal Bureau of Prisons, 21

Ferlinghetti, Lawrence, 124

Fijnje, Bobby, 132

Flower Children, The, 76

Gacy, John Wayne, 76-79

Galhey, James (Former Law Professor), 98

Gangs, 23-25, 221

Gates, Richard (Public Defender), 95

Genes (As a cause of substance abuse), 43

Golding, Susan, 94

G.R. (General Relief), 15

Graffiti, 26

Greene, Harold (Judge), 95

Haight Ashbury District, 76

Harper, Robert, 2

"Hitting Bottom", 34

Homeless, 4, 52-55, 65-70, 95, 99, 101, 103, 117, 175, 268, 271, 284-286, 290, 300, 308, 326

Illegitimacy and Drugs, 47, 310-312

The Justice Department, 128, 132, 299, 310

Legalization, of Drugs, 38, 122

Link, Frederic, (Judge), 97

Marijuana, Effects of, 78, 122, 124, 126, 129, 182, 228-229

Markey, Vicki (Deputy Chief Probation Oficer, San Diego County), 133-163, 212, 214

Mental Illness, 61, 99, 101, 103, 152

Methadone, 27, 148, 229-230

Miller, Edwin (Dist. Attorney), 102

Miller, Jerome (Director of National Center on Institutions & Corrections, 222-223, 328

M.I.T.E. (McAllister Institute for Trainig), 165-185, 228-291

Mullen, Rod, 221, 310

Murray, Charles, 26

N.A. (Narcotics Anonymous), 44, 144, 225, 251, 319

Narcotic Addiction Act, 30

N.A.C.C. (Narcotic Addiction Control Commission), 30-31

The National Academy of Sciences, 28

The National Institute of Drug Abuse, 304

The New York Times, 304

Nightmares, Cure of, 239-240

Nilsen, Dennis, 80-81

Paraquat, 1, 41

Peed, Garland (Assistant District Attorney), 110

Pfingst, Paul (Civil Defense Lawyer), 100

P.I.R. Program (Probationers in Recovery), 142-143

Potty Watch, 11

Prescription Drug Abuse, 313

Prisons, as nursing homes, 21

Rand Corporation, 97, 100

Reyes, Kristy, 202

Sanctuary Trauma, 280

San Quentin Prison, 14

Schizophrenia, 60-61, 65-66, 153

Singapore, Drug Policies in, 28

Smith, Peter, 310

"Sober Forever" Program, 19, 46, 52, 59, 63-64, 150-155, 161, 225, 228, 248-299, 327-328

Sober Living (Phase Houses), 196, 204-205, 215-216

Speck, Richard, 73

Stay 'N Out (Drug Treatment), 18, 20, 90, 260-265, 272, 280, 293

Stutman, Robert M., 304

Street Drug Markets, 206

Swank, Bill (Probation Officer), 97

Sutton, Paul (Professor), 98

Synanon, 86, 292

Taggers, 24-26

T.A.S.C. (Treatment Alternatives to Street Crimes, 316

Terminator Two: Judgement Day, 245

The Therapeutic Community, 18, 35, 38, 86-92, 264, 272, 292-294, 299

"Three Strikes You're Out", 321

T.M. (Transcendental Meditation), 221

"Tough Love," 226, 302

"Toxic Psychiatry," 104, 314 - 317

Twinkie, 81

Valenzuela, Francis (Probation Officer), 200-201

VisionQuest, 96

Wardens, Prison, 92

"Weed and Seed," 286

Westfork Prison Honor Camp, 16-17

Whorehouse, 9

Work and Work Training in Prison, 17

Work Furlough, 72

World-Wide Imprisonment rates, 127-128

POSTSCRIPT

NOW WE'VE DONE IT. THREE STRIKES AND YOU'RE OUT. LOCK THEM UP FOR THE REST OF THEIR LIVES FOR THEIR THIRD FELONY. ALL ACROSS AMERICA WE CAN SMUGLY SAY WE WON'T PUT UP WITH BEING HELD HOSTAGE BY OUR DRUG ADDICTED AND SUBSTANCE ABUSING CRIMINALS. WE DON'T WANT TO SOLVE THE PROBLEM BY SOBERING THEM UP AND STOPPING CRIME. INSTEAD, WE WANT TO GET EVEN.

WHAT WE HAVE DONE IS ESCALATE THE DRUG WARS TO A NEW AND EXTREMELY DANGEROUS LEVEL. WE AMERICANS SHOULD PREPARE OURSELVES FOR A BLOODBATH THAT WILL MAKE THE CHICAGO MOBSTER KILLINGS OF THE TWENTIES LOOK LIKE A BAMBI MOVIE.

INSIDE THE PRISONS ACROSS THE UNITED STATES THE GAUNTLET THAT AMERICANS HAVE THROWN DOWN HAS BEEN PICKED UP BY THE CRIMINALS. THEY HAVE ACCEPTED THE CHALLENGE. THEIR RESPONSE: "AFTER I'M OUT, IF I GET CAUGHT DOING JUST ONE MORE CRIME, I'LL GO BACK TO JAIL FOR THE REST OF MY LIFE. YOU BETTER BELIEVE THAT I WILL MAKE IT WORTH MY WHILE." WHAT THEY MEAN BY THAT IS THAT THE NEXT TIME THEY ROB A LIQUOR STORE TO GET SOME DOPE MONEY, JUST FOR FUN, THEY'LL SHOOT THE SALES CLERK ON THEIR WAY OUT. THIS WILL RESULT IN NO MORE TIME IF THEY ARE CAUGHT THAN IF THEY LEAVE EVERYBODY ALIVE.

"WE'LL GIVE THEM ALL THE CHAIR!" AMERICANS ARE SURE TO SCREAM. THAT SOLUTION WOULD BE YET ANOTHER ESCALATION OF THIS VERY DANGEROUS GAME. IT WILL BE ENGAGING IN A NEW

KIND OF LETHAL POKER. "IF YOU RAISE THE ANTE I WILL CALL YOUR HAND, NO MATTER HOW HIGH THE STAKES GET IN THIS GAME." GUARANTEEING THE DEATH PENALTY FOR THE COMMISSION OF MURDER DURING A ROBBERY WILL ALSO GUARANTEE THAT THEY WILL ALL FIGHT TO THE DEATH.

"YOU'LL NEVER TAKE ME ALIVE!" WILL BE THE DRUGGIE CRIMINALS VOW AS HE IS BEING HUNTED DOWN AFTER HIS THIRD FELONY. THEY WILL GO OUT IN A BLAZE OF GLORY AND TAKE AS MANY PEOPLE WITH THEM TO THE HEREAFTER AS POSSIBLE. THIS WILL BE PREFERRED TO FACING CERTAIN DEATH IN THE ELECTRIC CHAIR FOR KILLING DURING A ROBBERY.

BEING LAW ENFORCEMENT OFFICERS OR CONVENIENCE STORE OPERATORS WILL BECOME EXTREMELY HIGH RISK PROFESSIONS. GETTING MONEY FROM THE ATM MACHINE WON'T

JUST MEAN YOU GET ROBBED, IT WILL MEAN YOU GET SHOT AND ROBBED.

THERE IS NOT MUCH TIME LEFT. THE ABOVE DANGEROUS AND TRAGIC SCENARIO MUST NOT BE ALLOWED TO BE PLAYED OUT. IMMEDIATE IMPLEMENTATION OF THE "SOBER FOREVER" PROGRAM DETAILED IN CHAPTER 11 WILL AVOID THE BLOODBATH AND AN EVEN FURTHER DESCENT INTO CHAOS. IF THE "SOBER FOREVER" PROGRAM IS SPREAD ACROSS THE LAND THE "THREE STRIKES AND YOU'RE OUT" LAWS WILL BECOME OBSELETE AND NO LONGER NEEDED. OUR SUBSTANCE ABUSING CRIMINALS WILL BE SOBERED UP, REHABILITATED AND TURNED INTO LAW ABIDING, WORKING, TAX PAYING CITIZENS AFTER THEIR FIRST STRIKE, OR CRIME. STRIKES TWO AND THREE WILL NEVER HAPPEN.